DCE
SECURITY
Programming

DCE
SECURITY
Programming

WEI HU

O'Reilly & Associates, Inc.
103 Morris Street, Suite A
Sebastopol CA 95472

DCE Security Programming
by Wei Hu

Cover design by Edie Freedman
Cover illustration by Chris Reilley

Editor: Andy Oram

Production Editor: Mary Anne Weeks Mayo

Printing History:

     July 1995:   First Edition.

This book is printed on acid-free paper with 85% recycled content, 15% post-consumer waste. O'Reilly & Associates is committed to using paper with the highest recycled content available consistent with high quality.

ISBN: 1-56592-134-8

Table of Contents

Chapter 3: Overview of the DCE Security Application Programming Interface

Examples

Preface

Whether you're reading the daily newspapers, the computer journals, or the memos from your corporate head, security is on everybody's mind nowadays. Security becomes even more of an issue when you run your applications over a network. Here the Open Software Foundation Distributed Computing Environment (DCE) offers the strongest and most comprehensive package in the industry.

DCE Security provides strong user authentication, secure communications, and access control lists. These are the fundamental services you need to build secure, production-quality, distributed applications. Because DCE Security is designed to solve a hard problem, it is complex. The lack of tutorial material and sample applications makes it hard for users and application developers to take advantage of the powers of DCE Security.

My goal in writing this book is to help you cut through this complexity and understand what DCE Security is all about. I will explain the security threats in a network, how DCE Security helps you address these threats, and how to take advantage of the DCE Security services in your applications. In addition to showing you how to use the programmatic interfaces, I will also explain the rationale and design decisions behind DCE Security. This will allow you to gain the insight that's needed to make the right design tradeoffs.

Audience

If you just want to understand how DCE Security works, then you can start with this book directly. You should have a reading knowledge of C.

If you want to follow the examples, then you are expected to be able to program a simple DCE RPC application before reading this book. The

Guide to Writing DCE Applications should give you all the background you need, but of course you can get the information from courses and books put out by OSF and DCE vendors as well. As a kind of review, I develop a non-secure application as the first programming step.

Although this book focuses on DCE Security, the concepts and techniques are generally applicable to distributed applications in general.

Typographical Conventions

The following are the conventions for fonts used in this book.

Italic

Denotes command names, filenames, function names, users, principals, groups, and cells

Bold

Introduces new terms or concepts.

Courier

Indicates user input, sample code fragments, and examples. A reference to a code example or code fragment within text is also shown in Courier.

Courier Italic

Indicates variables within code examples and fragments for which a context-specific substitution should be made. (The variable *filename*, for example, would be replaced by an actual filename.)

...

Stands for text (usually computer output) that's been omitted for clarity or to save space.

Book Organization

Some chapters of this book are conceptual, while some have more hands-on programming information. You really need both to get the job done. The concepts help you plan your approach to security, so you give your users something reasonable and don't leave any unnecessary holes. The programming details show you how to get DCE to do what you want.

Chapter 1, *Security and the Distributed Computing Environment*, explains the concerns that lead to DCE's security model, and the major elements of that model. It explains why DCE demands the complicated activities described in the following chapters. Topics include types of security, and the Kerberos model of the trusted third party.

Chapter 2, *What Does a DCE Security Server Do?*, explains what the DCE Security Service does. I will explain how a client and server can make use of a Security Service in a network to authenticate each other's identities and obtain the privilege information that is needed to make access control checks. As part of this, I will also describe the messages that are exchanged over the wire (the protocol).

Chapter 3, *Overview of the DCE Security Application Programming Interface*, gives you an overview of the DCE Security application programming interface (API). These are the routines your application would issue to obtain security services. Topics include logging in, key management, authenticated RPC, registry, and access control lists. The APIs are described in terms of the major tasks that you need to do to develop an application.

Chapter 4, *How to Write an Application That Uses Security*, illustrates the use of the DCE Security API to develop a complete application: the employee database. The applications are developed in stages, starting first without any security. The next stages add in authenticated RPC, authorization by name, and authorization using the privileged attribute certificate. Finally code is added to make the server standalone (so it can have its own identity).

Chapter 5, *A Programmer's View of Access Control Lists*, gives an overview of access control lists (ACLs). ACLs are the primary mechanisms for protecting data in a distributed environment. In DCE, you implement ACLs by writing a piece of code called an ACL manager. In this chapter, I describe what ACLs are, how they are used, and how ACL managers allow ACLs to be managed via a common interface. I also describe ACL manager design issues such as ACL storage and the use of namespace junctions.

Chapter 6, *Writing an Application That Uses ACLs*, shows you how to add ACLs to an existing application. We start with the employee database application, modify it to store ACLs, and then implement a reference monitor that uses ACLs in making authorization decisions.

Chapter 7, *Writing the Remote ACL Management Interface*, adds the final touches to the employee database application by adding the remote ACL management interface. We do this by implementing the *rdaclif* remote procedure interface that allows *acl_edit* to set and modify our ACLs.

Chapter 8, *DCE 1.1 Security Enhancements*, describes the features provided in DCE 1.1. Topics covered include delegation, the generic security services API, the ACL library, and the audit API. As part of the description, I will also show you how to structure your application to use these features.

The appendixes contain the full source code for all the examples.

Obtaining Online Examples

The example programs in this book are available electronically in a number of ways: by FTP, Ftpmail, BITFTP, and UUCP. The cheapest, fastest, and easiest ways are listed first. If you read from the top down, the first one that works for you is probably the best. Use FTP if you are directly on the Internet. Use Ftpmail if you are not on the Internet, but can send and receive electronic mail to Internet sites (this includes CompuServe users). Use BITFTP if you send electronic mail via BITNET. Use UUCP if none of the above works.

The examples from this book are stored in four files:

unauth.jun95.tar.Z
> The examples from Appendix A.

name_based.jun95.tar.Z
> The examples from Appendix B.

pac_based.jun95.tar.Z
> The examples from Appendix C.

acl_based.jun95.tar.Z
> The examples from Appendix D.

In the sections that follow, *unauth.jun95.tar.Z* is used as an example; you should use the name of the actual file that you want to retrieve.

FTP

To use FTP, you need a machine with direct access to the Internet. A sample session is shown, with what you should type in **boldface**.

```
% ftp ftp.uu.net
Connected to ftp.uu.net.
220 FTP server (Version 6.21 Tue Mar 10 22:09:55 EST 1992) ready.
Name (ftp.uu.net:joe): anonymous
331 Guest login ok, send domain style e-mail address as password.
Password: joe@ora.com  (use your user name and host here)
230 Guest login ok, access restrictions apply.
ftp> cd /published/oreilly/dce/security
250 CWD command successful.
ftp> binary  (You must specify binary transfer for compressed files.)
200 Type set to I.
ftp> get unauth.jun95.tar.Z
200 PORT command successful.
150 Opening BINARY mode data connection for unauth.jun95.tar.Z.
226 Transfer complete.
ftp> quit
221 Goodbye.
%
```

The file is a compressed *tar* archive; extract the files from the archive by typing:

```
% zcat unauth.jun95.tar.Z | tar xvf -
```

System V systems require the following *tar* command instead:

```
% zcat unauth.jun95.tar.Z | tar xof -
```

If *zcat* is not available on your system, use separate *uncompress* and *tar* or *shar* commands.

```
% uncompress unauth.jun95.tar.Z
% tar xvf unauth.jun95.tar.Z
```

Ftpmail

Ftpmail is a mail server available to anyone who can send electronic mail to, and receive it from, Internet sites. This includes any company or service provider that allows email connections to the Internet. Here's how you do it.

You send mail to *ftpmail@online.ora.com*. In the message body, give the FTP commands you want to run. The server will run anonymous FTP for you and mail the files back to you. To get a complete help file, send a message with no subject and the single word "help" in the body. The following is a sample mail session that should get you the examples. This command sends you a listing of the files in the selected directory and the requested example files. The listing is useful if there's a later version of the examples you're interested in.

```
% mail ftpmail@online.ora.com
Subject:
reply-to janetv@xyz.com      Where you want files mailed
open
cd /published/oreilly/dce/security
dir
mode binary
uuencode
get unauth.jun95.tar.Z
quit
   .
```

A signature at the end of the message is acceptable as long as it appears after "quit."

BITFTP

BITFTP is a mail server for BITNET users. You send it electronic mail messages requesting files, and it sends you back the files by electronic mail. BITFTP currently serves only users who send it mail from nodes that are directly on BITNET, EARN, or NetNorth. BITFTP is a public service of Princeton University. Here's how it works.

To use BITFTP, send mail containing your ftp commands to *BITFTP@PUCC.* For a complete help file, send HELP as the message body.

The following is the message body you send to BITFTP:

```
FTP   ftp.uu.net   NETDATA
USER  anonymous
PASS  myname@podunk.edu   Put your Internet email address here
                          (not your BITNET address)
CD    /published/oreilly/dce/security
DIR
BINARY
GET   unauth.jun95.tar.Z
QUIT
```

Once you've got the desired file, follow the directions under FTP to extract the files from the archive. Since you are probably not on a UNIX system, you may need to get versions of *uudecode, uncompress, atob,* and *tar* for your system. VMS, DOS, and Mac versions are available. The VMS versions are on *gatekeeper.dec.com* in */pub/VMS.*

Questions about BITFTP can be directed to Melinda Varian, *MAINT@PUCC* on BITNET.

UUCP

UUCP is standard on virtually all UNIX systems and is available for IBM-compatible PCs and Apple Macintoshes. The examples are available by UUCP via modem from UUNET; UUNET's connect-time charges apply.

You can get the examples from UUNET whether you have an account there or not. If you or your company has an account with UUNET, you have a system somewhere with a direct UUCP connection to UUNET. Find that system, and type (on one line):

```
uucp uunet\!~/published/oreilly/dce/security/unauth.jun95.tar.Z
     yourhost\!~/ yourname/
```

The backslashes can be omitted if you use the Bourne shell (*sh*) instead of *csh*. The file should appear some time later (up to a day or more) in the directory */usr/spool/uucppublic/yourname*. If you don't have an account, but would like one so that you can get electronic mail, contact UUNET at 703-204-8000.

It's a good idea to get the file */published/oreilly/ls-lR.Z* as a short test file containing the filenames and sizes of all the files available.

Once you've got the desired file, follow the directions under FTP to extract the files from the archive.

Acknowledgments

First, I want to thank my editor, Andy Oram, for lending his eyes (and mind) in reviewing countless drafts of this book. His exhaustive reviews and suggestions are instrumental in making this book user-friendly and approachable. (You may, of course, form your own conclusions after reading the book.)

Thanks also to my external reviewers. Jonathan Chinitz gets the award for being first to return review comments. Mike Burati gets the award for the most logistically complex review—complete with late night readings and a hotel lobby drop-off of marked-up drafts. I wish to thank Walt Tuvell for his detailed review on the DCE security services and protocols. John Wray and Rich Salz provided great comments on the DCE 1.1 features. And last but not least, I would like to thank David Magid for his comments on the initial chapters.

Besides my reviewers, I wish to thank the many people from Digital, HP, IBM, Transarc, and the Open Software Foundation with whom I worked in creating DCE. Our (sometimes heated) discussions expanded my understanding of distributed computing in general and DCE in particular.

I wish to thank the production staff at O'Reilly & Associates for making my manuscript into this book. Sheryl Avruch managed the production team. Mary Anne Weeks Mayo served as project manager/copyeditor and was ably assisted by John Files. Thanks to Norm Walsh and Lenny Muellner, the tools experts, who wrote and tweaked the scripts that converted my manuscript into the format you see. Kismet McDonough was responsible for quality assurance during the production process. Nancy Priest was responsible for much of the book's design, and Chris Reilley and Hanna Dyer rendered my complex and detailed figures with precision and elegance. Edie Freedman designed the cover, and all the other O'Reilly DCE covers that form a familiar pattern along the shelves of DCE developers across the industry.

Like all projects of any size, this book is a family effort. I want to first thank my wife Irene for her support. In addition to her own full-time job, Irene created the "spare" time that allowed me to work on this book. I would never have undertaken this effort without her encouragement. In addition to Irene, I want to thank our parents: Fu-Sen Hu, Kwang-Cheng Hu, Kenneth Yeung, and Fanny Fan Yu Yeung Fung for all they've done. Finally, I want to thank my children Martin and Kevin who bring balance to my life and allow me to call myself a "Daddy."

1

Security and the Distributed Computing Environment

Distributed computing is today's solution to the need to share data. Hoping to get rid of the constant interchange of floppy disks and tapes (not to mention bulky paper documents), more and more businesses are networking their computers and providing client/server applications that transfer data at the click of a button. The widespread use of these applications brings with it pressing concerns for security—for programs that know who is asking for data and whether it is all right to supply that data.

The Distributed Computing Environment (DCE) from the Open Software Foundation (OSF) covers more platforms and offers more features than any other client/server technology. Security is one of its strongest selling points. But for security to be effective, programmers have to understand how it works and how to use it in their programs. And that, as you can see by the size of this book, is a large topic.

This book gives you both the understanding and the tools to use security properly in a DCE application. It explains what and how to write an application that makes the best use of its features. When you're done with the book, you'll be able both to design security into your application and to carry it out in your code.

The Role of Security in Distributed Computing

The technologies used in distributed computing have evolved over the years. The initial prototypes and research projects did not address security. The environment was typically isolated from the wide area network and all the users were "friendly." More significantly, these prototypes did not hold production data.

All these conditions change when one deploys client/server computing for production applications. Unlike a research environment, where the information is generally freely available from other sources, production data is typically regarded as an asset that needs to be protected. Consider, for example, the value of a mail-order company's customer list—both to the company itself and to its competitors. Similarly, when data is used for financial decisions, the integrity of that data becomes very important. Production client/server applications also tend to be larger in scale and accessible from geographically dispersed sites. Frequently, the applications may also have interfaces to external software systems. Thus, many of the assumptions that rely on a small user community that knows all of its members do not apply to larger, dispersed production environments.

You might wonder why I place such an emphasis on security. After all, outside of the government/military context, security is rarely discussed in the design of local applications. You might reasonably consider security an optional feature to be added later. Experience shows, however, that you should consider security issues up front when designing distributed applications. Because the network is far more exposed than the traditional single-machine environment, a distributed application is subject to more potential security threats than local applications.

Consider a distributed database for employee information. Figure 1-1 shows a possible architecture for the application. The server is a front end over a database engine that stores the actual employee information. The server process accesses the database in response to queries and updates that it receives over the network.

Typically, there are a large number of clients. A client can be a forms-driven application that takes user input, validates it, and then issues remote requests to the server. The client is also responsible for taking any responses and making them visible to the user. If the application needs to be highly available, servers can also be replicated.

Given this application, here are some potential threats:

- Checkers R Us, a private investigation firm, provides employment histories, including the complete salary history and performance reviews, for any individual of your choice. They guarantee up-to-the-minute correctness.

- New Life, Unlimited will, for a suitable fee, give you any job history you want. One of their more popular packages is the Self-Made-VP package, which gives the customer a 10-year employment history that starts in the mailroom and ends in the corner office. The job history provided is so authentic that even the employer's own personnel department will vouch for its authenticity.

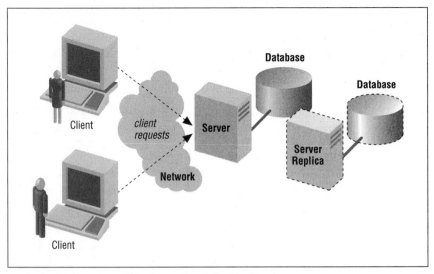

Figure 1-1: Distributed employee database application

- Jack More-is-Better has managed to earn double-digit pay increases every year, without fail. This occurs even though he has not gone to work for the last three years. He does, however, have a home computer that runs a customized version of the employee database client software that gives him the ability to update any record in the server.

- Open Networks, Inc., sells a line of network monitors that can decode and log all the messages that go across a network. One of their largest non-government customers is Headhunters, Inc., a recruiting firm known for its ability to locate candidates with specified skills. The firm is reputed to be working on an artificially intelligent application that automatically sifts through the voluminous data its monitors are accumulating.

  Open Networks is currently finishing a version of the monitor that can transparently insert any data stream of your choice and make it appear to have originated from any machine on the network. In its first demonstration, the prototype managed to artificially inflate the payroll of a firm by 300% and then eliminate all the new hires—all without going through any of the normal database interfaces.

These scenarios are hypothetical; but they are examples of situations that can arise when an application is not secure. The first threat is an example of an unauthorized client read access. The next two are instances of unauthorized client write accesses, and the last is an example of wiretapping and message stream modification. You may have noticed that all these examples exploit vulnerabilities in the network rather than in the operating system of any single machine. This is realistic because networks are much more vulnerable than operating systems.

The Root Cause

The fundamental problem that makes networks vulnerable is the lack of a common point of control. To explain this point, I'll contrast the distributed computing environment with the local operating-system environment. The operating system basically controls all the resources of the machine. All accesses to system resources must go through the operating system. It knows all the users that are logged on and all the processes that are running. The operating system isolates the processes so that one process cannot, for example, overwrite the memory of another process. The local file system works with the operating system to control access to files so that a malicious user cannot, for example, replace */bin/ls* with an "enhanced" version. All these factors combine to provide a very protected environment for local applications.

The protection inherent in a local environment changes when the application is spread across machines connected over a network. In a network, there is no single entity that "controls" the collection of machines and users that cooperate to run the application. An operating system's protection boundary ends at the network and there is nothing that extends across the operating systems. All a client or server computer sees is a stream of packets over the network.

Since all that is visible over the network are the packets that flow across it, it is quite feasible for a third party to emulate either a legitimate client or server system. All they would have to do is transmit the appropriate messages over the wire. In the absence of safeguards, messages from fake systems would be indistiguishable from those sent by real systems. Since one cannot apply security controls without knowing the identity of the entity, this renders the whole system vulnerable.

More sophisticated security mechanisms are needed. Fortunately for the future of distributed applications development, security is a component of modern distributed computing environments.

DCE Security Framework

The DCE Security framework (or model) is a way of describing and reasoning about the security problem in the abstract. We are going to spend some time with the model before going into the conrete details. A good grasp of the model will help you understand not only how DCE Security works but also what problems it can and cannot solve.

A model is simpler than real-life situations and omits implementation details that tend to obscure the underlying concepts. So if the details later in this book start of confuse you, come back to this abstract model and place the details in the context of the large picture.

In the rest of this chapter, I will describe the active entities in the system, the objects that are protected, privilege attributes, and general terminology. After this, I will describe what it means to write a secure application and review some of the fundamental techniques used in network security. This then lays the groundwork for a discussion of the components of DCE Security presented in Chapter 2.

Overview

Let's look at some of the terms and concepts used to explain computer security throughout the software industry. Figure 1-2 illustrates the general model.

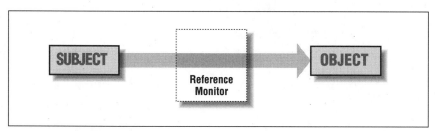

Figure 1-2: General security model

A person called the **subject** wants to refer to a file of data or some other resource, called the **object**. Since we don't want everyone to have access to every resource, we need a **reference monitor** that checks the identity of the subject and decides whether the reference to the object is allowed. On a standalone computer system, the operating system is the reference monitor; it checks permissions on files and other resources. On a network, the reference monitor is one of the tasks of an application server.

Objects represent the resources you want to protect. Typically, this would be the application data. In an operating system, for example, the objects are things like files and peripherals. In DCE, the objects are the data or services an **remote procedure call (RPC)** server offers. In the employee database application, for example, you can model either the RPC interface or the underlying database as an object.

Subjects are the entities that reference the data (e.g., a process that reads or writes the records in a database). In the employee database example, the users accessing the application are subjects. Every access to an object must go through a reference monitor. Intuitively, the reference monitor contains the access control code of the application. There usually are multiple reference monitors, each tailored to the object being protected. This model assumes, of course, that the reference monitor knows the true identity of the subject that is attempting to access the object. In the employee database example, the reference monitor is a piece of software in the database server. This software screens all client requests to make sure the client is authorized to see the requested data before allowing the call to proceed.

DCE has adopted a variant of this general model, shown in Figure 1-3. We do not want to make each client and server reinvent the wheel by defining their own security system, so we centralize security activity in a **security server**. The security server provides, over the network, the security services normally provided by an operating system. All other clients and servers trust the security server and what it tells them (although as we shall see later, there are ways to verify the security server itself).

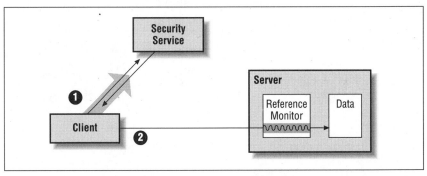

Figure 1-3: DCE security model

The security server maintains a **registry** that stores information about principals, privilege attributes, and secret keys. This registry is the equivalent of the */etc/passwd* and */etc/group* files in UNIX systems. While the UNIX registry is stored as text files that can be accessed directly, the DCE security registry is accessible only via an RPC interface. Every cell has its own registry that can be replicated along with the security server. Since the security server knows all the users of the DCE cell, it is in a position to vouch for the identity of another user. An implication of storing all the passwords and security information in the registry is that it must be protected against attack. If someone can gain control of the system with the security server and its registry, that individual would have access to all the accounts in the DCE cell. Thus, the machine that is running the DCE security registry should be stored in a locked room and should not contain any other software that may subvert the integrity of DCE security.

A user must log in to DCE before he or she can access DCE services. The DCE login operation involves communicating with the security server. During login, the user proves his or her identity by supplying a secret key that is known only to the user and the security server. Then, whenever the user wants to access a remote object, he or she must first ask the security server to issue a **certificate** that certifies the identity of the user. The certificate, also called a **credential**, is a message issued by a trusted authority in such a manner that the server can independently verify the client's authenticity. The client then passes the certificate as part of the RPC call to the server. When the server receives the call, it passes the certificate to the reference monitor for the object. The reference monitor examines the certificate and decides whether the client is authorized to make the call. If so, the call is accepted, processed, and the results are returned. Otherwise, the call is rejected.

I will now describe the parts of the model in greater detail.

Principals

The most important entities from a security perspective are **principals**. In DCE, principals are people, server processes, cells, and hosts (machines). An operational definition of a principal is an entity that can participate in an authentication exchange with another principal. **Authentication** is the act of verifying that a principal is who it claims to be. A principal is therefore either an entity with an identity that someone else would be interested in knowing or an entity that needs to know someone else's identity.

People are clearly principals because the identity of the user that initiated an RPC call is usually needed for determining whether access should be allowed. RPC servers are also principals, primarily because they need to authenticate the client that is making the RPC. In addition, a server's identity is also of interest to clients (running on behalf of principals) so that they can decide whether to trust the results of an RPC. Cells are also principals because two cells can exchange secret keys to support cross-cell authentication.

The less intuitive case is that of the host principal. The host, representing the local operating system on a computer, is made a principal because there are some cases where the local operating system needs to authenticate the DCE Security Service. Since you need to be a principal to authenticate another principal, it was necessary to create a principal for the local machine. As you may have inferred by now, the servers that offer the DCE security services are also principals.

Thanks to the **Cell Directory Service (CDS)** every DCE principal has a **principal name**. For example, */. . ./cell_x/bradford* is the global name of a principal. Within a cell, the principal can be named via a cell-relative name like *bradford*. Using global names allows you to unambiguously specify a principal regardless of the cell from which the name is encountered. This allows you to, for example, include names of users from other cells in your **access control lists (ACLs)**.

The name of a principal can change. What remains constant for every principal is its **universally unique identifier (UUID)**. Thus, DCE security uses UUIDs when security credentials are passed around the network. These

UUIDs are mapped to principal names when needed. This split between the name and the UUID is similar to the situation in UNIX where every user has both a name and a user-id. Although user names are used in utilities, the system data structures all store and check uids. When the operating system checks to see whether you are running as root, it is not checking whether your user name is root; rather, the system is checking whether your uid is that of the root uid.

Every principal also has a **password** or **secret key** that is used for authentication. You supply your password when you log in. The assumption is that if you know the password for user X, then you must be X. When you login to DCE, a secret key is generated based upon your password. Passwords and secret keys are equivalent, and we will use them interchangeably in this book. Passwords are primarily used by people, while keys are used by server programs.

Proxies

Proxies are processes that act on behalf of principals. For example, when you run a program like *cat* to examine the contents of a file, the shell forks a subprocess to execute the command. In this case you, the originator of the command, are the principal and the shell subprocess that executes the *cat* program is a proxy. (The system needs to know your identity to determine whether you should be allowed to read the file; the identity of your subprocess is irrelevant.) Because of the way UNIX executes commands, most RPC client programs are executed by proxies. What we care about from the perspective of security are the identities of the principal that invoked the client program. Proxies, therefore, do not have their own identities. Instead, a proxy assumes the identity of the principal on whose behalf they act. DCE 1.1 also provides delegates. We will describe them in Chapter 8.

Groups

The principal identity is a privilege attribute. Privilege attributes are what the operating system and applications use to make **authorization** decisions—i.e., determine whether you are allowed to perform certain actions. For example, you are allowed to write to certain system directories only if you are executing as root, or more precisely, if your current user ID is the same as that of the root principal. Standard UNIX just uses the user and group IDs combination as a process' privilege attributes. Other operating systems allow you to assign explicit roles and privileges.

DCE provides, in addition to the principal identity, the set of **groups** as a privilege attribute. A group is a collection of principals that can be treated identically for security purposes. Groups makes it easier for you to set and administer security policies.

For example, consider how you would allow some users administrative privileges to the employee database. One approach, the brute force way, is to list all the administrators' principal names directly in each ACL. This works, but it requires you to update each list if a new administrator joins the company. If you have multiple applications and objects each maintaining their own lists, they can get very difficult to maintain.

The other approach would be to define a group called *db_administrators* and add that group as an entry in the ACL. You would then make everyone who needs administrative access to the employee database a member of this list. If you did this, it would be much easier to make changes when a person changes roles. For example, if a person no longer needs administrative privileges, it is easy to go through the registry and remove him or her from all administrative groups. The alternative of going through all the ACLs in the network looking for entries containing his or her name is just impractical.

In general, you should feel free to define groups as necessary to represent each of the classes to which a principal belongs. For example, a user who belongs to both the administrator and the release engineering groups should be made a member of both groups. Since group membership can convey important access rights, the information about the groups to which a principal belongs must be obtained from a trusted source, i.e., the security service. Groups, like principals, have UUIDs in addition to the group name. And the UUID is what's passed around in security credentials.

Because DCE has only principals and groups as privilege attributes, you need to express all your security policies in these terms. For example, you can specify "Anthony, Yannik, and all members of the *supervisor* and *admin* groups have read and write permission." You cannot specify "Kelly, if she logged in from a physically secured device, has write permission." This policy cannot be implemented because it requires an attribute—the login location—that is not maintained and transmitted by DCE Security. Your application can, of course, define its own attributes. In this case, these extra attributes must be stored, managed, and protected outside of DCE Security. DCE 1.1 includes some extensions that make it possible to add user-defined attributes to the registry (see Chapter 8).

Components of DCE Security

Now we can look at what you need to do to write a secure DCE application. In addition to the application logic, you need to write client code that obtains the proper certificates and forwards them to the server. You also need to write server code that gets the privilege attributes of the calling client and determines whether the call should be allowed to proceed. DCE simplifies the process by providing two services: authenticated RPC ACLs.

Authenticated RPC

I said earlier that an application on a network has nothing but the data sent by a correspondent to determine whether access is permitted. So an RPC client needs to pass information about its identity in the form of a certificate. Before making a remote procdure call, a client has to contact the security server and get a certificate that proves the client's identity. The certificate is then passed to the server as part of the client's call. The server must then decode and verify the information.

This is a fair amount of work, especially when you consider all the different threats against which your code must guard. Authenticated RPC takes care of all this automatically. Your client code need only specify the server's principal name plus some additional parameters, and the RPC runtime automatically does the rest. DCE RPC will automatically obtain the required certificate, pass it along to the server as part of setting up the RPC call, and encrypt the messages so that the certificates cannot be tampered with.

Authenticated RPC does more than authenticate and convey privilege attributes. It can add a checksum and encrypt the RPC call arguments so that an application determine when its data has been tampered with and can protect the data against wire-tapping. Thus, DCE offers a protected RPC service.

DCE Access Control Lists

Authenticated RPC conveys the client's identity to the server, but the real work in security is finding the access rights of that client. The job of a reference monitor is to match the information in the certificate against an access control list (or some other data structure) that describes who may access the data.

It may surprise you to know that DCE Security does not provide a reference monitor. Instead, DCE provides the tools for you to implement your own reference monitors. Reference monitors are custom-made because each application has a different definition of the objects that it protects and the types of accesses that are defined. CDS, for example, defines directories and entries as objects and uses filesystem-like accesses such as read, write, etc. Your application may have completely different notions of what an object is and what the appropriate accesses should be.

Another reason that reference monitors are custom-made is that each application needs to define its own storage model. For example, a distributed UNIX-like file system will probably store its security attributes in the inode (a per-file data structure that stores file attribute information) while a database management system may choose to store it in some other data structure.

DCE does not provide a standard reference-monitor implementation. Instead, it defines a standard RPC management interface for an ACL facility. A common interface allows a management tool like *acl_edit* to manage all DCE ACLs, including those implemented by applications. Since only the interface is specified, an application is free to implement the ACLs in a manner most appropriate for the application. DCE, however, does supply sample code that shows how the privileges should be interpreted.

DCE allows you to use ACLs in many ways. For example, users can be checked both as individuals and as members of groups. Because most organizations assign roles to groups, groups are used in ACLs much more than individuals are. Applications can also choose their own kinds of permissions. Every application should support a "c", or control permission that determines who can update the ACL. Probably every application will have an "r" and "w" too. Another common permission is "d" for delete.

We can now see how all the pieces of DCE security fit together. The security server authenticates all the principals in the cell. It also generates certificates that can be passed from clients to servers to authenticate their identities. An authenticated RPC facility is provided to make this easy and transparent to the application. Finally, a standard interface is defined for implementing reference monitors using DCE ACLs. In the next chaper, we will examine the components of DCE Security in greater detail. This will be followed by concrete examples of how to write applications to use all of these services. Before we do that, however, we will describe some of the underlying technologies.

Fundamental Techniques

In the descriptions given so far, I avoided explaining *how* this all works. For example, I did not describe how certificates are generated and how a principal can determine the authenticity of a certificate. In this section, I will review the underlying techniques that are used by DCE Security: encryption and the Kerberos authentication system. For comparison, I will also describe public key based systems.

Cryptography

The most important technology used in distributed systems security is **cryptography**. Cryptography is the transformation of data in such a manner that it is impossible to retrieve the original data without the possession of another piece of information, the **key**. **Secret key cryptography** uses a secret key to transform your original message (the **plaintext**) into a new message (the **ciphertext**). The transformation is such that you cannot perform the reverse operation (**decryption**) without possesing of the same secret key. Because secret key cryptography uses the same key for encryption and decryption, it is also sometimes call **symmetric cryptography**. DCE uses the secret key based system called the **Data Encryption Standard (DES)**.

I used the terms "cannot" and "impossible" loosely in the sentences above. A more precise definition would have used the term "computationally difficult" to perform. For example, an encryption algorithm is generally considered strong if it takes a supercomputer centuries to decrypt a message without the use of the decryption key. Since computers are getting faster, what is acceptably secure today may not be adequate tomorrow.

The counterpart to secret key cryptography is **public key cryptography**, or **asymmetric cryptography**. Public key cryptography uses a pair of keys: one for encryption and a different one for decryption. The key pair is designed so that you cannot derive the other key given one of the pair. The best known example of a public key system is the **Rivest-Shamir-Adleman (RSA)** system. Public key systems are interesting because they are superior to private key systems in terms of manageability and also in terms of security capabilities. Although DCE currently is based upon a secret key system, it is helpful to understand how public key systems work to understand some of the implications of DCE's choice.

Cryptography performs several basic operations:

Privacy
> This is the traditional use of secret key cryptography. You and the intended reci pient of your message both agree on a key to use. This key is known only to the two of you. Before sending a message, you first encrypt it using the secret key. You then transmit the ciphertext to the recipient. The recipient would then decrypt the received message using the same secret key and retrieve the original message. Because the key is kept secret and only the encrypted text is transmitted, the message is safe from wiretaps.

Integrity
> Integrity refers to making sure that no one has modified the message after it was created by the sender. For example, if you want to transmit a request to transfer money from your bank account, it would be useful to ensure that no one else can tamper with the message to change the recipient of the funds. You can use encryption directly to ensure message integrity; just encrypt the entire message as before. This works because someone who wants to tamper with an encrypted message would need to decrypt the message back to the plaintext, modify the plaintext, and then reencrypt the message. If that individual does not know the encryption and decryption keys, he or she usually cannot succeed at modifying an encrypted message. A message that changes enroute will not make sense when decrypted using the original decryption key.

Applications tend to use encryption only when privacy is important. This is because encryption algorithms like DES are still relatively slow. A better technique to ensure integrity is to compute a cryptographic checksum of the original message and then encrypt the checksum. This method is more efficient since there are good checksum algorithms that are much faster than encryption algorithms. Unlike the privacy case where you transmit the ciphertext, you would transmit the plaintext message plus the encrypted checksum to the intended recipient. The recipient would then compute the checksum over the received message, decrypt the original checksum, and verify that the two checksums are the same. For this to work, of course, it must be impossible (i.e., computationally infeasible) for two distinct messages have the same checksum. DCE uses Message Digest 5 (MD5) for its integrity checksum.

Authentication

You can use encryption for authentication. For example, a shared secret key can authenticate two parties to each other. In the case of DCE, each principal has a secret key that is known only to itself and the security server. Thus, you can authenticate yourself to the security server by sending a message encrypted with your secret key. The security server would verify that you are who you claim to be by decrypting your message using your secret key. If the expected plaintext is recovered, that proves you know the secret key and are therefore authentic.

Authentication using public key systems is slightly different. In a public key system, every principal has a secret key that is only known to him or herself. A corresponding public key is made known to everyone. The property of public key systems is that if you encrypt a message using your secret key, it can be decrypted only with your public key. Likewise, a message encrypted with your public key can only be decrypted using your secret key. To authenticate you to someone else, all you need to do is to encrypt some text using your private key. The recipient does not need to know your private key. All that he or she needs to do is to retrieve your public key and decrypt the ciphertext. If the result looks OK, then you are who you claimed to be.

Digital signature

A digital signature is a means of verifying that you are the author of a message. It is easiest to illustrate this using public key cryptography. To "sign" a message in a public key system, you would compute a checksum of the message and encrypt the checksum with your secret key. You would then attach the encrypted checksum (signature) to the message. To verify that you signed the message, the recipient would just decrypt the checksum using your public key and compare it against a checksum computed from the message text.

Digital signature are implemented using public key systems because the secret key is known to only one individual. Thus, if the message is verified using that individual's public key, that individual must have "signed" it. This property is called **non-repudiation**. Secret key systems do not have this property because each secret key is known to at least two parties. If a message is signed using a secret key, the original signer could deny having signed it and accuse the other principal that shares the key as the signer.

Trusted Third Party

Secret key systems, because they rely upon sharing keys, are complex to manage. For example, for n people to authenticate each other, they would need n^2 keys. This is because each pair of communicating principals needs a unique secret key. The problem associated with generating all these keys, distributing them to the right principals, and storing them in a protected manner makes the direct use of secret key authentication non-scalable. This is an area where public key systems have an advantage. Public key systems scale because everyone can communicate with a principal using that principal's public key. You therefore do not need a separate pair-wise key. Thus, you would only need $2n$ keys (one public and one private key per principal). In addition, the public keys can be easily distributed since it is not a secret.

You can reduce the number of keys required, and improve scalability, in a secret key system if all the communicating parties are willing to share their secret keys with a common third party. If everyone trusts a principal, then everyone can just register a single key with the trusted principal and rely upon it to generate keys on a demand basis when two parties want to communicate. This reduces the number of keys required from $n\ 2$ to 2^n. This is the idea behind the Kerberos authentication service that is incorporated in DCE Security.

Kerberos Authentication Service

The Kerberos authentication service was developed by the Massachusetts Institute of Technology as part of Project Athena. It provides a trusted third party for key distribution and authentication. All the principals register their secret keys with the Kerberos authentication server. Then, when two parties want to authenticate each other, they step through a complicated process called the Kerberos authentication protocol. This just means a series of messages containing secret keys and other information that help clients and servers identity each other securely.

The Kerberos authentication protocol involves three parties: the client, the server, and the **key distribution center (KDC)**. The credentials or certificates mentioned earlier are here called **tickets**. The Kerberos protocol uses the various cryptographic operations that we described earlier as primitive operations and adds a layer of messages to foil certain attacks. For example, the Kerberos protocol avoids encrypting the same plaintext with your secret key for authentication; this prevents a wiretapper from taking the recorded results of an authentication exchange and retransmitting them to authenticate as you (the replay attack). Figure 1-4 shows the flow of messages that are required to establish an authenticated conversation between a client and a server. I have simplified the message exchange to make it easier to see what's going on. The shaded boxes are encrypted.

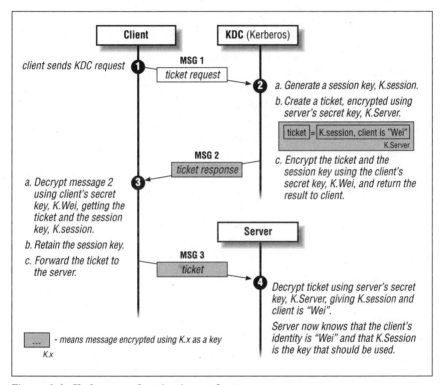

Figure 1-4: Kerberos authentication exchange

As you read about the rather complicated steps performed by the three parties, keep the security goals in mind. Neither the client nor the server should learn the other's key. However, they both get a new key that no one else in the world knows (except the key distribution center). Even the key distribution center forgets the key as soon as it is returned to the client. This key's lifetime is very short (a small number of hours); it enables them to carry out their shared task. The goal is to get the key to both client and server without letting anyone else learn it.

❶ A client starts the authentication exchange by sending a message to the KDC to request a new ticket. This is message 1 in Figure 1-4. The request specifies the identity of the client as well as that of the server that the client wishes to contact.

The KDC creates a ticket by generating a random **session key**, adding the identity of the client as well as some other information, and encrypting all of it using the server's secret key. The session key is a secret key whose only purpose is to authenticate one conversation between a client and server. It is not used beyond this conversation. In DCE, a conversation corresponds to an RPC connection between a client and a server. (A single RPC connection can be used for multiple RPC calls.) Figure 1-5 shows what the structure of a ticket looks like.

❷ The KDC then encrypts the ticket and another copy of the session key using the client's secret key and sends the result to the client. This corresponds to message 2 in Figure 1-4. The actual structure of the ticket response message is shown in Figure 1-6.

The KDC includes another copy of the session key because the client cannot access the copy in the ticket; only someone who has the server's secret key can decrypt and make sense of the information within the ticket.

❸ When the client receives the KDC's reply, it decrypts the message using the client's secret key. This yields the ticket as well as a copy of the session key the client can use. Since the KDC's reply is encrypted with the client's secret key, only the client can recover the session key and the ticket from the message. Note that at this point, even the client cannot take apart the ticket itself. This is because the ticket is encrypted using the server's secret key.

The client retains the session key for later use and forwards the ticket (which is still encrypted with the server's secret key) to the server as is. The ticket is message 3 in Figure 1-4.

❹ When the server gets the ticket, it decrypts it using its own secret key. Because the ticket was originally encrypted with the server's key, the server can decode the contents. The server therefore gets the identity of the client and the session key. This identity is certified by the KDC. The server knows that the ticket is authentic because only the KDC (besides the server itself) knows the server's secret key. Furthermore, only the true client could decode message 2, because it was encrypted with the client's secret key. This is how the server authenticates the client.

If the client requested mutual authentication (i.e., the client wants to know the authenticated identity of the server also), the server would send back a message encrypted with the session key. Since the session key was in the ticket encrypted using the server's secret key, possession of the right session key is proof that the server is the intended principal.

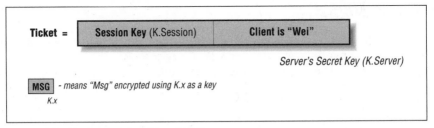

Figure 1-5: Kerberos ticket (simplified)

Figure 1-6: Kerberos ticket response message

The exchange described above is a basic model of the authentication protocol used by Kerberos and DCE Security. For clarity, I have omitted the processing used to detect the reuse of old messages. (To make sure clients and servers issue fresh responses, messages contain timestamps and unique markers called nonces.) The actual protocol also uses a session key, obtained from a **ticket-granting ticket** (TGT), instead of the client's secret key. The client would obtain a TGT from the ticket-granting server prior to acquiring tickets for any application servers. The ticket-granting server is also a component of Kerberos. The TGT is used instead of the secret key so that the secret keys themselves are not exposed more than needed. The initial acquisition of the TGT still involves the client's secret key. But once this is done, subsequent tickets are obtained using the TGT.

After the authentication exchange, the client and the server share a common secret key (the session key). This session key can be used for all the purposes described earlier. It can be used to individually authenticate the messages that are sent between the client and the server. It can be used to provide integrity protection. And it can be used as the encryption key to ensure the privacy of messages.

We can therefore see how the use of a trusted third party, in this case Kerberos, can address the scaling problems associated with managing secret keys. The tradeoff is that by storing all the keys at the KDC, it now becomes a single point of failure for the whole network. However, it is the commonly accepted way at present to make secret key based systems scale.

Single Logins

I want to take a slight detour now and discuss **single logins**, one of the benefits of network-based authentication services such as Kerberos. Single login allows you to log into some central authority once and not have to log in again regardless of which operating systems, machines, or applications you run after the initial login.

Single login addresses a common problem faced by people who run network applications. It is quite common today, for example, for a user to first log in to his or her local machine, *telnet* to another machine, then run a database application on the other machine. Because the individual operating systems and the database management system maintain their own security information, the user needs to log in (and produce a password) multiple times. Multiple logins are insecure because people cannot remember many different passwords and tend to write them down. In addition, because most passwords are transmitted across the network unencrypted, this mode of operation is vulnerable to someone monitoring packets that go across a network (wiretap attacks).

The single login solves this problem. When single login is implemented across your systems, you need to log into the network only once. Thereafter, whenever a local computer or software subsystem (e.g., a database management system) needs to verify your identity, it just queries the security server in the network for your identity. Single login is available for UNIX systems as part of Network Information Systems (NIS). Single login is also available as part of Novell's Netware.

DCE Security provides all the network services required to implement single login. First, it supplies all the information that local operating systems need. All the information that is normally stored in the */etc/passwd* files is available from the DCE Security Registry. At present, the registry is limited to local security attributes for UNIX-style systems. But DCE 1.1 will extend it to support arbitrary attributes that may be needed by non-UNIX operating systems and application subsystems. To implement single login, vendors have to change their local login programs to go over the network and query the security registry. The DCE Security APIs contain hooks to make this possible.

In today's DCE environments, single logins are available in a restricted form. Usually, single logins are integrated with the local operating system login. This allows a user to log into DCE once without having to separately log into the local operating system. As DCE becomes more widely deployed, you can expect to see single logins integrated with remote operations so that you don't need to reenter your password when you do a *telnet* or *rsh*. As more applications become DCE-ized, you can also expect to see single logins integrated into the application software that you run: database applications, mainframe links, etc.

Summary

This chapter dealt primarily with the background of distributed system security. I started by explaining why security is important in a distributed computing environment. I then covered some of the concepts and terminology used in the field (and DCE). I followed this with a description of the role that cryptography plays, and described the Kerberos authentication protocol that serves as the basis for DCE authentication. I concluded the chapter by discussing single logins. In the following chapters, I will show how all these concepts are applied to building secure distributed applications.

I want to end with a reminder. In this chapter, we've gone through a number of security mechanisms. These mechanisms were developed to address certain threats and are generally believed to be sound. One must not forget, however, that all these mechanisms depend upon the security of the underlying software and hardware. For example, we assume that the operating system would not take our secret keys and covertly transmit them to another user somewhere else. Since the operating system is only as secure as the underlying hardware, this in turn implies that we must trust the underlying hardware. For example, if someone has access to the physical machine, they can just load in a different operating system, or modify the hardware to cause an otherwise correctly functioning operating system to behave incorrectly.

Thus, the security of your distributed applications depends on the security of the local operating system and the physical security of the underlying computer hardware. In short, the machine hosting the security server (key distribution center) should be in a locked room.

2

What Does a DCE Security Server Do?

In Chapter 1, I gave an overview of the key concepts in distributed systems security. I described the model, terminology, and some of the underlying technologies that are used. I concluded the chapter by describing the Kerberos authentication protocol and single logins. With this background out of the way, we are now ready to look at DCE Security itself. We will start with the security servers upon which all the DCE security services are based.

Everyone knows that the security servers play a key role in making DCE and their distributed applications secure. But not many people know what these servers actually do. In this chapter, I will help you understand what they do. Because the security servers are network services that are accessed by remote clients, I will concentrate on the DCE security services as seen from a client system in the cell. Since what a client computer sees over the network are data packets, this chapter will concentrate on describing what these data packets are and how they are used to provide authentication and authorization services.

Most tutorials on DCE focus on using the **security application programming interface (API)**. This is because the API is what the application programmer sees. The API provides abstractions like binding handles, login contexts, etc. that allow applications to use the DCE security services. Indeed, you can develop simple, secure applications by using the API as a black box. If, however, your application needs to implement sophisticated mechanisms, or if you just want to understand why the API is structured the way it is and how it is designed to be used, then you must look beyond the API. This is because the API does not implement all the security mechanisms. Instead, they are implemented by the API code working in conjunction with the security servers in the cell. You must also look at the interaction between the API code and the security server to understand why DCE is secure.

The Security API and the Network Interface

Like any DCE server, the security server does its job by providing an interface that can be called by other programs. Whether you're writing the client or the server side of your application, you're a client of the security server. The calls that you use are called the **Security API**.

The security API, as you see it, is a subroutine library (*libdce*) that you link with your application code. When you call one of the functions, the underlying stub sends an RPC over the network to a security server. The security server processes the call and returns the results over the network. The **network interface** describes how these request/response messages are formatted; it tells you what bytes you need to send to the server in order to request services and what the resulting response message looks like. In DCE, these network interfaces are described using IDL. Figure 2-1 below illustrates the relationship between the API and the network interface.

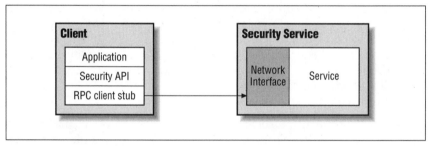

Figure 2-1: Relationship between the network interface and the API

If this still feels fuzzy, it may help to think of the DCE Security network interface as a specification of the code you must write if you want to implement a security server. The network interface is also what you must look at if you want to write another security server that interoperates with DCE Security. To replace a DCE security server, you would need to look at each of the DCE Security IDL files and implement all the remote procedures contained within them. Once you've done this, you should be able to plug your server into a DCE cell instead of a regular DCE security server and have things work as before. If you want to implement a proprietary security server that also interoperates with DCE security servers, your security server would need to translate between DCE Security's and your own network interfaces (that is assuming your own security servers support a different protocol.) All of this is possible because all that the other computers in a network see is the flow of messages as defined by the network interface.

Earlier, I said that DCE network interfaces are written in IDL. You might ask at this point why do we need an API library for DCE applications. In

particular, why don't clients just directly call the remote procedures specified in the server's IDL file? The first answer is that most API calls are not
implemented simply as an RPC to some server; they might, for example,
perform local operations. The other reason for having an API is that
servers usually implement low-level operations. For example, the DCE
security servers offer a ticket-granting service. If we export the remote
procedures directly as the client API, then the client applications would
have to do a fair amount of work to use the services. By providing a
higher level of service, such as authenticated RPC, that builds on top of
the primitive network interfaces, DCE greatly reduces the amount of work
that applications need to do. In addition, because we have added a layer
of API code over the network interfaces, we can change the network interface without affecting applications that use the current APIs.

DCE Security Services

A DCE Security server implements three network services. Each of these
services is a collection of RPC interfaces. The security services are: the
Authentication Service, the **Privilege Service**, and the **Registry Service**. The
Authentication Service provides mutual authentication for clients and
servers. It allows your server application to know the exact identity of the
client that is requesting a service. The DCE Authentication Service is the
key distribution service in the Kerberos model; it provides tickets and session keys.

Before we go further, you should know that my use of the term *Authentication Service* is different from that used by Kerberos. The Authentication
Service in Kerberos is just a component of the key-distribution service.
(The other part is the ticket-granting service.) I chose to combine them in
this book because separating out the functions of the ticket-granting service is not important for our purposes.

The Privilege Service supplies the authorization information about the
client that is calling your server. This is the information that your server
needs to decide whether the client is allowed to make the request. Privilege Service issues **Privilege Attribute Certificates** (**PACs**) and privilege tickets. And the Registry Service is the database that keeps track of the
security-relevant information about everyone in the cell. It is where the
names of your client and server principals and their secret keys are stored.

Note that although I talk about DCE Security as three separate security services, all the services are typically implemented by a single RPC server
usually called the security daemon, *secd*, that listens over all these RPC
interfaces. As you will see, these services have fairly simple network interfaces. The richness of DCE comes from building high level services on top
of these network primitives.

Authentication Service

The DCE Authentication Service is the trusted third party that authenticates clients and servers in a network. The primary mechanisms it uses are session keys and tickets.

A session key is a temporary secret key that is generated by the Authentication Service. The idea is that when two parties want to authenticate, they ask the Authentication Service to assign them a shared session key. This key is made known only to the two parties (and the Authentication Service itself). For security, the Authentication Service also forgets the session key as soon as it is returned to the requesting client. Then, when one side (say the client) sends a message to the other side (the server), the client would encrypt the message using the assigned session key. The server would then decrypt the message using its copy of the session key. If the message decrypts properly, the sender must be the client since the client is the only other principal that knows the key. If a client calls many servers, it should wind up with a different session key for each server with whom it communicates. Note that DCE provides facilities for clients and servers to generate their own session keys. However, I'm not going to discuss that aspect in this book.

The problem with the session keys, of course, is in getting the key to both the client and the server in such a manner that:

- The key cannot be tampered with.

- Both the client and server can verify that the session key was generated by the Authentication Service.

- No one else can get the session key even if they were to intercept the message that carried the session key. The DCE Authentication Service accomplishes all this through the use of tickets.

A ticket is an encrypted message that carries a session key and some other identifying information. Part of the ticket is encrypted (using a key that is shared only between the issuer and the final recipient of the ticket) to allow the intended recipient to verify the authenticity of the ticket. We are therefore putting the shared session key into another message that is encrypted using another key. Note that the requestor of the ticket (the client) cannot open a ticket targeted for the recipient since the requestor does not know the secret key of the recipient of the ticket. The Authentication Service passes some additional information outside of the ticket to let the requestor know what the session key is. What this means is that if I (the client) hand you (the server) a ticket, you can:

1. Verify that the ticket came from a legitimate authority (e.g., a security server).

2. Verify that I am who I claim to be.

3. Get a secret key (the session key) that we can use to authenticate each other and also to encrypt subsequent messages between us. Since the ticket is encrypted, you can't use a ticket that is directed to some other recipient.

The Service Ticket and the Ticket-Granting Ticket

The DCE Authentication Service supports two kinds of tickets. The ticket that a client passes to a server as part of an RPC is called a **service ticket** (**STkt**). It is called a service ticket because it is used by clients to obtain services. In DCE, service tickets are passed as part of authenticated RPC protocols. A service ticket carries a session key for use between a client and a server. Thus, a client must obtain an STkt in order to authenticate with a server. The other kind of ticket is the ticket-granting ticket (TGT). The TGT is what you use to obtain a service ticket. The TGT carries a session key for use between the client and the Authentication Service. A client must therefore have two tickets (and two session keys) in order to engage in authenticated communications with a server—the TGT and the STkt. Note that DCE uses more complicated forms of these tickets to support authorization. I'll describe them later in the chapter.

How the TGT and the STkt are used

Figure 2-2 shows how the TGT and the STkt are used at a high level. I will describe the parts in greater detail later. As we go through the flow, you should pay attention both to the tickets that are passed as well as the session keys that are carried by these tickets.

Get session key for use with the Authentication Service

❶ When a client, *Marty* say, starts up, it needs to get a shared session key between itself and the Authentication Service so that it can verifyfuture communications with the Authentication Service. To get the session key, the client makes a TGT request RPC to the Authentication Service.

❷ The Authentication Service generates a session key and puts it into a TGT. The TGT is then returned to the client *Kevin.* The client saves both the session key and the TGT so that they can be used when the client wishes to obtain service tickets to servers. At this point, the client has a session key that it can use for authenticating itself to the Authentication Service (and vice versa).

Get a session key for use with server

❸ Whenever the client *Marty* makes an authenticated RPC to a server, the client's RPC runtime must get a session key for use

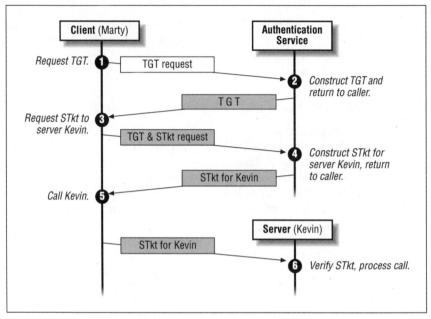

Figure 2-2: High level use of the TGT and STkt

with the server. This is done by obtaining an STkt on behalf of the client. To request an STkt, the client sends the TGT to the Authentication Service. Since DCE Security caches tickets, a client does not need to contact the Security Service on every RPC.

❹ The Authentication Service generates a session key for client *Marty* to authenticate with server *Kevin*, puts it into an STkt, and returns the STkt to the client. At this point, Marty knows the session key that it needs to use with Kevin.

Pass the session key to the server

❺ Marty makes the RPC to server *Kevin*. The STkt is passed as part of the RPC protocol. Inside the STkt is the session key.

❻ Server *Kevin's* RPC runtime validates the STkt. If it is valid, then the session key is extracted from the STkt. At this point, the client has been authenticated, and Kevin knows the session key to use when communicating with Marty. the RPC is allowed to proceed to its authorization step (discussed below). If there are any output arguments, they are encrypted using the session key so Marty can verify that they came from Kevin.

The client repeats steps 3 (request an STkt) for each distinct server it wants to call. The TGT and STkts can be cached and reused until they expire (as determined by the timestamps carried in the tickets). This, at a high level, is how TGTs and STkts are used.

Trust chain

In the flow above, notice how the client first obtains a session key for every server that it talks with before getting any information it needs from the server to go to the next step. What this does is allow the client to authenticate a server before using the information returned by the server. If there are multiple intervening servers, the client needs to establish a **trust chain**. A trust chain is a series of trust relationships that lead you to trust the final principal. Informally, the trust chain captures the notion of, If I trust C because B says it's okay, I have to make sure I can trust B. And I have to work this all the way back to someone I can really trust. In the case of the STkt, we have to make sure to authenticate the source of every piece of information that we use to authenticate the next principal in the chain.

The client verifies the authenticity of the TGT using its own long-term secret key. This allows it to trust the session key in the TGT. Then the client authenticates the STkt using the session key from the TGT. This allows the client to trust the next session key—the key in the STkt. And finally, the session key in the STkt is used to authenticate the server.

Now that we see how the tickets are used, we can look at what is carried in these tickets.

The ticket-granting ticket (TGT)

Figure 2-3 shows how the **TGT** and the **STkT** look. You may find it helpful to refer to this figure when I go over how these tickets are constructed and used.

TGTs are issued for use by specific clients. Every TGT has the well-known (fixed) name of the Authentication Service that issued the TGT plus an encrypted portion. The encrypted portion, shaded in the figure, is encrypted using K.AS. K.AS is the secret key of the DCE Authentication Service. The encrypted portion contains the name of the client, *Marty*, a TGT session key that is shared between the client and the Authentication Service, and the ticket **lifetime** (period during which this TGT is valid).

The most important part of the TGT is, of course, the TGT session key. This session key is generated by the Authentication Service for this TGT. I named this key *K (Marty, AS)* to indicate that this key is shared between Marty and the Authentication Service. This key will be used by Marty to authenticate its future STkt requests to the Authentication Service.

TGTs lifetimes are used like password expiration times. Limiting the lifetime of TGTs limits the amount of damage that can be caused by a compromised TGT. In DCE, there is currently no way to revoke a TGT once it has been issued. Thus, limiting the TGT lifetime implicitly sets a deadline after which the TGT becomes useless. (An expired TGT cannot be used to obtain tickets.)

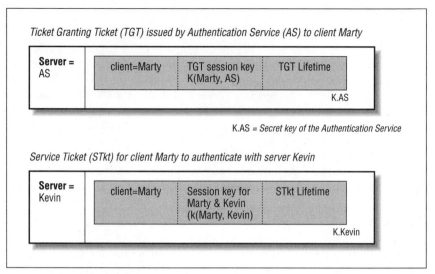

Figure 2-3: Structure of the TGT and STkt

The TGT also serves as a place where the Authentication Service can store any information it will later need for servicing STkt requests from this client. This is important because the Authentication Service does not remember past requests; it does not even keep copies of the session keys it assigns. Thus, the Authentication Service has to make sure it saves whatever context information it needs in the TGT. The Authentication Service will get the TGT back when the client makes an STkt request. At that point, the Authentication Service can retrieve the information that it put into the ticket earlier and use that in conjunction with any additional information in the request message to issue the STkt.

For ticket authentication to work, the Authentication Service needs to make sure that Marty cannot tamper with the information in the TGT to impersonate someone else. We protect the TGT against tampering by encrypting the TGT with the secret key of the Authentication Service, K.AS. This is an example of the use of encryption to protect the integrity (as well as the confidentiality) of a piece of information. We encrypt the TGT to ensure that someone else (who does not know the secret key of the Authentication Service) is not able to modify the TGT undetectably. This works because you can't generate a packet that, when decrypted using K.AS, will yield a legitimate TGT without knowing the value of K.AS.

The other threat to address is that someone else could intercept the message the Authentication Service sends to Marty, extract the TGT from the message, and then use the TGT to get service tickets. We prevent this possibility by encrypting portions of the message that holds the TGT using Marty's secret key before sending it back to Marty. This ensures that should the message be intercepted by someone else, that person (who presumably does not know Marty's secret key) would be unable to extract the session key from the message.

The Service ticket (STkt)

A service ticket is issued to a specific client for use with a specific server. An STkt issued by the Authentication Service to client *Marty* for authenticating with server *Kevin* contains two parts. The first part is the principal name of the target server, Kevin. The second part of the ticket is opaque to the client. It is encrypted under the secret key of the target server, *K.Kevin*. The encrypted portion of the STkt contains the name of the client, Marty, a session key generated by the Authentication Service that Marty and Kevin can use, and a lifetime during which the STkt is valid.

You can think of the service ticket as a passport that does not have a picture of the person to whom the passport is issued. The passport is issued by some trusted authority (i.e., some recognized government) to a traveler (the client). The traveler produces the passport to a customs officer (the server) to gain admission to a country. We assume that the admitting country trusts the issuing country of the passport (by an international agreement of some sort). The first problem that need to be solved is how to verify that the person who holds the passport is really the person to whom it was issued. The second problem is in creating a passport such that the customs officer can reliably determine that the passport is genuine and has not been tampered with by someone else, including the traveler holding the passport.

The solution, of course, is to give the traveler a code word and to write the code word itself in the passport. To prevent someone from impersonating this traveler should the passport be stolen, we must also write the code word itself using another secret code that only the customs officer can read. The customs officer then asks the traveler to give the code word to prove that he or she is really the person to whom the passport is issued. You can refine this example further by adding a step that requires the customs officer prove he is genuine by having him demonstrate knowlege of his own secret key.

The service ticket is therefore the data structure that the Authentication Service uses to pass the client identity and session key to the server through an intermediary (the client). Like the customs officer, the server cannot trust the client until the client's identity has been verified by the service ticket the client is holding. We resolve this problem by encrypting the service ticket with the secret key of the intended server (*K.Kevin* in this case). Encrypting the information using Kevin's secret key protects the ticket against tampering (because the client would not know Kevin's secret key), and allows Kevin to believe that the information in the ticket really came from the Security Service (because only the Security Service knows Kevin's secret key besides Kevin himself). Finally, encrypting the ticket also ensures that someone who gets a copy of the ticket by monitoring the network will not be able to use the session key contained within the ticket. Since the session key will be used by the client and server to authenticate each other's messages later, this prevents someone else from impersonating either the client or the server.

Obtaining the TGT

A client needs a TGT to get two pieces of data: a TGT session key for authenticating itself with the Authentication Service in future ticket requests and some context information that needs to be supplied in these requests. A principal typically asks the security server for a TGT when the principal logs into DCE. In the case of a user, this would be during *dce_login* (or an integrated login program.) Once a TGT has been obtained, it can be reused until it expires. Figure 2-4 shows the process involved in getting a TGT.

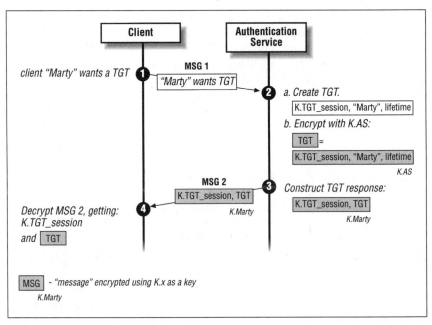

Figure 2-4: Obtaining a TGT

❶ The client logs in. As part of logging into DCE, the login program requests a TGT on behalf of the client. This results in a TGT-request RPC to the DCE Authentication Service (the security server). This is Message 1. The request message includes the principal name of the client, *Marty*; the desired lifetime of the ticket; and some other miscellaneous information.

❷ The Authentication Service creates a TGT. The TGT contains the identity of the client, a randomly generated session key (the TGT session key), and the lifetime of the TGT. The entire TGT is encrypted under the secret key of the Authentication Service.

❸ The Authentication Service then constructs a response message containing the TGT, a copy of the TGT session key, and some other information. The message is then encrypted using the client's secret key, *K.Marty* (that is known to the Security Service) so that some other process that is masquerading as the client would not be able to use the TGT or obtain the TGT session key.

Because the response message is encrypted under Marty's secret key, the Authentication Service can return Marty's TGT to anyone who asks for it. This is secure because only Marty can decrypt the TGT response message to get the TGT session key or the TGT.

In any case, the result (Message 2) is returned to the client.

❹ The client decrypts the message from the Authentication Service using the client's secret key *K.Marty*. If the client principal is really Marty, it will successfully get the TGT (that is still encrypted under the Authentication Service's secret key) and a copy of the TGT session key.

At this point, the client has a TGT (still encrypted under the Authentication Service's secret key) and a copy of the TGT session key. This is enough for the client to authenticate with the Authentication Service.

Obtaining the STkt

Whenever the client needs to talk to a particular server, the client needs to request a service ticket targeted to that server. The objective of the STkt request is to get a new session key for the client to use in authenticating with the server. The TGT is forwarded as part of this request. Figure 2-5 shows the messages that are exchanged to obtain an STkt. For clarity, I have omitted some fields from the tickets.

❶ The client, *Marty*, decides to make an authenticated RPC to a server whose principal name is *Kevin*.

Before the RPC is made, the client must first indicate that it wants to use authenticated RPC. This causes the client's RPC runtime to ask the Authentication Service for an STkt. This is Message 1; it includes the name of the server, Kevin, and the TGT. This message is integrity-protected via an encrypted checksum using the session key between the client and the Authentication Service.

❷ The Authentication Service receives the STkt request. It extracts the TGT from the request and decrypts it using its own secret key, *K.AS*. Since the TGT contains data encrypted using the Authentication Service's secret key, this operation has to fail if the TGT was forged.

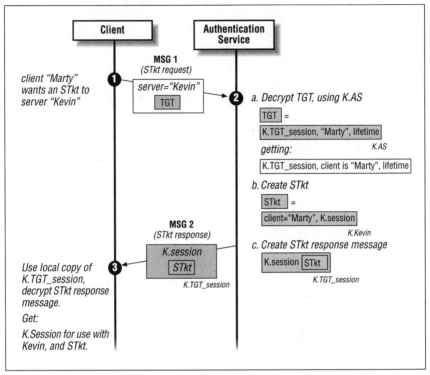

Figure 2-5: Obtaining an STkt

After the TGT is decrypted, the Authentication Service gets back the information that it put into the ticket when the TGT was issued—the identity of the client to whom the TGT was issued, the lifetime of the TGT, and the TGT session key. Now the Authentication Service has all the information it needs to create the STkt.

The Authentication Service now constructs the STkt that would allow the client to authenticate with the target server, *Kevin*. The Authentication Service first generates a session key for use between the client and the target server, *K (Marty, Kevin)*. This key, along with the identity of the client, *Marty*, are put into the STkt. The STkt is then encrypted using the target server's secret key, *K.Kevin*, thus insuring that only the server, *Kevin*, can decrypt the STkt and assuring the target server that the ticket is genuine. (Kevin can believe that the received STkt is genuine if it decrypts properly using Kevin's secret key because besides Kevin itself, only the Security Service knows Kevin's secret key.)

The Authentication Service then encrypts the STkt and a copy of the session key using the TGT session key and sends the resulting message back to the client. This procedure corresponds to Message 2 shown in Figure 2-5. Note that the encryption used is different from the TGT response, which was encrypted using the client's secret key. I'll discuss the importance of this point later.

❸ The client receives the STkt response. It decrypts the message using its copy of the TGT session key (obtained from the previous TGT request). Once the client decrypts the message, he gets the session key for it to use with the server Kevin, *K (Marty, Kevin)* and the STkt.

If the response decrypts properly using the TGT session key, the client can believe that the response really came from the Authentication Service. This is because the message would decrypt properly only if it was encrypted using the same TGT session key. The TGT session key was stored in the TGT that was encrypted under the Authentication Service's secret key. The fact that the sender of the STkt response encrypted the message using the TGT session key meant that the sender must have been able to decrypt the TGT and hence must know the Authentication Service's secret key.

In addition to authenticating the sender of the STkt response message, the encryption also ensures that only the client to whom the TGT was sent can use the STkt. This is because only the real client (or someone who knows its secret key) could have decrypted the original TGT response message to get the client's copy of the TGT session key.

At this point, the client Marty has once again a session key it can use to authenticate with the next server in the trust chain. In addition, Marty has a copy of the STkt that it cannot read. Marty cannot read the contents of the STkt itself since that is encrypted under Kevin's secret key. As I mentioned before, the STkt is a way for the security server to pass information about Marty to Kevin in such a way that Marty cannot alter what the security server said.

Using the STkt

Now that Marty has an STkt and a session key for use with Kevin, Marty must inform Kevin of the session key. This is done as part of the RPC. The RPC runtime sends the STkt as part of the RPC connection setup. Figure 2-6 illustrates what happens next.

❶ The client makes the actual RPC to the server. The STkt is passed to the server when the RPC connection is set up.

❷ The server receives the RPC call. It decrypts the STkt using its secret key, *K.Kevin*, and gets back the shared session key and the identity of the client.

Now the server knows that the authenticated identity of the client is *Marty* and the session key that it should use to authenticate with the client. The server performs the requested remote operation and then uses the shared session key to encrypt the results of the RPC.

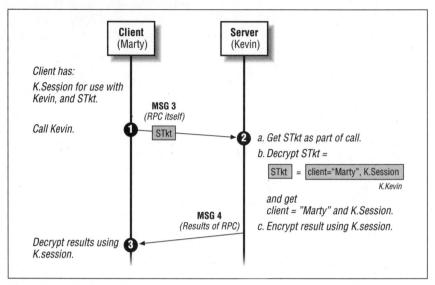

Figure 2-6: Using an STkt

The server Kevin trusts both the identity and the session key because the STkt was encrypted using the Kevin's secret key; and only the security server knows that key (besides Kevin). Since Kevin knows that the session key was issued by the Security Service for use with Marty, Kevin can safely authenticate Marty's subsequent communications using that session key.

❸ The client Marty receives the call results. It decrypts the results using the shared session key. If the RPC packet decrypts successfully, then it knows that the server is really Kevin. Had the server not been Kevin, it would not have been able to decode the STkt to get the session key. Thus, the fact that the server was able to use the session key demonstrates to the client that the server is Kevin.

At this point, both Marty and Kevin have copies of a shared session key that they can safely use to authenticate each other's communications. And we are done.

This then, is how a client uses the STkt to authenticate with a server. As you'll see later, the entire sequence of message exchanges is what takes place (under the covers) when you use authenticated RPC with name-based authorization.

Now that we've gone through how TGTs are used, we can discuss why TGTs are good to have. DCE uses TGTs so that a client only needs to use its secret key when obtaining the initial TGT. Thereafter, the client just uses the TGT to obtain tickets instead of the client's secret key. DCE could have implemented an entire authentication system that used only service tickets. This means that the Authentication Service would encrypt the STkt response message using the requesting client's secret key and the client would use its secret keys to decrypt the STkt response message. However, that would not be as safe as using TGTs. Reducing the need to use the client's secret key is important because the more often a key is used, the easier it becomes for someone else to figure out what the secret key is. The other reason for reducing the direct use of the client's secret key is that the chance of accidentally disclosing the secret key increases as the key is handled (read, stored, etc.) by more pieces of software.

Now that we've seen how the client and server authenticate each other's identities, the next topic to address is authorization. The STkt conveys authentication information. It does not, however, convey all the principal's security attributes. For example, group membership information is not part of the STkt. To see how a server gets a client's full security attributes, we need to look at the second of the three security services—the Privilege Service.

Privilege Service

While authentication answers the question, "who is Marty?", authorization answers the question, "Is Marty allowed to perform this operation?" The Authentication Service issues session keys to authenticate clients and servers. The Privilege Service issues PACs that describe a client's security attributes. PACs are what servers use to determine whether a given client is authorized to perform a specific operation. PACs are therefore created to support authorization.

What is a PAC?

In Chapter 1, I introduced the concept of a certificate that carries a principal's security attributes. In DCE, such a certificate is called a PAC. The PAC carries the authorization information that is used to make access-control decisions. In DCE, these security attributes are the principal's identity and the group information. DCE supports two types of PACs. DCE 1.0.x uses version 1 PACs while DCE 1.1 has extended the PAC to incorporate additional security information related to delegation. I will discuss the extended PAC format when we discuss delegation.

A version 1 PAC is depicted in Figure 2-7.

The *authentication flag* shows whether this PAC was authenticated by DCE Security. This Flag is necessary because clients can supply unauthenticated PACs. Since anyone can create an unauthenticated PAC, you are basically trusting the client to be whom it claims to be. Unauthenticated PACs are therefore used only for migrating applications designed to work with older security mechanisms to DCE. As you might expect, servers normally

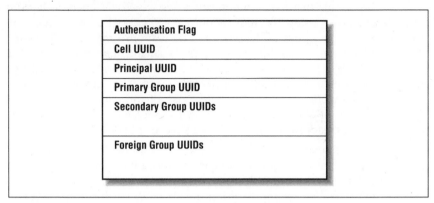

Figure 2-7: Version 1 privilege attribute certificate (PAC)

grant only restricted access to clients who use unauthenticated PACs. The next field, the *cell UUID*, is the UUID of the principal's home cell, i.e., the cell in whose registry the principal is registered. This Field is followed by the *principal UUID*, the UUID of the principal whose security attributes are described by this PAC.

The rest of the PAC describes the various groups to which the principal identified by the PAC belongs. Although the PAC provides for both local and foreign groups, DCE currently supports only local groups. Local groups are groups registered in the principal's home cell. For purposes of checking for access, all the local groups are treated the same. For example, you will be granted access if any of your groups are authorized. For administrative purposes, one of these groups is the primary group. This is the group whose UUID is stored in the *primary group UUID* field of the PAC. The other local groups are then stored in a variable-length list following the primary group UUID.

The last part of the PAC is the list of foreign groups. These are groups registered in remote cells to which this principal belongs. Each entry in this list specifies the foreign cell UUID as well the foreign group UUID. This list will always be empty in DCE 1.0 and DCE 1.1.

I want to emphasize at this point that DCE applications should use PACs instead of just the client principal name that is available in the STkt for authorization. This is because PACs contain the UUIDs that are needed to work with DCE access control lists. In addition, group information is available only in PACs. Name-based authorization does have a role, however, in working with non-DCE applications and also in situations where access control lists are not appropriate.

How PACs Are Used

DCE uses a client-initiated model for conveying privilege information. With this model, it is the client that obtains the PAC from the Privilege Service and then forwards the PAC to the server. The server then uses the authorization information in the PAC to make access-control decisions. Usually, the server compares the principal and group UUIDs in the PAC against those stored in access control lists. Since the PAC contains all the authorization information, the server can make its access control decisions without having to contact the Privilege Service again.

The Authenticaton Service uses tickets to pass session keys and other authentication information. The Privilege Service extends these tickets to carry privilege information. These extended tickets are called PTGT. A privilege ticket is a ticket (issued by the Authentication Service) that contains a PAC in addition to the normal authentication information. The Privilege Service does not directly issue privilege service tickets for client to talk with servers. Instead, the Privilege Service issues a modified version of the TGT called **privilege ticket-granting ticket (PTGT)** that will include PACs in all the tickets generated from the TGT. Such a privileged service ticket will be called a **privilage service ticket (PSTkt)**.

We can now look at how a client obtains and passes the PAC to the server. Figure 2-8 shows how this is done at a high level.

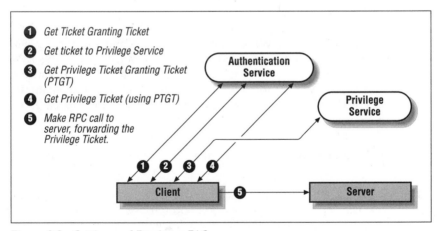

Figure 2-8: Getting and Passing a PAC

❶ Establish authenticated communications with the Privilege Service. To get a PAC, the client must contact the Privilege Service. To make sure that it is calling a genuine Privilege Service, the client will first obtain a session key to the Privilege Service by using the normal Authentication Service protocol.

The client obtains a TGT from the Authentication Service using the protocol described in the first part of this chapter. This gives the client an initial session key that it shares with the Authentication Service.

❷ The client then asks the Authentication Service for an STkt to the Privilege Service. The Privilege Service is treated like any other server. The client passes the TGT to the Authentication Service as before. The Authentication Service returns an STkt for the client to pass to the Privilege Service. As part of this, the client also gets a session key that it should use with the Privilege Service.

❸ Ask Privilege Service for a PTGT (with PAC). At this point, the client has a session key for use with the Privilege Service. The client can safely ask the Privilege Service for the PTGT:

The client sends the STkt to the Privilege Service to ask for a PTGT. The PTGT is a TGT that can be used to obtain a PSTkt; i.e., STkts that contain PACs.

The Privilege Service authenticates the client by decrypting the STkt. As part of this operation, the Privilege Service gets its copy of the session key to use with the client. Assuming that the client has been authenticated, the Privilege Service creates the client's PAC and puts it in the PTGT. The PTGT is returned to the client.

At this point, the client has a PTGT that can be used to obtain STkts with PACs.

❹ Get session key and PAC for use with server. Now the client wants to make an RPC to the server. To get a session key and PAC for use with the server, it needs to get a PSTkt for that server. It issues the PSTkt request by sending the PTGT to the Authentication Service. Because of the way the PTGT is formed, the resulting ticket will contain the client's PAC. I'll describe how this is done later. In any case, the Authentication Service returns an STkt that contains an imbedded PAC in addition to a session key—a PSTkt.

Now the client has a session key that can authenticate the server and a PAC.

❺ Pass session key and PAC to server. The client sends the PSTkt to the server. The server decodes the ticket and retrieves the session key and the PAC. The server uses the PAC to make authorization decisions. The call completes if the client is authorized and the server's responses are authenticated via the session key passed in the PSTkt.

Notice how the client needs to build a trust chain as before. The client gets an initial session key using the TGT, then uses it to authenticate the next ticket, and so forth until it obtains the final session key to the server. This chain is longer than the TGT/STkt one described before because we have to talk to the Privilege Service in addition to the Authentication Service.

As you can see, DCE implements the Privilege Service as another network service that uses the services offered by the Authentication Service. This is why a client must first obtain a TGT (that has no PAC) and an STkt to the Privilege Service to ask for a PTGT. Separating the Privilege and Authentication Services instead of creating an integrated service that only deals with privilege tickets is a good approach because it allows us to replace these components independently. We can, for example, replace the current secret key-based Authentication Service with a public key-based system and still retain the existing Privilege Service architecture.

There are other advantages for separating the services: the Privilege Service is simpler since it does not need to provide a general ticket-granting service. This makes it more reliable. Having each of the services provide a small, well-defined set of functions make them easier to analyze for correctness—a prerequisite for security.

Now that I've sketched out the high-level flow of privilege tickets, we can look in detail at what they contain.

Structure of a PTGT and PSTkt

The PTGT and the PSTkt are TGTs and STkts that carry PACs. It is important to know that a PTGT is treated as a TGT by the Authentication Service; the same goes for the PSTkt and STkt. If I were to pass the PTGT to the Authentication Service as part of an STkt request, for example, the resultant STkt will be a PSTkt because of the way certain values are set in the PTGT. To help you refer to the various pieces of the privilege ticket-granting ticket and the privilege service ticket, I refer to Figure 2-9, which depicts the structure of these privilege tickets.

As you can see, the PTGT looks like a TGT while the PSTkt looks like the STkt. For example, privilege tickets also contain session keys and ticket lifetimes. If you look closely, however, you will notice two differences. First, both the PTGT and the PSTkt contain a client PAC. For example, the PAC describes Marty's security attributes. The presence of the PAC is the primary thing that makes privilege tickets different from normal tickets.

The other difference is that the privilege tickets specify the Privilege Service as the client while the TGT and STkt specify the real client (Marty). As we'll see later, this is done so that the recipient of the PAC can determine that the PAC really originated from a legitimate Privilege Service. (The identity of the real client can be found in the PAC itself.)

How PACs Are Propagated by PTGTs

In describing how the PSTkt is generated (step 4 in Figure 2-8), I said that when the Authentication Service gets a PTGT, it automatically generates an STkt with that PAC. (This STkt becomes a PSTkt.) This is a feature of

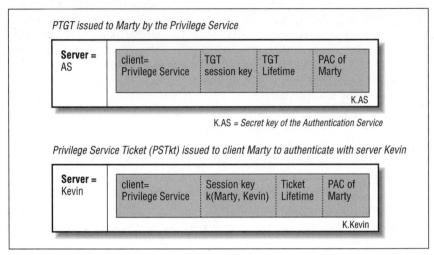

Figure 2-9: Format of the PTGT and PSTkt

Kerberos V5 that was inherited by the DCE Authentication Service. Basically, the Authentication Service has reserved an **authorization data field** in the tickets that it uses. The Authentication Service only provides the space; it does not interpret the contents of this field. The meaning of the data in this field is left to the authorization service to define. What the Authentication Service will do, however, when it gets a TGT non-null authorization data field, is copy the contents of the field into the STkts that is generated.

The objective of the Privilege Service is therefore to generate a TGT that has a PAC in the authorization data field. Once we have this TGT, we will automatically get service tickets that contain the PAC. This should become clearer as I go through the steps of how the privilege tickets are obtained and used.

Obtaining the PTGT

We assume that the client *Marty* wants to make an authenticated RPC using PAC-based authorization to server *Kevin*. When the RPC call is made, the RPC runtime checks to see if Marty already has a PTGT. (A PTGT, like the TGT, can be reused until it expires.) Let's assume that this is the first time, and Marty has no PTGT. Figure 2-10 shows how the client passes the PTGT request to the Privilege Service. The purpose of the PTGT request is to get back a TGT that will allow the client to get STkts with PACs in them (or PSTkts).

❶ Since Marty does not have a PTGT, we will start with the TGT. (If Marty does not have a TGT, then he can get one by logging in.) The RPC runtime uses the TGT and asks the Authentication Service for an STkt to the Privilege Service.

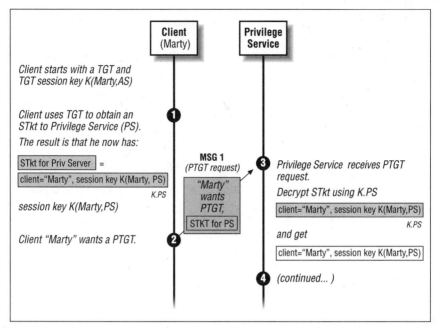

Figure 2-10: Obtaining a PTGT

Marty gets back the usual STkt response message, decrypts it, and gets both an STkt it can forward to the Privilege Service and a session key, *K (Marty, PS)* to be used for authenticated communications with the Privilege Service. All these steps are part of the Authentication Service protocol we saw earlier.

❷ Now that Marty has a session key for communicating with the Privilege Service, it can ask that Service for the PTFT. Marty sends a PTGT request (Message 1) to the Privilege Service. This PTGT request contains the STkt obtained from step 1. As I described before, this STkt passes the session key *K (Marty, PS)* to the server (the Privilege Service in this case). The STkt is encrypted as usual under the server's (the Privilege Service) secret key by the Authentication Service.

❸ The Privilege Service decrypts the STkt and gets a copy of the session key, *K (Marty,PS)*, and the identity of the client, *Marty*.

At this point, the Privilege Service has all the information it needs to construct the PTGT and a session key that it should use to authenticate the results of this call. Figure 2-11 shows the remaining steps:

❹ The Privilege Service constructs the PTGT. The purpose of the PTGT is to hold a session key and a PAC that describes Marty's security attributes so that the Authentication Service can use it to generate PSTkts. The Privilege Service uses the name specified in the PTGT

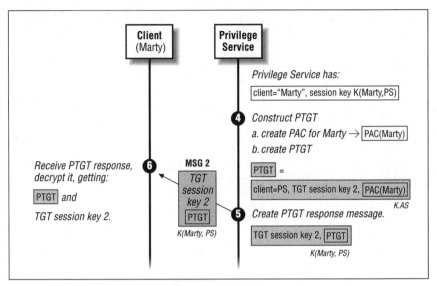

Figure 2-11: Creating and returning the PTGT

request, Marty, and asks the security registry to get his identity and the list of groups to which he belongs. The Privilege Service then generates a new session key, the **PTGT session key**.

Now the Privilege Service copies this information into a TGT. The Privilege Service copies the PAC into the authorization data field of the ticket. In addition, the PTFT session key is also copied. The Privilege Service then sets the client field of the TGT to be itself (i.e., the Privilege Service) instead of the real client. I'll explain why this is done shortly. At this point, the TGT is a PTGT because it contains privilege information.

After filling in all the fields of the PTGT, the Privilege Service encrypts the PTGT using the Authentication Service's secret key. The Privilege Service uses the Authentication Service's secret key because regular TGTs are encrypted in that way. As we saw earlier, the Authentication Service will reject any STkt request should the submitted TGT not decrypt properly using its secret key. (The Privilege Service can get the Authentication Service's secret key because they are really part of the same Security Service.)

❺ The Privilege Service now constructs the PTGT response message (Message 2). The PTGT response message contains the PTGT from step 3 and a copy of the new session key, the PTGT session key. The entire message is encrypted under the session key passed to the Privilege Service in step 2, *K (Marty, PS)*. This allows the Privilege Service to make sure that only Marty can read the response and get the STkt and session key. It also allows Marty to know the response really came from the Privilege Service as only the Privilege Service could have extracted the session key from the STkt.

❻   The client, Marty, gets Message 2 and decrypts it. He obtains the PTGT session key and the PTGT. He saves both for later use.

Obtaining the PSTkt

At this point, the client has a PTGT and the associated PTGT session key. Now the client has all it needs to get PSTkts; Figure 2-12 shows how the PTGT can be used to acquire a PSTkt.

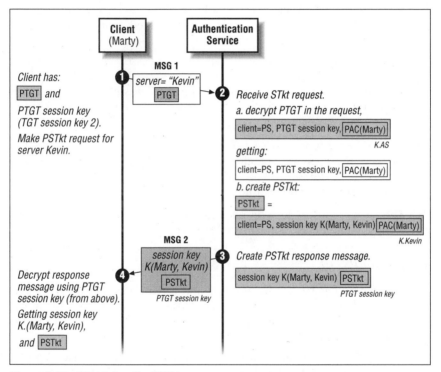

Figure 2-12: Obtaining the PSTkt

❶   The client asks the Authentication Service for a PSTkt to server *Kevin* using a regular STkt request message. The request message (Message 1) contains the name of the server, Kevin, and a copy of the client's PTGT. (We can use the STkt request because a PSTkt is also an STkt.)

❷   The Authentication Service gets the STkt request. It decrypts the PTGT in the request using its secret key, *K.AS* and gets: Privilege Service as the client, Kevin as the server that the client wants to talk to, and a non-null authorization data field (containing the PAC). It proceeds to generate an STkt as usual.

The Authentication Service sets the STkt's client to be the Privilege Service (as specified in the PTGT) and generates a new session key, *K (Marty, Kevin)*. Since the authorization data field in the PTGT is non-null, the Authentication Service copies the contents of the authorization data field from the PTGT to the STkt. This results in the PAC being transferred to the STkt. Since the STkt now contains a PAC, it becomes a PSTkt. Note that the Authentication Service copies the contents of the authorization data field blindly; it does not know the internal structure of the PAC. The PSTkt is encrypted using the intended server's secret key, *K.Kevin.*

Note how the Authentication Service processes the PSTkt request exactly as it would a normal STkt request. The differences result from the way the Privilege Service has set up the fields in the PTGT (adding a PAC and setting the Privilege Service as the client) that is passed as part of the request.

❸   The Authentication Service constructs the PSTkt response message. In essence, the message contains the PSTkt and a copy of the new session key, *K (Marty, Kevin)*. The entire message is encrypted using the PTGT session key and returned to the requestor.

❹   The client receives the STkt response, decrypts it, and obtains the session key and the PSTkt for use with Kevin.

Using the PSTkt

The client now has both a session key and a PSTkt targeted for the server Kevin. The client now needs to pass the PSTkt (containing the session key and PAC) to Kevin. This is done when the RPC connection is set up. Figure 2-13 shows what happens.

Note that DCE RPC handles tickets differently when running over connection-oriented and connection-less transports. In the example below, I'll describe the way it works over the connection-oriented transport.

❺   The client makes the RPC to the server Kevin and forwards the PSTkt when the RPC connection is set up.

❻   Kevin's RPC runtime receives the PSTkt and decrypts it using Kevin's secret key. At this point, it needs to verify that the PAC was really issued by the Privilege Service. It does so by verifying that the client specified in the PSTkt is the Privilege Service. If you recall, the Privilege Service set the client to be itself when the PTGT was created. This

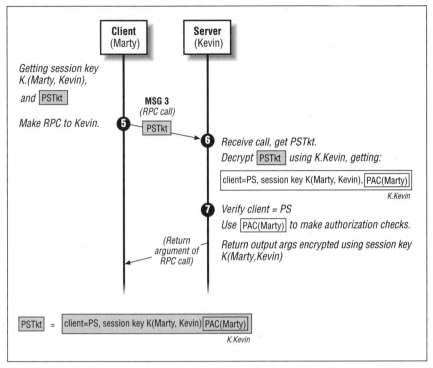

Getting session key
K.(Marty, Kevin),

and PSTkt

Make RPC to Kevin.

Figure 2-13: Using the PSTkt

name was then copied into the PSTkt by the Authentication Service when the PSTkt was created. Since the ticket is encrypted using Kevin's secret key, Kevin knows that it has not been forged.

❼ "How," you might ask, "does the server get the identity of the real client if the PSTkt names the Privilege Service as the client?" The answer is that the server gets it from the PAC. The information in the PAC can be used as soon as the server has verified that the PSTkt carrying the PAC was issued by a trusted Privilege Service.

Review

The DCE Authentication Service allows clients to authenticate with servers by issuing session keys that are carried in tickets. Encryption is used so that both the client and server can trust the key and so that no one else can read the key. DCE uses a TGT to generate an initial session key for the client to communicate with the Authentication Service. The client thus can avoid using its own secret key for each ticket request. After obtaining the TGT, the client uses it to request additional tickets to individual servers. These additional tickets are called service tickets. Each of these service tickets in turn carries a new session key that can be used to authenticate with the named server. The whole purpose of the authentication service exchange is therefore to securely pass the client's identity and a session key to the server the client wants to authenticate.

The DCE Authorization Service (or Privilege Service) enhances the Authentication Service by adding Privilege Attribute Certificates (PACs) to tickets. PACs provide the security attributes that are used by servers to make authorization checks. The tickets that carry PACs are called privilege tickets—the Privilege Ticket-Granting Ticket (PTGT) and the Privilege Service Ticket (PSTkt).

DCE applications only use unprivileged tickets to talk with the Privilege Service to get an initial privilege ticket-granting ticket. From that point on, the PTGT is used to get other privilege tickets. This, at a very high level, is the set of network services that the Authentication and Privilege Services provide. You may have noticed that I did not really describe how authorization is really done. For example, I did not describe access control lists and how servers check a client's privileges. I'll discuss these aspects in later chapters.

The Authentication and Privilege Services are really the core network service offered by DCE Security. These services, however, cannot exist in a vacuum. For example, these servers need to know the secret keys of all the principals in the cell. Where are these keys kept? The Privilege Service needs a client's security attributes to create a PAC. Where are the list of groups to which a principal belongs kept? The answer to these questions is the Registry Service.

Registry Service

The Registry Service is the third network service offered by DCE Security. You can think of the DCE Registry Service as the network's analog of the UNIX */etc/passwd* and */etc/group* files. The Registry Service maintains a database of all the principal, group, and account information for a cell. The Registry also stores information about the cell as a whole. This information is used by the Authentication Service and the Privilege Service as well as application programs. The following is a summary of the information stored in the Registry:

Cell information

This is information about the Security Service itself as well as information that is not specific to the other objects. This includes the cell name and UUID, the version of the software that the Registry itself is running, and the bounds on the UNIX IDs that the Registry can assign to accounts. (When the Registry creates a DCE account for a principal, it also assigns a corresponding local UNIX ID.) Cell information also includes general cell-wide security policy information. This includes the minimum ticket lifetime and the default lifetime of TGTs.

Principal, group, and organization information

The registry stores a list of all the principals, groups, and organizations (PGO for short). For each PGO entry, the registry stores its UUID, its name, and its UNIX ID. In the case of a principal, for example, this would be the principal UUID, the principal name, and the corresponding UNIX ID for the principal. (As an optimization, UNIX IDs are embedded in the UUIDs.) Note that the organization concept is a local-cell administrative convenience that can be used on a site-specific basis, but is generally irrelevant for UNIX systems. Groups also do not have UUIDs, since they are not included in PACs.

Account information

DCE accounts are like local system accounts—you must log into an account before you can use DCE services. An account represents a principal to DCE. Each account has an associated principal and a list of groups to which the principal belongs. The account information consists of a network portion and a local system portion. The network portion contains the information necessary to acquire tickets and other services. For example, it includes the principal's secret key.

The local portion of the account information contains the entries normally stored in the */etc/passwd* file. It includes information such as the home directory and the shell to run. The local portion is designed to support network-wide single login, whereby logging into DCE automatically logs a user into all the local accounts also. This is usually accomplished by integrating the local system login with DCE login such that, if the user successfully logs into DCE, the login program would query the security registry for the local account information and automatically log the user into the local system and set up his or her environment.

All the security services are replicated; there is a primary server where updates can take place and multiple read-only replicas of the server. This is important because of the key role the security service plays in DCE. If your cell has a single security service and it crashes, for example, no client can obtain new tickets. This means that authenticated communications cannot take place. Since the DCE services communicate among themselves using authenticated RPC also, the whole cell would quickly grind to a halt.

DCE Security is designed so that you can manage it from anywhere in the network. To do this, all the data stored in the security registry are accessible through remote interfaces. For example, you can add a new account by making an RPC to one of the registry interfaces. For convenience, API functions have been implemented on top of the client stub to make it easier for programs to access the data in the registry. Because there is such a large variety of information that is stored in the registry, the Registry Service has the most network interfaces (and API calls) among the security services.

The Registry APIs are the only exposed interfaces to the registry. Even *rgy_edit*, the program you run to edit the contents of the registry, makes use of these APIs. *rgy_edit* is just a command-line front-end that makes calls on the Registry API. These APIs, in turn, issue RPC calls to the interfaces exported by the security registry. When you run *rgy_edit* to list the groups in the cell, for example, the *rgy_edit* program makes procedure calls to the *sec_rgy_pgo_* routines that internally make RPC calls on the PGO management interface of the Registry Service to get the information. Structuring the management interface this way has several advantages. First, the program can be run anywhere in the network instead of directly on the server machine. Secondly, having a clean API means that you can develop alternate user interfaces to the Registry. This is in fact what DCE 1.1 has done with the *dcecp* program. (*dcecp* is the single control program that replaces several DCE administrative control programs, such as *rpccp*, *cdscp*, and *rgy_edit*.)

Because entries in the security registry are accessed via RPCs, they need to perform authorization checks to ensure that the caller is authorized to view or update the data item. (This is analogous to the way the */etc/passwd* file itself is protected with permission bits, normally restricting access to root. The registry does this by using ACLs. The default ACL that is placed on all the data in the registry allows the cell_administrator to read and write the data. In order to attach ACLs to a DCE object, you have to specify the name of the object. This name is what you pass to *acl_edit*, for example, when you want to look at an object's ACLs. To make this possible, the Registry Service presents an external interface of a tree-structured directory under which all the data items can be named. For example, if one creates a group named *admin*, */.:/sec/group/admin* is the name that one would specify to modify the ACL on that object. I will describe how this is done when I discuss the implementation of DCE ACLs.

Management Interface

One issue that cuts across all the security services is remote management. DCE servers are unique in that all administration is done remotely via RPCs. The tools that manage these services are standard RPC client applications. Even if you run the control program locally on the server's machine, it still goes through the RPC interfaces. This means you can manage the server from anywhere within the DCE cell, not just on the local server machine. Interestingly enough, it is the availability of DCE security services that makes it possible for you to safely manage critical network resources like the security registry from a remote site. The lack of a distributed Security Service is one of the reasons why most traditional, non-DCE systems require all administration to be done on the servers themselves.

Another benefit of defining an RPC-based management interface is that we now have a well-defined interface between control programs such as *rgy_edit* and the underlying management operations. Since the RPC interfaces are public, vendors can supply value-added replacement for the standard tools supplied with DCE.

Differences Between DCE AS and Standard Kerberos

If you are familiar with the Kerberos message exchange, you would have recognized that a lot of the protocols (flows of messages) I described are identical to those used by MIT Kerberos V5. This is not surprising given that DCE Authentication Service was built upon the MIT Kerberos V5 source code. What, then, are the differences between the DCE Security and Kerberos?

Actually, DCE Security is a superset of Kerberos V5. Kerberos provides key-distribution and ticket-granting services; it corresponds to the DCE Authentication Service. Kerberos does not provide the Privilege Service or the Registry Service. In addition, Kerberos does not provide some of the DCE facilities like authenticated RPC and DCE ACLs. A more meaningful question to ask is therefore, what are the differences between the Authentication Service component of DCE and Kerberos? We can answer this question more easily.

The DCE Authentication Service differs from Kerberos V5 services in two major ways: First, the DCE Authentication Service interprets DCE principal names (e.g., */.../cell_a/name*) in addition to the MIT Athena names (*name@realm*). This allows the DCE Authentication Service to work with principals that have DCE names. The second difference between the Kerberos and the DCE Authentication Service is that Kerberos uses UDP/IP while DCE in addition uses DCE RPC for communications. Kerberos clients send ticket requests to a well-known UDP/IP port and receive responses back in UDP packets. As we have seen, the equivalent operations in DCE are performed by making RPCs to the Authentication Service. In other respects, the DCE Authentication Service is wire-protocol-compatible with Kerberos and, in fact, can receive requests from Kerberos clients over UDP/IP. This means that a DCE Authentication Service can replace a Kerberos V5 server in existing Kerberos installations.

Since the reference implementation of the DCE Authentication Service uses the Kerberos source code, the native Kerberos APIs still exist. However, the Kerberos API is not made available to applications. DCE 1.0.x does not support an API to the Authentication Service. Instead, the use of the Authentication Service is integrated with the DCE login and RPC facilities. DCE applications invoke the Authentication Service indirectly when they login and when they make authenticated RPCs. DCE 1.1, however, includes an implementation of the GSSAPI over the DCE security services as mentioned above; I will describe this further in Chapter 7.

Summary

In this chapter, we looked at the network services offered by DCE Security. I described the creation and use of session keys, tickets, and privilege attribute certificates. We saw how the Authentication Service provides session keys for clients and servers to authenticate each other. I explained how the session keys are encrypted within tickets that make it possible for clients and servers to use them securely. Following this, we saw how the Privilege Service extends the tickets to also hold privilege information. This way, a server gets both authentication as well as authorization information in the same ticket when it gets an RPC call. Once the server has this information, it can decide whether the client should be granted access. This, in a nutshell, are the basic network services offered by DCE Security.

At this point, we are ready to move to the APIs. The APIs are how applications use the network services we studied in this chapter. DCE supplies APIs that allow a server to login, manage its secret key, and participate in authenticated RPC with clients. In addition, there are APIs for managing DCE Security itself and also DCE ACLs. We will look at these APIs in greater detail starting in the next chapter.

3

Overview of the DCE Security Application Programming Interface

In Chapter 2, I described how the DCE security servers provide the basic authentication and authorization services that DCE applications use. Your applications are not going to directly call the services I described. Instead, you will use a higher layer, the Security API. In this chapter, I will explain what the API does, the key abstractions that it uses, and how it is designed to be used.

The DCE Security API is extensive. This makes it possible to build tools that integrate local security with network security and augment, or even replace, the admininstration tools supplied by DCE. The drawback of a large API, of course, is that an application developer can easily get lost among the services provided. To help you navigate through these calls, I have structured this chapter into two parts. In the first part, I will preview the API at a very high level so that you can see what the major functional groupings are and how they relate. My goal is to convey the big picture so that you can get a sense of what the API as a whole does.

The second part of this chapter describes the API again, this time structured around the basic programming tasks that involve DCE Security. This will be done with enough detail so that you can actually use the API to write useful programs. I will concentrate on those API calls you need to write client and server applications; there will be much less detail on calls that are only used by administrative utilities. As I go along, I will also make sure to point out those functions you can ignore. This allows you to concentrate on understanding the key API calls that you will actually use in developing applications.

I recommend that you go through this chapter in two passes. First, read the API overview and skim the rest of the chapter. Then, skip ahead to the next chapter to see how the APIs are used in sample applications. After this, come back and reread this chapter in detail.

Overview of the DCE Security API

The DCE Security API consists of five separate APIs:

- The *authenticated RPC API* allows clients and servers to establish secure communications and transmit security attributes. This is the central API applications use the most.

- The *sec_login* API allows principals to set up their DCE identity and security attributes.

- The *key management API* allows servers to manage their secret keys.

- The *Registry API* offers access to information stored in the security registry.

- The *sec_acl API* allows management applications to control remote access control lists.

Figure 3-1 shows how these APIs relate to the services I described in Chapter 2. The lines show the remote services each of these APIs communicate with.

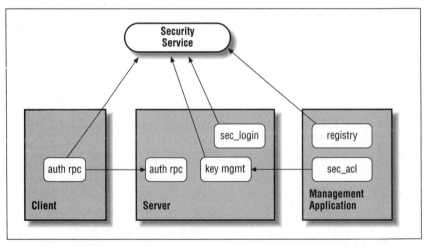

Figure 3-1: DCE Security API

As you can see, I've classified the five APIs into three categories (client, server, and management application) to indicate who is most likely to use the particular API. Authenticated RPC is used by both clients and servers, the *sec_login* and key management APIs are used primarily by servers, and the registry and *sec_acl* API are used primarily by management applications. Note that this grouping is inexact. In particular, you will see that management applications tend to use all the APIs. This grouping, however, is still helpful in that it shows which APIs applications programmers should focus on.

In a typical application, the server starts up and uses the key management API to obtain its secret key. Then it uses the *sec_login* API to get an identity for itself. When the client and server communicate, each uses the authenticated RPC API to set up a secure connection. The server then uses a set of calls (described in other chapters) to check the client's access rights against an access control list.

Authenticated RPC

Authenticated RPC makes sure that a client's call succeeds only if it represents the principal it claims to represent, and if the server is really the server that the client wants to contact. In addition, it can protect the call from corruption and snooping. To carry out authenticated RPC, the RPC runtime adds some extra fields to the packets that are sent, and makes some hidden calls to the security server. The process was described in Chapter 2, but I'll summarize the main activities here. The enhancement in authenticated RPC is to take as much work as possible out of the application programmer's hands and put it into the RPC runtime.

Authenticated RPC uses the PSTkt issued by the security servers. The process starts when the client initiates an authenticated RPC to the server. The RPC runtime contacts the Privilege Service for a PSTkt targeted for the server the client wants to call. As we saw in Chapter 2, the PSTtk contains the client's PAC and a session key. The entire ticket is also encrypted using the targeted server's secret key. The ticket is then passed to the server when the RPC connection is made.

Encrypting the PSTkt with the server's secret key allows the server to trust the information in the PAC; this is how it authenticates the client. It also assures the client that no one except for the intended server can complete the call. The PAC contains the client's security attributes the server needs to make its access control checks.

In addition to its role in the PSTkt, the session key is used to encrypt the data passed between the client and server as part of this call. The session key also allows the client to verify that the response to the call came from the server the client called. All of this is done automatically by the RPC facility; your application just needs to tell RPC what kind of protection and authentication it needs, and RPC does the rest.

Since authenticated RPC involves two parties, both clients and servers use the API. Client programs use the API to tell the RPC runtime how to set up the authenticated connection. The client specifies the server principal to which the client wants to authenticate, the client's identity, and how heavily to protect the data that is passed between the client and server.

A server uses the API to set up its end of the RPC connection. The server tells the RPC runtime its principal name and its secret key so that the runtime can decode the tickets that are sent to this server. The API also provides a function that allows the server to retrieve the client's PAC. This function should be called whenever an incoming RPC has been received so the server can find out who the client is and use that information to decide whether the call should be processed.

The authenticated RPC API therefore allows the application to pass all the information the underlying RPC facility needs to acquire and decode tickets, transmit and decode PACs, and protect the data that is passed between the client and server. The API also returns information that allows servers to perform its access control checks.

sec_login API

The *sec_login* API allows a process to establish its DCE identity; that is, to log in to DCE so that it can make authenticated RPC calls. Given its purpose, you might expect that this API is intended for clients. However, it turns out that it is usually the servers that make calls on the *sec_login* API. Client applications do not need to make *sec_login* calls because client applications typically inherit the DCE identity of the user that runs the application. A user usually establishes his or her DCE identity by logging in via either a DCE or operating-system login. Server applications, on the other hand, do not run the DCE login program. Therefore, if a server wants to make authenticated RPC calls, it must use the *sec_login* API to establish its identity.

A server does not need to establish its identity if it does not intend to use authenticated RPC. If you can guarantee that the server will not make an authenticated RPC either directly or indirectly, then it does not need to set up an identity. This turns out to be very restrictive as many DCE APIs internally make authenticated RPC. Thus, servers tend to establish their identities by default as a part of normal initialization.

Internally, the *sec_login* API communicates with the Security Service to obtain a principal's identity and security attributes.

Key Management API

The key management API was created to solve two problems. First, servers need to keep a local copy of their secret keys so that they can authenticate themselves. Unlike people who remember their passwords, servers need some storage mechanism. The key management API solves this problem by allowing a server program to store its secret keys in a local file (the keytab file) and providing operations to retrieve and update their values. Because a server's secret key is also stored in the Security Registry, the key management API also communicates with the Security Server.

The second problem the key management API solves is the need to change a secret key periodically, to minimize the damage cause by a stolen key. This is analogous to having users change their passwords on a periodic basis.

The key management API is primarily a local API. A local API is a collection of calls that operate only on local data; local APIs do not make RPCs.

Registry API

The Registry API is a collection of APIs (the *sec_rgy* and the *sec_id* functions) that allows an application to retrieve and update the information stored in the Security Registry. This is mostly for use by administrative utilities such as *rgy_edit*, the management tool for creating accounts; principals; and other DCE Security configuration information.

sec_acl API

The *sec_acl* API allows an application to manipulate ACLs on remote objects. You can use the API, for example, to view, replace, or remove ACLs. As you might expect, this is primarily for use by the DCE ACL administration tool, *acl_edit*.

Note that there is no API defined for ACLs themselves, i.e., there is no server-side API to manipulate and check ACLs. In DCE 1.0, each application must define its own ACL checks. DCE 1.1 provides an ACL library API. We will describe this in Chapter 8.

This concludes our overview. We will now look at the entire API again in detail, from a task-oriented perspective.

Tasks in Security Programming

Every DCE program needs to perform certain fundamental tasks. For example, you already know that an RPC server program needs to register its interfaces and export its bindings. DCE Security imposes its own tasks.

Manage server keys

To be a principal in DCE, you must have a secret key. People remember their passwords; server processes store their secret keys in local files called keytab files. The programmer or administrator who configures the server uses *rgy_edit* to create the keytab file. After a keytab file has been created, the server application must periodically change its secret key in the keytab file just as users should change their passwords.

The key management API allows a server to get and set the keys stored in its keytab file and refresh the keys when they expire.

Setting up and managing a login context

Servers, like people, must log in before they can use DCE. Logging into DCE associates a server with its principal name and security attributes. When you log into a local computer, you are given access to certain system resources such as a terminal, files, etc. When you log into DCE, you are given a set of tickets that can be used to access other DCE services. In DCE, these tickets (along with your identity information) are stored in a data structure called a **login context**. A principal needs to provide a valid login context before it can make use of authenticated RPC.

A login context remains valid only so long as the tickets within it are valid. Remember that tickets have finite lifetimes. A server needs to renew its tickets regularly; this can be done by a simple operation called **refreshing** a login context.

Authenticated RPC setup

The RPC runtime handles most of the complicated work of authentication. But to do so, it has to know something about the client and server. So servers must register their principal names and secret keys with the authenticated RPC facility. A client needs to tell the RPC runtime the principal name of the server that it wants to talk to and the level of security to apply to the messages passed during the call. These two client calls tell the RPC runtime how to set up the authenticated RPC connection between the client and server when an actual RPC is made. The rest of the processing occurs automatically when RPCs are made.

Per-call processing and the reference monitor

Clients make authenticated RPCs just like normal RPCs; all the extra work is done transparently by the RPC runtime. When the server gets the RPC call, the server manager code (code that implements the remote procedure being called) needs to do a bit more work. It needs to verify that the level of security the client has selected for the call is acceptable. For example, the server might insist that each client authenticate itself on each call. Assuming that the level of security the client has selected is acceptable to the server, the server manager code should extract the client's privilege attributes from the PAC, check the PAC against any access control lists, and then complete the RPC if the client is authorized. Programmers generally separate the code making the security checks into its own routine, called a **reference monitor**.

The basic tasks in security programming are therefore:

- Setting up and managing a server's DCE identity
- Managing keys

- Using authenticated RPC

- Writing a reference monitor in the server

I will describe how to write a reference monitor later since it is a major topic by itself. For now, we will now look at each of the other tasks.

Managing Server Secret Keys

Every principal ultimately identifies his or her identity with a secret key. In DCE, keys and passwords are equivalent. Given a string password, DCE can derive a secret key. Servers use keys while people use passwords. It's easy to see why people use passwords; they are easier to remember than strings of numbers. Processes use keys since fixed-size bitstrings are easier to manipulate in software than variable-length character strings.

People remember their passwords. Processes need to store their secret keys in some protected, nonvolatile local storage so that they can be retrieved on demand to authenticate themselves. The registry, of course, knows all the secret keys. However, the registry won't tell a principal its secret key unless the principal has authenticated itself, and the principal cannot authenticate itself without the key. Thus, a local key storage area separate from the registry is needed.

The Keytab File

DCE has adopted the Kerberos approach of using keytab files to store keys locally. The keytab file is protected using the local operating system's facilities. In UNIX, for example, the keytab file should be owned and accessible only by the process that owns the secret keys. In general, every server should use a separate keytab file. Multiple servers can share a keytab file; however, that is not recommended as it opens the possibility for one process to improperly impersonate another process. Remember, a process that can get to your secret key can *become* you as far as DCE is concerned.

As the name indicates, the keytab file stores a table of keys. This is because each principal must keep track of both its current key and previous keys. If a principal only keeps track of its current key, then all the PTGTs and PSTkts targeted to this server would become immediately invalid as soon as the principal changes its key. This is because the security server encrypts these tickets using the server's secret key at the time it issues the tickets. Since tickets are kept around and reused until they expire, a server is quite likely to be presented with tickets that are still encrypted with an older key version. We therefore must keep enough versions of the key around to decrypt the oldest outstanding ticket designated for this server.

Since we are storing multiple keys in the keytab file, we identify each key with a distinct version number. The version number is incremented each time the principal changes its key. By default, a server gets the most current key version when it asks for its secret key. The key management interface, however, allows an application to specify the exact version number of the key that is needed. The key management API also allows you to iterate through all the keys in a keytab file.

You should note, however, that the Registry Service stores only the latest version of each principal's key. The Registry Service does not need old key versions because the Authentication Service only needs the latest version of the requesting principal's secret key to create its tickets.

The key-management functions are shown in the three lists below. I have divided the calls by function: looking up keys, changing and deleting keys, and miscellaneous. I have also highlighted the calls you are likely to use.

The first four calls allow you to look up keys from the keytab file. *sec_key_mgmt_get_key* allows a server to get the latest key version from its keytab file. This is used by a server during initialization. I will show how this is used in an example later. The other calls allow you to get all the keys from the keytab file. These calls take a cursor as a parameter. The cursor in this case is just a variable in which the key-management routines maintain their current state so that you can cycle through all the keys in the keytab file by making successive calls to *sec_key_mgmt_get_next_key*. As you might expect, the calls that iterate through the keytab file are of interest only to people who want to write administrative utilities.

> ***sec_key_mgmt_get_key***
> *sec_key_mgmt_get_next_key*
> *sec_key_mgmt_initialize_cursor*
> *sec_key_mgmt_release_cursor*

The functions listed above are local operations. They work with local keytab files and do not communicate with the Registry Service.

The next set of calls allows you to delete and change keys.

> *sec_key_mgmt_delete_key*
> *sec_key_mgmt_delete_key_typ*
> *sec_key_mgmt_garbage_collect*
> *sec_key_mgmt_change_key*
> *sec_key_mgmt_gen_rand_key*
> ***sec_key_mgmt_manage_key***

The first· three calls delete keys from the local keytab file. *sec_key_mgmt_garbage_collect*, although not normally used by applications, is interesting because it illustrates the relationship between key versions and tickets. This routine figures out which of your key versions can be safely deleted. It does this by using the cell's ticket-expiration policy to figure out which is the oldest valid ticket (presumably acquired by some client) and then deleting any older keys.

The *sec_key_mgmt_change_key* function changes a principal's key; the *sec_key_mgmt_gen_rand_key* function generates a random key. The second call is primarily used by servers to generate new key values when they need to change their keys. Note that both functions change the key in the Registry Service as well as the local keytab file. This turns out to be important. If the registry were not updated with the new key when the local key is updated, the security server would start issuing tickets to the principal using the wrong key. This would not be catastrophic if the local keytab file still had a copy of the old key, and the server knew enough to use it. But if the old key was deleted from the local keytab file, or if the server tried to use the new key, clients' calls would be rejected and the server would not be able to authenticate itself.

Secret keys (and passwords) should be changed frequently. This is because the more often a key is used, the more likely it is that someone can figure out the key. Thus, each server should periodically generate a new key and then change its key in the keytab file and the Registry Service. Because this is such a common operation, DCE provides a function, *sec_key_mgmt_manage_key*, that does it for you. This is what applications should use. *sec_key_mgmt_manage_key* blocks the calling thread for a period of time, then wakes up and changes the principal's key to a new random value. It is designed to be called from a dedicated thread. I will show you how to use it when we write our server.

In the last group of functions, *sec_key_mgmt_get_next_kvno* returns the version number of the caller's key that is stored by the Registry Service. *sec_key_mgmt_free_key* frees the memory used for a key. This is needed because the key management routines return keys from heap memory. The final call, *sec_key_mgmt_set_key*, is used by replicated servers (ones that share a common secret key) to synchronize their local copies of the key prior to changing the key that is stored in the Registry.

> *sec_key_mgmt_get_next_kvno*
> *sec_key_mgmt_free_key*
> *sec_key_mgmt_set_key*

Setting Up and Maintaining a Login Context

The *sec_login* API allows a principal to log into DCE. To log in means to authenticate yourself to the Security Service and acquire a TGT in order to access other DCE services. People who run DCE applications use the *sec_login* API indirectly through login programs such as *dce_login*. Server programs use the *sec_login* API directly to log in. Other users of the *sec_login* API may include the local operating-system login program and the code that starts up a DCE cell.

The *sec_login* API uses the Authentication and the Privilege Services to obtain the TGT. The main data structure that the login API manipulates is the **login context**. The login context is a place where the principal's security information is stored. A client must have a login context before it can make an authenticated RPC. The internal structure of the login context is not exposed; applications always refer to them via opaque handles. But I'll explain what is inside so you can understand the role the login context plays. The login context contains information about the principal and the cell, the **credentials cache**, the state of the login context, UNIX login information, and whether the login context was authenticated by the Security Service or the local operating system. The credentials cache stores all the credentials that have been issued to this principal; both the TGT and PTGT are stored there.

Acquiring a Login Context

You acquire a login context when you log into DCE. A DCE login works differently from a UNIX login. When you log into the UNIX operating system, the login program prompts you for your user name and password. The password is then encrypted and compared against the encrypted password stored in the local password file. If they match, you are authenticated and are allowed to use the system.

When you log into DCE, the *dce_login* program still needs your principal name and password. However, the actual login processing will usually take much longer than local system logins. This is because the program needs to do more processing and make RPCs to the Security Service. The *dce_login* program could ask the user to type the principal name and password up front. This would mean, however, that the password would be stored in the local computer's memory for potentially a long time if we should experience network delays. This increases the likelihood of someone else getting at the user's secret key.

DCE therefore splits the login into two parts (getting a login context and validating it). The user is asked to type in the password only after all network communications have taken place. This ensures that the password is kept around for only a short period of time. In addition, DCE login is carefully crafted so that it never transmits the user's password over the wire. This prevents unauthorized people from getting users' passwords just by monitoring the network traffic. Figure 3-2 illustrates the steps involved in a DCE login. Even though we are not going to write a new *dce_login* program, I will describe how it works because it is the best example of how to use the *sec_login* API.

❶ The user starts by running the *dce_login* program on the local computer. (If the operating system supports an integrated login program, then this might be done as part of the local login.) *dce_login* prompts the user for a principal name.

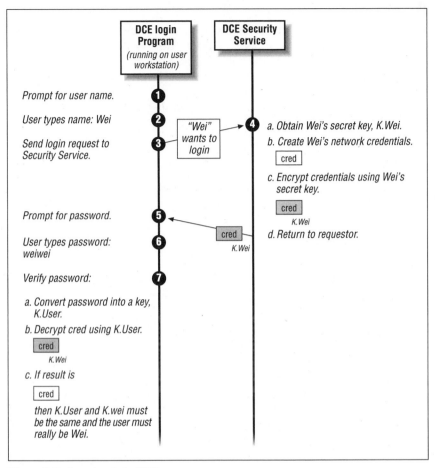

Figure 3-2: Logging into DCE

❷ The user then enters his or her principal name.

❸ The *dce_login* program sends the user name to the Security Service.

❹ The Security Service returns a TGT for the principal the user claims to be. As explained before, this TGT is encrypted with the principal's secret key. The TGT is sealed with the principal's secret key and is not directly usable.

❺ After the *dce_login* program receives the credentials from the Security Service, it prompts the user for a password. As I mentioned earlier, the login program waits until this point because there may be a delay between steps ❷ and ❺ (during which messages are exchanged with the Security Service). Asking for the password immediately before it's needed reduces the amount of time that the password needs to be kept around.

❻   The user now types in the password.

❼   The program converts the password into a secret key through a hash
     function and then attempts to use the key to decrypt the TGT. The
     program can tell if the key is the right one because the decrypted TGT
     contains certain known fields. If the decrypted TGT looks like a real
     TGT, the user is assumed to be the principal he or she claimed to be.
     At this point, the user has successfully authenticated himself or herself
     to the Security Service (or the network) and is logged into DCE.

The initial login context, created after the sealed credentials have been
received from the Security Service, is called an **unvalidated login context**.
An unvalidated login context cannot be used for authenticated RPC. The
login context becomes **validated** after the credentials within it have been
properly decrypted using the user's secret key. In the login sequence
shown in Figure 3-2, the login context becomes validated after step 7c.

The list below shows the API calls that acquire (set up) and validate login
contexts.

```
boolean32 sec_login_setup_identity (
      [in, string]      unsigned_char_p_t    principal,
      [in]              sec_login_flags_t    flags,
      [out, ref]        sec_login_handle_t   *login_context,
      [out, ref]        error_status_t       *st   );

boolean32 sec_login_validate_identity (
      [in]              sec_login_handle_t   login_context,
      [in, out, ref]    sec_passwd_rec_t     *passwd,
      [out, ref]        boolean32            *reset_passwd,
      [out, ref]        sec_login_auth_src_t *auth_src,
      [out, ref]        error_status_t       *st   );

void sec_login_valid_from_keytable (
      [in]              sec_login_handle_t          login_context,
      [in]              unsigned32                  authn_service,
      [in]              void                        *arg,
      [in]              unsigned32                  try_kvno,
      [out]             unsigned32                  *used_kvno,
      [out]             boolean32                   *reset_passwd,
      [out]             sec_login_auth_src_t        *auth_src,
      [out]             error_status_t              *st   );
```

sec_login_setup_identity takes a principal name and a flags argument that
specifies whether the login context can be inherited by subprocesses. It
returns an unvalidated login context. *sec_login_validate_identity* validates
a login context using the specified password. The function will let you
know if the password has expired and whether the login context was validated by the Security Service. (The local operating system can validate a
login context when the network is unavailable). If the login context was
validated by the local operating system, it cannot be used to access
network resources. This is because the local operating system does not
issue TGTs.

sec_login_valid_from_keytable is meant for servers that maintain their keys in keytab files. It is the equivalent of *sec_login_validate_identity* except that instead of requiring the caller to get the key from the keytab file, this function will do the lookup automatically in the keytab file. It will first try the specified key version number; if that fails, it will iterate through all the keys in the keytab file. The *arg* input parameter is used to specify the name of the keytab file.

The calls I've described so far are used by application programs after the DCE cell has started. While the cell is starting up, however, the host principal itself needs to set up its login context. This is done through the calls *sec_login_init_first*, *sec_login_setup_first*, and *sec_login_validate_first*. As you would expect, these calls are very specialized and we mention them only for completeness.

Certifying the Login Context

If a user needs only to access network resources through RPC, a validated login context is sufficient. If you want to use the login context as a basis for setting the user's local identity, however, more is required. The problem is that the local operating system needs to know the login context is genuine before it can use the information within it to set up the user's local identity. You might want to do some more checking, for example, if the login context says that the principal should have the local identity of *root*.

Recall that the login context was sealed (encrypted) by the Security Service using the user's secret key and unsealed (decrypted) by the user using that same key. This allows the user to verify that the tickets in the login context really came from a genuine Security Service. It does not, however, allow the operating system to trust the login context. For example, a malicious user could work in conjunction with a fake Security Service to produce a login context that improperly grants the user root permission on the local operating system. This would open the entire operating system to attack. To prevent this, the local operating system needs to establish the authenticity of the Security Service directly through some message exchange.

If you can somehow get a login context that is encrypted with the secret key of the local operating system, the local operating system would be able to decrypt the login context and verify for itself whether the login context is valid. You could, in theory do this by adding more information to the tickets. DCE has chosen a simpler way. DCE establishes the trustworthiness of a login context by **certifying** the login context.

To certify the login context, an independent authority—a daemon called *sec_clientd*—tests the PTGT in the login context to see if the issuer is really the Security Service. The certify-identity API call tests the validity of the login context by making an authenticated RPC to a special process on the local computer, the *sec_clientd* daemon. (Since the target server is really a local process, this RPC is local.) *sec_clientd* represents the machine principal; each machine in DCE has one of these processes. It has the principal name of the form */cell_name/hostname*/self. As with any other process, *sec_clientd* has a secret key that is known only to itself and the Security Service.

When the certify-identity call makes an authenticated RPC to *sec_clientd*, the RPC runtime asks the Security Service for a PTGT and PSTkt to the target server, *sec_clientd*. It does so by taking the TGT from the login context and passing it to the Security Service. Since the Security Service will only accept requests made with valid TGTs, the caller will obtain a PTGT and PSTkt only if the TGT is valid. The RPC runtime will also complete an authenticated call only if it succeeds in obtaining a PSTkt. Therefore, if the RPC to *sec_clientd* completes, the caller (in this case the *sec_login_certify_identity* code) knows that the TGT (hence the login context) was issued by a legitimate Security Service.

Earlier, I said that the login context does not need to be certified if you are accessing only network services and are not using the DCE identity to set up your local operating-system identity. We can now see why. If your login context contains credentials that were issued by a fake Security Service, your authenticated RPC calls will fail. This is because the fake PTGT will not allow you to obtain privilege tickets and session keys that are encrypted using the target server's secret key. Thus, you will know that your login context is invalid as soon as you try to make your first authenticated RPC using that login context.

The above explanation may be tedious; however, it illustrates the step-by-step style of reasoning that is required to decide if something can be trusted. One of the nice things about using security facilities like DCE is that someone else has already gone through the laborious reasoning to make sure it's secure. All you have to do is to use the services as intended. However, if in doubt, it is still very important to be able to retrace these steps to ensure that DCE is indeed secure.

The list below displays the functions that allow you to certify a login context.

```
boolean32 sec_login_certify_identity (
    [in]          sec_login_handle_t    login_context,
    [out, ref]  error_status_t        *st    );
boolean32 sec_login_valid_and_cert_ident (
    [in]                 sec_login_handle_t    login_context,
    [in, out, ref]  sec_passwd_rec_t      *passwd,
    [out, ref]         boolean32              *reset_passwd,
    [out, ref]         sec_login_auth_src_t  *auth_src,
    [out, ref]         error_status_t        *st    );
```

sec_login_certify_identity certifies a previously validated login context. *sec_login_valid_and_cert_ident* combines the validate and certify operations into a single call. Since this call requires a password as input, servers need to first call *sec_key_mgmt_get_key.*

Refreshing Login Contexts

Login contexts, like passwords, expire. Or more precisely, the TGT within the credentials cache of the login context expires. (The expiration times of TGTs are attributes that can be configured by the *rgy_edit* utility.) When a login context expires, all authenticated RPC calls that use this login context will fail. A user can easily recover from an expired login context; he or she can simply run the *kinit* command.

Servers also need to refresh their login contexts. DCE provides the call *sec_login_refresh_identity*, which allows servers to refresh an existing login context.

```
boolean32 sec_login_refresh_identity (
     [in]          sec_login_handle_t  login_context,
     [out, ref]    error_status_t      *st   );
```

This routine is designed to be called periodically from a dedicated thread that has a built-in timer. It should be called before the login context is due to expire. The login context that is returned is unvalidated. Thus, it should be followed by the appropriate *sec_login_validate_* call. We will illustrate its use when we develop our sample application.

Sharing Login Contexts

A process can create and use several login contexts. However, at any given moment, the process has a single **current login context**. A process' current login context is the login context whose credentials cache is used by the DCE runtime when it looks for tickets. The current login context of a process is inherited by all of its child processes. This is very convenient as it allows all the DCE applications that you run after you have logged into DCE to use your login context. (A program can make a login context private to the current process, i.e., not allow it to be inherited by subprocesses, by setting a flag when the context is set up.) The routines *sec_login_set_context* and *sec_login_get_current_context* allow you to set and get the current login context.

```
void sec_login_set_context (
     [in]          sec_login_handle_t  login_context,
     [out, ref]    error_status_t      *st   );
void sec_login_get_current_context (
     [out, ref]    sec_login_handle_t  *login_context,
     [out, ref]    error_status_t      *st   );
```

The vast majority of applications use a single, default login context. Multiple login contexts are used in more complex situations where you are working with multiple identities. For example, they are useful if you want to implement a clerk process that needs to assume the identity of the principal on whose behalf it is acting. Another situation in which multiple login contexts are useful is where a client may act in two roles: a "normal" role in which it gets a restricted set of privileges, and a "super user" mode where it gets extra access. In this case, you would associate a distinct login context for each of these cases and use the appropriate one.

In addition to subprocesses, you can pass a login context to another process on the same host computer by calling *sec_login_export_context*. This function creates a byte string that contains the external representation of a login context. You can then pass this byte string to the target process via local interprocess communications mechanisms such as pipes or sockets. The target process converts the byte string back into a usable login context by calling *sec_login_import_context*.

The *sec_login_export_context* and *sec_login_import_context* calls are shown in the example below.

```
void sec_login_export_context (
    [in]        sec_login_handle_t  login_context,
    [in]        unsigned32          buf_len,
    [out, size_is(*len_used)] byte  buf[],
    [out]       unsigned32          *len_used,
    [out]       unsigned32          *len_needed,
    [out]       error_status_t      *st   );
void sec_login_import_context (
    [in]        unsigned32          buf_len,
    [in, size_is(buf_len)] byte     buf[],
    [out]       sec_login_handle_t  *login_context,
    [out]       error_status_t      *st   );
```

Note that you cannot use the export/import calls to pass a login context to a process on another host computer. This is because a login context contains network credentials (e.g., the PTGT) that are usable only on the system to which it is issued. DCE 1.1 allows you to pass your identity to a process on another system through a separate mechanism called delegation. We will discuss delegation in Chapter 8.

Least Privilege

Least privilege is a concept first developed for local system security. Basically, it means that you want to accomplish your tasks using the least amount of privileges that are needed. For example, if you do not need to be root to run a certain program, you should not *su* to root. This helps prevent mishaps because more privileged processes can typically cause more damage if something goes wrong. In the case of UNIX, for example, accidentally typing `rm -rf /` is far more destructive when you are acting as root than if you were just a normal user. If your default privileges are very powerful, then the principal of least privilege says that you should try to reduce (or temprarily disable) unneeded privileges when you perform unprivileged commands.

DCE allows applications to implement least privilege by controlling the set of groups that are propagated across RPCs. This is done by changing the set of groups in a client's login context prior to an RPC. The cell administrator, for example, can temporarily remove certain group attributes from his or her login context prior to making an authenticated RPC to prevent unintended side effects resulting from propagating powerful privileges. The list below shows the calls that can be used to do this.

```
void sec_login_get_groups (
[in]              sec_login_handle_t  login_context,
[out, ref]        unsigned32          *num_groups,
[out, ref]        signed32            **group_set,
[out, ref]        error_status_t      *st   );


boolean32 sec_login_newgroups (
[in]              sec_login_handle_t  login_context,
[in]              sec_login_flags_t   flags,
[in]              unsigned32          num_local_groups,
[in, length_is(num_local_groups)]
                  sec_id_t             local_groups[],
[out]             sec_login_handle_t  *restricted_context
[out, ref]        error_status_t      *st   );
```

A client program would call *sec_login_get_groups* to get the current groups that are associated with a login context, selectively create a new group list, and then call *sec_login_set_groups* to create a restricted login context that contains only the specified groups. Since a process can maintain multiple login contexts, these restricted contexts can be set up and put aside for later use.

Miscellaneous sec_login Calls

We are ready to wrap up the *sec_login* API. In the list below, I have grouped the remaining *sec_login* calls.

sec_login_get_expiration
sec_login_release_context
sec_login_purge_context
sec_login_get_pwent
sec_login_inquire_net_info
sec_login_free_net_info

Out of this group of calls, you will most likely use only the first three.

sec_login_get_expiration
> Returns the time when the login context is due to expire. When you start a thread with the job of refreshing the login context, it issues this call.

sec_login_release_context
> Frees the memory associated with a login context. It should be called when you no longer need the login context. Because multiple processes may be sharing the same login context (e.g., when a subprocess uses the default login context of its parent process), each login context has a reference count.

sec_login_release_context
> Decrements the reference count on the login context and destroys the contents of the credentials cache only if there are no other references to this login context.

If you need to destroy the credentials regardless of who else may be sharing it, you should use:

sec_login_purge_context
> This call is normally used for cleaning up after an error or by servers when they exit.

In terms of the other calls:

sec_login_get_pwent
> Extracts the */etc/passwd* file information (local identity information) from the login context. It is primarily used for integrating the local system login with the DCE login.

sec_login_inquire_net_info
> Returns the network (or DCE) information in the login context. This includes the PAC, the DCE account associated with this login context, and when this login context will expire.

sec_login_free_net_info
> Frees the data structure returned by *sec_login_inquire_net_info* to heap.

In summary, the *sec_login* API allows you to maintain and manipulate login contexts. The login context is where a process's DCE credentials (tickets and PACs) are stored. It must be set up prior to making authenticated RPCs. Because we want to ensure that the login context is genuine and only usable by the principal for which it is intended, DCE goes through a complex login context setup procedure. However, the code sequence to do so is fairly straightforward and typically does not change from application to application. You will see this as we develop sample applications.

Authenticated RPC Setup

Using authenticated RPC is quite routine; you just call a function defined in an IDL file. But you *control* and *set up* the authenticated RPC connection through the authenticated RPC API. To use authenticated RPC, the client and server have to agree up front on the level of security desired and the server principal name. Once this is done, the server needs to register itself with the RPC runtime under that principal name. The client needs to set up certain fields in the binding handle to be used for the RPC. The server then gets to decide if the values are acceptable when the call is received. Note that the security information is carried in the binding and has nothing to do with the interface.

Setting up Authenticated RPC by Modifying Binding Handles

The client program controls how an authenticated RPC connection is set up by modifying the binding handle it uses for the RPC. Recall that a binding is defined as a relationship between a client and server. If you want the RPC connection between a client and server to be authenticated, you must modify the binding handle you use to make the RPC call.

Authenticated RPC is set up and controlled through the set of APIs listed below.

```
void rpc_binding_set_auth_info (
    [in]        rpc_binding_handle_t    binding_handle,
    [in]        unsigned_char_p_t         server_princ_name,
    [in]        unsigned32              protect_level,
    [in]        unsigned32              authn_svc,
    [in]        rpc_auth_identity_handle_t auth_identity,
    [in]        unsigned32              authz_svc,
    [out]       unsigned32              *st);

void rpc_binding_inq_auth_info(
    [in]        rpc_binding_handle_t    binding_handle,
    [out]       unsigned_char_p_t         *server_princ_name,
    [out]       unsigned32              *protect_level,
    [out]       unsigned32              *authn_svc,
    [out]       rpc_auth_identity_handle_t *auth_identity,
    [out]       unsigned32              *authz_svc,
    [out]       unsigned32              *st);

void rpc_binding_inq_auth_client (
    [in]        rpc_binding_handle_t    binding_handle,
    [out]       rpc_authz_handle_t      *privs,
    [out]       unsigned_char_p_t         *server_princ_name,
    [out]       unsigned32              *protect_level,
    [out]       unsigned32              *authn_svc,
    [out]       unsigned32              *authz_svc,
```

```
         [out]          unsigned32          *st);

void rpc_server_register_auth_info (
         [in]          unsigned_char_p_t          server_princ_name,
         [in]          unsigned32          auth_svc,
         [in]          rpc_auth_key_retrieval_fn_t get_key_func,
         [in]          void                *arg,
         [out]         unsigned32          *st);

void rpc_mgmt_inq_server_princ_name (
         [in]          rpc_binding_handle_t          binding_h,
         [in]          unsigned32          authn_svc,
         [out]         unsigned_char_p_t          *server_princ_name,
```

Three of these calls form the core of the authenticated RPC API. Figure 3-3 shows how they are used.

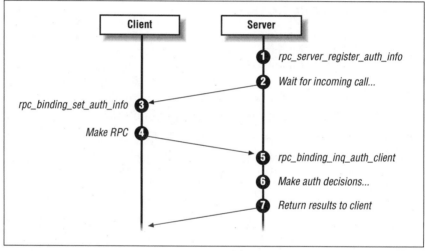

Figure 3-3: Flow of control among the key RPC calls

❶ The server starts by calling *rpc_server_register_auth_info* to register its principal name and secret key with the DCE runtime. This is done when the server starts up. Internally, this call enables a series of extra processing that will take place when an incoming RPC is received. At this point, the server can go into the RPC listen loop (by calling *rpc_server_listen*) to start accepting authenticated RPCs.

The server's secret key is not passed directly to the runtime. This is because the secret key can be changed while the server is running. So the call takes as input a call-back routine (the *key retrieval function*) the DCE runtime can invoke when it actually needs the server's key. The default key-retrieval function takes it from a local keytab file (provided by the key management API). The name of this server's keytab file is specified in the *arg* parameter to *rpc_server_register_auth_info*.

❷ The server finishes its other initialization tasks and enters its wait loop.

❸ The client obtains a binding handle to the server as usual, e.g., by importing it from CDS or by using a string binding. It then calls *rpc_binding_set_auth_info* to set the desired security characteristics for the RPC calls to be made using this binding handle. The client specifies the principal name of the server it wants to talk to, the client's login context (*rpc_auth_identity_handle_t*), and the type of security it wants (authentication and authorization service). Once this call is made, any subsequent RPCs using this binding handle will be protected using the parameters specified.

❹ The client then makes an RPC. Internally, this causes the client's DCE runtime to contact the DCE Security Service to obtain tickets and a PAC. These security attributes are then transmitted as part of the RPC setup messages. When the call gets to the server's RPC runtime, it gets the server's secret key and tries to decrypt the ticket. If the ticket decrypts successfully, then the client is authenticated, and the RPC is allowed to proceed. Otherwise, the call is rejected.

❺ If the client is authenticated, the server remote procedure (the server manager routine) gets control. At this point, the server passes the client's binding handle to *rpc_binding_inq_auth_client* to retrieve the security attributes of the client. This call returns the authenticated identity of the client, its PAC, and the security characteristics the client has chosen for the call (e.g., whether encryption was used, etc.).

❻ The server then makes its authorization decisions based on the values returned by *rpc_binding_inq_auth_client*. If the client is authorized to perform the operation, the call is processed. Otherwise, the call is rejected. As I mentioned before, the code that makes this decision is called the reference monitor.

❼ If the server accepts the call, results are returned as in any remote procedure call. If the level of protection is high enough, chechsums or encryption ensure that the results are from the true server

This captures the basic flow of an authenticated RPC. A client specifies authenticated RPC by modifying its binding handle and a server finds out who it's talking to by making an inquiry operation on the binding handle. Now that I've described the flow of control, I'll detail how to set up an authenticated connection.

Parameters for Setting up Authenticated RPC

A client program calls *rpc_binding_set_auth_info* to specify how an authenticated RPC connection is set up. The important parameters are the authentication service, the authorization service, and the protection level.

Selecting the authentication service

The authentication services are *dce_private*, *dce_public*, and *none*. *dce_private* uses the private key authentication protocol I described earlier. This is the default for DCE applications. *dce_public* was defined for future use when we incorporate public-key authentication into DCE. *none* means not to use any authentication at all. This means the client can claim to be whomever it wants to be. This feature was added to support legacy applications that are not fully integrated with DCE Security. Note that this is not as insecure as it sounds because *rpc_binding_inq_auth_client* tells the server the authentication service that was selected by the client and the server can therefore either reject the call or allow restricted access (such as read-only access).

Selecting the authorization service

An application can specify three possible values for the authorization service: *dce*, *name*, and *none*. *dce* authorization means to pass a PAC. *name* means to pass just the user's principal name. *none* does what it says. As I mentioned earlier, DCE applications should use PACs. All of these options might at first appear to be confusing (especially since only a few are truly useful). However, they were designed into the API so that DCE can plug in a different security service (for instance, one based on public keys) in the future without having to introduce new function calls.

Selecting a protection level

DCE allows an application to specify just how much the data in an RPC should be protected. There are six distinct protection levels:

none

Communication is unauthenticated.

connect

Clients and server will mutually authenticate when the RPC connection is established. Subsequent calls over the same connection will not be individually authenticated.

call

Client and server will mutually authenticate on every call. In addition, RPC will compute a checksum on the protocol header of the *first* packet of each call to ensure that the header has not been modified by a third party. Note that subsequent packets are not protected. Since you cannot, in general, determine the number of RPC packets transmitted for each call, you cannot tell how much of your message stream is protected when you select call-level protection. This level is therefore not very useful. RPC automatically upgrades this level to the next, packet, when you run over a connection-oriented transport like TCP.

packet

> Client and server will mutually authenticate on every call. In addition, a checksum is computed on *every* packet header to ensure that the headers have not been modified in transit.

integrity

> Client and server will mutually authenticate on every call. In addition, a checksum is computed over each RPC packet; this includes the user data. This level will detect any tampering of either the RPC header or the user data. This is the level that is currently specified when an application selects the default protection level.

privacy

> Similar to integrity level, except that the user data is encrypted using DES to guard against wiretapping.

The amount of overhead increases as you select higher protection levels. In a typical implementation, for example, level *privacy* is about five times slower than level *none*. The other levels fall in between. (Note that the overhead is not linear: the overhead for the various flavors of integrity protection is much less than that for privacy.) You must therefore decide whether the extra protection level is worth the performance penalty. You should select the lowest protection level that suffices.

When you are picking a protection level, it helps to realize that there are really only three levels from which to choose: *connect*, *integrity*, and *privacy*. Level *none* is almost never used, as an unauthenticated RPC should not be calling *rpc_binding_set_auth_info* in the first place. Level *connect* is used when the client and server want to mutually authenticate, and you do not need to worry about your packets being modified by someone else while they are transmitted over the network. Levels *call* and *packet* do not offer much additional security. Level *integrity* should be used where malicious modification of the data being passed is an issue but privacy is not. Level *privacy* should be selected where the data is sensitive. The default protection level in DCE is *integrity*.

The U.S. government maintains export controls on data encryption technologies. This means you can export equipment and software that encrypt user data only after obtaining an export license. Because authenticated RPC running at protection level *privacy* offers encryption of user data, it is subject to the same export restrictions. This makes it more expensive and slower to sell such products. Therefore, most U.S.-based vendors support level *privacy* only in versions of DCE that are sold in the United States. For this reason, level *privacy* may not be available in all DCE implementations.

Other Authenticated RPC API Calls

The three API calls described earlier form the core of the authenticated RPC API. For completeness, I will describe the last two calls here.

rpc_binding_inq_auth_info

> This call allows a client application to retrieve the security parameters that were previously set via *rpc_binding_set_auth_info*. Servers need to call *rpc_binding_inq_auth_client* to get the client's security attributes.

rpc_mgmt_inq_server_princ_name

> This call allows a client to ask the server for its principal name. The name returned is that which is registered by the server via *rpc_server_register_auth_info*. This is useful when the client does not care about the exact identity of the server but is interested only in a class of servers. This call should be used with care, because asking a server for its principal name is not secure without additional checks. We'll see how this call can be safely used when a sample application is presented in Chapter 4.

What's Missing?

You can implement a bare-bones authenticated RPC application using just the APIs described here. However, the server needs to do a few more things if you want to implement a full-blown application. (The client does not need more work.) I'll point out the missing server pieces so you can see why the other APIs are needed.

First, the server did not log in. It is using the default login context of the process that started it. This works. However, the server should be given its own identity in order to perform access checks on its operations. This capability is provided by the *sec_login* API. The server also does not change its secret key; it just uses the key version stored in the keytab file. This is workable but insecure. The server should really use the key management API to periodically modify its key.

Besides these API issues, the server is missing a reference monitor. Some piece of code, perhaps based upon DCE ACLs, needs to be written to decide whether a given client is authorized to make a given call. In addition, I have left out all the operations you need to do with *rgy_edit* to set up the principal names and accounts in order to run the application.

Using the Security Registry

The Registry API is the collection of APIs that allows you to access the information in the security registry. This includes all the calls that begin with *sec_rgy*. In general, you will need to use these calls only if you are writing a new version of *rgy_edit*. The term *rgy_edit* refers to registry editor, or a program used to update the contents of the security registry. So most of these calls will not be of general interest. I summarize them below to give you a better feel for what they do.

sec_rgy_bind Calls

The *sec_rgy_bind* calls manage bindings to the Registry Service. As with any other RPC service, you need to establish a binding before you can call any of the remote procedures exported by the Registry Service. This binding handle (termed a *rgy_handle*) is then passed to each of the other Registry API calls. The list below enumerates the *sec_rgy_* calls.

> *sec_rgy_site_open*
> *sec_rgy_site_open_update*
> *sec_rgy_site_open_query*
> *sec_rgy_cell_bind*
> *sec_rgy_site_bind*
> *sec_rgy_site_bind_update*
> *sec_rgy_site_bind_query*
> *sec_rgy_site_bind_from_towerv*
> *sec_rgy_site_binding_get_info*
> *sec_rgy_site_get*
> *sec_rgy_site_close*
> *sec_rgy_site_is_readonly*

The first set, the *sec_rgy_site_open_* calls, allows you to establish a binding to a registry site. If you need only read access, you should call *sec_rgy_site_open_query*, which returns a binding to a read-only site. *sec_rgy_site_open_update* returns a binding to the master, or update site. These calls take as an input parameter the name of the registry server to which you want to bind. The Registry Service can be specified in three ways: by the cell name, by the name of an entry in CDS that contains the binding of a Registry Service replica, or by the string binding of the Registry Service. If you pass in a null name, the routine will pick an arbitrary replica of the Registry Service. The *sec_rgy_site_open_* calls are the most convenient means for establishing a binding to a registry because they can default all the arguments.

A sample CDS entry name for the Registry Service is /.../adlman_cell/subsys/dce/sec/master. If you break this name down into its components, you find that /.../adlman_cell is the name of the cell, /subsys/dce/sec is the security subsystem, and *master* is the name for the master Security Service for the cell.

The *sec_rgy_site_bind_* and *sec_rgy_cell_bind_* calls allow the caller to specify the level of authentication to use in communicating with the Security Service. These calls are used by DCE Security internally; few application programs need to worry about them.

sec_rgy_site_get returns the name of the registry site to which a registry handle refers; *sec_rgy_site_close* frees the binding to the registry. *sec_rgy_site_is_readonly* tells the caller whether the bound registry site is a read or update site.

The most common way for applications to use the *sec_rgy* interface is therefore through the sequence:

1. Call *sec_rgy_site_open_open_query* or *sec_rgy_site_open_update* depending on whether you're performing a read or update operation.

2. Perform some other registry lookup or update operations.

3. Call *sec_rgy_site_close* to release the binding acquired in step 1.

The example below (taken from our first sample application) shows the calls that you need to make to see if a principal is a member of a group:

```
/*
 * Establish a binding to the registry interface of the
 * Security Server.
 */
sec_rgy_site_open_query(NULL, &rgy_handle, &status);
CHECK_STATUS (status, "rgy_site_open failed", ABORT);

/*
 * Check to see if the client principal is a member of
 * the personnel department group.
 */
is_teacher = sec_rgy_pgo_is_member (rgy_handle,
        sec_rgy_domain_group, "personell_dept",
        client_principal_name, &status);
CHECK_STATUS (status, "is_member failed", ABORT);

/*
 * We are done with the Security registry; free the handle
 * now.
 */
sec_rgy_site_close(rgy_handle,&status);
CHECK_STATUS (status, "rgy_site_close failed", ABORT);
```

You should treat the *rgy_handle* as a normal RPC handle. Therefore, once you've obtained a *rgy_handle* from a *sec_rgy_site_open* call, you should save and reuse it instead of calling *sec_rgy_site_open* each time you need to contact the registry. This allows you to spread out the overhead of the binding operation over a large number of calls.

Now that you know how to bind to a Registry Service, we can look at how you access the information stored in the registry.

Cell Information Calls

The following series of calls allows you to get and set cell and policy information. Note how they match the operations supported by *rgy_edit.*

> *sec_rgy_properties_get_info*
> *sec_rgy_properties_set_info*
> *sec_rgy_plcy_get_info*
> *sec_rgy_plcy_get_effective*
> *sec_rgy_plcy_set_info*
> *sec_rgy_plcy_get_override_info*
> *sec_rgy_plcy_set_override_info*
> *sec_rgy_auth_plcy_get_info*
> *sec_rgy_auth_plcy_get_effective*
> *sec_rgy_auth_plcy_set_info*

These calls are used to implement the properties, policy, and authpolicy subcommands in *rgy_edit.*

PGO Calls

PGO calls let you access and modify the principal/group/organization (PGO) entries in the Registry. I have grouped them into four categories below.

The first group deals with individual PGO entries. You can add, delete, replace, and rename PGO items.

> *sec_rgy_pgo_add*
> *sec_rgy_pgo_delete*
> *sec_rgy_pgo_replace*
> *sec_rgy_pgo_rename*

The second group allows you to look up PGO entries using a number of lookup keys.

> *sec_rgy_pgo_get_by_name*
> *sec_rgy_pgo_get_by_id*
> *sec_rgy_pgo_get_by_unix_num*
> *sec_rgy_pgo_get_next*

The third group deals with groups and organizations. They allow you, for example, to check whether a principal is a member of a specified group.

> *sec_rgy_pgo_add_member*
> *sec_rgy_pgo_delete_member*
> *sec_rgy_pgo_is_member*
> *sec_rgy_pgo_get_members*

The last group of calls lets you convert among the various lookup keys supported by the PGO database.

> *sec_rgy_pgo_name_to_id*
> *sec_rgy_pgo_id_to_name*
> *sec_rgy_pgo_name_to_unix_num*
> *sec_rgy_pgo_unix_num_to_name*
> *sec_rgy_pgo_id_to_unix_num*
> *sec_rgy_pgo_unix_num_to_id*

We will use the *sec_rgy_pgo_is_member* function later on for clients to determine whether they can trust a given server. Other than that, the other calls are normally used only by *rgy_edit*.

Account Calls

The account calls allow you to administer the accounts database in the registry. These calls are directed towards management applications for the security registry and are not normally used by general DCE applications.

> *sec_rgy_acct_add*
> *sec_rgy_acct_user_replace*
> *sec_rgy_acct_admin_replace*
> *sec_rgy_acct_replace_all*
> *sec_rgy_acct_delete*
> *sec_rgy_acct_rename*
> *sec_rgy_acct_passwd*
> *sec_rgy_acct_get_projlist*
> *sec_rgy_acct_lookup*

If you look at the list of *rgy_edit* commands for creating, modifying, and deleting user accounts, you should find a very close correspondence between the command and these functions.

Mapping Between UUIDs and Names

I mentioned earlier that DCE uses UUIDs to identify principals and groups. People, on the other hand, prefer to deal with string names. The ID map API converts between the string names and the UUIDs.

> *sec_id_parse_name*
> *sec_id_gen_name*
> *sec_id_parse_group*
> *sec_id_gen_group*

sec_id_parse_name breaks a global principal name, for example */.../my_cell/ASmith*, into a cell-name (*my_cell*), the cell-relative name (*ASmith*), the cell UUID, and the principal UUID. *sec_id_parse_group* is the equivalent operation for groups. *sec_id_gen_name* and *sec_id_gen_group* are the inverse operations. They convert from UUIDs back to string names. These routines are useful because they allow you to employ user-friendly string names instead of UUIDs in your user-interface programs. They are also helpful during debugging.

You should be aware that the *sec_id* routines are implemented as remote procedures to the Registry Service. This is because the Registry is the only place where the mapping information is kept. The *sec_id* API is described in the DCE documentation as a separate API. I have, however, included it in the Registry API in Chapter 2 because it uses the Registry to perform its mappings.

Managing ACLs

The *sec_acl* API allows a management application such as *acl_edit* to update ACL entries. Internally, the *sec_acl* calls use a set of remote procedures called the *rdacl* interface. *acl_edit* uses the *rdacl* interface to tell your server what to do with an ACL.

You won't have to learn about the *sec_acl* interface unless you are writing a management application like *acl_edit*. However, you do have to concern yourself with the *rdacl* interface. You need to write your own versions of these calls, using the models presented in this book, so that users can modify your ACLs.

Figure 3-4 shows how these APIs relate. The list below details the operations that are part of the *rdacl* interface.

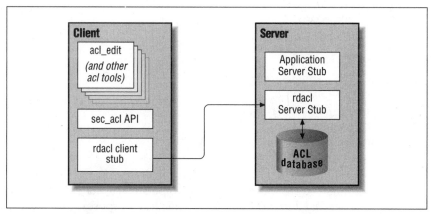

Figure 3-4: Relationship between the sec_acl API and ACLs

> *rdacl_lookup*
> *rdacl_replace*
> *rdacl_get_access*
> *rdacl_test_access*
> *rdacl_test_access_on_behalf*
> *rdacl_get_manager_types*
> *rdacl_get_printstring*

> *rdacl_get_referral*
> *rdacl_get_mgr_types_semantics*

I will describe what each of these calls do when I talk about ACL managers. However, just by looking at the function names, you can tell that the *rdacl* interface allows you to remotely perform the usual operations one would expect to be able to do with ACLs, i.e., replace an ACL entry, look at one, check whether someone can access the object protected by the ACL, etc.

Because every server that implements DCE ACLs supports this common RPC interface, a single RPC application can manipulate all ACL types.This is why DCE can use a single utility, *acl_edit*, to manage all the ACLs in a cell, regardless of how each server implements ACLs internally. Because DCE has standardized only the interface, each application is free to implement ACLs internally as it sees fit.

Management applications do not call the *rdacl* client stubs directly. Instead, they call the *sec_acl* API that is layered on top of the client stub. I will describe this API very briefly. The functions in the *sec_acl* API are:

> *sec_acl_bind*
> *sec_acl_bind_to_addr*
> *sec_acl_release_handle*
> *sec_acl_lookup*
> *sec_acl_get_access*
> *sec_acl_test_access*
> *sec_acl_test_access_on_behalf*
> *sec_acl_replace*
> *sec_acl_get_manager_types*
> *sec_acl_calc_mask*
> *sec_acl_get_printstring*
> *sec_acl_release*
> *sec_acl_get_error_info*
> *sec_acl_get_mgr_types_semantics*

I have grouped the *sec_acl* calls into three categories. In the first set, the *sec_acl_bind* and *sec_acl_bind_to_addr* manipulate *sec_acl_handle_t* data structures. A *sec_acl_handle_t* is, for all practical purposes, just the RPC binding handle to a server's *rdacl* interface. All the ACL query and update functions require a *sec_acl_handle_t* as an input; it is used to determine the server to operate on. The *sec_acl* API allows you to bind to the server by either its CDS name or its RPC string binding. *sec_acl_release_handle* just releases the storage taken up by a *sec_acl_handle_t* after you are done with it.

The second group of calls operate on a server's ACLs. *sec_acl_lookup* retrieves a copy of the server's access control list. You can perform permission checks using the ACL by any of three calls: *sec_acl_get_access* returns the permissions that the caller has to the object protected by the ACL, *sec_acl_test_access* tells the caller whether the requested type of access is allowed, and *sec_test_access_on_behalf* allows the caller to determine if another principal can have the requested type of access to the object. The last call is useful for an administrator to test the access permitted to another user, for example. The last call, *sec_acl_replace*, replaces an existing ACL with a new one. This is how you would add or delete ACL entries.

The last group of calls return various information related to the implementation of an ACL manager. They will make more sense after I describe how you would actually write an ACL manager. We will therefore skip them for now.

The first three chapters of this book were a long journey through the mechanics of DCE Security. Finally, we are ready to write an application. In the next three chapters, we will explore how to program DCE Security.

4

How to Write an Application
That Uses Security

In this chapter, we will look at how to use the DCE Security API in a complete application using the employee database described in Chapter 1. First, we will implement the application without security. Then, we will enhance it to use authentication and name-based authorization. This is mostly done as a transition to a PAC-based server because it's fairly simple, but name-based authorization is not secure enough for production applications. After this, we will add the use of groups and DCE authorization, and make the server standalone. These improvements will be added incrementally, so that we have a complete application at every stage. Note that the complete sources for these programs are in the Appendixes.

Employee Database Application

In Chapter 1, I introduced the employee database application. This application consists of a server that stores a database of employee information (name, mailstop, and phone number) and a client that allows employees to query and update records in this database over a network. This example is a simplified version of a remote query/update application. Figure 4-1 shows how this application is divided into client and server pieces.

The client and server are conventional DCE RPC programs. The server provides an RPC interface to the back-end database. It receives RPCs and executes the requested operations against the database. We assume there are multiple clients in the network, each running its own copy of the client program.

Figure 4-2 shows the pieces of code that make up the client and server programs. I have shaded the code we have to write.

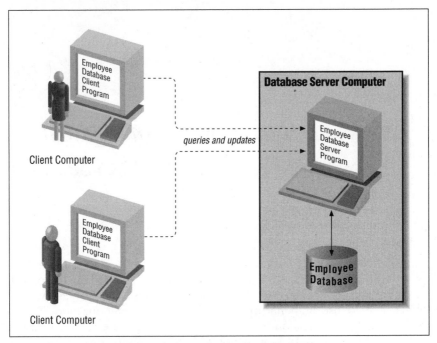

Figure 4-1: Overview of the employee database application

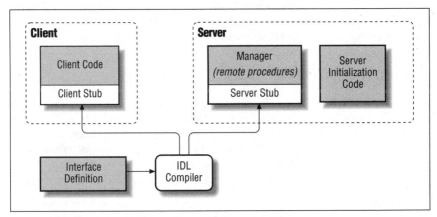

Figure 4-2: Structure of the employee database application

As you can see, we need to write the interface definition, the client code, the server manager, and the server-initialization code. The interface definition is used by the stub compiler to generate the client and server stubs, which are then linked with the client and server code. We will now look at each of these pieces in turn.

Interface Definition

Our server supports a single remote interface, *emp_db*, containing four remote procedures: *emp_db_insert*, *emp_db_update*, *emp_db_delete*, and *emp_db_query*. They allow you to add a record to the database, change an existing record, remove a record, and search for a record. Example 4-1 shows the IDL file for this application.

The handle that is the first argument of each remote procedure shows you are using explicit binding. It isn't necessary for the trivial, nonsecure version of the example, but will be important later when you add security because you specify the level of security you want by modifying the binding handle used as part of the call. Note that we've also chosen to return all information (including errors) in arguments, so the procedures are declared as returning type void.

Example 4-1: Interface Definition for Employee Database

```
[uuid(70340588-a9a0-11cd-838b-69076147ce07),
    version(1.0)]
interface emp_db
{
        const unsigned32        emp_s_ok                = 0;
        const unsigned32        emp_s_not_found         = 100;
        const unsigned32        emp_s_exists            = 101;
        const unsigned32        emp_s_nospace           = 102;
        const unsigned32        emp_s_not_authorized    = 103;

        const unsigned32        EMP_DB_MAX_LEN = 40;
        typedef [string] char emp_db_field_t[EMP_DB_MAX_LEN];

        typedef struct {
                emp_db_field_t          emp_name;
                emp_db_field_t          emp_mailstop;
                emp_db_field_t          emp_phone_number;
        } emp_record_t;

        void emp_db_insert (
                [in]    handle_t        handle,
                [in]    emp_record_t    emp_record,
                [out]   unsigned32      *emp_status
        );

        void emp_db_modify (
                [in]    handle_t        handle,
                [in]    emp_record_t    emp_record,
                [out]   unsigned32      *emp_status
        );

        void emp_db_delete (
                [in]    handle_t        handle,
                [in]    emp_db_field_t  emp_name,
```

Example 4-1: Interface Definition for Employee Database (continued)

```
                    [out]    unsigned32       *emp_status
         );

         [idempotent]
         void emp_db_query (
                    [in]     handle_t         handle,
                    [in]     emp_db_field_t   emp_name,
                    [out]    emp_record_t     *emp_record,
                    [out]    unsigned32       *emp_status
         );
}
```

Server Manager Code

We are now ready to implement the remote procedures themselves. Except for the mutexes they use to protect against multithreaded access, the procedures look just like nondistributed applications. DCE calls this body of code a manager because it manages the abstract object or resource exported by the interface. For example, the manager code for the employee database manages the abstract datatype (*emp_record_t*) of our application. As we'll see later, a server may act as a manager for multiple interfaces. The employee database example will have only one manager. Example 4-2 shows a simple *emp_db* manager.

Example 4-2: Server Manager Code for the Employee Database

```
#include <stdio.h>
#include <string.h>
#include <bstring.h>
#include <pthread.h>

#include "emp_db.h"
#include "chk_stat.h"

/*
 * Make our database just an array of DATABASE_SIZE entries.
 */
#define DATABASE_SIZE 1000
emp_record_t    emp_database[DATABASE_SIZE];

/*
 * Mutex to serialize access to the database.
 */
pthread_mutex_t emp_db_mutex;


void
emp_db_init (void)
{
```

Example 4-2: Server Manager Code for the Employee Database (continued)

```
        unsigned        i;

        pthread_mutex_init (&emp_db_mutex, pthread_mutexattr_default);

        bzero (emp_database, sizeof(emp_record_t) * DATABASE_SIZE);

        ... more initialization code ...

}


void
emp_db_insert (
        handle_t handle,
        emp_record_t emp_record,
        unsigned32 *emp_status)
{
        unsigned        i;

        pthread_mutex_lock (&emp_db_mutex);

        /*
         * Make sure entry is not already in the database.
         */
        for (i=0; i < DATABASE_SIZE; i++) {
                if (strcmp (emp_database[i].emp_name,
                        emp_record.emp_name) == 0) {
                        *emp_status = emp_s_exists;
                        pthread_mutex_unlock (&emp_db_mutex);
                        return;
                }
        }

        /*
         * Now copy the record into the first empty entry.
         */
        for (i=0; i < DATABASE_SIZE; i++) {
                if (emp_database[i].emp_name[0] == '\0') {
                        emp_database[i] = emp_record;
                        *emp_status = emp_s_ok;
                        pthread_mutex_unlock (&emp_db_mutex);
                        return;
                }
        }

        *emp_status = emp_s_nospace;
        pthread_mutex_unlock (&emp_db_mutex);
        return;
}

void
emp_db_modify (
        handle_t handle,
```

Example 4-2: Server Manager Code for the Employee Database (continued)

```
        emp_record_t emp_record,
        unsigned32 *emp_status)
{
        unsigned        i;

        pthread_mutex_lock (&emp_db_mutex);

        for (i=0; i < DATABASE_SIZE; i++) {
                if (strcmp (emp_database[i].emp_name,
                        emp_record.emp_name) == 0) {
                emp_database[i] = emp_record;
                *emp_status = emp_s_ok;
                pthread_mutex_unlock (&emp_db_mutex);
                return;
            }
        }

        *emp_status = emp_s_not_found;

        pthread_mutex_unlock (&emp_db_mutex);
        return;
}


void
emp_db_delete (
        handle_t handle,
        emp_db_field_t emp_name,
        unsigned32 *emp_status)
{
        unsigned        i;

        pthread_mutex_lock (&emp_db_mutex);

        for (i=0; i < DATABASE_SIZE; i++) {
                if (strcmp (emp_database[i].emp_name,
                        emp_name) == 0) {
                bzero (&emp_database[i], sizeof(emp_record_t));
                *emp_status = emp_s_ok;
                pthread_mutex_unlock (&emp_db_mutex);
                return;
            }
        }

        *emp_status = emp_s_not_found;
        pthread_mutex_unlock (&emp_db_mutex);
        return;
}


void
emp_db_query(
        handle_t handle,
```

Example 4-2: Server Manager Code for the Employee Database (continued)

```
            emp_db_field_t emp_name,
            emp_record_t *emp_record,
            unsigned32 *emp_status)
{

    unsigned        i;

    pthread_mutex_lock (&emp_db_mutex);

    for (i=0; i < DATABASE_SIZE; i++) {
            if (strcmp (emp_database[i].emp_name,
                    emp_name) == 0) {
                *emp_record = emp_database[i];
                *emp_status = emp_s_ok;
                pthread_mutex_unlock (&emp_db_mutex);
                return;
            }
    }

    *emp_status = emp_s_not_found;
    pthread_mutex_unlock (&emp_db_mutex);
    return;

}
```

Note that the manager code uses a mutex to control access to the database because the server is multithreaded and may be concurrently servicing requests from several clients. The routine, *emp_db_init*, initializes the database; it is designed to be called from the server *main* routine, and shouldn't be in the interface.

Server Main

The server *main* program initializes the database and then sets itself up as an RPC server. Initialization involves the steps described in the *Guide to Writing DCE Applications*, also by O'Reilly & Associates. The server program needs to register the *emp_db* interface, create the binding information, advertise the server and manage the endpoints. When these tasks are finished, the server needs to call *rpc_server_listen* to transfer control to the RPC runtime so that incoming RPC calls will be dispatched to the server manager code.

Example 4-3 shows the server main program. Before you look at the example, I want to emphasize that the server main program is mostly boiler-plate code. I wrote this version by taking one of my other main programs and then changing the interface name and the namespace entry to which I want to export the servers bindings.

Example 4-3: Unauthenticated Server Main Procedure

```
#include <stdio.h>
#include <pthread.h>
#include <bstring.h>
#include <string.h>
#include "emp_db.h"
#include "chk_stat.h"

extern void emp_db_init (void);

int
main(
    int                         argc,
    char                        *argv[])
{
    rpc_binding_vector_t        *bind_vector_p;
    unsigned32                  status;

    /* Initialize local state. */
    emp_db_init();

    /* Register interface with rpc runtime. */

    rpc_server_register_if(emp_db_v1_0_s_ifspec, NULL, NULL, &status);
    CHECK_STATUS (status,"unable to register i/f",ABORT);

    /* We want to use all supported protocol sequences. */

    rpc_server_use_all_protseqs(rpc_c_protseq_max_reqs_default, &status);
    CHECK_STATUS (status,"use_all_protseqs failed",ABORT);

    /* Get our bindings. */

    rpc_server_inq_bindings(&bind_vector_p, &status);
    CHECK_STATUS (status,"server_inq_bindings failed",ABORT);

    /* Register binding information with the endpoint map. */

    rpc_ep_register(emp_db_v1_0_s_ifspec, bind_vector_p,
        NULL,
        (unsigned_char_t *)"Employee database server, version 1.0",
        &status);
    CHECK_STATUS (status,"ep_register failed",ABORT);

    /*
     * Export binding information into the namespace.
     */
    rpc_ns_binding_export(rpc_c_ns_syntax_dce, "/.:/subsys/emp_db",
        emp_db_v1_0_s_ifspec, bind_vector_p,
        NULL, &status);
    CHECK_STATUS (status,"export failed",ABORT);

    /* Listen for remote calls. */
    fprintf(stderr, "Server ready.\n");
```

Example 4-3: Unauthenticated Server Main Procedure (continued)

```
    rpc_server_listen(rpc_c_listen_max_calls_default, &status);
    CHECK_STATUS (status,"server_listen failed",ABORT);
}
```

Client

Now that the server is complete, you can write the client. Example 4-4 shows part of the code that implements the client application. It prompts the user for a command and then calls the corresponding remote procedure. The complete source code is in Appendix A. Basically, the client establishes a binding to the server by querying the DCE CDS, and then makes the appropriate remote procedure call based on the user's command.

Example 4-4: Basic Employee Database Client Program

```
#include <stdio.h>
#include <stdlib.h>
#include "emp_db.h"
#include "chk_stat.h"

void print_status (unsigned  status);

/*
 *      main()
 *
 *      Get started, and main loop.
 */

int
main(
        int                             argc,
        char                            *argv[])
{

        unsigned32                      status;
        handle_t                        binding_handle;
        rpc_ns_handle_t                 import_context;
        emp_db_field_t                  emp_name;
        emp_record_t                    emp_record;
        char                            command[5];

        /*
         * Get server binding from the name space.
         */

        rpc_ns_binding_import_begin(rpc_c_ns_syntax_dce,
                "/.:/subsys/emp_db", emp_db_v1_0_c_ifspec,
                NULL, &import_context, &status);
```

Example 4-4: Basic Employee Database Client Program (continued)

```
CHECK_STATUS (status, "Import begin failed", ABORT);

rpc_ns_binding_import_next(import_context,
    &binding_handle, &status);
CHECK_STATUS (status, "Import next failed", ABORT);

rpc_ns_binding_import_done(&import_context, &status);
CHECK_STATUS (status, "Import done failed", ABORT);

/*
 * Enter our command loop.
 */
while (1) {

        ... get user command ...


        switch (command[0]) {
                case 'q':        /* query */
                    ...


                        emp_db_query (binding_handle,
                                emp_name, &emp_record, &status);

                        ... print out the information ...

                        break;

                case 'i':
                    ...


                        emp_db_insert (binding_handle,
                                emp_record, &status);
                        break;

                case 'm':
                    ...


                        emp_db_modify (binding_handle,
                                emp_record, &status);
                        break;

                case 'd':
                    ...


                        emp_db_delete (binding_handle,
                                emp_name, &status);
                        break;
```

Example 4-4: Basic Employee Database Client Program (continued)

```
                    case 'e':
                         exit(0);
                         break;

                    default:
                         ...


              }
         }
}
```

Now that we've seen the implementation, let's build and run the application.

Running the Basic Employee Database Application

The employee database application is built as a normal DCE application. The full Makefile is in Appendix A.

Configuring the application

Because this version of the employee database does not use DCE Security, you can omit many of the usual configuration steps. You merely need to configure CDS so that the employee database server can export its bindings to its CDS entry. By default, DCE is configured so that anyone can read from a CDS entry; this allows unauthenticated client programs to import server bindings. A program, however, needs write permission to create a CDS entry or to export its bindings into a CDS entry. The example below shows how to modify the CDS ACL.

```
 adlman 8% dce_login cell_admin -dce-             ❶
 adlman 1% cdscp create obj /.:/subsys/emp_db     ❷
 adlman 2% acl_edit -e /.:/subsys/emp_db          ❸
 sec_acl_edit> list                               ❹

 # SEC_ACL for /.:/subsys/emp_db:
 # Default cell = /.../adlman_cell
 unauthenticated:r--t-
 user:cell_admin:rwdtc
 group:subsys/dce/cds-admin:rwdtc
 group:subsys/dce/cds-server:rwdtc
 any_other:r--t-                                  ❺
 sec_acl_edit> modify any_other:rwt               ❻
 sec_acl_edit> modify unauthenticated:rwt
 sec_acl_edit> list

 # SEC_ACL for /.:/subsys/emp_db:
```

```
# Default cell = /.../adlman_cell
unauthenticated:rw-t-
user:cell_admin:rwdtc
group:subsys/dce/cds-admin:rwdtc
group:subsys/dce/cds-server:rwdtc
any_other:rw-t-                                    ❼
sec_acl_edit> exit                                 ❽
adlman 4% exit

adlman 5% adlman 12% server &
[1] 6325
adlman 13% Server ready.
```

❶ First log into DCE as `cell_admin` so that you have all needed permissions.

❷ Create the CDS entry */.:/subsys/emp_db* to which the server will export its bindings.

❸ Run *acl_edit* to change the ACL associated with the CDS entry. Normally, when you specify an entry, *acl_edit* assumes you want to change the ACL on the server that stores its bindings there. But here, you must change the ACL on the CDS entry itself so that the server can store its bindings there. The *-e* option tells *acl_edit* you wish to operate on the CDS entry itself and not on the server whose bindings are stored there.

❹ *acl_edit list* shows that the default ACLs on this CDS entry allows the *cell_admin* and members of the *cds-admin* and the *cds-server* groups full access; everyone else has only read and test permissions.

❺ Modify the *any_other* ACL entry to have read, write, and test permission on the CDS entry. This allows your server (and anyone else) to export bindings to that entry.

❻ The *any_other* ACL entry still requires an authenticated identity. To allow servers that are not authenticated to run, you should modify the *unauthenticated* ACL entry to read, write, and test permission. Combined with the *any_other* ACL entry, this modification allows anyone to write to this entry. This is not a secure situation, of course. Someone could run a bogus server that impersonates yours. In another chapter, we'll improve the security with respect to our use of CDS. I will explain in detail what the different ACL entries mean when I describe DCE ACLs in the next chapter.

❼ Exit out of the current shell. This destroys the *cell_admin* login context and returns to the original shell. You do this so that the server would not run under the *cell_admin*'s identity.

❽   The server should start up correctly.

Running the application

At this point, the server is up and ready to receive client requests. Here is a sample session.

```
adlman 12% server &
[1] 6325
adlman 14% Server ready.
adlman 15% client
Ready> insert
name: wei_hu
mailstop: 7L-802
phone: 3-1511
Status: Ok
Ready> query
name:wei_hu
mail stop: 7L-802, phone: 3-1511
Status: Ok
Ready> delete
name:wei_hu
Status: Ok
   ...
```

Using Authentication and Name-Based Authorization

The basic employee database application I have described so far is not secure. Any client that can reach the server can read and write any record in the database. Let us now improve our application by having the client and server authenticate each other and use the authenticated identity to make authorization decisions. this is called **name-based authorization** because only the client's name (instead of PACs) is used to determine whether the client is authorized to make the request.

You need to make three changes to the application to support authentication and name-based authorization. First, change the client to request authentication. Then you need to change the server main program to register its principal name and secret key with the RPC runtime. Finally, you should write a reference monitor the server can call on every incoming RPC to see if the client is authorized for the operation. As you will see, this is not very much work.

Before we make these changes, however, we must first decide upon the security policy that our application will implement.

Defining a Security Policy

The security policy defines the types of access that are allowed. Since the only thing we have to work with are the identities of the client and server, you need to express the security policy in these terms. For the employee database application, a reasonable security policy based solely upon principal names would consist of the following rules.

Only employees can query the database.
> If you assume that only employees are in the database, you can implement this rule easily by making sure that the client is in the database.

Every client can update his or her own record.

The personnel manager can update any record in the database.
> You can implement this by giving the personnel manager a reserved name and granting this access if the client has that name.

That covers the security needs of the server. The client, however, also needs to protect itself against a fake server. We therefore add another statement.

A client will call only the genuine employee database server.
> You implement this by giving the server the reserved name *emp_db_server*; the client authenticate with the server under that identity.

Modifying the Client to Request Authentication

To make an authenticated RPC, all that a client needs to do is request authentication before calling the remote procedure. This can be done in one call, *rpc_binding_set_auth_info*.

Recall from Chapter 2 what has to pass between a client and server for authentication to work. The client must obtain a set of credentials from the Security Service, which will be sent to the server from each call. The server's secret key must be used to encrypt the client's information. Since the binding handle is the data structure tying the two sides together, that is where the client places the authentication information. All this work is done by *rpc_binding_set_auth_info*; the action is called annotating the binding handle.

The client has to specify the server it wants to communicate with by giving the server's name to the Authentication Service. The server's job is to provide its secret key; this will be shown later when we discuss the code of the server.

Example 4-5 shows how the binding handle is annotated for authenticated RPC in the employee database client.

Example 4-5: Client code

```
unsigned32                    status;
handle_t                      binding_handle;
rpc_ns_handle_t               import_context;
emp_db_field_t                emp_name;
emp_record_t                  emp_record;

/*
 * Get server binding from the name space.
 */

rpc_ns_binding_import_begin(...                              ❶
rpc_ns_binding_import_next(...
rpc_ns_binding_import_done(...


/*
 * Annotate our binding handle for authentication.
 */
rpc_binding_set_auth_info(binding_handle,                    ❷
    "/.:/emp_db_server", rpc_c_protect_level_default,
    rpc_c_authn_dce_secret, NULL /*default login context*/,
    rpc_c_authz_name, &status);
CHECK_STATUS (status, "binding_set_auth_info failed", ABORT);



emp_db_query (binding_handle, emp_name, &emp_record, &status); ❸
```

❶ The client obtains a server binding as before. This can be done either by importing it from the name service (as done here), or by using a string binding.

❷ The client then annotates the binding handle for authenticated RPC. Here is a description of what each argument means in the call to *rpc_binding_set_auth_info*:

Binding handle
> The binding handle for the RPC.

Server principal name
> Specifies the name of the employee database server to identify the principal for the STtk. Later I'll explain what to do if the client does not know the server's principal name.

Protection level
> DCE RPC can protect the data sent over the network to prevent unauthorized modification or reading. For this call, you are requesting the default protection level; this causes a checksum to be computed for each packet so that RPC can detect any unauthorized modifications. Please refer back to Chapter 3 for a discussion of the various protection levels.

Selecting integrity protection allows you to detect fake client or server principals and to guarantee that the data transmitted are not tampered with. It does not, however, prevent a wiretapper from reading the messages that are exchanged. If you want to protect your application against wiretaps, you need to select privacy protection. I chose not to do so because I don't consider that threat to be significant enough to warrant the extra overhead. (Privacy protection adds overhead because the RPC runtime will encrypt the user data that is sent as part of the RPC.) In addition, this ensures that the application will run on all DCE implementations. Remember, because of export restrictions, you cannot count on privacy protection being available.

Authentication service

DCE RPC is designed to support multiple authentication services. Thus, this argument is provided to allow the application program to select one. At present the only supported authentication services are *none* and *DCE private key* authentication; *DCE private key* is the default.

Login context for this principal

Use NULL to specify the default login context. This causes RPC to use the login context of the process that is running the client application. Recall that this is the desired behavior since the real principal is the process that is running the client program as opposed to the client program itself.

Type of authorization

Specify authorization by name. This causes RPC to pass the client's authenticated principal name as the privilege attribute when the RPC is initiated. The name is authenticated because the Authentication Service is still involved in generating the ticket. The only thing missing is the privilege information normally supplied by the Privilege Service.

❸ Call the remote procedure. The call will be authenticated, the client's principal name will be passed for authorizaton, and the messages that go over the network will be integrity-protected.

Modify Server Main to Initialize Authenticated RPC

The server main program needs to register its authentication information before it calls *rpc_server_listen*. This tells the DCE runtime the server's principal name and how to get the server's secret key. The DCE runtime will then use this information to decrypt service tickets directed to this server. Note that Example 4-6 uses the keytab file described in Chapter 3 to store the server's secret key.

Example 4-6: Register Authentication Information with RPC

```
#define SERVER_PRINC_NAME "/.:/emp_db_server"
#define KEYTAB_FILE "/usr/people/emp_db_server/emp_db_keytab"

        /*
         * Register authentication info with RPC.
         */
        rpc_server_register_auth_info(SERVER_PRINC_NAME, ❶
            rpc_c_authn_dce_secret, /* authn protocol */ ❷
            NULL /*default key retrieval function*/,    ❸
            KEYTAB_FILE, /* server keytab file */
            &status);
        CHECK_STATUS (status,"server_register_auth_info failed",ABORT);
```

The arguments specify:

❶   A **server principal name**. This is the name of the server as it is regis-
    tered with DCE Security. A full principal name includes the cell name.
    If it is not specified, DCE will automatically prepend the name of the
    local cell to the principal name. So you could have used
    emp_db_server, a name specifying the local cell as */.:/emp_db_server*,
    or the precise cell name as */ . . . /adlman_cell/emp_db_server*.

❷   An **authentication protocol**. This picks the Authentication Service to
    use. At present, the only supported authentication protocol is the
    secret key based protocol described in Chapter 2. In the future, this
    may include others.

❸   A **key retrieval function** and **argument**. *NULL* is specified for the key
    retrieval function to indicate the use of the standard keytab mecha-
    nism to store the server's secret key. The name of this server's keytab
    file is passed as the next argument. As we'll see later, this keytab file
    is created by the administrator as part of this server's configuration.

If a server operates under multiple identities, this routine must be called
once per identity. In the future, should DCE support multiple authentication services, this call should be called once per identity per supported
authentication service.

Choosing a server principal name

Sometimes people have trouble picking principal names for their servers. I
tend to first pick a local identity for the server and then use the same
identity as its principal name. For UNIX systems, the local identity of
servers usually consists of invocation names such as *rpcd* and *nfsd*. All
you need do is add the cell name to the front of the invocation name.
This is a good approach because you will want to associate a local operating system identity (or UNIX process name) with every server principal
you create. (The local identity thus becomes the owner of the server's
keytab file.)

Naming servers becomes slightly trickier when your servers are replicated. If your servers are really totally interchangeable, you can make them all instances of the same principal and have them share the same name. The drawback of this approach is that you cannot pinpoint the exact server that is responsible should something go wrong. In addition, you cannot use the key management API or the *rgy_edit* keytab commands to set a random key for your servers because there is no way to set the same random key in each server's keytab file if the server instances are on separate computers in a network.

An alternative approach in handling replicated servers is to assign them individual names and then make them members of the same group. This way, you can still hold individual servers accountable and yet treat them collectively as a group for those cases where you don't care. I'll show you how to do this in a later section.

Implementing a Reference Monitor

The reference monitor is the piece of code that performs authorization checks. The initialization code described previously is called during startup, before the main server thread calls *rpc_server_listen*; it is called only once. The reference monitor, by contrast, must be called at the start of every remote procedure call. Figure 4-3 shows the flow of control. Notice how the reference monitor logically intercepts all calls to the server. This is crucial; any RPC that bypasses the reference monitor will bypass the server's security checks.

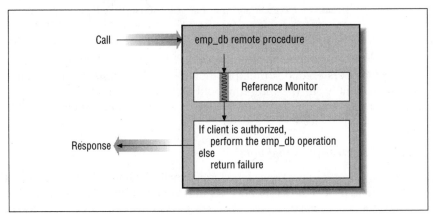

Figure 4-3: Reference monitor

Example 4-7 shows how the server manager code makes calls to the reference monitor.

Example 4-7: Calling the Reference Monitor

```
typedef enum { OP_READ, OP_WRITE } access_type_t;
extern int client_is_authorized (
        handle_t        handle,
        access_type_t   operation,
        emp_db_field_t  emp_name);                    ❶

void
emp_db_insert (
        handle_t handle,
        emp_record_t emp_record,
        unsigned32 *emp_status)
{
        pthread_mutex_lock (&emp_db_mutex);

        if (! client_is_authorized(handle, OP_WRITE, ❷
                                emp_record.emp_name)) {
                *emp_status = emp_s_not_authorized;
                pthread_mutex_unlock (&emp_db_mutex);
                        return;
        }

        ... rest of insert code ...

}

void
emp_db_modify (
        handle_t handle,
        emp_record_t emp_record,
        unsigned32 *emp_status)
{
        ...

}


void
emp_db_delete (
        handle_t handle,
        emp_db_field_t emp_name,
        unsigned32 *emp_status)
{
        ...

}


void
emp_db_query(
        handle_t handle,
        emp_db_field_t emp_name,
        emp_record_t *emp_record,
        unsigned32 *emp_status)
```

Example 4-7: Calling the Reference Monitor (continued)

```
{
        pthread_mutex_lock (&emp_db_mutex);

        if (! client_is_authorized (handle, OP_READ, emp_name)) {
                *emp_status = emp_s_not_authorized;
                pthread_mutex_unlock (&emp_db_mutex);
                return;
        }

        ... rest of query code ...

}
```

❶ The reference monitor is implemented by a single procedure, *client_is_authorized*. This call takes the binding handle, the type of operation (read or write), and the name of the entry to be operated upon as input. It returns 1 if the client is authorized for the operation and 0 if not. As you'll see shortly, the reference monitor needs all of these inputs to make its access control checks.

❷ Here is a call to the reference monitor. Note how *emp_db_insert* checks to see if the client is authorized before inserting the record.

Now that we've seen how the reference monitor is called, let's look at an implementation. A reference monitor needs to see whether the authentication parameters specified by the client are acceptable, and then perform the actual access check.

Checking authentication parameters

Authenticated RPC guarantees that if the server's manager code is invoked, the client is who it claims to be. (Since DCE supports mutual authentication, the server is also authenticated to the client.) But there is more to security than knowing who you're talking to. The server must still determine if the other aspects of the authenticated call are acceptable. In particular, the server needs to decide if the values the client selected in its call to *rpc_binding_set_auth_info* are acceptable. These parameters include the protection level, the authentication protocol, and the authorization protocol. The server can retrieve these values by calling *rpc_binding_inq_auth_client*. Example 4-8 shows how this call is used.

Example 4-8: Checking Authentication Parameters

```
extern int emp_db_present (char    *client_name);
extern char *emp_db_cell;

int
client_is_authorized (
```

Example 4-8: Checking Authentication Parameters (continued)

```
        handle_t        handle,
        access_type_t   operation,
        emp_db_field_t  emp_name)
{
        unsigned_char_t    *server_principal_name;
        unsigned_char_t    *client_principal_name;
        unsigned32         protection_level;
        unsigned32         authn_svc;
        unsigned32         authz_svc;
        unsigned32         status;
        char               *client;

        /*
         * Check the authentication parameters that the client
         * selected for this call.
         */
        rpc_binding_inq_auth_client (handle,                          ❶
        (rpc_authz_handle_t *) &client_principal_name,
                &server_principal_name, &protection_level, &authn_svc,
                &authz_svc, &status);
        CHECK_STATUS (status, "inq_auth_client failed", ABORT);

        /*
         * Make sure that the caller has specified the required
         * level of protection, authentication, and authorization.
         */
        if (! ((protection_level == rpc_c_protect_level_pkt_integ) &&  ❷
                (authn_svc == rpc_c_authn_dce_secret) &&
                (authz_svc == rpc_c_authz_name)))
                return 0;

        ... perform the access checks ...
```

❶ The server first retrieves the parameters the client used to set up the authenticated RPC. *rpc_binding_inq_auth_client* gets the values the client specified in its call to *rpc_binding_set_auth_info*.

The most important output argument is the *rpc_authz_handle_t* parameter. This is a pointer to the client's privilege information. The exact data structure to which it points depends upon the type of authorization that is used. In the case of name-based authorization, it points to the client's authenticated principal name. If PAC-based authorization is used, then it points to a PAC. This call also returns the server principal name the client specified, the protection level, the authentication service, and the authorization service.

The server principal name argument is useful when the server process has registered several principal names. The protection level, authentication, and authorization service parameters specify those actually used for the current call.

❷ The server must now check that the authentication, authorization, and protection levels specified by the client are acceptable. DCE RPC relies upon the server to check these values so that it can decide what to do when the values are unacceptable. A common action to take in this case is to audit the failure and reject the call.

For this version of our application, the reference monitor requires that the transmitted data be integrity-protected, the authentication service be DCE private key, and the authorization protocol be name-based. If the checks fail, the call fails. It would actually be OK if a client specified a protection level that is even stronger than the one I checked for, but I omitted checks for other protection levels in order to keep the example simple.

Performing the access check

After the reference monitor is satisfied with the authentication parameters specified by the client, it can proceed to check to see if the security policy permits this particular remote procedure call. We use the authenticated client identity returned earlier by *rpc_binding_inq_auth_client* to do so. The code is somewhat messy because *rpc_binding_inq_auth_client* returns a full principal name that includes the cell name. The names stored in the employee database, on the other hand, are just simple principal names.

To handle this mismatch, our reference monitor will first convert the full name into a simple principal name before making the comparison. To make this efficient, also change the server initialization code to obtain the cell name, and store it in *emp_db_cell*. The access checking code will compare that cell name to the one passed by the client. Example 4-9 shows the resultant code.

Example 4-9: A Reference Monitor for Name-based Authorization

```
extern int emp_db_present (char    *client_name);
extern char *emp_db_cell;       /* Our cell name, initialized during
                                   server startup. */

int
client_is_authorized (
       handle_t        handle,
       access_type_t   operation,
       emp_db_field_t  emp_name)
{

       ... Check authentication parameters ...


       /*
        * Strip off the cell name from the client principal name
        * if it matches the local cell name.
```

Example 4-9: A Reference Monitor for Name-based Authorization (continued)

```
    */
    if (strncmp (client_principal_name, emp_db_cell, strlen(emp_db_cell))
            == 0) {
            client = &client_principal_name[strlen(emp_db_cell)+1];
    }
    else
            return 0;

    /*
     * The administrator can read or write any record.
     */
    if (strcmp (client, "emp_db_administrator") == 0)
            return 1;

    if (operation == OP_READ) {
            /*
             * We allow read access to any client that is in the
             * database.
             */
            return (emp_db_present (client));
    }
    else {
            /*
             * A client can also update its own record,
             * provided that the client is already in the
             * database.
             */
            return ((emp_db_present (client)) &&
                    ((strcmp (client, emp_name)) == 0));
    }

}
```

Note that I have implicitly made the assumption that all the employees in the database are in a single DCE cell. If this were not the case, it would be better to store the full principal name in the database.

The reference monitor is the last piece of code needed to make the example use name-based authorization. To help you place the code fragments in context, I have summarized the changes in Figure 4-4.

As you can see, the changes are minimal. First, the client needs to request authentication by calling *rpc_binding_set_auth_info*. The server shows three changes. During initialization, it calls *rpc_server_register_auth_info* to set up its authentication state. A new function, the reference monitor, calls *rpc_binding_inq_auth_client* and the information returned is used to make access control decisions. Each remote procedure is changed to call the reference monitor on every incoming RPC it receives. This is the extent of the changes. As I go on to the next examples, I will be enhancing various aspects of this application. You will quickly see, however, that all the versions of this example will retain the same structure.

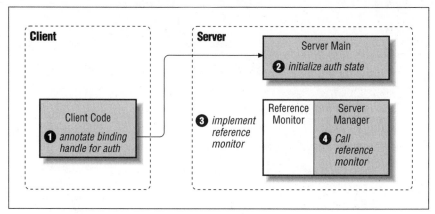

Figure 4-4: Changes to make for name-based authorization

Running the Application

When your application uses security, configuration is as important as the code itself. The code for the employee database application assumes that principals and accounts have been created for:

- The server, so that it can have an identity and therefore other attributes of security, like a secret key

- An administrator of the database. If you don't create this, the application will still run, but you won't be able to create any employee records, because only the administrator can do this.

The server now needs a keytab file. As before, the server assumes that it can export its bindings to CDS. These operations are done outside of the program by an administrator, when installing the application, using the management utilities supplied with DCE.

The administrative activities are divided into two parts: those dealing with security and those dealing with CDS. (In DCE 1.1, they are controlled through different commands.) Let's start with security, since those steps create the principal identities needed for the namespace operations.

Configuring security

Let's assume that the server will execute with the local identity of *emp_db_server*, and that it owns the directory */usr/people/emp_db_server*. On UNIX systems, this means adding an entry to */etc/passwd* for the *emp_db_server*. You can either do this directly or by running the *passwd_export* command. The server needs the local identity so that it can access its keytab file.

To run this application, you must create the principals for the *emp_db_server*, the *emp_db_administrator*, and the employees. In addition, you should create the keytab file for the server. The example below shows a sequence of *rgy_edit* commands I used to configure the application.

```
% dce_login cell_admin -dce-                              ❶
% rgy_edit
Current site is: registry server at /.../adlman_cell/subsys/dce/sec/master
rgy_edit=> domain principal                               ❷
Domain changed to: principal
rgy_edit=> add emp_db_server
rgy_edit=> add emp_db_administrator
rgy_edit=> domain account                                 ❸
Domain changed to: account
rgy_edit=> add emp_db_server -g none -o none -pw -dce- -mp -dce-
rgy_edit=> add emp_db_administrator -g none -o none -pw -dce- -mp -dce-
rgy_edit=> ktadd -p emp_db_server -pw -dce- \
-f/usr/people/emp_db_server/emp_db_server_tab    ❹
rgy_edit=> quit
bye.
%
% chown emp_db_server /usr/people/emp_db_server/emp_db_server_tab
% chmod 0600 /usr/people
/emp_db_server/emp_db_server_tab                 ❺
%
```

❶ Log in as *cell_admin.*

❷ Create the principal that runs the server and a principal for people who administer the database.

❸ Create accounts for the principals.

❹ Create a keytab file for the *emp_db_server* principal.

❺ Change the file permissions on the keytab file so that it is accessible only by the server process.

Configuring CDS

The employee database server exports its bindings into the CDS entry named */.:/subsys/emp_db* via a call to *rpc_ns_binding_export*. In the unauthenticated version of this application, set the permissions on the CDS entry to allow anyone to write to it. You had to do that since that version of the server did not have an identity. Now that the server is its own identity, we can do better. The example below shows how to change the ACLs on the entry so that only this server can write to it.

```
csh> cdscp delete obj /.:/subsys/emp_db    ❶
csh> cdscp create obj /.:/subsys/emp_db    ❷
csh> acl_edit -e /.:/subsys/emp_db         ❸
```

```
sec_acl_edit> modify user:emp_db_server:rw ❹
sec_acl_edit> list

# SEC_ACL for /.:/emp_db:
# Default cell = /.../mycell
unauthenticated:r--t-
user:cell_admin:rwdtc                                    ❺
user:emp_db_server_1:rw---
group:subsys/dce/cds-admin:rwdtc
group:subsys/dce/cds-server:rwdtc
any_other:r--t-
sec_acl_edit> exit
csh>
```

❶ Delete the */.:/subsys/emp_db* entry in CDS. This is the entry to which
the server exports its bindings. This undoes all the CDS configuration
you did for the unauthenticated version of this application. If you did
not run the unauthenticated version of the application, skip this step.

❷ Recreate the */.:/subsys/emp_db* entry in CDS.

❸ Run *acl_edit* to examine and change the ACL associated with this
name space entry.

❹ Modify the ACL to allow the *emp_db_server* principal read and write
access.

❺ List the current ACL again and verify that *emp_db_server* is now
included.

Running the application

At this point, we are ready to run the application. The following example
shows the transcript of a session.

```
adlman 3% dce_login emp_db_server -dce-)        ❶
adlman 1% server &
adlman 2% exit                                  ❷
adlman 4% dce_login emp_db_administrator -dce-  ❸
adlman 1% klist                                 ❹
DCE Identity Information:
  Warning: Identity information is not certified
  Global Principal: /.../adlman_cell/emp_db_administrator
  Cell:     67d3cdf6-af0e-11cd-8aa8-69076147ce07/.../adlman_cell
  Principal: 0000006a-b628-21cd-9800-69076147ce07 emp_db_administrator
  Group:     0000000c-af0e-21cd-8a01-69076147ce07 none
  Local Groups:
           0000000c-af0e-21cd-8a01-69076147ce07 none

        ... other klist information ...

adlman 2% exi                                   ❺
adlman 2% dce_login wei_hu -dce-                ❻
```

```
adlman 1% klist
DCE Identity Information:
  Warning: Identity information is not certified
  Global Principal: /.../adlman_cell/wei_hu
  Cell:      67d3cdf6-af0e-11cd-8aa8-69076147ce07 /.../adlman_cell
  Principal: 0000006b-b628-21cd-9800-69076147ce07 wei_hu
  Group:     0000000c-af0e-21cd-8a01-69076147ce07 none
  Local Groups:
              0000000c-af0e-21cd-8a01-69076147ce07 none

          ... other klist information ...

adlman 2% client                            ❼
Ready> query
name:wei_hu
mail stop: mmmm, phone: ppppp
Ready> modify
name: wei_hu
mailstop: 7L-802
phone: 3-1511
Ok
Ready> query
name:wei_hu
mail stop: 7L-802, phone: 3-1511
Ready> delete
name:wei_hu
Ok
Ready> insert
name: wei_hu
mailstop: 8L-802
phone: 4-1511
Not authorized for operation
Ready> exit
```

❶ Log into DCE as the *emp_db_server*. This establishes a login context for the server process. Start up the server; it inherits the login context and runs under the *emp_db_server* identity.

❷ Exit out of the shell so that your own process no longer uses that identity.

❸ Log into DCE as the *emp_db_administrator*. This allows you to create the *emp_db* entry you'll be using. Note that although a client can modify his or her own record in the *emp_db*, the client cannot create an initial record. Don't allow someone to add themselves to the database because that would allow unauthorized clients to appear as an employee.

❹ Type *klist* to show your current DCE identity. As expected, it shows you are the *emp_db_administrator*.

❺ Exit the current shell so that you no longer have the server's login context. This does not affect the server since the login context won't actually be destroyed until there are no more references to it.

❻ Log into DCE as yourself and type *klist* again to verify that you are logged in as yourself.

❼ Run a few test cases.

Why is the emp_db Application Secure?

Now that I've described the application, let's see why it is secure. First, we can trust the cell administrator who configured the Security Service in the first place. Trusting the cell administrator in turn implies that you can trust everything the administrator configures. For this example, the most important information are the principals, their passwords, and keytab files. Since the cell administrator is the one that assigns secret keys to principals, you can trust the identity of a principal if it produces a secret key/password that matches the one configured by the cell administrator. Thus, you can translate trust in the cell administrator into trust that a principal is who it says it is.

The DCE client program trusts the identity of the process that is running the client program because the process has a valid login context. If you recall, a client can obtain a valid login context only by logging in with the right password. Chapter 3 described how encryption is used by DCE to ensure that you can only get a valid login context if you have the correct secret key.

The client program then passes the identity of the client process to the server as part of the RPC. This information is packaged as a service ticket which the Security Service and RPC runtime created when the client called *rpc_binding_set_auth_info*. The server can trust the client identity it received from the client because of the way the service tickets are constructed. As discussed in Chapter 2, the server can believe the identity of the client if the server can decrypt the service ticket using its secret key.

The client program can trust the server that processed the call is the real *emp_db_server* because authenticated RPC guarantees that only the server that has the real server's secret key can decode the service ticket transmitted by the client. In this case, the *emp_db_server* can get the right key because the cell administrator put it into its keytab file after setting the key value in the security registry. This guarantees that the server will be able to use the same secret key the Security Service used to encrypt the ticket. The central rule of the keytab file, by the way, shows how important local UNIX security is. You must set the mode bits on the keytab file so that only the *emp_db_server* can access it; otherwise, anyone that could read the keytab file could get the *emp_db_server*'s secret key and authenticate as the server.

Note that your application must trust the integrity of the DCE runtime it is using. For example, if a malicious user replaces the standard DCE runtime with one of his own, he could conceivably change it to falsely authenticate a server or client. You can prevent this by using the local operating system's security features—e.g., setting the protection bits on *libdce.so*—such that only *root* can write it. As you can see, the security of DCE depends upon the security of the underlying operating system (and hardware).

You may have noticed that I did not include CDS in the list of things that we need to trust. In fact, CDS is not trusted. Since the client and server authenticate each other directly through secret key exchanges, the worst that a compromised CDS server can do is to deny service. For example, if a fake *emp_db_server* were to bypass CDS' access controls and export its bindings into */.:/subsys/emp_db*, it might fool clients into calling it. However, the call would still fail since the fake server would fail the authentication exchange. The worst that the fake server could do is to overwrite the bindings exported by the genuine *emp_db_server* into that CDS entry and prevent clients from reaching the real server—hence the term **denial of service attack**. DCE does not address denial of service attacks because they are extremely difficult to address in general. (You can trivially prevent other clients from using the services of a server by flooding the server with your own requests, for example.)

An important design goal lies behind the rule that you don't have to trust CDS. One way DCE makes security tight is by isolating the security-relevant software (i.e., the code that must work correctly for your application to be secure) into a few key modules and then carefully examine them for security flaws. Thus, the less code you put into the trusted category, the more you can be confident that it all works securely.

Using PAC-based Authorization

The previous example uses only a principal's name for making authorization checks. Now I'll change the example to use PACs. PACs allows you to make an application more flexible and easier to administer because they let you combine users into groups. In addition, using PACs opens up the possibility of using ACLs in the future.

Security Policy Using Groups

A **group** is an abstraction that lets you collect individuals and treat them consistently. For instance, your employee application has a special provision for those allowed to modify any entry. These people can therefore be placed in a group. Groups allow us to express our security policy differently. Assume that you have two groups: *emp_db_user_group*, containing all employees, and *emp_db_admin_group*, to which all employees who work in the personnel department belongs. You can now reformulate your security policy:

Any client that belongs to the *emp_db_user_group* group can read any entry in the employee database. Any client can modify his or her own entry in the database. And any client that belongs to the *emp_db_admin_group* group can modify any entry in the database.

To make the application more independent of the server principal name, let's also create a new group, *emp_db_server*, to which all the *emp_db* servers will belong. We then modify the client to accept responses from any server that belongs to the *emp_db_server* group.

Here's how to implement this version of the application, you need to do the following:

1. Change the reference monitor to use the client's PAC for its access control checks. As you'll see, this change has some side effects.

2. Change the client to select PAC-based authorization so that the client's PAC would be transmitted to the server.

3. Change the client to check the server's group instead of the server principal name.

Modify the Reference Monitor to Use PACs

To use PACs, you need to change the current reference monitor to retrieve the client PAC and then use its contents to decide whether the client should be allowed access. The changes are pretty straightforward; the biggest change is the use of UUIDs. Remember, a PAC contains the client's UUID instead of the client principal name. Since our current reference monitor uses client principal names, you need to change both the data structures and the code.

DCE does provide calls that allow you to map between UUIDs and principal names. For example, *sec_id_gen_name* returns the principal name associated with a UUID. You can therefore convert the UUID in the PAC into the client's principal name and then compare the name against the database entries. The drawback of this approach is that most of these calls involve RPCs to the Security Service. Since you may need to perform this operation whenever a record is updated, it can become expensive if you do lots of updates.

Because of caching, the actual performance hit associated with mapping between UUIDs and principal names may be quite low. However, you can eliminate this runtime overhead entirely by asking the Security Service for the employee's UUID when an employee's record is first inserted into the database, then store that UUID with the record. This approach allows you to pay the penalty of the RPC only when the record is created and not during every update. The cost is the extra storage for the UUIDs. It's interesting to compare the role of the UUID stored in your record with an ACL. Because the UUID lets you know who can change the record, it functions as a single-entry ACL.

For the employee database application where you don't expect many updates, the two approaches are comparable in efficiency. For simplicity, let's adopt the former approach and dynamically convert the UUID into the principal name when you need to make an access control check for an update.

There is a similar decision to make with respect to the tests for group membership. Given a PAC, take the principal UUID and call *sec_rgy_pgo_is_member* to see if the principal is a member of a certain group. This is simple to do but involves an RPC. The alternative is to explicitly check the list of group UUIDs in the client PAC against the list of group UUIDs that you care about. In this case, the second approach is clearly better since it eliminates an RPC on each call and requires very little storage. So we will take this approach.

Initializing the reference monitor

As just discussed, the initialization code for the *emp_db* reference monitor needs to obtain the UUIDs for the *emp_db_admin_group* and the *emp_db_user_group*. Example 4-10 shows the code that does this:

Example 4-10: Reference Monitor Initialization

```
void
emp_db_init (void)
{
    ...

    /*
     * Establish a binding to the registry interface of the
     * Security Server.
     */
    sec_rgy_site_open ("/.:", &emp_db_rgy_handle, &status);  ❶
    CHECK_STATUS (status, "rgy_site_open failed", ABORT);

    /*
     * Convert the group names into UUIDs and save it for
     * later use by the reference monitor.
     */
    sec_rgy_pgo_name_to_id (emp_db_rgy_handle,              ❷
            sec_rgy_domain_group,
            "emp_db_user_group",
            &emp_db_user_group_uuid,
            &status);
    CHECK_STATUS (status, "pgo_name_to_id failed", ABORT);

    sec_rgy_pgo_name_to_id (emp_db_rgy_handle,
            sec_rgy_domain_group,
            "emp_db_admin_group",
            &emp_db_admin_group_uuid,
```

Example 4-10: Reference Monitor Initialization (continued)

```
                &status);
        CHECK_STATUS (status, "pgo_name_to_id failed", ABORT);


    ...


}
```

❶ Before querying the security registry, you must first establish a binding to the Security Service. The security code could have established this binding internally on every call, but that would be rather inefficient. Instead, the application is given full control of the binding process, which gives you a binding to any available Security Service instead of the master replica. (You must bind to the master replica if you want to update the security registry.)

The first argument is the name of the specific Security Service to which you want to bind. Pass in /.: because you are willing to bind to any available Security Service in the cell. The output of this call, the second argument, is a binding handle to the Security Service.

Note that you do not free the binding handle but, instead, save it in a global variable *emp_db_rgy_handle*. This is an optimization that lets you make subsequent queries without having to first rebind to the security registry.

❷ Call *sec_rgy_pgo_name_to_id* to convert the group names to the group UUIDs. We save them in *emp_db_admin_group_uuid* and *emp_db_user_group_uuid* so that the reference monitor can use them directly without having to contact the security registry each time.

Now that you've made the necessary changes to the initialization code, we can proceed to the main body of the reference monitor.

Main Body of Reference Monitor

Example 4-11 shows the part of the reference monitor that makes the access checks for every client request. The flow of the code should look familiar.

Example 4-11: Reference Monitor That Uses PACs

```
extern sec_rgy_handle_t emp_db_rgy_handle = NULL;

/*
 * uuid for the emp_db_admin and emp_db_user groups.
 */
extern uuid_t emp_db_user_group_uuid;                              ❶
extern uuid_t emp_db_admin_group_uuid;
```

Example 4-11: Reference Monitor That Uses PACs (continued)

```
int
client_is_authorized (                                                   ❷
        handle_t        handle,
        access_type_t   operation,
        emp_db_field_t  emp_name)
{
        unsigned_char_t    *server_principal_name;
        sec_rgy_name_t     client_principal_name;
        sec_id_pac_format_v1_t *pac;
        unsigned32         protection_level;
        unsigned32         authn_svc;
        unsigned32         authz_svc;
        unsigned32         status;
        char               *client;

        /*
         * Check the authentication parameters that the client
         * selected for this call.
         */
        rpc_binding_inq_auth_client (handle,                             ❸
                (rpc_authz_handle_t *) &pac,
                &server_principal_name, &protection_level, &authn_svc,
                &authz_svc, &status);
        CHECK_STATUS (status, "inq_auth_client failed", ABORT);

        /*
         * Make sure that the caller has specified the required
         * level of protection, authentication, and authorization.
         */
        if (! ((protection_level == rpc_c_protect_level_pkt_integ) &&
                (authn_svc == rpc_c_authn_dce_secret) &&
                (authz_svc == rpc_c_authz_dce)))                        ❹
                return 0;

        /*
         * An administrator can read or write any record.
         */
        if (is_member (pac, &emp_db_admin_group_uuid)) {               ❺
                return 1;
        }


        if (operation == OP_READ) {
                /*
                 * We allow read access to any client that is in the
                 * database.
                 */
                return (is_member (pac, &emp_db_user_group_uuid)); ❻
        }
        else {
```

Example 4-11: Reference Monitor That Uses PACs (continued)

```
              ... check to see if client is authorized to perform write ...


    }

}
```

❶ These are the *emp_db_user_group* and *emp_db_admin_group* UUIDs that were initialized during server init in Example 4-10.

❷ Note that the interface to the reference monitor stays the same. You can get the client's security attributes from the binding handle.

❸ Call *rpc_binding_inq_auth_client* as before to retrieve the parameters the client selected for this call.

❹ This time, you check to make sure the Authorization Service is *authz_dce*, or PAC-based authorization.

❺ Make the membership check by calling a subroutine, *is_member*. If the client is a member of the *emp_db_admin_group*, read or write access are both allowed.

❻ If the client is a member of the *emp_db_user_group*, read access is allowed.

Using a PAC to check for group membership

Let's now look at the implementation of *is_member*. This function takes a PAC and a group UUID. Its purpose is to check to see if the group UUID is in the list of groups specified in the PAC. If so, the client belongs to this group and *is_member* returns 1. Otherwise, the function returns 0. Before you go into this routine, look at the structure of a PAC. Example 4-12 is the IDL declaration for the version 1 PAC. This structure is declared in */usr/include/dce/id_base.idl*.

Example 4-12: Structure of a Version 1 PAC

```
typedef struct {
    sec_id_pac_format_t pac_type;                    ❶
    boolean32           authenticated;               ❷
    sec_id_t            realm;                        ❸
    sec_id_t            principal;                    ❹
    sec_id_t            group;                        ❺
    unsigned16          num_groups;                   ❻
    unsigned16          num_foreign_groups;           ❼
    [size_is(num_groups), ptr]                        ❽
        sec_id_t        *groups;
    [size_is(num_foreign_groups), ptr]               ❾
```

Example 4-12: Structure of a Version 1 PAC (continued)

```
        sec_id_foreign_t *foreign_groups;
} sec_id_pac_t, sec_id_pac_format_v1_t;
```

The first part of the PAC has a fixed size. It consists of:

❶ The version of the PAC. DCE 1.0 uses Version 1 PACs, of which this is an example. DCE 1.1 supports the use of Version 2 PACs.

❷ A flag that indicates whether this PAC was authenticated. Recall that it is possible for a client to pass an unauthenticated PAC. It is up to the server to determine whether that is acceptable. The reference monitor already checked to make sure that the client is authenticated.

❸ A **realm field**. The realm is the Kerberos term for cell. This field identifies the cell that issued the PAC.

❹ The principal UUID. Note that although the *sec_id_t* contains fields for both an UUID and a string name; the principal's name is not filled in.

❺ The primary group UUID. This is the main group to which the named principal belongs. Note that in spite of the term, all the groups to which the principal belongs to should be treated identically.

❻ The number of local groups (i.e., groups defined by the local security registry) included in the variable-length part of the PAC.

❼ The number of foreign groups (i.e., groups defined by security servers in foreign cells) that are included in this PAC. These UUIDs will also be in the variable part of the PAC. Since foreign groups are not supported in DCE 1.0, this will be zero in Version 1 PACs.

The rest of the PAC contains the variable-length data:

❽ The list of local groups (including the primary group) to which this principal belongs.

❾ The list of foreign groups, if any, to which this principal belongs.

Since the primary group is included in the list of groups, the code only needs to check the group list. The code for this routine is presented in Example 4-13.

Example 4-13: Checking the Group List in a PAC

```
/*
 * See if group_uuid is among the local group list in the pac.
 */
int
is_member (sec_id_pac_t              *pac,
           uuid_t                    *group_uuid)
{
```

Example 4-13: Checking the Group List in a PAC (continued)

```
int              i;
sec_id_t         *group;
unsigned32       status;

group = pac->groups;
for (i=0; i < pac->num_groups; i++) {
        if (uuid_equal (&group->uuid, group_uuid, &status))
                return 1;
        CHECK_STATUS (status, "uuid_equal failed", ABORT);
        group++;
}
return 0;
}
```

Now that I have described the code that does the group membership checks, we can look at the last part of the reference monitor. This is the code that determines whether a client that is not a member of the *emp_db_admin* group should be allowed to update a specific record. Recall that in this case, you will allow the update only if the client is a member of *emp_db_users* and is trying to update its own record in the database.

Checking for client update of own record

To determine whether the client is updating its own record, convert the client's principal UUID (from the PAC) into a string name and compare it to the name in the record the client is trying to update. Note that when you use PAC-based authorization, *rpc_binding_inq_auth_client* returns the client PAC instead of the client's principal name in the second argument. You can get the identity of the real client by looking inside the PAC. (Please refer to Figure 2-9 for a detailed breakdown of the fields of a privilege ticket.) Example 4-14 shows the code that checks to see if the client is authorized to make the update.

Example 4-14: Checking to See if the Client is Authorized for Update

```
/*
 * A client can also update its own record,
 * provided that the client is already in the
 * database.
 */

/*
 * Convert the principal uuid into a name.
 * Note that this call returns a cell-relative name.
 */
sec_rgy_pgo_id_to_name (emp_db_rgy_handle,              ❶
            sec_rgy_domain_person,
```

Example 4-14: Checking to See if the Client is Authorized for Update (continued)

```
          &(pac->principal.uuid),
          client_principal_name,
          &status);
CHECK_STATUS (status, "pgo_id_to_name failed", ABORT);

return ((is_member (pac, &emp_db_user_group_uuid)) && ❷
        ((strcmp (client_principal_name, emp_name)) == 0));
```

❶ Call *sec_rgy_pgo_id_to_name* to convert the principal UUID taken from the client PAC into the principal's string name. Note that the code reuses the registry handle *emp_db_rgy_handle* that was established during server initialization. This allows you to avoid the overhead of reestablishing the binding handle to the security registry each time. Note that this call returns a cell-relative name; you therefore do not need to strip off the cell name.

❷ See if the client is a member of the *emp_db_user_group* and is updating its own record. If so, allow access.

This is it for the reference monitor. Note that the current version of the reference monitor allows a client to create its own initial record. This is because a create is treated as a write and any employee can do it. The earlier version of the reference monitor let clients modify their records but did not them create those records. This restriction was needed so that you could use the database itself to see if the client is an employee. Allowing anyone to add a record would allow any one to access to the database. Thus, the previous version of the reference monitor only allowed administrators to create records. Since this version of the reference monitor uses the *emp_db_user_group* to decide whether a client is an employee, you can eliminate this restriction (and also make the administrator's life easier).

Now that we are done with the server, let us look at the client. The client needs to request PAC-based authorization and do a membership check on the server.

Modifying the Client to Request PAC-based Authorization

The client code needs to specify PAC-based instead of name-based authorization in its call to *rpc_binding_set_auth_info*. The example below shows the new parameters. Note that only the authorization service is affected; all other parameters remain the same as before.

```
rpc_binding_set_auth_info(binding_handle,
      server_princ_name, rpc_c_protect_level_default,
      rpc_c_authn_dce_secret, NULL /*default login context*/,
      rpc_c_authz_dce, &status);
```

Modifying the Client to Inquire the Server Principal Name

At present, the client authenticates to a named server, *emp_db_server*. This works but is somewhat inflexible. For example, if you want to replicate the server, you must give each server the same principal name. Otherwise, existing clients would not be able to authenticate with the new servers. You won't need to assign the same name to all the servers, of course, if you are willing to modify all the employee database client programs in existence.

A way to avoid imbedding the server's principal name in the client application is to have the client ask the server for its principal name. The client would then look in the CDS for a server that offers the required interface, bind to that server, and ask the server for its principal name. Once the client has the server's principal name, the client can then annotate its binding handle with that principal name and use authenticated RPC and PAC-based authorization as before.

The danger of this approach is, of course, that even if the client gets the real name of the server, the client still has no idea whether the server can be trusted. Anyone who gets a copy of the IDL file can write a server that correctly exports the interface. Example 4-15 shows how we solve this problem. Create a group, *emp_db_server*, and make every bona fide server a member of this group. Since adding a principal to a group can be done only by an administrator, an imposter will not be able to masquerade as a member of this group.

Example 4-15: Inquiring for Server's Principal Name and Group

```
unsigned32              status;
handle_t                binding_handle;
sec_rgy_handle_t        rgy_handle;
unsigned_char_t         *server_princ_name;
sec_rgy_name_t          princ_name;
int                     is_member;



/*
 * Determine the server's principal name.
 */
rpc_ep_resolve_binding (binding_handle, emp_db_v1_0_c_ifspec, ❶
        &status);
CHECK_STATUS (status, "resolve_binding failed", ABORT);

rpc_mgmt_inq_server_princ_name (binding_handle,                  ❷
            rpc_c_authn_dce_secret,
            &server_princ_name, &status);
CHECK_STATUS (status, "inq_princ_name failed", ABORT);

/*
```

Example 4-15: Inquiring for Server's Principal Name and Group (continued)

```
 * Find out if the principal is a member of the emp_db_server
 * group.
 */

/*
 * Open a registry site for query.
 */
sec_rgy_site_open ("/.:", &rgy_handle, &status);              ❸
CHECK_STATUS (status, "rgy_site_open failed", ABORT);

/*
 * Ask the security registry to translate the global principal
 * name into a simple principal name.
 */
sec_id_parse_name (rgy_handle, server_princ_name,            ❹
       NULL, NULL, princ_name, NULL, &status);
CHECK_STATUS (status, "sec_id_parse_name failed", ABORT);

/*
 * The group membership check.
 */
is_member = sec_rgy_pgo_is_member (rgy_handle,              ❺
        sec_rgy_domain_group, "emp_db_server",
        princ_name, &status);
CHECK_STATUS (status, "is_member failed", ABORT);

/*
 * We are done with the registry; we can release the rgy_handle.
 */
sec_rgy_site_close(rgy_handle, &status);                     ❻
CHECK_STATUS (status, "rgy_site_close failed", ABORT);

if (! is_member) {
        fprintf (stderr, "Got an imposter, please report this!\n");
        exit (1);
}

/*
 * Annotate our binding handle for authentication.
 */
rpc_binding_set_auth_info(binding_handle,                   ❼
    server_princ_name, rpc_c_protect_level_default,
    rpc_c_authn_dce_secret, NULL /*default login context*/,
    rpc_c_authz_dce, &status);
```

❶ The binding handle is returned from CDS is normally a partially bound handle, i.e., it does not contain the endpoint. Before you can get the server's name, however, you must first resolve the binding handle to a particular server. Do this by calling *rpc_mgmt_ep_resolve_binding*. This routine contacts the *rpcd* at the server's machine to fully resolve the binding to the emp_db interface. For an Internet address, this would fill in the dynamic endpoint portion of the binding. For instance, *rpcd* would put the *[2067]* into *ncacn_ip_tcp*, giving us an address of the form ncacn_ip_tcp:136.12.125[2067].

❷ Get the principal name of the server that is listening at the specified endpoint. This results in a call to the RPC management interface that is built into all DCE servers. *rpc_mgmt_inq_server_princ_name* returns the full principal name; e.g., */ . . ./adlman_cell/emp_db_server.*

❸ Establish a binding to the security registry by calling *sec_rgy_open.*

❹ Check to see if the server listening at that endpoint is a member of the *emp_db _server* group. The routine that checks for group membership, *sec_rgy_pgo_is_member*, takes a cell-relative name. (This is an artifact of the way the current DCE Security works. It does not allow a group to include principals from foreign cells.) The server principal name returned in (2) is a fully qualified name; it contains the cell name as well as the relative name within the cell. You therefore need to extract the last part of the name. For this application, *sec_id_parse_name* will return emp_db_server.

❺ Contact the security registry to see if the server is a member of the *emp_db_server* group. If so. proceed with the call; otherwise, you've bound to the wrong server.

❻ The query is done; you can close the registry site. This frees the underlying binding handle to the Security Service.

❼ Annotate your own binding handle (as opposed to the one used to contact the security registry) for authentication as before, except you now pass in the server principal name you've obtained dynamically.

This concludes the changes needed to create this version of the *emp_db* application. You've changed the reference monitor to use PAC-based authorization and the client to ask the server for its principal name. You can now configure and run the application.

Configuring the Application

This version of the application runs just like the previous version. The only differences are in how the application is configured. You now have to create the necessary groups and make the appropriate principals members of this group. The example below shows the necessary steps.

```
rgy_edit <<EOF
domain principal                                    ❶
add emp_db_server
add emp_db_administrator
add wei_hu
add marty_hu
```

```
domain group                                                              ❷
add emp_db_user_group
add emp_db_admin_group
add emp_db_server
domain account
add emp_db_server -g emp_db_server -o none -pw -dce- -mp -dce-            ❸
add wei_hu -g emp_db_user_group -o none -pw -dce- -mp -dce-              ❹
add emp_db_administrator -g emp_db_admin_group \                         ❺
-o none -pw -dce- -mp -dce-                                              ❻
add marty_hu -g emp_db_user_group -o none -pw -dce- -mp -dce-
ktadd -p emp_db_server -pw -dce- \                                       ❼
-f /usr/people/emp_db_server/emp_db_keytab
quit
EOF                                                                      ❽
cdscp create obj /.:/subsys/emp_db                                       ❾
acl_edit -e /.:/subsys/emp_db -m user:emp_db_server:rw
```

❶ Create four principals named *emp_db_server*, *emp_db_administrator*, *wei_hu*, and *marty_hu*.

❷ Create the groups you need.

❸ Create an account for *emp_db_server*. Specify that it belongs to the *emp_db_server* group and its password is −dce−.

❹ Create an account for *wei_hu* and make him a member of the *emp_db_user_group*.

❺ Create an account for *emp_db_administrator* and make him or her a member of the *emp_db_admin_group*.

❻ Create an account for *marty_hu* and make him a member of the *emp_db_user_group*.

❼ Create a keytab file for the *emp_db_server*.

❽ Run *cdscp* to create the namespace entry to which the *emp_db_server* will export its bindings.

❾ Modify the permissions on the namespace entry so that the *emp_db_server* can read and write to that entry. This allows it to export its bindings into that entry. By default, everyone else has read access.

Discussion

As you can see, it takes more code to use PAC-based authorization and each side must make more time-consuming RPCs to the Security Service. You now have to work with UUIDs, understand the internal structure of PACs, and use more of DCE Security. The code is indeed more complicated; however, there is a gain in terms of configurability. You can now freely make anyone an administrator just by adding him or her to the *emp_db_admin_group.* You can likewise give query access to anyone (even someone that is not in the database) just by making him or her a member of the *emp_db_user_group.*

In general, I believe that reducing configuration complexity by making the code slightly more complex is a worthwhile trade-off. This is because the harder it is to configure an application, the greater the chance that a mistake could be made. When you are working with applications that must be secure, these configuration mistakes can be very costly.

Making the Server Standalone

In the examples so far, the server uses the login context of its parent process. This is why you explicitly logged in as the server before running the server program. Relying upon the parent process to establish the server's login context is a bad idea because it is error-prone. For example, if you want to start the server automatically, you have to include the server password in the script. If the password were changed, then the script would be out of sync. You can solve these problems if you make the server standalone; in other words, have the server maintain its own login context and password. DCE provides the *sec_login* and the *key_mgmt* APIs to allow a server to set up its own identity. Let's see how we can add them to our application.

As an aside, I treat the code that makes a server standalone as boiler-plate code along with the rest of the server initialization code. The code is somewhat lengthy but is pretty straightforward. I tend to reuse the same code sequence in all my servers. I deliberately saved it for now because I did not want it to get in the way of the really important issue: how to use authenticated RPC and how to write a reference monitor. However, with the other issues out of the way, we can now address this aspect of the application.

There are three security-related tasks involved in making a server standalone: establishing a login context, keeping that login contex refreshed, and keeping the server's secret key refreshed.

Establishing the Server's Login Context

In the previous chapter, I described how users log into DCE. Recall that a DCE login consists of two operations. First, you ask the security registry for your sealed network credentials. You then use your password to unseal the credentials. If you supplied the correct password, the network credentials result in a usable login context. Otherwise, the result is unusable. A server can follow the same login sequence by using the *sec_login* API calls I described in Chapter 3. Example 4-16 shows how the *emp_db_server* uses these calls.

Example 4-16: Establishing a Login Context

```
#define SERVER_PRINC_NAME "emp_db_server"
#define KEYTAB "/usr/people/emp_db_server/emp_db_keytab"

        sec_login_handle_t      login_context;
        sec_login_auth_src_t    auth_src;
        void                    *server_key;
        error_status_t          status;
        boolean32               identity_valid;
        boolean32               reset_passwd;

            ...


        sec_login_setup_identity(SERVER_PRINC_NAME,                    ❶
                              sec_login_no_flags,
                              &login_context, &status);
        CHECK_STATUS (status,"unable to set up identity",ABORT);

        /*
         * Retrieve the server's secret key from the private keytab
         * file.
         */
        sec_key_mgmt_get_key(rpc_c_authn_dce_secret, KEYTAB,          ❷
                          SERVER_PRINC_NAME,
                          0,  /* return most recent version */
                          &server_key, &status);
        CHECK_STATUS (status,"unable to retrieve key",ABORT);

        /*
         * Unseal the network identity using the server's secret key.
         */
        identity_valid = sec_login_validate_identity(login_context, ❸
                      server_key, &reset_passwd, &auth_src, &status);

        /*
         * Free the secret key as soon as we are done with it.
         */
        sec_key_mgmt_free_key (&server_key, &status);                ❹
        CHECK_STATUS (status,"unable to free key",ABORT);

        if (identity_valid) {                                        ❺
              /*
               * Make sure that the server identity was validated by
               * the network -
               * i.e., the security server, instead of local data.
               */
              if (auth_src != sec_login_auth_src_network) {          ❻
                  fprintf (stderr, "Server has no network credentials\n");
                  exit (1);
              }

              /*
               * We make this login context the default for this process.
```

Example 4-16: Establishing a Login Context (continued)

```
                  */
                  sec_login_set_context(login_context, &status);        ❼
                  CHECK_STATUS (status,"unable to set login context",ABORT);
      }
      else {
                  /* Fail and cleanup */
      }
```

❶ The Security Service encrypts the credentials and seals them in a ticket. Begin by getting the encrypted network credentials for the *emp_db_server*. By setting the second argument, *flags*, to *sec_login_no_flags* you indicate that the credentials may be inherited by any children of the current process. The call returns a handle to the login context.

❷ Retrieve the server's secret key by calling *sec_key_mgmt_get_key*. For extensibility, this routine allows the caller to specify an authentication protocol. At present, the only supported authentication protocol is the secret key protocol. Also specify the keytab file as well as a key version number; specify 0 to indicate that the most recent key should be used. The output of this call is the server's secret key.

❸ You now have the network credentials, but they are encrypted by the server's secret key. The next step is to decrypt them; this step simultaneously verifies the server's password. Pass in a handle to the current login context (that contains the sealed network credentials from *sec_login_setup_identity*) and the server's key/password obtained from *sec_key_mgmt_get_key*. If the key is valid, the credentials in the login context will be decoded and made usable. As discussed earlier, this is a local operation; the secret key is not transmitted over the network, thus eliminating another potential security threat.

In addition to indicating whether the key is valid, *sec_login_validate_identity* will set the third argument, *reset_passwd*, to let the caller know if the key has expired and should be changed. Notification of an expired key is informational only; DCE 1.0 Security does not force you to change the key immediately. Thus, the server can let the key management thread (to be discussed shortly) handle it.

The login context will be validated by the network unless the Security Service is unavailable or if the local system has explicitly disabled this capability. The fourth argument, *auth_src*, lets the caller know whether the login context was validated by the network (i.e., the Security Service) or by the local operating system.

❹ Secret keys, like passwords, should not be kept around because that increases the chances of them being compromised. Hence, the key should be freed as soon as it has been used for validating the login context.

❺ Before continuing, check to make sure that the identity is valid.

❻ Check that the login context was validated by the Security Service.

Note that the *emp_db_server* only validates the login context, which ensures that the server has an identity during RPCs. It does not certify the login context because you aren't going to set the *emp_db_server's* local identity using the login context. If you need to certify the login context, use *sec_login_validate_and_cert_identity* instead. Please refer to Chapter 2 for a brief discussion of how DCE Security certifies a login context.

❼ Make the validated login context the default login context. This allows it to be selected by default when, for example, the server calls *rpc_binding_set_auth_info* to annotate binding handles for making authenticated RPCs.

Refresh Server's Login Context

The credentials within a login context have expiration times. When a login context expires (or more precisely, when the credentials within a login context expire), the login context is no longer valid. This means, for example, that authenticated remote procedure calls using this login context will fail. To maintain uninterrupted service, servers must refresh their login contexts before they expire by calling *sec_login_refresh_identity*.

sec_login_refresh_identity should be run from a dedicated thread. A dedicated thread is needed because the routine repeatedly sleeps until it is time to refresh the login context. Example 4-17 below shows how to create the thread and the code that the thread executes.

Example 4-17: Starting Up a Thread to Maintain the logincontext

```
sec_login_handle_t      login_context;
pthread_t               refresh_login_context_thread;
void                    refresh_login_context_rtn();

/* login code */

/*
 * Start up a thread to refresh the login context when it
 * expires.
 */
if (( pthread_create (&refresh_login_context_thread,          ❶
        pthread_attr_default,
        (pthread_startroutine_t) refresh_login_context_rtn,   ❷
```

Example 4-17: Starting Up a Thread to Maintain the logincontext (continued)

```
        (pthread_addr_t)login_context) ) == -1)
        exit (1);

/* rest of code in server initialization */



/*
 * A thread to periodically refresh the credentials contained in a
 * login context.
 */
#include <sys/time.h>

void refresh_login_context_rtn (sec_login_handle_t  login_context)   ❸
{
        struct timeval  current_time;
        struct timezone tz;
        struct timespec delay;
        signed32                expiration;
        signed32                delay_time;
        unsigned32              used_kvno;
        boolean32               reset_passwd;
        boolean32               identity_valid;
        void            *server_key;
        sec_login_auth_src_t auth_src;
        error_status_t  status;

#define MINUTE 60

        fprintf (stderr, "refresh login context thread started up\n");

        while (1) {

            /*
             * Wait until shortly before the login context expires...
             */

#ifdef _BSD_COMPAT
            /* BSD version of gettimeofday has a timezone parameter. */
            gettimeofday (&current_time, &tz);
#else
            gettimeofday (&current_time);
#endif

            sec_login_get_expiration (login_context,
                    &expiration, &status);                           ❹
            if ((status != rpc_s_ok) &&
                (status != sec_login_s_not_certified)) {
                    fprintf (stderr,
                            "Cannot get login context expiration time\n");
                    exit (1);
            }
```

Example 4-17: Starting Up a Thread to Maintain the logincontext (continued)

```
        delay_time = expiration - current_time.tv_sec - (10*MINUTE);

        if (delay_time > 0) {
                delay.tv_sec = delay_time;
                delay.tv_nsec = 0;
                pthread_delay_np (&delay);                              ❺
        }

        /*
         * Refresh the login context.
         */
        sec_login_refresh_identity (login_context, &status);          ❻
        CHECK_STATUS (status, "cannot refresh identity", ABORT);

        /*
         * Retrieve the server's secret key from the private keytab
         * file.
         */
        sec_key_mgmt_get_key(rpc_c_authn_dce_secret, KEYTAB,          ❼
                SERVER_PRINC_NAME,
                0,  /* return most recent version */
                &server_key, &status);
        CHECK_STATUS (status,"unable to retrieve key",ABORT);

        /*
         * The refreshed login context still needs to be validated.
         */
        identity_valid = sec_login_validate_identity(login_context,
                server_key, &reset_passwd, &auth_src, &status); ❽

        /*
         * Free the secret key as soon as we are done with it.
         */
        sec_key_mgmt_free_key (&server_key, &status);                 ❾
        CHECK_STATUS (status,"unable to free key",ABORT);

        if (! identity_valid) {

                /* Fail and cleanup */

        }

    }
}
```

❶ Create a separate thread to keep the login context refreshed. It will start execution at *refresh_login_context_rtn* ❷, which is defined at ❸. *refresh_login_context_rtn* takes a single argument, the login context.

❸ The thread starts execution at *refresh_login_context_rtn*. The thread repeatedly calls *sec_login_get_expiration* ❹ to see when the login context will expire, computes a new wakeup time that is 10 minutes before that time, and calls *pthread_delay_np* ❺ to suspend itself until shortly before the login context would expire.

❻ When the proper amount of time has elapsed, the thread wakes up and calls *sec_login_refresh_identity* to refresh the login context. Since the wake time was computed to be earlier than the expiration time, the current login context should still be valid.

The login context returned by *sec_login_refresh_identity*, like that returned by *sec_login_setup_identity*, needs to be validated. You need to acquire the key from the keytab file ❼ and make a call to *sec_login_validate_identity* ❽. As before, destroy the server's secret key as soon as you are finished. ❾

Refresh Server Key

Since anyone who knows a principal's secret key can become that principal and access any resource the principal can access, the keys must be kept secret. Servers should therefore periodically change their keys to reduce the chance of compromising the server key. Like maintaining the login context, this is done by creating a separate thread that periodically changes a server's key. *sec_key_mgmt_manage_key* automatically changes a principal's key to a random value before it expires and updates both the Security Service's registry and the keytab file. Example 4-18 shows how to create the key management thread from the initialization thread and how to change the key automatically.

Example 4-18: Starting Up the Key Management Thread

```
#include <pthread.h>
#include <dce/sec_login.h>

pthread_t       key_mgmt_thread;
void            key_mgmt_rtn();

/* Login code */

/* Start up a thread to refresh the login context */

/*
 * Start up a thread to manage our secret key.
 */
if (( pthread_create (&key_mgmt_thread,                    ❶
        pthread_attr_default,
        (pthread_startroutine_t) key_mgmt_rtn,            ❷
        (pthread_addr_t)NULL) ) == -1)
        exit (1);
```

Example 4-18: Starting Up the Key Management Thread (continued)

```
/* rest of code in server initialization */



/*
 * A thread to periodically change the server's secret key.
 */
void key_mgmt_rtn ()                                      ❸
{
        error_status_t  status;

        sec_key_mgmt_manage_key (rpc_c_authn_dce_secret,(4) ❹
                    KEYTAB, SERVER_PRINC_NAME, &status);
        CHECK_STATUS (status,"key mgmt failure",ABORT);
}
```

❶   Create a separate thread to perform the key management operation.

❷   This thread executes *key_mgmt_rtn* shown at ❸.

❹   The only operation this thread needs to do is repeatedly call *sec_key_mgmt_manage_key*. This routine never returns unless it encounters an error. *sec_key_mgmt_manage_key* causes the thread to sleep until shortly before the key expires, change the key randomly, update this server's key, and then sleep again.

This concludes the code that you must add to the server to make it standalone. The code that refreshes the login context and changes the secret key is the same for all servers. I usually put it into a single procedure and call it all from the server main program.

Running the Application

This version of the application does not require any configuration beyond that done before for PAC-based authorization. The only difference now is that you can start up the server without having to log into DCE; the server logs in.

Summary

The employee database application is a good example because it included a lot of the commonly used security techniques and exercises enough of the DCE Security API to give you a feel of what they can do. It uses authentication, name-based and PAC-based authorization, and implements a reference monitor. Note that the actual steps that I would go through in developing the application would be a bit different. I presented some of the steps out of order for clarity. The steps that I normally follow are:

1. Write and debug the application logic without authentication. This involves writing an IDL file, the server main program, the server manager, and the client code. The resulting code allows you to debug the logic of the application.

2. Change the client and the server main programs to use authenticated RPC. Both the client and the server need to be altered at the same time because both sides must use the same authentication protocol. This involves using *rpc_binding_set_auth_info* in the client and *rpc_server_register_auth_info* in the server. If you plan on asking the server for its principal name, this would also be a good time to add that code to the client. You can also put in the code that makes a server standalone since that is pretty standard code. After you've completed this step, you can be pretty sure that your code has properly set up the security framework.

3. Implement the reference monitor. You need to write the code that checks an incoming call to see if the client is authorized for the requested operation, and then modify the server manager code to call the reference monitor on every incoming call.

5

A Programmer's View of Access Control Lists

The two major facilities provided by DCE Security are authenticated RPC and DCE ACLs. In Chapter 4, we saw how authenticated RPC is used in the employee database application. Now we will cover the concepts and terminology associated with DCE ACLs. We will then apply these concepts to add ACLs to our sample application in the next chapter.

In the employee database application, you used a simple reference monitor that checked a client's PAC to decide whether the requested access should be allowed. The reference monitor allows read access to members of *emp_db_users_group*, write access to members of *emp_db_admin _group*, and update access to the owner of a database entry. The policy is simple and the code was straightforward to implement. But configuration by users was limited.

The employee database application allows an administrator to customize the set of people that are allowed to access the database by adding and removing people from two groups. For example, if an administrator wants to allow a principal read access to the database, he or she would make the principal a member of the *emp_db_users* group. This is all supported by the reference monitor implementation. What it can't do is set access control policies on individual database entries.

Suppose you have a principal, Irene, who wants her secretary, Kevin, to maintain her employee database entry. As the application currently works, only Irene and the administrators can update Irene's database entry. You could give Irene's password to Kevin and allow him to log in as Irene when Kevin needs to update Irene's record. But this procedure would be unsafe as it would allow Kevin to act as Irene for all other DCE applications also. The other choice would be to make Kevin a member of *emp_db_admin_group*. This would also be undesirable as this would allow Kevin to update everyone's record in the employee database.

What we would like to do with the application is allow finer-grained and decentralized administration of the access control policies. A finer-grained security policy would allow you to grant a person access to a part of the database without having to give that person access to the rest of it. Decentralized administration implies the ability for someone other than the administrator to decide who can access the database entries. You might like to allow, for example, a person to set the list of principals that can access his or her database entry. You can achieve all of this by using access control lists.

What Is an Access Control List?

An ACL is a data structure that describes the set of principals that can access a piece of data and the type of access that should be allowed. They were originally designed for protecting files and directories in filesystems. For each principal or group that has its own set of access rights, the ACL contains an **access control list entry** (ACLE). The ACL is used by the reference monitor. This is how you program with ACLs:

1. First, you must decide on the objects (or data) you want to individually protect. In the employee database application, for example, a good choice would be the individual database entries.

2. You then create an ACL for every object that needs to be protected. Each ACL would specify the set of clients that can access the object and the permissible types of access (e.g., read or write). Usually, you would store the ACL with the object it is protecting. In the case of the employee database, a reasonable approach would be to store it as an extra field in the database entry itself.

3. When the server gets a client request to access an object, the server passes the client's authorization information to the reference monitor as before. The reference monitor retrieves the ACL associated with the object and checks the client's authorization information against the ACL. If the ACL lists the client among its set of permitted principals for the type of access that the client is making, then the call is processed. Otherwise, access is denied.

4. Finally, the server needs to implement a piece of code called an **ACL manager** that provides an RPC-based management interface. This RPC interface allows an authorized user to set and change the application's ACLs.

As you can see, the use of ACLs shifts more of the specification of the security policy away from the reference monitor code into a data structure—the ACL. The ACL now describes the set of people that can access a given object. Once the ACLs are in place, all that the reference monitor needs to do is retrieve the ACL associated with an object, compare the client's authorization information against the entries in the ACL, and then either grant or deny access based upon what the ACL says. All the real decisions about who can have what type of access are determined by the ACLs. Since we can change the ACLs without rewriting our application, we can easily change the set of people that can access an object.

ACLs solve the problem that Irene encountered when she tried to give Kevin update access to her record. If the employee database application used ACLs, then all that Irene would need to do is modify the ACL associated with his employee database entry to add an entry that allows Kevin write access.

The DCE ACL Data Structure

You are going to be extracting and manipulating parts of the ACL data structure in your code, so let's take a look at it here. A DCE ACL contains an ACL manager type UUID, a default cell UUID, and a list of ACL entries. Figure 5-1 shows what a DCE ACL looks like.

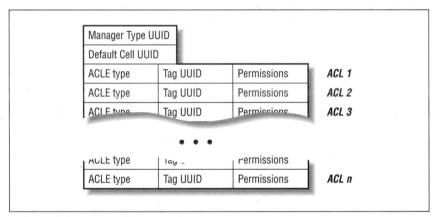

Figure 5-1: A DCE access control list (ACL)

The **ACL manager type** UUID identifies the ACL manager of this ACL. When the program creates each ACL, it stores the UUID that identifies the ACL manager that you have written. Why does each ACL have to "know" what its manager is? Because only your particular manager knows which access rights you have defined. So when someone invokes *acl_edit*, it uses this field to find your ACL manager. All ACLs of the same type share the same ACL manager. In the employee database application, for example, all the ACLs might share a single ACL manager.

The **default cell** UUID identifies the cell to which local users belong. If an ACL has an entry that specifies a local user *John*, for example, then John is assumed to belong to the cell specified by the default cell UUID (the default cell). Note that although DCE allows you to specify a foreign cell as the default cell for an ACL, I will adopt the convention that the default cell corresponds to the local cell.

The most important part of an ACL is the last part—the actual list of ACL **entries** (ACLEs). These entries describe who can access the object protected by this ACL and what type of access should be granted.

Structure of an ACL Entry

As Figure 5-1 shows, each ACL entry contains three fields: the ACL **entry type**, the **tag** UUID, and the **permissions**. Before I describe what each of these fields are, let us look at a sample ACL. Figure 5-2 shows an ACL with two ACL entries. Fields in the ACLE are separated by a colon. For clarity, I have used names instead of UUIDs.

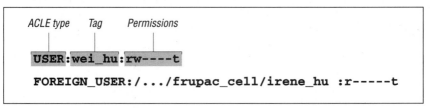

Figure 5-2: Two sample ACL entries

The first entry is a *USER* type ACL entry. It means that the ACL entry specifies the permissions to be granted to a principal from the default (local) cell. This type of ACLE has a single tag UUID—that of the user to which this entry applies. In this case, the UUID is the principal UUID of *wei_hu*. This is followed by the permissions field, *rw----t*, which means that the named principal should be allowed *read*, *write*, and *test* access to the object. These permissions are entirely chosen by your application. Note that, just as in C++ where it is possible for you to define a + operator that performs subtraction, your application can define the permission bit *r* to be *write* and *w* to be *read*. However, at least for applications intended for use by English-speakers, you should avoid doing so.

The second entry is an example of an ACL entry where the tag UUID field contains two UUIDs. This entry is a *FOREIGN_USER* entry. It specifies the permissions to be granted to a user from a foreign cell. The tag UUID field contains the cell UUID and the principal UUID of the foreign user. In this case, the entry applies to the principal *irene_hu* from the *frupac_cell*. The last field is the permission field as before. This ACL entry grants *read* and *test* permissions to the named principal.

The ACL entry therefore identifies the type of information contained in this ACL entry, whether it describes the permissions to be applied to a group, principal, or other entity. The tag UUID field identifies the specific group or principal to which this ACL entry applies, and the permissions field specifies the types of access this principal or group has to the object being protected by this ACL entry.

Now that we've seen a couple of examples of ACL entries, let us look at all the ACL entry types defined by DCE 1.0. I've divided the ACL entry types into the **core** and the **compatibility** types. (Note that I will describe the DCE 1.1 ACL entry types in Chapter 7.)

Core ACL Entry Types

The core ACL entry types specify the access to be granted to all types of principals and groups. It even lets you say, "apply these rights to anyone who doesn't match a specific entry." This should become clearer as I go through each of the core ACL entry types.

USER (U)
> Permissions to be granted to a user from the local cell. For example, *U:wei_hu:rw----t* grants the local user *wei_hu* the *read, write*, and *test* permissions.

GROUP (G)
> Permission to be granted to members of a local group. For example, *G:emp_db_users:r-----t* grants all members of the local group *emp_db_users read* and *test* permissions.

OTHER_OBJ (O)
> Permissions to be granted to anyone else from the local group. This is useful for establishing the default permissions for any other local users or groups that do not have explicitly USER or GROUP ACL entries. For example, *O::r------* means to give *read* access to anyone from the local cell that does not have an explicit USER or GROUP ACL entry that applies.

FOREIGN_USER (FU)
> Permissions to be granted to a principal from another cell. The tag UUID field specifies the UUIDs for the cell as well as the principal. For example, the ACLE *FOREIGN_USER:/.../frupac_cell/irene_hu:r-----t* allows the principal *irene_hu* from the *frupac_cell* the *read* and *test* permissions.

FOREIGN_GROUP (FG)
> Permissions to be granted to a principal that belongs to a foreign group. The tag UUID field specifies the UUIDs for the cell and the group. The ACLE *FOREIGN_GROUP:/.../frupac_cell/testers:r-----t*, for example, allows members of the *testers* group in cell *frupac_cell read* and *test* permissions.

FOREIGN_OTHER (FO)

Permissions to be granted to a member of a foreign cell that is not otherwise covered by either a FOREIGN_USER or FOREIGN_GROUP ACL entry. For example, *FOREIGN_OTHER:frupac_cell:------t* allows members of the *frupac_cell* not covered by a FOREIGN_GROUP or FOREIGN_USER entry *test* permission.

ANY_OTHER (AO)

Permissions to be granted to anyone else not covered by any of the above ACL entries. For example, *ANY_OTHER:-------* says that anyone else not covered by any of the previous ACL entry types shouldn't have access.

An example of an ACL that contains entries of each type is shown below.

```
USER : wei_hu : rwxcidt
USER : irene_hu : rwxcidt
FOREIGN_USER : /.../marty_cell/marty_hu : rwxcidt
GROUP : cell_admin : rwxcidt
FOREIGN_GROUP : /.../marty_cell/cell_admin : rwxcidt
OTHER_OBJ : r-----t
FOREIGN_OTHER : marty_cell : r-----t
ANY_OTHER : -----
```

The local users *wei_hu,* *irene_hu* and the foreign user */.../marty_cell/marty_hu* should be allowed all types of access to the object protected by this ACL. In addition, members of the *cell_admin* groups from both the local cell and the foreign cell *marty_cell* also should be granted complete access. Other than the users and group just mentioned, all members of the local cell and *marty_cell* are allowed *read* and *test* access. Everyone else is denied access.

Discussion

You might ask at this point, "Why does DCE support so many different types of ACL entries? Is all this complexity justified?" It turns out that having all these ACL entry types actually makes it easier to administer ACLs. They allow you to express the access-control policy more succinctly (i.e., with fewer ACL entries). Consider what would happen if you didn't have all these ACL entry types.

Assume that you have an ACL-based security system that uses only a single type of ACL entry. This ACL entry lists a principal and the type of permissions that he or she should have. (For sake of generality, we assume that the principal can be from either the local or a foreign cell.) To create an ACL in this environment, an administrator would first create an entry for everyone that should be permitted access. This may not be bad if the set of authorized users is small. The problem comes when he or she want to control what everyone else (those not given explicit access) can do. If we only have a single ACL entry type, an administrator would then need to add separate entries for everyone else. In effect, this would force everyone to name all the principals (in all the cells) on every ACL. This is clearly impractical. This example may be a bit extreme, but it illustrates the problem that can arise if you do not have a comprehensive set of ACL entry types.

The USER, GROUP, FOREIGN_USER, and FOREIGN_GROUP ACL entry types allow you to specify the set of clients you want to single out. Use these entries to specify people to whom you want to give extra access or less access. The various OTHER ACL entry types (ANY_OTHER, FOREIGN_OTHER, and OTHER_OBJ ACL) allow you to easily specify the types of access to be given to groups of users without having to name them individually.

Compatibility ACL Entry Types

The core ACL entry types are flexible enough for most applications. DCE, however, has defined some additional ACL entry types for compatibility with non-DCE applications. The first one is the **UNAUTHENTICATED** ACL entry type. It is used as a mask to specify the maximum privileges that can be granted to a client whose security attributes are not authenticated by DCE Security. (This can happen, for example, if the client called *rpc_binding_set_auth_info* and selects DCE authorization without any authentication.) Since the client's security attributes are not authenticated, the client could have chosen any principal name and group. For example, the client can assert that his or her identity is that of the cell administrator, *cell_admin*. The example below shows an ACL entry that grants read access to anyone who passes an unauthenticated PAC.

```
UNAUTHENTICATED:r------
```

Obviously, you should avoid using this ACL entry type.

The other special ACL entry types are defined for compatibility with POSIX ACLs. The IEEE POSIX 1003.6.1 committee has been working on a standard for local system ACLs. Their design center is the UNIX filesystem. For compatibility, they have carried forward traditional UNIX filesystem concepts such as owners and owning groups. To make it easier to distribute applications that use POSIX-style ACLs, DCE Security has included these POSIX ACL entry types. Since the POSIX draft is still evolving, there are differences between what DCE Security provides and the current POSIX draft. Listed below are the DCE ACL entry types that were defined for POSIX compatibility.

USER_OBJ (UO)
> Identifies an ACL entry that specifies the permissions to be granted to the owning user of the object. This is the DCE equivalent of a file's owner.

GROUP_OBJ (GO)

Identifies an ACL entry that specifies the permissions to be granted to the owning group. This is the DCE equivalent of the file's owning group.

MASK_OBJ (M)

Identifies an ACL entry whose permissions should be used to mask (i.e., logical AND) permissions granted by all other ACL entries except for USER_OBJ and OTHER_OBJ. It is used for subtracting permissions.

The compatibility ACL entry types are therefore defined so that DCE Security can remain indirectly compatible to the traditional, non-ACL-based filesystem protection model. I personally find them very complicated and recommend that you avoid them. Of course, you will have no choice if you are doing something like writing a distributed filesystem that needs to emulate POSIX-style ACLs.

ACL Entry Permissions

So far, I've described the type and tag UUID fields of an ACL entry. Let us now look at the last field—the permissions field. Each DCE ACL entry has 32 permission bits. This means that each user can have 32 separate permissions associated with each ACL. This is plenty for most applications; UNIX, for example, has only nine file access permission bits. If, however, your application really needs more than 32 separate permissions, you can do this by defining multiple ACL managers and then associating one ACL of each type per object.

All that is stored in an ACL entry are *bits*. It is the ACL manager that gives meaning to these bits. It decides, for example, that if bit 0 is on, then that means the named principal or user should have read access. It is also the ACL manager that associates the bit with the printstring representation; e.g., bit 1 means *r*, for example.

To get some consistency across applications, DCE has defined seven permission bits, their meanings, and their print representations. The predefined bits are listed below.

r (read)

Gives read permission on the object protected by the ACL.

w (write)

Gives write permission on the object protected by the ACL.

x (execute)

Gives execute permission on the object protected by the ACL.

c (control)

Gives write permission on the ACL itself, which allows you to change an object's ACL. Irene uses this permission to add Kevin to the ACL on her database entry.

i (insert)

Gives the client permission to add an object into the container (e.g., create a directory entry). A container is an advanced concept needed by applications that organized objects into hierarchies, like DFS and CDS.

d (delete)

Gives permission to remove an object from a container (e.g., delete a directory entry).

t (test)

Gives permission to compare an input value against the current value of an object. This call will tell you if they match, but will not return the actual value of the object.

Besides these seven predefined permissions, applications are free to define others. You can, for example, define bit 8 to have the print representation of *R* (for *Reduce*) and have that mean that the specified principal can reduce the set of permissions on an object. So long as your ACL manager supports all the required management interfaces and authorization checks, this new permission will have the same level of support as the predefined permissions.

ACL Manager Overview

Now that I've described what ACLs are, let us move on to the ACL manager. The ACL manager is the server code that works with ACLs. An ACL manager has three parts as shown in Figure 5-3.

❶ A **storage** component that stores and retrieves the ACL associated with an object

❷ An **authorization** component that compares a client PAC against an object's ACL and determines whether the client should be allowed to access the object

❸ A **management** component that allows the DCE *acl_edit* utility to administer these ACLs through an RPC interface.

The most important part of the ACL manager is the authorization component. This piece of code compares a client PAC against an object's ACL and decides whether the client should be allowed to perform the requested operation on the object; it is the guts of an ACL-based server's reference monitor. The authorization module is therefore the part of the ACL manager that is directly used by the server application.

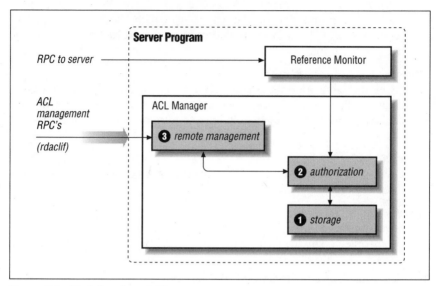

Figure 5-3: Modules of an ACL manager

To do its work, the authorization module must locate and retrieve the ACL associated with the object being accessed. Usually, an application's data and objects are stored on disk. Therefore, the ACLs that protect them must also be persistent. The ACL manager's storage component is the collection of procedures that store and retrieve ACLs using the filesystem or other persistent storage. This component is used by the other two ACL manager components.

The last part of the ACL manager is the management component. This module allows a client to modify the ACLs maintained by the ACL manager. When the user asks for an ACL, the management component uses the storage component to get it, and after the user makes a change, the manager writes the modified ACL back to persistent storage.

Unlike the authorization component, the management component is not directly called by the server applications. It is involved only when a client wants to modify the ACLs maintained by this server. Although applications do not use the management component directly, it is still very important because the main advantage of ACLs is that you can change them. Notice how the management component also goes through the authorization component in order to prevent clients from making unauthorized changes to our ACLs.

Now, we should consider how to change an application's ACLs. Traditional filesystems have commands that set and modify ACLs on files. You can follow the same model and write your own management utilities to control your application's ACLs. You can easily see how every application developer would need to do this also.

The designers of the DCE ACL facility recognized the need for managing ACLs that are implemented by user applications. DCE therefore provides a utility, *acl_edit*, that can work with all server programs that implement DCE ACLs. For example, DCE uses *acl_edit* to manage ACLs implemented by the DCE security registry, CDS, DTS, and DFS. *acl_edit* can also manage user applications' ACLs. DCE makes this possible by defining a standard RPC interface for managing ACLs and then requiring that all ACL-based servers implement this interface uniformly. The calls in the API all have names that begin with *rdacl*. This RPC interface is one of several ACL manager APIs.

ACL Manager APIs

DCE defines three ACL manager APIs. In order of importance, they are:

- The *rdaclif* RPC interface, which defines the management interface all ACL managers must export for *acl_edit* to work on their ACLs.

- The *sec_acl* client API, which is a client-side library that *acl_edit* uses to bind to and call a server's *rdaclif* remote procedures.

- The *sec_acl_mgr* server API, which provides source code for a sample memory-based ACL manager.

Figure 5-4 shows how these APIs are related. The shaded areas are the library and source code DCE provides; some are used for writing ACL managers and some are used by client applications such as *acl_edit* that work with ACL managers.

The central API is the *rdaclif* interface, which consists of remote procedures called by *acl_edit*. Each ACL manager is expected to provide routines that match the operations requested by *acl_edit*. I represent this interface in Figure 5-4 by the client and server stubs that are generated by the IDL compiler. The *rdaclif* interface includes remote procedures to retrieve an ACL, replace an ACL, test whether a given client is allowed to perform a given operation, etc.

A server that wants to implement ACLs will export the *rdaclif* interface in addition to its normal interfaces. For example, the *emp_db_server* would export both the *rdaclif* interface and its *emp_db* interface. A client that wants to run the application would call the *emp_db* interface; a client that wants to change the ACLs associated with the application would call the *rdaclif* interface.

Although anyone can write a client application that calls the *rdaclif* interface, the primary client of the interface is *acl_edit*. Because *rdaclif* is an RPC interface, *acl_edit* becomes just another RPC client application. When *acl_edit* starts up, it first establishes a binding to the server's *rdaclif* interface. It then makes RPC calls on that interface to manipulate the ACLs. When it is done, *acl_edit* releases the binding.

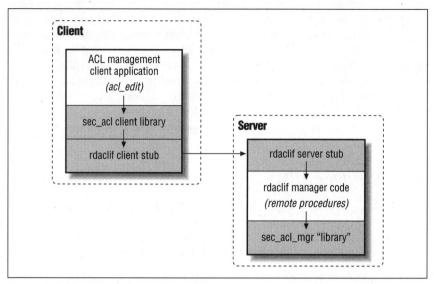

Figure 5-4: The three ACL manager APIs

Actually, *acl_edit* does not call the *rdaclif* remote procedures directly; instead, it uses a client-side library. Establishing a binding to an ACL manager can be complex (more detail later). The *sec_acl* API is the client-side library *acl_edit* uses. DCE exposes this interface so that DCE vendors can write improved ACL management tools. As you might expect, the *sec_acl* API is layered over the *rdaclif* client interface.

I refer to the *sec_acl_mgr* as an API because that is how the DCE documentation describes it. In reality, the *sec_acl_mgr* API is simply a collection of source code that illustrates how to write a simple ACL manager. This sample code is supplied to show an application developer how the various arguments to the *rdaclif* routines should be set and so forth. The actual code itself is not meant to be used without change.

DCE provides the *sec_acl_mgr* routines in source form instead of as a general runtime library because ACL managers are highly application-specific. Every application stores its ACLs differently. Even in DCE itself, for example, CDS and DFS represent and store ACLs differently. A distributed filesystem, for example, will probably integrate DCE ACLs with the filesystem inode data structure. Some implementations may also choose to store ACLs in compressed form. It is impossible to provide a single ACL back-end for all applications. DCE 1.1 partially addresses this need by providing an ACL manager library that supplies a single, coarse-grained ACL storage mechanism. I'll describe it in Chapter 7.

We are almost ready to go into each of the ACL manager APIs in detail. Before we do so, however, let us look at how *acl_edit* works. I want to cover this topic because the ACL manager APIs were designed to support the needs of *acl_edit*. Looking at how *acl_edit* runs will explain why some of these APIs are structured the way they are.

How Does acl_edit Work?

The ACL manager APIs were geared towards the needs of *acl_edit*. Consider what actually happens when you enter the command detailed below:

```
acl_edit"> /.:/subsys/emp_db/wei_hu  ❶
acl_edit> list                       ❷
....

...
acl_edit> modify unauthenticated:-   ❸
acl_edit> exit                       ❹
```

❶ Start *acl_edit* by passing it the name of the object whose ACL we want to modify. In this case, the first part of the name is the CDS entry to which the server exported its bindings, */.:/subsys/emp_db*, followed by the name of the object that we want to modify, *wei_hu*. The first thing *acl_edit* needs to do is locate the server that manages the ACL. This is done by importing the server's bindings from CDS. The import is done using the CDS entry name that was passed to *acl_edit*, */.:/subsys/emp_db*. After obtaining the server's bindings, *acl_edit* makes an RPC to the *emp_db* server and passes it the name of the object, *wei_hu*, whose ACL we want to modify. Notice how *acl_edit* allows you to name an object (*wei_hu*'s *emp_db* entry) as if it were stored in CDS. This is accomplished by the use of namespace junctions that I'll discuss later.

❷ Type a *list* command to display the ACL protecting this database entry. To process this command, *acl_edit* first asks the ACL manager for some configuration information. For example, it finds out how the ACL's permission bits should be displayed. *acl_edit* then asks the ACL manager to return the ACL so it can be displayed. As you might expect, this is done using authenticated RPC. The ACL manager will also check the identity of the client that is running *acl_edit* to ensure that it is allowed to work with this server's ACLs.

After this is done, *acl_edit* displays the current ACL.

❸ Type a *modify* command to change the unauthenticated ACL entry type so it denies access to everyone. *acl_edit* makes the changes to the local copy of the ACL. This update will be sent to the ACL manager when you type either the *commit* or the *exit* command.

❹ Exit the program. This causes *acl_edit* to make an RPC to the *rdacl_replace* remote procedure, passing in the updated ACL entry. If the client is authorized to replace ACLs, the server would replace the ACL entry with the one specified by the user. If the ACLs are stored on disk, this will also cause the on-disk version to be updated.

acl_edit then releases its binding to the *emp_db* server's *rdaclif* interface.

As you can see, the work that *acl_edit* does to update and manage ACLs is pretty straightforward. The *rdacl* interface basically supports a remote procedure for each ACL operation. *acl_edit* makes RPCs to request operations on ACLs. The actual changes to the ACLs are made by the *emp_db* server. The most complex part of *acl_edit* lies in how *acl_edit* obtains a binding to the right ACL. The two issues of interest here are namespace junctions and generic RPC interfaces.

Namespace Junctions

In the previous section's example, you specified the object whose ACL you wished to modify as */.:/subsys/emp_db/wei_hu*. At the time, I said that */.:/subsys/emp_db* is the CDS entry to which the server exports its bindings and *wei_hu* is the name of the database entry maintained by the *emp_db* server. How does this actually work? After all, the *emp_db* server exported its bindings to */.:/subsys/emp_db*. There are no CDS entries that are named */.:/subsys/emp_db/wei_hu*, */.:/subsys/emp_db/irene_hu*, or */.:/subsys/emp_db/marty_hu*. What you are seeing is the use of namespace junctions.

A **namespace** is a collection of names managed by some name server such as CDS. Most of the DCE names that we deal with are in the CDS namespace. A **namespace junction** is an interface that allows an application to join its own namespace to the CDS namespace. Namespace junctions allow you to use CDS names to refer to objects that are not stored in CDS. Normally, when you specify a namespace entry, say */.:/subsys/emp_db*, that entry is stored in some CDS directory. When a client imports a binding from that entry, CDS looks up that namespace entry and returns the binding stored at that entry. This is how RPC servers normally export their bindings.

What happens if you pass CDS an entryname that does not exist in some CDS directory, for example, */.:/subsys/emp_db/wei_hu*? In this case, since the named entry does not exist in CDS, CDS will fail to resolve the name. However, CDS will return the portion that it can resolve, */.:/subsys/emp_db*, and the portion that it failed to resolve, *wei_hu*. (This is actually done through two separate calls.) If CDS resolves a portion of the name to a namespace junction, it will return a binding to the server at that junction. The client will also get back the unresolved portion of the name. The client should then use the binding to contact the server at the junction and then pass it the unresolved portion of the name to resolve. The server at the junction can then use the unresolved portion of the name as a lookup key to find the object of interest.

A namespace junction server can use its namespace to name whatever objects it chooses. The *acl_edit* utility, for example, uses namespace junctions so that you can specify ACLs by using a single CDS name instead of having to specify the ACL manager and the name of the object it is protecting separately. Other examples of namespace junctions in DCE include DFS, which allows you to name files using CDS names, and the security registry, which allows you to specify individual entries in the security registry database using CDS names. As you can imagine, namespace junctions can also allow you to splice together different directory services. For example, vendors could connect a NIS+ name service to CDS by implementing a namespace junction.

It turns out that most of the work involved with using namespace junctions lies in the client. A client application that is not aware of junctions expects that the bindings it imports from CDS will resolve directly to a server. A junction-aware application, like *acl_edit*, knows to explicitly ask for the portion of the name that is not resolved by CDS. (This is done by the RPC call, *rpc_ns_entry_inq_resolution*.) For example, an application would resolve a full name like */.:/subsys/emp_db/wei_hu* by first calling *rpc_ns_entry_inq_resolution* to determine which portion can be resolved within CDS. In the case of the *emp_db* application, the resolved portion would be the namespace junction */.:/subsys/emp_db*. This namespace entry contains the *emp_db* server's ACL manager.

After calling *rpc_ns_entry_inq_resolution*, the client should then obtain a binding to the server junction by doing an *rpc_ns_import* on the resolved portion. The client should then bind to the junction and pass the unresolved portion, *wei_hu*, to the server at the junction for futher processing. *acl_edit*, for example, saves the last component, *wei_hu*, and passes it to the *emp_db* ACL manager so that it can use it to locate the *emp_db* record whose ACL the user wants to modify. All the *rdaclif* remote procedures accept a component name as an input argument; it specifies the unresolved portion of the name.

The whole issue of namespace management can be very complex. Fortunately, most of this complexity is handled by the *sec_acl* API. If you are interested only in writing an ACL manager (as opposed to writing a replacement for *acl_edit*), then all that you need do is write your ACL manager so that it can use the unresolved portion of the name to locate the ACL of interest. I'll illustrate this when we develop our sample ACL manager in chapter seven.

Note that namespace junctions are really intended for those applications that need to maintain more objects than are practical to store in CDS. Junctions are not always needed. If your application maintains only a few

ACLs, for example, then you might as well store their entry names directly in CDS. If my database consisted of only two entries, say *marty_hu* and *kevin_hu*, then it would be much easier for me to export the ACL manager's bindings into the CDS entries */.:/subsys/emp_db/marty_hu* and */.:/subsys/emp_db/kevin_hu*. Doing so would enable CDS to directly resolve these names to the proper ACL manager. The ACL manager can select the appropriate database entry depending upon where the binding was obtained from.

The namespace junction is the first issue associated with binding to an ACL manager. The other issue involves distinguishing among different servers that all export the same *rdaclif* interface.

Generic rdaclif Interfaces

Earlier, I said that all ACL managers export the same *rdaclif* remote interface. This consistency is what allows a single client application, *acl_edit*, to manage all ACLs. For example a new banking application and the *emp_db* application would export the same *rdaclif* interface into their CDS entries (along with their other interfaces). A client would get the server's binding by doing an *rpc_ns_import* operation from the right CDS entry. For example, *acl_edit* would retrieve the binding for the *emp_db* server's *rdaclif* interface when it binds to */.:/subsys/emp_db* and the binding for the banking application's *rdaclif* interface when it binds to */.:/subsys/bank*.

The problem comes when you have two servers (e.g., the banking and the *emp_db* servers) on the same host that export identical interfaces. Recall that bindings in the namespace are partial bindings, they contain only the host addresses but not the endpoints. The endpoints are stored by *rpcd* at the server node. Each server registers with the *rpcd* by calling *rpc_ep_register* or *rpc_ep_register_no_replace*. When the client makes an RPC using a partial binding, the call is first sent to the endpoint mapper (*rpcd*) at the server node. *rpcd* looks into its own database and uses the interface UUID to locate the endpoint for the server that exported that interface. The *rpcd* then forwards or redirects the call to the right server. This breaks down when multiple servers export the same interface. The interface UUID would be ambiguous in this case. If both the banking and *emp_db* servers export the same *rdaclif* interface (as required to support *acl_edit*), then *rpcd* would be unable to dispatch the call to the right ACL manager.

DCE solves this problem by having each ACL manager export a distinct object UUID with its *rdacl* interface. You can use the ACL manager type UUID for this purpose (see Figure 5-1). This object UUID is exported along with the server's bindings into the CDS. When *acl_edit* imports this ACL manager's bindings from CDS, the binding contains the ACL manager's object UUID. When the client uses this binding to make an RPC, the *rpcd* at the server node can use the object UUID (along with the interface UUID) to select the right server to process the call. The *rpcd* will use the object UUID if the interface UUID is ambiguous in resolving bindings.

ACL Storage

We are now finished with the ACL manager APIs. Before we end this chapter, however, I would like to talk about how you can store ACLs. The ACL storage code is the most application-specific part of an ACL manager. By constrast, the reference monitor and the *rdaclif* manager code are pretty similar across implementations. Programmers custom-build ACL storage code because ACLs usually need to be integrated with the application data (for example, filesystems usually store a file's ACLs in the directory structure) and also to reduce the space taken up by ACLs.

Reducing the size of stored ACLs is important because ACLs are large data structures. If you have only a few ACLs, overhead is not an issue. When you are using lots of ACLs to protect many fine-grained objects, however, you can easily wind up using most of your disk space for storing ACLs rather than the objects that the ACLs protect. This kind of overhead is clearly unacceptable. So what should you do? Well, a good approach is to look at how ACLs are used in real situations and try to optimize for those cases.

I have learned a great deal by looking at how people use filesystem ACLs. Filesystems are interesting because they are still the most common application in which ACLs are used. The following are some observations derived from them:

Most files have short ACLs

The reason that most files have only a few ACL entries is that people tend to organize users into groups. For example, the set of people who are interested in a file typically work on the same project or are in the same department. Thus, the ACL on the file would usually have a single ACL entry for the group as opposed to an ACL entry for every individual that belongs to the project team. For example, in one of my former projects where the program source code was protected by ACLs, all the files had two ACLs: one for the project group and one for the system (for backups and so forth).

By the way, people tend to use groups in administering ACLs because it is just too cumbersome to enter and update individual ACL entries when you have lots of files.

Most files in a directory subtree have the same ACL

People have learned to use directories to group related files. In practice, this also means they share the same access-control information. You can see this even in filesystems that do not support ACLs. For example, files in the same UNIX directory tend to have the same user and group ID bits.

ACLs tend to be referenced far more frequently than they are updated

ACLs are referenced frequently because the reference monitor needs to check them on every access to the protected object. However, they don't tend to be updated very often. When people create new files, for example, they usually take the default ACL inherited from the parent directory. If a user explictly sets an ACL, it's usually done when the file is first created; people almost never modify an ACL afterwards. (You can think about how seldomly you need to run *chmod* on an existing file to get an idea of how often ACLs are changed.)

From these observations, we can pick up a couple of traits that let us optimize the use of ACLs: most ACLs have very few entries, and different objects often share entries.

Optimizing ACL Implementations

We can take advantage of this pattern of ACL usage to implement several optimizations. First, we can reduce the storage required for duplicate ACL entries by storing the full ACL entries out-of-line in a separate data structure, an ACL table. Then, instead of storing a full ACL with every object, we store pointers to the ACL entries. When we add an ACL entry to an object, we first search the ACL table. If the ACL entry exists in the table, we just store a pointer to that ACL entry in our object. If the ACL entry does not exist, we would add a new entry to the ACL table. We also add a reference count to each ACL entry in the ACL table to keep track of the number of references to that ACL entry so that we can safely reclaim the storage associated with that ACL entry. Figure 5-5 illustrates how we can use references to entries in an ACL table to represent an equivalent implementation that stores the ACLs inline.

Sharing ACL entries in this manner can save significant amounts of storage because pointers take up much less space than the actual ACL entries themselves. In the extreme case where all the objects have the same ACL, they would all share a single copy of that ACL. For simplicity, I have defined an ACL table that allows applications to share individual ACL entries. In some cases, you can compact your ACLs even more by sharing groups of ACL entries (or even entire ACLs).

The next optimization is to store a small, fixed number of ACL entries (or pointers to entries in the ACL table) in the data structure that the ACL is protecting. When the number of ACL entries exceeds this limit, the ACL manager allocates an indirect overflow data structure. This gives us very fast ACL lookup for objects with short ACLs; relatively slower lookups for those objects that have long ACLs. It therefore optimizes for the common case.

The two optimizations described so far are primarily space optimizations. You can also reduce ACL evaluation time by caching the outcome of

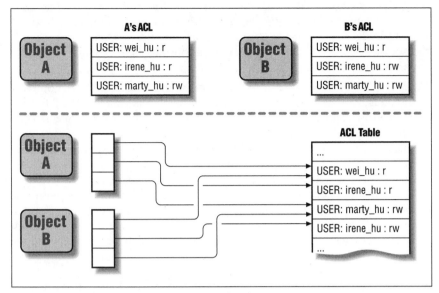

Figure 5-5: Sharing ACL entries via an ACL table

previous ACL evaluations. Whenever the reference monitor checks a client's PAC against an ACL, the results of the access-control decision can be saved. Then, whenever the reference monitor is asked to compare a client's PAC against another ACL, the ACL manager first uses the ACL and the client PAC as a lookup key in the ACL result cache. If there is a match, the cached result is returned. This allows the reference monitor to quickly determine whether access should be granted when a client is referencing objects with the same ACLs. This works very well, for example, when you are sequentially scanning through the files in the same directory. We will not be implementing this optimization in our example.

These examples give you an idea of what can be done to make ACLs efficient. How much effort you should spend on optimizing ACLs really depends upon your application. If you have only a few ACLs, for example, it is probably not worth the effort to implement any of these optimizations. On the other hand, if you are designing a high-performance application where both efficient storage and performance are critical, then designing a highly optimized ACL facility would clearly be worthwhile.

Summary

DCE ACLs offer a more flexible way to implement authorization than the methods I introduced earlier. ACLs gives you greater flexibility in controlling who can access your data. By using ACLs, you can set up access controls on a per-object basis. You don't need to grant more access than necessary to perform a given task. You can, for example, give someone access to a part of the data without having corresponding access to the rest of the data. Since the ACL is just a data structure, you can even change the set of people who can access your application's data while the application is up and running.

However, as we have seen in this chapter, ACLs can also be very complex. Fortunately, we as implementors of ACL managers are shielded from a great deal of this complexity. For example, *acl_edit* and the *sec_acl* API handle all the client-side work that's required to work with namespace junctions. When you write an ACL manager, all that you really need to worry about is making sure it fits properly within the framework expected by *acl_edit*. The job is analogous to writing device drivers. The typical UNIX I/O subsystem is very complex, involving interactions with the buffer cache and virtual memory. However, this complexity is shielded from device drivers because of the well-defined driver interface. The *rdaclif* interface plays a similar critical function. It is the interface that you must implement faithfully to enable your ACL manager to "plug" into *acl_edit*.

Writing an ACL manager really involves only three major steps. First, you must include ACLs in your data structures. Next, you need to write a reference monitor that uses ACLs to make authorization decisions. Finally, you must implement the *rdaclif* interface. Taken as a whole, it can be a fair amount of work. However, it becomes much more tractable when handled a piece at a time. But that's enough hand-waving. Let us now go on to the next chapter where I'll take you step by step through a complete implementation.

6

Writing an Application That Uses ACLs

Conventional wisdom says that writing an ACL manager is the hardest part of developing a DCE application. ACL managers are hard because you have to use several APIs, write an additional RPC interface, and then make sure that they all work together and with your application logic. The lack of documentation on this subject makes the whole process even harder. As with many projects, however, writing an ACL manager becomes easier if you understand the underlying principles and approach the task systematically. By reading Chapter 5, you've already gotten the required concepts. Now I will take you the rest of the way and show you how to build an ACL manager for our employee database application.

I use a five-step approach to writing an ACL manager:

1. Decide on how the application will use ACLs. Issues to consider include what these ACLs protect and what access rights they grant.

2. Make room for ACLs in the application's data structures. If the application stores data in persistent storage, make space there also.

3. Write a reference monitor that uses the ACLs to make authorization decisions. This reference monitor takes a client PAC, retrieves the appropriate ACL, and compares them to see if the requested access can be granted.

4. Implement the *rdaclif* management interface. This allows a client to set and change this application's ACLs.

5. Integrate and test all the pieces together.

In this chapter, we will go through steps 1 through 3 and modify the employee database application to use ACLs. We will store ACLs and use them to make authorization decisions. Then in the next chapter, we will add the ACL management interface to our application.

Using ACLs in the Employee Database Application

Before writing any ACL manager code, you must first decide how to use ACLs. Specifically, you need to decide which objects these ACLs will protect and the permissions that these ACLs will grant to clients.

As you learned in Chapter 5, you must associate an ACL with every object you wish to give separate protection. For the employee database application, this would be the individual database entry. Having an ACL for each database entry allows you, for example, to selectively grant a client access to an entry in the database without having to grant him or her access to the rest of the database. That was easy. Now let's look at the types of access (or permissions) that you need to support on each database entry.

The following are the permissions I would define in these ACLs:

read
Allows someone to query the database entry protected by an ACL.

write
Allows someone to modify the fields in an existing database entry. This includes the ability to delete an entry.

control
Allows someone to modify the ACL associated with a database entry. Every ACL manager should implement some permission like this because it controls who can change the ACLs.

A permission that I've left out is *insert*. This permission controls who can add a new entry to the database. You need to control creation of database entries because anyone who can add new entries to the employee database would be able to create fake employee records. In the previous version of the employee database, we solved this problem by allowing only members of the *emp_db_users* group to insert entries. For this version of the application, we will make this more flexible by using an ACL for this.

You may have noticed that the *write* permission only allows a client to modify a database entry; it does not allow a client to add a new database entry. This is intentional. I did not want to put the *insert* permission on an ACL that is attached to the entry itself. Making the *insert* permission part of each database entry's ACL would be hard to administer as you would have to modify the ACLs on all the empty database entries if you want to change who can create new entries. A better approach is to associate an ACL with the database as a whole. This would allow you to work with a single ACL when you want to change who can create database entries. Logically, this also makes sense because all the unused database entries are equivalent from a security perspective.

This ACL would have two permissions:

insert
> Allows a principal or group to add a new database entry.

control
> Allows a principal or group to modify the database ACL itself.

Therefore, we will implement two kinds of ACLs: one for each database entry and one on the database as a whole. Now you have enough information to proceed to the next step, which is to figure out where and how to store your ACLs.

Writing an ACL Storage Library

In Chapter 5, I discussed some ACL storage design issues. For this application, you will use an external ACL table to reduce the space needed for ACL storage. Every entry in this ACL table will contain a full ACL entry and a reference count. You then store a compact ACL in each database entry. A compact ACL is just an ACL in which the ACL entries are replaced by indices to entries in the ACL table. For simplicity, each compact ACL will store a maximum of 10 ACL table indices. Although we have not done so, it would be a straightforward task to extend this data structure to include an overflow field that points to additional storage for large ACLs as needed. Example 6-1 shows the declaration for the compact ACL. For comparison, I have also included the declaration for the full ACL and an ACL entry.

Example 6-1: The Compact ACL

```
/*
 * One entry in the ACL table.
 */
typedef struct acl_table_entry_s {
        sec_acl_entry_t acl_entry;
        int             ref_count;
} acl_table_entry_t;


#define MAX_ACLS_PER_OBJ 10

/*
 * The compact ACL.
 */
typedef struct {
        sec_acl_id_t    default_realm;
        int             num_entries;
        int             acl_indices[MAX_ACLS_PER_OBJ];
} compact_acl_t;
```

Example 6-1: The Compact ACL (continued)

```
/*
 * The full ACL as defined by DCE.
 */
typedef struct {
    sec_acl_id_t            default_realm;        /* the default cell */
    uuid_t                  sec_acl_manager_type;
    unsigned32              num_entries;
    [ptr, size_is(num_entries)]
        sec_acl_entry_t     *sec_acl_entries;
} sec_acl_t;


/*
 * An ACL entry.
 */
typedef struct {
    sec_acl_permset_t       perms;
    union sec_acl_entry_u
            switch (sec_acl_entry_type_t entry_type) tagged_union {

        case sec_acl_e_type_mask_obj:
        case sec_acl_e_type_user_obj:
        case sec_acl_e_type_group_obj:
        case sec_acl_e_type_other_obj:
        case sec_acl_e_type_unauthenticated:
        case sec_acl_e_type_any_other:
            /* ... just the permset_t ... */;

        case sec_acl_e_type_user:
        case sec_acl_e_type_group:
        case sec_acl_e_type_foreign_other:
            sec_id_t        id;

        case sec_acl_e_type_foreign_user:
        case sec_acl_e_type_foreign_group:
            sec_id_foreign_t foreign_id;

        case sec_acl_e_type_extended:
        default:
            [ptr] sec_acl_extend_info_t *extended_info;
    } entry_info;
} sec_acl_entry_t;
```

You may have noticed that the compact ACL does not store all the fields present in an ACL. This is another optimization. Do not store the ACL manager type because it is the same for all the ACLs supported by an ACL manager. Instead, fill them in when a compact ACL is expanded into a full ACL. Also, I would normally store the *default_realm* field out of line in a separate table because most ACLs will have the same value. For clarity, I've decided to keep it in the compact ACL.

You might ask why bother to work with full ACLs at all. The answer is that the *rdaclif* wire protocol uses full ACLs, so it is easier to write the ACL manager modules in terms of full ACLs.

Now you're ready to look at the procedures that implement your ACL storage facility. Example 6-2 shows *acl_store_init*. This routine is called when the ACL manager starts up. It reads the ACL table from the ACL file.

Example 6-2: Initializing the ACL Store

```
#include <sys/types.h>
#include <dce/uuid.h>
#include <sys/stat.h>
#include <unistd.h>
#include <stdlib.h>
#include <stdio.h>
#include <fcntl.h>
#include <string.h>
#include <errno.h>

#include <dce/rpc.h>
#include <dce/aclbase.h>
#include <dce/dce_cf.h>
#include <dce/binding.h>
#include <dce/secidmap.h>
#include <dce/idlbase.h>
#include "chk_stat.h"
#include "aclstore.h"


static acl_table_entry_t acl_table[ACL_STORE_SIZE];

#define ACL_DB_FILE "/usr/people/emp_db_server/acl_db_file"
static int acl_db_fd;


/*
 * Initialize the ACL store.
 */
void
acl_store_init (void)
{
        int                    n, db_size, fd;

        db_size = ACL_STORE_SIZE*sizeof(acl_table_entry_t);

        /*
         * If the file exists, read it in. Otherwise, create one.
         */
        fd = open (ACL_DB_FILE, O_RDWR|O_SYNC);
        if (fd != -1) {
                /*
                 * File exists, read it in.
                 */
```

Example 6-2: Initializing the ACL Store (continued)

```
                        n = read (fd, acl_table, db_size);
                        if ((n == -1) || (n < db_size))
                                PERROR_EXIT ("acl_store_init, open failed");
        }
        else if (errno == ENOENT) {
                /*
                 * File does not exist; create it.
                 */
                if ((fd = creat (ACL_DB_FILE, S_IRUSR|S_IWUSR)) == -1)
                        PERROR_EXIT ("acl_store_init, create failed");

                memset (acl_table, 0, db_size);
                n = write (fd, acl_table, db_size);
                if ((n == -1) || (n < db_size))
                        PERROR_EXIT ("acl_store_init, write failed");
        }
        else {
                PERROR_EXIT ("acl_store_init, open failed");
        }

        /*
         * Save the file descriptor for later use.
         */
        acl_db_fd = fd;
}
```

Example 6-3 shows the code that retrieves an ACL from the in-memory
ACL table. This routine is called by the server on every RPC because it
needs the ACL to figure out whether the client is authorized to make the
call. *acl_store_read_acl* takes a compact ACL as input, retrieves each ACL
entry from the ACL table, and returns a full ACL containing those entries.
Note that you fill in the ACL header information before returning the full
ACL to the caller.

Example 6-3: Retrieving an ACL from the ACL Store

```
/*
 * Read in an ACL.
 */
extern void
acl_store_read_acl (uuid_t            *acl_mgr_type,    /* IN */
                    compact_acl_t     *compact_acl,     /* IN */
                    sec_acl_t         **acl_p)          /* OUT */
{
        sec_acl_t       *acl;
        unsigned        i, acl_table_index, size;
        sec_acl_entry_t *acl_entry_p;
        unsigned32      st;

        /*
```

Example 6-3: Retrieving an ACL from the ACL Store (continued)

```
 * Allocate space for the ACL.
 */
acl = (sec_acl_t *) malloc(sizeof(sec_acl_t));
memset (acl, 0, sizeof(sec_acl_t));

/*
 * Allocate space for the ACL entries.
 */
acl->num_entries = compact_acl->num_entries;
size = compact_acl->num_entries * sizeof(sec_acl_entry_t);
acl_entry_p = acl->sec_acl_entries =
        (sec_acl_entry_t *)malloc (size);
memset (acl_entry_p, 0, size);

/*
 * Fill in the ACL entries with information from the ACL table.
 */
for (i=0; i < compact_acl->num_entries; i++) {
        acl_table_index = compact_acl->acl_indices[i];
        memcpy (&acl_entry_p[i], &acl_table[acl_table_index],
                sizeof(sec_acl_entry_t));
}

acl->default_realm = compact_acl->default_realm;
if (acl_mgr_type)
        acl->sec_acl_manager_type = *acl_mgr_type;
else
        uuid_create_nil (&acl->sec_acl_manager_type, &st);

*acl_p = acl;
}
```

The inverse operation to *acl_store_read_acl* is *acl_store_write_acl*. This routine (shown in Example 6-4) is called whenever you create a new ACL. It is also called whenever *acl_edit* replaces an ACL. *acl_store_write_acl* takes a full ACL and writes each ACL entry into the ACL table and the ACL file. It then returns a compact ACL containing the ACL table indices to which each ACL entry was written. If the ACL entry being written already exists in the ACL table, *acl_store_write_acl* just increments the reference count on that entry. If the entry does not exist, a new entry is added.

Example 6-4: Writing an ACL to the ACL Store

```
/*
 * Write an ACL.
 */
extern void
acl_store_write_acl (sec_acl_t          *acl,          /* IN */
                     compact_acl_t      *compact_acl)   /* OUT */
{
```

Example 6-4: Writing an ACL to the ACL Store (continued)

```
        unsigned        i;
        sec_acl_entry_t  *acl_entry_p;

        acl_entry_p = acl->sec_acl_entries;
        for (i=0; i < acl->num_entries; i++) {
                acl_store_write_acl_entry (&acl_entry_p[i],
                        &compact_acl->acl_indices[i]);
        }
        compact_acl->num_entries = acl->num_entries;
        compact_acl->default_realm = acl->default_realm;
}


/*
 * Internal procedure to write an ACL entry and update the backing store.
 * This routine returns the ACL table index to which this ACL entry was
 * written.
 */
static void
acl_store_write_acl_entry (sec_acl_entry_t      *acl_entry,      /* IN */
                           int                  *acl_index)      /* OUT */
{
        unsigned        i, found;
        int             n;

        /*
         * See if entry is already in the table.
         */
        found = 0;
        for (i=0; i < ACL_STORE_SIZE; i++) {
                if (memcmp (acl_entry, &acl_table[i].acl_entry,
                        sizeof(sec_acl_entry_t)) == 0) {
                        /*
                         * It exists, just increment the reference count.
                         */
                        acl_table[i].ref_count++;
                        *acl_index = i;
                        found = 1;
                        break;
                }
        }

        if (! found) {
                /*
                 * This acl entry does not exist in the table; add it.
                 */
                for (i=0; i < ACL_STORE_SIZE; i++) {

                        /*
                         * Free entries have reference counts of 0.
                         */
                        if (acl_table[i].ref_count == 0) {
                                memcpy (&acl_table[i].acl_entry, acl_entry,
```

Example 6-4: Writing an ACL to the ACL Store (continued)

```
                                sizeof(sec_acl_entry_t));
                    acl_table[i].ref_count = 1;
                    *acl_index = i;
                    found = 1;
                    break;
                }
            }

        if (! found)
            PERROR_EXIT (
                "acl_store_write_acl_entry, no space in acl_table");
    }

    /*
     * Write the acl entry to the backing store.
     */
    if (lseek (acl_db_fd, i*sizeof(acl_table_entry_t), SEEK_SET) == -1)
            PERROR_EXIT ("acl_store_write_acl_entry, seek failed");

    n = write (acl_db_fd, &acl_table[i], sizeof(acl_table_entry_t));
    if ((n == -1) || (n < sizeof(acl_table_entry_t)))
            PERROR_EXIT ("acl_store_write_acl_entry, write failed");

}
```

Whenever the server deletes an object, it must also delete the associated ACL. *acl_store_delete_acl* deletes an ACL from both the in-memory ACL table and the ACL file. This routine simply decrements the reference count on the ACL table entries. An entry becomes free when its reference count goes to zero. Example 6-5 shows the implementation.

Example 6-5: Deleting an ACL from the ACL Store

```
/*
 * Delete an ACL.
 */
extern void
acl_store_delete_acl (compact_acl_t     *compact_acl)          /* IN */
{
    unsigned     i;

    for (i=0; i < compact_acl->num_entries; i++) {
            acl_store_delete_acl_entry (compact_acl->acl_indices[i]);
    }
    memset (compact_acl, 0, sizeof(compact_acl_t));
}



/*
 * Internal procedure to delete an ACL entry.
```

Example 6-5: Deleting an ACL from the ACL Store (continued)

```
 */
static void
acl_store_delete_acl_entry (int          acl_index)      /* IN */
{
    int    n;

    /*
     * Decrement the reference count. A reference count of 0
     * implicitly frees this entry.
     */
    acl_table[acl_index].ref_count--;
    if (acl_table[acl_index].ref_count == 0)
            memset (&acl_table[acl_index], 0, sizeof(acl_table_entry_t));

    /*
     * Write the empty acl entry to the backing store.
     */
    if (lseek (acl_db_fd, acl_index*sizeof(acl_table_entry_t), SEEK_SET)
        == -1)
            PERROR_EXIT ("acl_store_delete_acl_entry, seek failed");

    n = write (acl_db_fd, &acl_table[acl_index], sizeof(acl_table_entry_t));
    if ((n == -1) || (n < sizeof(acl_table_entry_t)))
            PERROR_EXIT ("acl_store_delete_acl_entry, write failed");

}
```

Note that the ACL storage library does not include an *acl_store_modify_acl* routine. An ACL manager that needs to modify an existing ACL must first delete the original ACL and then write back the new ACL. This sequence of steps automatically handles shared ACL entries correctly since *acl_store_delete_acl* would leave the old version intact if there are any other references to it.

You should also note that a production implementation would probably use a hash function for fast lookup instead of the linear search that is used here.

Writing the Employee Database Manager Code

Now that you've written the code to store ACLs, let's look at the code that uses ACLs. We will start with the *emp_db* manager. This is the server code that implements the remote procedures for the employee database application. I have already shown a version of the employee database manager code in Chapter 4 (see Example 4-2). For this chapter, we are going to change it to use ACLs and also to keep a copy of the employee database itself in a file. Example 6-6 shows the type definition of the employee database record stored.

Example 6-6: The emp_record_t Structure

```
typedef idl_char emp_db_field_t[EMP_DB_MAX_LEN];

typedef struct {
        emp_db_field_t          emp_name;
        emp_db_field_t          emp_mailstop;
        emp_db_field_t          emp_phone_number;
} emp_record_t;

typedef struct {
        emp_record_t     emp_record;
        compact_acl_t    compact_acl;
} emp_store_record_t;

extern emp_store_record_t       emp_database[DATABASE_SIZE];
```

Initializing the emp_db Manager

The *emp_db server* initializes the employee database manager code from
main(). Example 6-7 shows what this routine does.

Example 6-7: Initialization Code for the emp_db Manager Code

```
#include <pthread.h>
#include <stdio.h>
#include <string.h>
#include <dce/dce_cf.h>

#include <dce/binding.h>
#include <dce/pgo.h>
#include <dce/secidmap.h>

#include "emp_db.h"
#include "aclstore.h"
#include "empstore.h"
#include "ref_mon.h"
#include "chk_stat.h"

/*
 * The in-memory copy of the employee database.
 */
emp_store_record_t      emp_database[DATABASE_SIZE];

static unsigned32 create_default_entry_acl (char *db_entry_name,
        compact_acl_t *compact_acl);

static void create_default_db_acl (compact_acl_t *compact_acl);

/*
 * Mutex to serialize access to the database.
 */
```

Example 6-7: Initialization Code for the emp_db Manager Code (continued)

```
pthread_mutex_t emp_db_mutex;

/*
 * Cached binding to the Security Registry.
 */
sec_rgy_handle_t  emp_db_rgy_handle = NULL;

/*
 * UUIDs for the emp_db_admin and emp_db_user groups.
 */
uuid_t  emp_db_admin_group_uuid;
uuid_t  emp_db_user_group_uuid;

#define EMP_DB_USER_GROUP "emp_db_user_group"
#define EMP_DB_ADMIN_GROUP "emp_db_admin_group"

/*
 * Our cell name and UUID.
 */
static char          *emp_db_cell_name;
static uuid_t         emp_db_cell_uuid;

/*
 * ACL manager type UUIDs for our ACL managers.
 */
static char emp_db_acl_mgr_uuid_str[] =
       "73c3d2fc-0966-11ce-9968-69076147ce07";
static char emp_db_entry_acl_mgr_uuid_str[] =
       "b5a7d9ac-0966-11ce-82e5-69076147ce07";
uuid_t  emp_db_acl_mgr_uuid;
uuid_t  emp_db_entry_acl_mgr_uuid;


void
emp_db_init (void)
{
        int            initial_db;
        error_status_t  status;

        pthread_mutex_init (&emp_db_mutex, pthread_mutexattr_default); ❶

        /*
         * Establish a binding to the registry interface of the
         * Security Server.
         */
        sec_rgy_site_open ("/.:", &emp_db_rgy_handle, &status);
        CHECK_STATUS (status, "rgy_site_open failed", ABORT);

        /*
         * Convert the group names into UUIDs and save it for
         * later use by the reference monitor.
         */
        sec_rgy_pgo_name_to_id (emp_db_rgy_handle,                    ❷
```

Example 6-7: Initialization Code for the emp_db Manager Code (continued)

```
                sec_rgy_domain_group,
                EMP_DB_USER_GROUP,
                &emp_db_user_group_uuid,
                &status);
    CHECK_STATUS (status, "pgo_name_to_id failed", ABORT);

    sec_rgy_pgo_name_to_id (emp_db_rgy_handle,
                sec_rgy_domain_group,
                EMP_DB_ADMIN_GROUP,
                &emp_db_admin_group_uuid,
                &status);
    CHECK_STATUS (status, "pgo_name_to_id failed", ABORT);

    /*
     * Initialize our cell name & UUID.
     */
    dce_cf_get_cell_name (&emp_db_cell_name, &status);
    CHECK_STATUS (status, "dce_cf_get_cell_name failed", ABORT);

    sec_id_parse_name (emp_db_rgy_handle, emp_db_cell_name, NULL,
                    &emp_db_cell_uuid, NULL, NULL, &status);
    CHECK_STATUS (status, "sec_id_parse_name failed", ABORT);

    /*
     * Read the ACLs in from the backing store.
     */
    acl_store_init();                                                    ❸

    /*
     * Read the emp_db database itself in from the backing store
     * into emp_database. If the database does not exist, zeroes
     * the emp_database.
     */
    emp_store_init(emp_database, &initial_db);                           ❹

    /*
     * Set up the ACL manager UUIDs.
     */
    uuid_from_string (emp_db_acl_mgr_uuid_str,                           ❺
            &emp_db_acl_mgr_uuid, &status);
    CHECK_STATUS (status, "uuid_from_string failed", ABORT);

    uuid_from_string (emp_db_entry_acl_mgr_uuid_str,
            &emp_db_entry_acl_mgr_uuid, &status);
    CHECK_STATUS (status, "uuid_from_string failed", ABORT);

    /*
     * If this is a new database, create the default database ACL.
     * We store the database ACL in reserved location 0 of the
     * employee database.
     */
    if (initial_db) {
        strcpy (emp_database[0].emp_record.emp_name, "emp_db_server");
```

Example 6-7: Initialization Code for the emp_db Manager Code (continued)

```
        create_default_db_acl (&emp_database[0].compact_acl);      ❻
    }
}
```

emp_db_init initializes a number of global variables that are used by the reference monitor and the *rdacl_if manager* code. It does the following:

❶ Initialize *emp_db_mutex*. You use this mutex to protect both the employee database and the ACLs against concurrent access by different threads. Any thread that wants to access either the employee database or the ACLs must first lock this mutex.

❷ Query the security registry to get the UUIDs for the *emp_db_admin* and *emp_db_user* groups. This will be needed by the reference monitor. Also get the cell name and cell UUID; they will be needed to create default ACLs.

❸ Read the ACLs in from the backing store. If the file does not exist, then initialize a new ACL table. This function was defined in Example 6-2.

❹ Read the employee database itself in from its backing store. If the file does not exist, you should initialize a new database.

❺ Get the ACL manager UUIDs. These UUIDs were generated by using *uuidgen* and are declared as text strings. Convert the strings into *uuid_t*s so that you can work with them. This will be needed by the *rdacl_if* manager code.

❻ If you have a brand new employee database, create a default ACL for it. This is the ACL that describes who can insert entries in this database. Note that this is just the default; the administrator can always change the ACL later. The default ACL also describes who can modify the ACL.

Modifying the emp_db Remote Procedures to Use ACLs

The rest of the code in the *emp_db* manager are the entry points defined in *emp_db.idl*, the RPC interface for the employee database application. These entry points are the remote procedures that allow clients to work with the employee database. They allow a client to insert entries, modify entries, delete entries, and make queries. Example 6-8 shows the code.

Example 6-8: Employee Database Manager Code

```
void
emp_db_insert (
    handle_t handle,
    emp_record_t emp_record,
    unsigned32 *emp_status)
{
    unsigned        i;

    pthread_mutex_lock (&emp_db_mutex);

    /*
     * Check the creation ACL on the database. We don't care which db
     * entry gets created, so we pass in NULL for the entryname.
     */
    if (! client_is_authorized (handle, OP_INSERT, NULL)) {          ❶
            *emp_status = emp_s_not_authorized;
            pthread_mutex_unlock (&emp_db_mutex);
            return;
    }

    /*
     * Make sure entry is not already in the database.
     *
     * Note how we start from index 1; index 0 is reserved for holding
     * the creation ACL for the database as a whole.
     */
    for (i=1; i < DATABASE_SIZE; i++) {
            if (strcmp (emp_database[i].emp_record.emp_name,
                    emp_record.emp_name) == 0) {
                *emp_status = emp_s_exists;
                pthread_mutex_unlock (&emp_db_mutex);
                return;
            }
    }

    /*
     * Now copy the record into the first empty entry.
     */
    for (i=1; i < DATABASE_SIZE; i++) {
            if (emp_database[i].emp_record.emp_name[0] == '\0') {
                /*
                 * Update the incore database.
                 */
                emp_database[i].emp_record = emp_record;
                *emp_status = create_default_entry_acl (             ❷
                        emp_record.emp_name,
                        &emp_database[i].compact_acl);

                if (*emp_status == emp_s_ok) {
                    /*
                     * Write to the backing stores.
                     */
                    emp_store_write (i);                             ❸
```

Example 6-8: Employee Database Manager Code (continued)

```
                            }
                    pthread_mutex_unlock (&emp_db_mutex);
                    return;
            }
    }

    *emp_status = emp_s_nospace;
    pthread_mutex_unlock (&emp_db_mutex);
    return;
}

void
emp_db_modify (
    handle_t handle,
    emp_record_t emp_record,
    unsigned32 *emp_status)
{
    unsigned        i;

    pthread_mutex_lock (&emp_db_mutex);

    if (! client_is_authorized(handle, OP_WRITE, emp_record.emp_name)) { ❹
            *emp_status = emp_s_not_authorized;
            pthread_mutex_unlock (&emp_db_mutex);
            return;
    }

    for (i=1; i < DATABASE_SIZE; i++) {
            if (strcmp (emp_database[i].emp_record.emp_name,
                    emp_record.emp_name) == 0) {

                    emp_database[i].emp_record = emp_record;
                    emp_store_write (i);                            ❺

                    *emp_status = emp_s_ok;
                    pthread_mutex_unlock (&emp_db_mutex);
                    return;
            }
    }

    *emp_status = emp_s_not_found;
    pthread_mutex_unlock (&emp_db_mutex);
    return;
}


void
emp_db_delete (
    handle_t handle,
    emp_db_field_t emp_name,
    unsigned32 *emp_status)
{
    unsigned        i;
```

Example 6-8: Employee Database Manager Code (continued)

```
        pthread_mutex_lock (&emp_db_mutex);

        if (! client_is_authorized (handle, OP_WRITE, emp_name)) {
                *emp_status = emp_s_not_authorized;
                pthread_mutex_unlock (&emp_db_mutex);
                return;
        }

        for (i=1; i < DATABASE_SIZE; i++) {
                if (strcmp (emp_database[i].emp_record.emp_name,
                                emp_name) == 0) {

                        /*
                         * Delete the ACL and the database entry.
                         */
                        acl_store_delete_acl (&emp_database[i].compact_acl);   ❻
                        emp_store_delete (i);
                        memset (&emp_database[i], 0, sizeof(emp_record_t));

                        *emp_status = emp_s_ok;
                        pthread_mutex_unlock (&emp_db_mutex);
                        return;
                }
        }

        *emp_status = emp_s_not_found;
        pthread_mutex_unlock (&emp_db_mutex);
        return;
}


void
emp_db_query(
        handle_t handle,
        emp_db_field_t emp_name,
        emp_record_t *emp_record,
        unsigned32 *emp_status)
{
        unsigned        i;

        pthread_mutex_lock (&emp_db_mutex);

        if (! client_is_authorized (handle, OP_READ, emp_name)) {          ❼

                /*
                 * Explicitly clear the output argument for those
                 * cases where we have nothing to return.
                 */
                memset (emp_record, 0, sizeof(emp_record_t));
                *emp_status = emp_s_not_authorized;
                pthread_mutex_unlock (&emp_db_mutex);
                return;
```

Example 6-8: Employee Database Manager Code (continued)

```
    }

    for (i=1; i < DATABASE_SIZE; i++) {
        if (strcmp (emp_database[i].emp_record.emp_name,
                    emp_name) == 0) {
            *emp_record = emp_database[i].emp_record;
            *emp_status = emp_s_ok;
            pthread_mutex_unlock (&emp_db_mutex);
            return;
        }
    }

    memset (emp_record, 0, sizeof(emp_record_t));
    *emp_status = emp_s_not_found;
    pthread_mutex_unlock (&emp_db_mutex);
    return;

}
```

The manager routines that were changed to support ACLs are: *emp_db_insert, emp_db_modify,* and *emp_db_delete.*

❶ *emp_db_insert* inserts a new employee entry into the database. After acquiring the mutex, first check to see if the database's ACL allows this client to add new entries. You do this by calling *client_is_authorized* with a null database entry name. The null entry name tells the routine to look for the database ACL as opposed to a database entry ACL.

❷ Assuming the client is authorized, create the database entry and a default ACL for this new entry. I will explain what *create_default_entry_acl* does later.

❸ Write the database entry to the backing store.

❹ *emp_db_modify* modifies an existing database entry. It first checks to see if the client is authorized to modify this database entry. Note that in this case, you pass *client_is_authorized* the name of the entry. This will cause the reference monitor to evaluate that entry's ACL.

❺ Assuming the client is authorized to change the employee's information, update the in-memory database entry and the backing store. Note that *emp_db_modify* does not modify the database entry's ACL. ACLs are only modified via the *rdacl_if* management interface.

❻ *emp_db_delete* deletes a database entry. This routine now deletes the ACL as well as the employee entry from the backing store.

❼ *emp_db_query* looks up a database entry. I chose to make the authorization check before you see if the entry exists. If it is important to return the *not_found* status even when the authorization check fails, then you can reorder the code.

The application manager code (i.e., the *emp_db* manager code in this case) needs to do three things to support ACLs:

1. Create an initial ACL whenever it creates a new object. In the case of the *emp_db* manager, it needs to create a database ACL when you initialize a new database and create an entry ACL whenever you make a new database entry.

2. Delete the ACL whenever the manager deletes object that the ACL protects.

3. Check the ACL to decide whether the client is authorized to perform a given operation.

Other than these operations and initialization code, the application manager should not modify ACLs. That job should be left strictly to the *rdacl_if* manager code.

Creating Default ACLs

You create an ACL as soon as a new database or database entry is created because you want to control access to an object as soon as it becomes available. Although ACLs are customizable by users, you should make the initial ACL reasonable so that users are not forced to change the ACLs before running the application.

In the case of the employee database application, you need two defaults ACLs: a default ACL for the database that determines who can add new entries into a database, and a default ACL for each database entry that determines who can access an individual database entry. A reasonable thing to do in this case is to set up the initial ACLs so that your application behaves the same as the earlier, non-ACL version.

Default database ACL

The example below shows the default creation ACL for the database.

```
GROUP : emp_db_users : i
GROUP : emp_db_admin : ic
```

This ACL gives members of the *emp_db_users* and *emp_db_admin* groups *insert* permission (i.e., they can create new entries). In addition, members of the *emp_db_admin* group also have *control* permission. This means that by default, administrators are the only ones that can change the set of people who can add new database entries. Since anyone who has *control* permission can also create an ACL entry that grants someone else *control* permission, this default ACL also allows an administrator to give someone else the ability to modify this ACL. Example 6-9 shows the implementation of *create_default_creation_acl.* This routine is called when the server initializes a new employee database. The code first creates a full ACL, writes it to the backing store, and then returns the compact version of the ACL to the caller.

Example 6-9: Setting Up the Initial Database Creation ACL

```
/*
 * Create the default ACL for the database as a whole. It allows:
 *    1. members of the emp_db_users group "w" access.
 *    2. members of the emp_db_admin group "wc" access.
 */
static void
create_default_db_acl (compact_acl_t      *compact_acl)
{
    sec_acl_t        acl;
    sec_acl_entry_t *acl_entry_p;
    error_status_t   status;

    /*
     * Initialize an ACL of 2 entries.
     */
    acl.num_entries = 2;                              ❶
    acl.sec_acl_entries = acl_entry_p =
            (sec_acl_entry_t *) malloc (
                    acl.num_entries * sizeof(sec_acl_entry_t));

    /*
     * Fill in the default realm.
     */
    acl.default_realm.name = strdup (emp_db_cell_name);
    acl.default_realm.uuid = emp_db_cell_uuid;

    /*
     * Note that we do not bother to fill in the ACL manager UUID
     * since we can infer it when we read the ACL back.
     */

    /*
     * Allow "i" access to emp_db_users group.
     */
    acl_entry_p->perms = sec_acl_perm_insert;         ❷
    acl_entry_p->entry_info.entry_type = sec_acl_e_type_group;
    acl_entry_p->entry_info.tagged_union.id.uuid = emp_db_user_group_uuid;
    acl_entry_p->entry_info.tagged_union.id.name = (idl_char *) "";

    /*
     * Allow "ic" access to emp_db_admin group.
     */
    acl_entry_p++;
    acl_entry_p->perms = sec_acl_perm_insert | sec_acl_perm_control;
```

Example 6-9: Setting Up the Initial Database Creation ACL (continued)

```
acl_entry_p->entry_info.entry_type = sec_acl_e_type_group;
acl_entry_p->entry_info.tagged_union.id.uuid = emp_db_admin_group_uuid;
acl_entry_p->entry_info.tagged_union.id.name = (idl_char *) "";

/*
 * Write this ACL to the ACL table and backing store.
 */
acl_store_write_acl (&acl, compact_acl);  ❸

/*
 * Since we now have the compact_acl, we don't need the full ACL
 * any more.
 */
free (acl.sec_acl_entries);
}
```

❶ Allocate the ACL entries from heap. Defines a pointer, *acl_entry_p*, that is used to step through and initialize the array.

❷ Set up the ACL fields. The ACL entry identifies the permissions granted by this ACL entry (*insert*), the type of this entry (*GROUP*), and the tag field. In this case, the tag field contains the group UUID. You do something similar for the second entry.

Don't bother to store the group name in the ACL because clients will only use the UUIDs. (They can get the group name by calling *sec-id_gen_name.*) So set the group name to the null string.

The constants for the permission bits, e.g., *sec_acl_perm_insert*, are defined in *aclbase.idl.*

❸ Call *acl_store_write_acl* to write this ACL to the backing store. This routine returns the equivalent compact ACL. Since the compact ACL is all you'll need, this routine frees up the storage associated with the full ACL.

Default Database Entry ACL

The default database entry ACL is similar to the default database ACL. The example below shows the ACL assigned to a new database entry.

```
GROUP : emp_db_users : r
GROUP : emp_db_admin : rwc
USER : entry_name : rwc
```

This ACL allows any member of the *emp_db_users* group to read this database entry. It also gives *write* and *control* permissions to administrators and the principal named by that database entry. The last ACL entry lets an employee modify his or her own database entry and also control who can access that entry. Example 6-10 shows the implementation.

Example 6-10: Creating Default ACLs

```
/*
 * Create the default ACL for an entry in the database. It allows:
 *   1. members of the emp_db_users group read access.
 *   2. members of the emp_db_admin group read+write+control access.
 *   3. the person named in this database entry read+write+control access.
 */
static unsigned32
create_default_entry_acl (char            *db_entry_name,
                          compact_acl_t *compact_acl)

{
    sec_acl_t       acl;
    sec_acl_entry_t *acl_entry_p;
    error_status_t  status;

    /*
     * Initialize an ACL of 3 entries.
     */
    acl.num_entries = 3;
    acl.sec_acl_entries = acl_entry_p =
            (sec_acl_entry_t *) malloc (
                    acl.num_entries * sizeof(sec_acl_entry_t));

    /*
     * Fill in the default realm.
     */
    acl.default_realm.name = strdup (emp_db_cell_name);
    acl.default_realm.uuid = emp_db_cell_uuid;

    /*
     * Allow "r" access to emp_db_users group.
     */
    acl_entry_p->perms = sec_acl_perm_read;
    acl_entry_p->entry_info.entry_type = sec_acl_e_type_group;
    acl_entry_p->entry_info.tagged_union.id.uuid = emp_db_user_group_uuid;
    acl_entry_p->entry_info.tagged_union.id.name = (idl_char *) "";

    /*
     * Allow "rwc" access to emp_db_admin group.
     */
    acl_entry_p++;
    acl_entry_p->perms = sec_acl_perm_read | sec_acl_perm_write |
                        sec_acl_perm_control;
    acl_entry_p->entry_info.entry_type = sec_acl_e_type_group;
    acl_entry_p->entry_info.tagged_union.id.uuid = emp_db_admin_group_uuid;
    acl_entry_p->entry_info.tagged_union.id.name = (idl_char *) "";

    /*
     * Allow the person named in the database entry "rwc" access.
     */
    acl_entry_p++;
    acl_entry_p->perms = sec_acl_perm_read | sec_acl_perm_write |
                        sec_acl_perm_control;
    acl_entry_p->entry_info.entry_type = sec_acl_e_type_user;
    sec_rgy_pgo_name_to_id (emp_db_rgy_handle, ❶
            sec_rgy_domain_person,
```

Example 6-10: Creating Default ACLs (continued)

```
                    db_entry_name,
                    &acl_entry_p->entry_info.tagged_union.id.uuid,
                    &status);
      if (status != rpc_s_ok)
              return emp_s_unknown_name;

      acl_entry_p->entry_info.tagged_union.id.name = (idl_char *) "";

      /*
       * Write this ACL to the ACL table and backing store.
       */
      acl_store_write_acl (&acl, compact_acl);

      /*
       * Since we now have the compact_acl, we don't need the full ACL
       * any more.
       */
      free (acl.sec_acl_entries);

      return emp_s_ok;
}
```

❶ The database entry identifies the owner of the entry by name. To create an ACL entry for that principal, however, you need his or her
   UUID. You can get the UUID by calling the security registry (via
   sec_rgy_pgo_name_to_id to convert the entry name into a principal
   UUID. This application assumes that all the entry names are names of
   properly registered principals in the cell.

This concludes the implementation of our ACL storage module and the
emp_db manager code. I decided not to show the code that implements
the backing store for the employee database itself because it is really not
particularly relevant to ACL managers. If you are interested in looking at it,
however, the code is included in Appendix D.

Writing a Reference Monitor That Uses ACLs

So far, I've shown you how to write an ACL store library and how to modify the employee database application to create and destroy ACLs. Now
let's use these ACLs to make authorization checks. We'll start by looking at
the function *client_is_authorized*. This is the reference monitor that the
manager code calls to see if a client is authorized to perform the
requested operation. In Chapter 4, I've already shown you two ways to
implement this reference monitor. Now we are going to change it to use
ACLs.

In DCE 1.0, the easiest way to implement *client_is_authorized* is to call a
routine named *sec_acl_mgr_is_authorized*. This function is provided in

source form as part of the *sec_acl_mgr* API (the sample ACL manager implementation that is supplied with DCE.) *sec_acl_mgr_is_authorized* implements the code that compares a PAC against an ACL to determine if the client is allowed to perform the requested operation. You need to customize it for your purposes. The example below shows the prototype for this function.

```
boolean32 sec_acl_mgr_is_authorized (
    [in]        sec_acl_mgr_handle_t    sec_acl_mgr,
    [in]        sec_acl_permset_t       desired_access,
    [in, ref]   sec_id_pac_t            *accessor_info,
    [in]        sec_acl_key_t           sec_acl_key,
    [in, ref]   uuid_t                  *manager_type,
    [in]        sec_id_t                *user_obj,
    [in]        sec-id_t                *group_obj,
    [out]       error_status_t          *st
);
```

The first argument, *sec_acl_mgr*, is a context to the ACL manager's backing store. For implementations that use a file to store the ACLs, for example, it might hold the file descriptor. In this case, the backing store maintains the file descriptor in a static variable, so we use NULL for this argument. *desired_access* describes the set of permissions that the client needs for access to be granted. This can be, for example, *read* or *write*.

accessor_info is the client PAC. *sec_acl_mgr_is_authorized* will use it to check the client's security attributes. The server retrieves this by calling *rpc_binding_inq_auth_client*.

sec_acl_key is a piece of information that tells the reference monitor where to look up the ACL. In the case of the *emp_db* application, this will contain the database entry name if you are checking the ACL associated with a database entry and will be NULL if you are checking the ACL on the database as a whole.

manager_type is the ACL manager UUID. You can distinguish the manager you want here when you have several ACL managers protecting the same object. Since you only have a single ACL manager for each of your objects, this will also be NULL.

The last two input arguments, *user_obj* and *group_obj*, are used when your application supports USER_OBJ and GROUP_OBJ ACL entry types. They tell *sec_acl_mgr_is_authorized* which identities and groups to use when it encounters ACL entries of these types. As I mentioned earlier, they were defined for compatibility with POSIX ACLs. Since we won't support either of these ACL entry types, set them to NULL.

How *client_is_authorized* calls *sec_acl_ mgr_is_authorized* is shown in Example 6-11.

Example 6-11: client_is_authorized

```
#include <stdio.h>
#include <stdlib.h>
#include <string.h>

#include "emp_db.h"
#include "empstore.h"
#include "aclstore.h"
#include "chk_stat.h"

#include <dce/binding.h>     /* binding to registry */
#include <dce/pgo.h>         /* registry i/f */
#include <dce/secidmap.h>    /* translate global name -> princ name */

#include <dce/id_base.h>
#include <dce/daclmgr.h>

#include "ref_mon.h"


int
client_is_authorized (
        handle_t              handle,
        sec_acl_permset_t     desired_access,
        emp_db_field_t        emp_name)
{
        unsigned_char_t    *server_principal_name;
        sec_rgy_name_t     client_principal_name;
        sec_id_pac_t       *pac;
        unsigned32         protection_level;
        unsigned32         authn_svc;
        unsigned32         authz_svc;
        unsigned32         status;
        boolean32          authorized;

        /*
         * Check the authentication parameters that the client
         * selected for this call.
         */
        rpc_binding_inq_auth_client (handle,                        ❶
                (rpc_authz_handle_t *) &pac,
                &server_principal_name, &protection_level, &authn_svc,
                &authz_svc, &status);
        CHECK_STATUS (status, "inq_auth_client failed", ABORT);

        /*
         * Make sure that the caller has specified the required
         * level of protection, authentication, and authorization.
         */
        if (! ((protection_level == rpc_c_protect_level_pkt_integ) && ❷
                (authn_svc == rpc_c_authn_dce_secret) &&
                (authz_svc == rpc_c_authz_dce)))
                return 0;
```

177

Example 6-11: client_is_authorized (continued)

```
        authorized = sec_acl_mgr_is_authorized (NULL, desired_access, ❸
            pac, emp_name, NULL, NULL, NULL, &status);

    /*
     * We can get sec_acl_object_not_found if the ACL is not found.
     * This can happen since we call the reference monitor before we
     * look up the entry in the emp_db.
     */
    if ((status != rpc_s_ok) && (status != sec_acl_object_not_found))
        CHECK_STATUS (status, "sec_acl_mgr_is_authorized failed",
                        ABORT);

    return authorized;
}
```

❶ Call *rpc_binding_inq_auth_client* to get the client's PAC and authentication parameters that are selected by the client for this RPC.

❷ Check the parameters of the authenticated RPC to see if they are acceptable. You need to do it here because these parameters are not checked by *sec_acl_mgr_is_authorized*.

❸ Call *sec_acl_mgr_is_authorized* to make the access-control decision. The only arguments that to use are the desired access bits, the client PAC, and the name of the database entry that the client is trying to access.

Now we can look at how *sec_acl_mgr_is_authorized* is implemented.

Implementing sec_acl_mgr_is_authorized

The standard implementation of *sec_acl_mgr_is_authorized* does more than most ACL managers need. You will have to pick out the needed pieces. For the employee database application, you should retain the interface to this routine but eliminate the code to check for those ACL entry types that you won't support. For this application, you won't be supporting POSIX compatibility or the UNAUTHENTICATED ACL entry types.

sec_acl_mgr_is_authorized basically looks up the ACL for the object the client is attempting to access and checks the client PAC against the entries in the ACL.

Looking Up the ACL

sec_acl_mgr_is_authorized starts by retrieving the ACL associated with the object the client is trying to access. *sec_acl_mgr_is_authorized* does this by calling an application-specific routine named *sec_acl_mgr_lookup*. The *sec_acl_mgr* API defines the interface to this routine; you provide the implementation. *sec_acl_mgr_lookup* is defined as a separate routine instead of as a part of *sec_acl_mgr_is_authorized* because there are other places where you need to look up ACLs. Example 6-12 shows how the lookup call is made.

Example 6-12: Retrieving the ACL

```
boolean32
sec_acl_mgr_is_authorized (
    sec_acl_mgr_handle_t    sec_acl_mgr,
    sec_acl_permset_t       desired_access,
    sec_id_pac_t            *accessor_info,
    sec_acl_key_t           sec_acl_key,
    uuid_t                  *manager_type_p,
    sec_id_t                *user_obj,
    sec_id_t                *group_obj,
    error_status_t          *st_p)
{
    sec_acl_list_t    *sec_acl_list;
    sec_acl_t         *sec_acl_p;
    int               i;            /* For traversing entry list. */
    unsigned int      j;            /* For traversing entry list. */
    int               user_entry,   /* For keeping track of entries... */
                      foreign_user_entry,
                      other_obj_entry,
                      foreign_other_entry,
                      any_other_entry;
    sec_id_t          *group_id, *realm_id;
    error_status_t    st;
    sec_acl_permset_t granted, group_access;
    boolean32         chk_loc_groups = false, one_group_found = false;
    boolean32         acc_granted;

    /*
     * Retrieve the ACL for this key.
     */

    sec_acl_mgr_lookup(NULL, sec_acl_key, manager_type_p, ❶
                  sec_acl_type_object, &sec_acl_list, st_p);
    if (*st_p != rpc_s_ok) {
        return false;
    }
    else
        sec_acl_p = sec_acl_list->sec_acls[0];

    ... check the ACL against the PAC ...
```

❶ *sec_acl_mgr_is_authorized* calls *sec_acl_mgr_lookup* to look up the ACL it should check. The call passes the following input arguments:

sec_acl_mgr

> Context to the ACL backing store. Here, it will always be NULL since the ACL storage module maintains its own state.

sec_acl_key

> The lookup key that identifies the object whose ACL you want. For the employee database application, this will be NULL if you want the ACL for the database as a whole or the employee name if the ACL is associated with a database entry.

manager_type_p

> The UUID for the ACL manager responsible for maintaining this ACL. Since there is only a single ACL manager per object, set it to NULL.

sec_acl_type

> The type of ACL; this is useful when you are working with container objects that have default creation ACLs as well as object ACLs. There aren't any container objects in this application, so set this to *sec_acl_type_object.*

sec_acl_list

> A pointer to the results of the lookup. *sec_acl_mgr_lookup* returns a list of ACLs in the event you have more than 32 permission bits. Your list will always have one element.

As you can see, the interface to *sec_acl_mgr_lookup* is also more general than needed. Since the *sec_acl_mgr* API is internal to your ACL manager, you won't need to adhere to its interfaces. For this sample application, I've decided to preserve the interface because I want to give you an idea of what the interface allows you to do. Example 6-13 shows my implementation of *sec_acl_mgr_lookup.*

Example 6-13: Looking up an ACL

```
/*
 * Retrieve the ACL associated with the object named by sec_acl_key.
 */
void
sec_acl_mgr_lookup(
        sec_acl_mgr_handle_t    sec_acl_mgr,
        sec_acl_key_t           sec_acl_key,
        uuid_t                  *manager_type,
        sec_acl_type_t          sec_acl_type,
        sec_acl_list_t          **sec_acl_list,
        error_status_t          *st)
{
        sec_acl_t               *acl_p;
        sec_acl_list_t          *acl_list;
        unsigned                i, found;
```

Example 6-13: Looking up an ACL (continued)

```
        if ((sec_acl_key == NULL) ||                                    ❶
            (((char *)sec_acl_key)[0] == '\0')) {
            /*
             * We are looking up the ACL for the database as a whole.
             * It is stored in reserved location 0 of the emp_database[].
             */
            acl_store_read_acl (manager_type,
                            &emp_database[0].compact_acl, &acl_p);
            found = 1;
        }
        else {
            /*
             * We are looking up the ACL for a single database entry.
             */
            found = 0;
            for (i=0; i < DATABASE_SIZE; i++) {
                if (strcmp (emp_database[i].emp_record.emp_name,
                        sec_acl_key) == 0) {

                    acl_store_read_acl (manager_type, ❷
                        &emp_database[i].compact_acl, &acl_p);
                    found = 1;
                    break;
                }
            }

            if (! found) {
                *st = sec_acl_object_not_found;
                *sec_acl_list = NULL;
                return;
            }
        }
        acl_list = malloc (sizeof(sec_acl_list_t));                      ❸
        acl_list->num_acls = 1;
        acl_list->sec_acls[0] = acl_p;

        *sec_acl_list = acl_list;

        *st = rpc_s_ok;
}
```

❶ If the *sec_acl_key* (or database entry name) is NULL, the caller wants the ACL for the database. In this case, you get the compact ACL stored at location 0 in the employee database (which is reserved for this ACL), and call *acl_store_read_acl* to expand it to a full ACL.

❷ If *sec_acl_key* refers to a database entry, then look up the ACL for that entry.

❸ Set the ACL as the only element of the ACL list output argument and return.

At this point, *sec_acl_mgr_is_authorized* has the right ACL and can proceed with the access checks.

Finding Matching ACL Entries

To check an ACL, you find those entries that match the client's security attributes and then check the matching entries to see if they grant the requested access. The rules observed by ACLs require you to check the possible entries in a certain order. Let's quickly review what you're looking for: USER_OBJ, USER, and FOREIGN_USER entries are searched first, in order. The group entries (GROUP_OBJ, GROUP, and FOREIGN_GROUP entries) are then searched together. The group entries are checked together because a client is given the sum of the permissions given to all of the groups to which it belongs. Finally, check the OTHER_OBJ, FOREIGN_OTHER, and ANY_OTHER entries.

Because the entries stored in an ACL are not sorted, you may need to make multiple passes through the ACL entries to perform checks. To eliminate this overhead, first make a single pass through the ACL to find all the non-group entries that match the security attributes in the client PAC. Example 6-14 below shows the code that does this.

Example 6-14: Finding Matching ACL Entries

```
/* continuation of sec_acl_mgr_is_authorized function */

    ... lookup ACL ...



/*
 * We will check for each of the following ACL types. Only
 * one entry of each will match the client.
 */
user_entry = foreign_user_entry = other_obj_entry = ❶
foreign_other_entry = any_other_entry = ENTRY_NOT_FOUND;

/*
 * Now find each type in the ACL, if it exists. Only one entry
 * in the ACL matches each type.
 */
for (i = 0; i < sec_acl_p->num_entries; i++) {        ❷

    /*
     * Check for existence of each type of entry, and keep track
     * of where each type was found in the entry list.
     * Don't mark type as found if the associated realm id's
```

Example 6-14: Finding Matching ACL Entries (continued)

```
        * are not the same.
        */
        switch(sec_acl_p->sec_acl_entries[i].entry_info.entry_type) {

            case sec_acl_e_type_user:                          ❸
                if ((uuid_equal(&accessor_info->principal.uuid,
                                &sec_acl_p->sec_acl_entries[i].entry_info.
                                tagged_union.id.uuid,
                                &st)) && (default_realm_eq(i)))
                        user_entry = i;
                break;

            case sec_acl_e_type_foreign_user:                  ❹
                if ((uuid_equal(&accessor_info->principal.uuid,
                                &sec_acl_p->sec_acl_entries[i].entry_info.
                                tagged_union.foreign_id.id.uuid,
                                &st)) && (foreign_realm_eq(i)))
                        foreign_user_entry = i;
                break;

            case sec_acl_e_type_other_obj:                     ❺
                if (default_realm_eq(i))
                        other_obj_entry = i;
                break;

            case sec_acl_e_type_foreign_other:                 ❻
                if ( uuid_equal( &accessor_info->realm.uuid,
                        &sec_acl_p->sec_acl_entries[i].entry_info.
                        tagged_union.id.uuid, &st))
                        foreign_other_entry = i;
                break;

            case sec_acl_e_type_any_other:                     ❼
                any_other_entry = i;
                break;

            default:
                break;
        }
    }
}
```

❶ The variables *user_entry, foreign_user_entry,* etc., are used to store each matching ACL entry type's position within the ACL. For example, if you find a USER ACL entry that matches this client, you would set *user_entry* to the index of that entry. Initialize them to *ENTRY_NOT_FOUND.* (You needn't keep track of group entries because they will be handled separately.)

❷ Loop through all the entries in this ACL. For each non-group entry in the ACL, do the appropriate checks, described below.

❸ If there is a USER entry, check to see if it matches your client. You have a match if the client's UUID matches the UUID in the ACL and if the client's cell is the same as the default (local) cell specified in the ACL. This second check is done by calling the *default_realm_eq* macro (shown below).

❹ If there is a FOREIGN_USER entry, check to see if the principal and the cell matches those specified by the ACL entry. The cell UUID check is done by calling the *foreign_realm_eq* macro (shown below).

❺ If you have an OTHER_OBJ entry, check to see if the client's cell is the same as the default cell of this ACL. (OTHER_OBJ applies to everyone in the local cell.) If so, you have a match.

❻ If there is a matching FOREIGN_OTHER entry, see if the client's cell matches that specified in the ACL entry. If so, you have a match.

❼ Finally, the ANY_OTHER ACL entry, if it exists, matches everyone.

Example 6-15 shows the macros used to check the cell in the client PAC against that in the ACL.

Example 6-15: Macros for Checking the Client's Cell

```
/* Compare default realm with accessor's realm */
#define default_realm_eq(entry) uuid_equal(&accessor_info->realm.uuid, \
                                 &sec_acl_p->default_realm.uuid, \
                                 &st)

/* Compare foreign realm with accessor's realm */
#define foreign_realm_eq(entry) uuid_equal(&accessor_info->realm.uuid, \
  &sec_acl_p->sec_acl_entries[entry].entry_info.tagged_union. \
  foreign_id.realm.uuid, &st)
```

At this point, you know the position of each non-group ACL entry that matches this client's identity within the ACL. (Groups are checked in a separate pass because they are handled differently from other ACL entry types.) In any case, you can start to check the matching ACL entries.

Checking USER and FOREIGN_USER Entries

The first two entry types you need to check are the USER and FOREIGN_USER entry types. Example 6-16 belows shows the code that does this.

Example 6-16: Checking USER Entry

```
/* continuation of sec_acl_mgr_is_authorized function */

    ... lookup ACL ...

    ... find matching ACL entries ...


/*
 * USER check
 */
if (user_entry != ENTRY_NOT_FOUND) {              ❶
    /* check the permsets to see if access is granted */
    acc_granted = access_granted(sec_acl_p->sec_acl_entries[user_entry],
                        desired_access, &granted);
    acl_store_free_acl(&sec_acl_p);
    return acc_granted;
}

/*
 * FOREIGN_USER check
 */
if (foreign_user_entry != ENTRY_NOT_FOUND) { ❷
    /* check the permsets to see if access is granted */
    acc_granted = access_granted(
                        sec_acl_p->sec_acl_entries[foreign_user_entry],
                        desired_access, &granted);
    acl_store_free_acl(&sec_acl_p);
    return acc_granted;
}

    ... check GROUP entries ...

}
```

❶ If you find an USER ACL entry that matches the client's identity, then call *access_granted* to see if the permissions in that entry includes that specified by *desired_access*. Return the result of that function.

❷ If you don't find a matching USER ACL entry, see if there is a matching FOREIGN_USER ACL entry. If so, find out if the permissions in that entry include those requested.

The *access_granted* macro is shown in Example 6-17. It takes as input the ACL entry and the permissions that the client need for access to be granted (the desired permission set).

Example 6-17: access_granted Macro

```
/* access_granted
 *
 * Private routine to compare an ACL entry permset against the desired
 * access permset, to determine if access should be granted
 */

boolean32
access_granted (
    sec_acl_entry_t      entry,
    sec_acl_permset_t    desired,
    sec_acl_permset_t    *granted)
{
    boolean32 grant_access = false;

    switch (entry.entry_info.entry_type) {
        case sec_acl_e_type_any_other:
        case sec_acl_e_type_user:
        case sec_acl_e_type_group:
        case sec_acl_e_type_other_obj:
        case sec_acl_e_type_foreign_other:
        case sec_acl_e_type_foreign_user:
        case sec_acl_e_type_foreign_group:
        case sec_acl_e_type_extended:
            *granted = entry.perms & desired;  ❶
            break;

        case sec_acl_e_type_group_obj:
        case sec_acl_e_type_user_obj:
        case sec_acl_e_type_mask_obj:
        case sec_acl_e_type_unauthenticated:
        default:
            /*
             * We do not support POSIX-compatibility or the
             * UNAUTHENTICATED ACL entry types.
             */
            *granted = (sec_acl_permset_t) 0;
    }
    if ( *granted == desired )
        grant_access = true;

    return grant_access;
}
```

❶ This function does a logical AND of the desired permissions against those allowed by the matching ACL entry. If all the desired permissions are allowed, then this function returns 1; otherwise it returns 0.

Therefore, if there is a USER ACL entry that matches this client's identity, the user is granted access if all the desired permissions are allowed by the ACL entry. If there are no matching USER entries, see if there is any matching FOREIGN_USER entry. If there are no matching USER or FOREIGN_USER entries, check GROUP entries next.

The code becomes slightly more complicated if you want to support the MASK_OBJ ACL entry type. In that case, you must first mask the permissions granted by the USER entry by the permission bits in the MASK_OBJ entry before comparing them against the requested permissions. But the structure of the code would be the same.

Checking Group Entries

If you couldn't find matching USER or FOREIGN_USER entries, then we check for matching group entries. The permissions granted to a client are the sum of the permissions granted by each of the groups to which the client belongs. So you need to find all the groups to which the client belongs (i.e., all the groups named in the PAC), and OR all the permission bits together. Example 6-18 shows the code that does this.

To do the group check, make a complete pass through the ACL again. Don't try to keep track of them during the first pass because an ACL may contain a variable number of GROUP and FOREIGN_GROUP entries.

For each GROUP and FOREIGN_GROUP entry, look to see if the specified group is in the client PAC.

Example 6-18: Checking Group Entries

```
/* continuation of sec_acl_mgr_is_authorized function */


    ... lookup ACL entry ...


    ... find matching ACL entries ...


    ... USER checks ...


    ... FOREIGN_USER checks ...



/*
 * GROUP checks
 */

/*
 * Initialize mask where we will store all permissions that we find.
 */
group_access = (sec_acl_permset_t) 0;

for (i = 0; i < sec_acl_p->num_entries; i++) {

  switch(sec_acl_p->sec_acl_entries[i].entry_info.entry_type) {
```

Example 6-18: Checking Group Entries (continued)

```
case sec_acl_e_type_group:
case sec_acl_e_type_foreign_group:                    ❶

    if (sec_acl_p->sec_acl_entries[i].entry_info.entry_type
                                == sec_acl_e_type_group) {
        /*
         * The PAC has 2 group lists: one for the local groups
         * to which the client belongs and one for the foreign
         * groups to which the client belongs. Figure out which
         * one we need to search as follows:
         *
         * If the client belongs to this ACL's default (local)
         * cell, then we need to look in the PAC's list of
         * local groups for a match. Otherwise, look in the
         * PAC's foreign group list.
         */
        chk_loc_groups = default_realm_eq(i);

        /*
         * The group that we want to match is stored in the
         * ACL entry and the cell is the ACL's default cell.
         */
        group_id = &sec_acl_p->sec_acl_entries[i].entry_info.
                    tagged_union.id;
        realm_id = &sec_acl_p->default_realm;

    } else {        /* sec_acl_e_type_foreign_group */

        /*
         * If the client belongs to the same cell as that
         * specified by the ACL entry, then we need to
         * look in the PAC's local group list. Otherwise,
         * look in the PAC's foreign group list.
         */
        chk_loc_groups = foreign_realm_eq(i);
        group_id = &sec_acl_p->sec_acl_entries[i].entry_info.
                    tagged_union.foreign_id.id;
        realm_id = &sec_acl_p->sec_acl_entries[i].entry_info.
                    tagged_union.foreign_id.realm;
    }

    /*
     * Check either the PAC's list of local groups or the
     * PAC's list of foreign groups.                       ❷
     */
    if (chk_loc_groups) {

        /*
         * We are checking the PAC's local group list.
         *
         * First, check the primary group.
         */
```

Example 6-18: Checking Group Entries (continued)

```
if (uuid_equal(&accessor_info->group.uuid,
              &group_id->uuid, &st) ) { ❸
    /* then check the perms to see if access is granted */
    if (access_granted(sec_acl_p->sec_acl_entries[i],
                       desired_access, &granted)) {
        acl_store_free_acl(&sec_acl_p);
        return true;
    }
    else {                                    ❹
        one_group_found = true;
        group_access = (group_access | granted);
    }
}

/*
 * Check the secondary groups.              ❺
 */

for (j = 0; j < accessor_info->num_groups; j++) {

    if (uuid_equal(&accessor_info->groups[j].uuid,
                   &group_id->uuid, &st) ) {

        /* check the perms to see if access granted */
        if (access_granted(sec_acl_p->sec_acl_entries[i],
                           desired_access, &granted)) {
            acl_store_free_acl(&sec_acl_p);
            return true;
        }
        else {
            one_group_found = true;
            group_access = (group_access | granted);
        }
    }
}
} else {

    /*
     * We are checking the PAC's foreign group list.
     */

    for (j = 0; j < accessor_info->num_foreign_groups; j++) {

        if ((uuid_equal(&accessor_info->foreign_groups[j].id.uuid,
                        &group_id->uuid, &st)) &&
            (uuid_equal(&accessor_info->foreign_groups[j].realm.uuid,
                        &realm_id->uuid, &st)) ) {

            /* check the perms to see if access granted */
            if (access_granted(sec_acl_p->sec_acl_entries[i],
                               desired_access, &granted)) {
                acl_store_free_acl(&sec_acl_p);
                return true;
```

Example 6-18: Checking Group Entries (continued)

```
                    }
                    else {
                        one_group_found = true;
                        group_access = (group_access | granted);
                    }
                }
            }
        }
        break;

    default:
        break;
                                        ❻
    } /* switch (entry type) */

    /* See if the union of multiple group entries granted access */
    if ((group_access & desired_access) == desired_access) {
    acl_store_free_acl(&sec_acl_p);
    return true;
    }

} /* GROUP check */

/*
 * At this point, we've gone through all the groups in the PAC without
 * having granted the client access. If we've gotten a matching group
 * entry, then deny any access.              ❼
 */

if (one_group_found) {
    acl_store_free_acl(&sec_acl_p);
    return false;
}

    ... check other entries ...
```

❶ The client PAC stores all groups to which a client belongs. Each group to which the client belongs is put into one of two lists in the PAC. If the group is defined in the client's home cell, then it is put in the PAC's local group list. Otherwise, if the group is defined in a foreign cell, then it is put into the PAC's foreign group list. Since a group may be in one of two group lists in the PAC, start by figuring out which of the PAC's group lists to look at.

The cell specified by a GROUP ACL entry is the default cell of the ACL. If the client belongs to the same cell, then the cell is local to the client. This means that if the client belongs to this group, the group UUID must be in the client PAC's local group list. Otherwise, if the cell specified by the ACL entry is not the client's home cell, you need to look in the PAC's foreign group list for a match.

If you have a FOREIGN_GROUP entry, see if the client is also from the same foreign cell. If so, look for the group in the PAC's local group list. Otherwise, look in the client PAC's foreign group list.

❷ Check the PAC's local group list. The local group list actually consists of the primary group (stored in the *group* field of the PAC) and list of secondary groups (stored in the *groups* field). Check both.

A principal's primary group is set when the account is created via *rgy_edit*. For all access-control decisions, however, the primary group is treated like any other local group.

❸ If the group UUIDs match, call *access_granted* to see which permissions are granted by the ACL entry. If *access_granted* returns 1, just return 1 because the desired access is explicitly granted by an ACL.

❶ If all the requested access bits are not granted by this ACL entry, then you can save it. Use a logical OR because a client should be granted the union of all the access granted to its groups.

❺ Check the foreign group list. The logic is similar to that of ❷.

❻ Check to see if the permissions granted by this group plus the permissions granted by other matching groups are equal to those requested. If so, you can grant access. Otherwise, continue and check more group entries.

❼ At the very end, if you have found at least one group to which the client belongs and the client is still denied access, then deny access.

At this point, you have not found any matching USER or GROUP entries. (Otherwise, you would have already decided to either grant or deny access.) You should now check the various kinds of OTHER entries.

Checking the OTHER Entries

The last entries to look at are the OTHER_OBJ, FOREIGN_OTHER, and ANY_OTHER checks. Example 6-19 shows the code that does this.

Example 6-19: Checking Other Entries

```
/* continuation of sec_acl_mgr_is_authorized function */

    ... lookup ACL ...


    ... do USER checks ...


    ... do GROUP checks ...
```

Example 6-19: Checking Other Entries (continued)

```
/* OTHER_OBJ check */
if (other_obj_entry != ENTRY_NOT_FOUND) {
  /* check the permsets to see if access is granted */
  acc_granted = access_granted(
                        sec_acl_p->sec_acl_entries[other_obj_entry],
                        desired_access, &granted);
  acl_store_free_acl(&sec_acl_p);
  return acc_granted;
}

/* FOREIGN_OTHER check */
if (foreign_other_entry != ENTRY_NOT_FOUND) {
  /* check the permsets to see if access is granted */
  acc_granted = access_granted(
                        sec_acl_p->sec_acl_entries[foreign_other_entry],
                        desired_access, &granted);
  acl_store_free_acl(&sec_acl_p);
  return acc_granted;
}

/* ANY_OTHER check */
if (any_other_entry != ENTRY_NOT_FOUND) {
  /* check the permsets to see if access is granted */
  acc_granted = access_granted(
                        sec_acl_p->sec_acl_entries[any_other_entry],
                        desired_access, &granted);
  acl_store_free_acl(&sec_acl_p);
  return acc_granted;
}

/*
 * No matching ACL entries were found, deny access.
 */
acl_store_free_acl(&sec_acl_p);
return false;

}
```

As you can see, each of the checks is like the USER check. If you have a match on any of the entries, then use that to determine the access. If you don't match any entries, then fall through to the end and return false, for access denied.

With this, you have all the new code needed to convert the application to use ACLs for authorization. The server main and the client programs are the same as in Chapter 4. The only piece of code that is missing is the management interface that allows you to change the ACLs. We will create this in the next chapter.

Running the Application

I find it helpful to actually build and run the application when I reach this point. Assuming you picked reasonable defaults for all the ACLs, the application should run correctly. Building and testing the application at this point is important because it allows you to debug the application before adding the ACL management interface. The example below shows how the current version of the *emp_db* application behaves. The Makefile to build this version of the application is in Appendix D.

```
adlman 328% server &
[4] 15363
adlman 329% refresh login context thread started up
key mgmt thread started up
Server ready.                                      ❶

adlman 32% dce_login emp_db_administrator -dce-
adlman 1% client
Ready> insert
name: wei_hu
mailstop: 7L-802
phone: 4-1511
Ok
Ready> insert
name: marty_hu
mailstop: 8L-191
phone: 4-1222
Ok
Ready> query
name:wei_hu
mail stop: 7L-802, phone: 4-1511
Ready> modify
name: marty_hu
mailstop: 8L-192
phone: 4-1223
Ok
Ready> query
name:marty_hu
mail stop: 8L-192, phone: 4-1223
Ready> exit                                        ❷
adlman 2% exit
adlman 3% adlman 33% dce_login wei_hu -dce-        ❸
adlman 1% client
Ready> insert
name: kevin_hu
mailstop: 3L-123
phone: 5-8788                                       ❹
Not authorized for operation
Ready> query
name:marty_hu                                       ❺
mail stop: 8L-192, phone: 4-1223
```

```
Ready> modify
name: wei_hu
mailstop: 7L-803
phone: 4-1511                                    ❻
Ok
Ready> delete
name:marty_hu
Not authorized for operation
Ready> exit
adlman 3%
```

❶ Log in as the *emp_db_administrator* and create a few new entries, make a query, and then modify an entry. All these operations are allowed by the default ACLs. Log out.

❷ Log back in as *wei_hu*, who is a member of the *emp_db_users* group but not a member of *emp_db_admin* group.

❸ Try to create a new entry in the database. As expected, you fail because you aren't authorized for the operation. (*wei_hu* is not on the default database ACL that controls who can create new entries.)

❹ Query a database entry. This request succeeds because the *emp_db_users* group is on the default ACL for each database entry.

❺ Try to modify your own database entry. As expected, here you succeed. The default ACL on the entry allows the person named in the entry (*wei_hu* in this case) to modify the entry.

❻ Finally, try to delete someone else's database entry. As expected, the operation fails.

As you can see, the current ACL-based version of the *emp_db* application runs just like the non-ACL based version. This should not be a surprise given that the default ACLs were chosen to make this happen. You'll start seeing differences once you start changing ACLs in the next chapter.

Summary

In this chapter, I started to show you how to convert an existing application to use ACLs. We began by figuring out where ACLs would fit in and how they would be used. We then added ACLs to our application's data structures. This also involved changing the application's management routines to initialize and destroy ACLs. When we created initial ACLs, we made sure that the application would behave properly even if these ACLs were never modified after they were created.

Once we changed our application to maintain ACLs, we changed our reference monitor to check the ACLs for authorization. Our reference monitor first checks to make sure that the client's authentication parameters are acceptable and then calls the ACL evaluation routine. I then showed you how to implement the ACL evaluation routine using the source code supplied with the *sec_acl_mgr* library.

In sum, what we've done is to implement the storage and authorization components of an ACL manager. We have a complete application that uses ACLs to describe the access control policy. The only remaining piece of the ACL manager that is not yet implemented is the management component that allows us to change the application's ACLs. We will cover that topic in the next chapter.

7

Writing the Remote ACL Management Interface

In Chapter 6, we converted a sample application to use DCE ACLs. We modified the application to store ACLs and to use them for making authorization decisions. We then ran the application and demonstrated that it behaves correctly. Now, we are ready to let someone use *acl_edit* to modify our ACLs. This involves implementing the *rdaclif* RPC interface and modifying our server main program to register and export this interface in addition to the *emp_db* interface.

An ACL editor is the user interface to manage ACLs. I use *acl_edit* (and *dcecp* in DCE 1.1) in this chapter because it is part of the DCE offering. Vendors may offer more attractive alternatives. To make it easy for users to invoke *acl_edit* anywhere in the network, it accesses ACLs by making remote procedure calls. This means that the application developer should to implement all the procedures that *acl_edit* can call. All the necessary calls are well-defined by the *rdaclif* IDL and ACF files.

Before I go into the implementation, I would like to start by showing you what should happen when you run *acl_edit* on the ACL manager. (You'll be able to do this for real once we complete the changes described in this chapter.) The example below demonstrates how a user can use *acl_edit* to allow someone else access to her database entry.

```
adlman 1% dce_login irene_hu -dce-          ❶
   ...
adlman 2% acl_edit /.:/subsys/emp_db/irene_hu ❷
sec_acl_edit> l
# SEC_ACL for /.:/subsys/emp_db/irene_hu:
# Default cell = /.../adlman_cell
user:irene_hu:crw
group:emp_db_user_group:-r-
group:emp_db_admin_group:crw
```

197

```
sec_acl_edit> modify user:kevin_hu:rw        ❸
sec_acl_edit> exit
adlman 3% exit                                ❹
adlman 4% adlman 2% dce_login kevin_hu -dce-  ❺
adlman 1% client
Ready> modify                                 ❻
name: irene_hu
mailstop: 9L-9999
phone: 3-1511
Ok
Ready> query
name:irene_hu
mailstop: 9L-9999
phone: 3-1511
Ready> exit
```

❶ Log in as *irene_hu*. This principal is a member of the *emp_db_users* group but not a member of the *emp_db_administrators* group.

❷ *irene_hu* uses *acl_edit* to look at her database entry. Note how she specifies the entry as */.:/subsys/emp_db/irene_hu*. This is an example of the use of namespace junctions. The */.:/subsys/emp_db* part is interpreted by CDS, but it passes the *irene_hu* trailing part to the server. *acl_edit* now makes an RPC to the *rdacl_lookup* remote procedure of the *emp_db* server. This remote procedure returns the ACLs associated with the object.

The *list* command shows that the entry has the default ACLs for a database entry. The ACL allows administrators and *irene_hu* herself *control, read* and *write* permission. Members of the *emp_db_users* group may read the entry. The *emp_db_admin* group has all types of access. But access is denied to everyone else.

❸ Add *kevin_hu* explicitly to the ACL. We do so by creating a USER ACL entry naming *kevin_hu* and granting him *read* and *write* permissions.

❹ *acl_edit* buffers up the changes until you either enter the commit command or exit. When you exit *acl_edit*, it makes an RPC to the *rdacl_replace* remote procedure to pass back the new ACL. The ACL manager changes the ACL and then returns to *acl_edit*. *acl_edit* then returns the user to the shell.

❺ Test that this change works by logging out and logging back in as *kevin_hu*.

❻ *kevin_hu* runs the *emp_db* client program and tries to modify *irene_hu*'s entry. Since you've changed the ACL to allow this operation, it succeeds.

Let's look at the server code that makes this interaction possible.

Implementing the rdaclif Manager Code

The *rdaclif* interface is the ACL management RPC interface. This interface specifies the remote procedures that each server must implement so that *acl_edit* can manage the server's ACLs. On UNIX systems, the IDL and ACF (attribute configuration) files are *rdaclif.idl* and *rdaclif.acf* in the */usr/include/dce/* directory. The ACF file specifies that all error status codes should be returned to the client in variables as opposed to being raised as exceptions.

You can divide the remote procedures in the *rdaclif* interface into two groups. The first group of remote procedures allows *acl_edit* to look up an ACL, update an ACL, and test the access granted by an ACL:

> *rdacl_lookup*
> *rdacl_replace*
> *rdacl_get_access*
> *rdacl_test_access*
> *rdacl_test_access_on_behalf*

The second group of calls allows *acl_edit* to find out about the ACL managers that protect an object:

> *rdacl_get_manager_types*
> *rdacl_get_printstring*
> *rdacl_get_referral*
> *rdacl_get_mgr_types_semantics*

Except for a few routines that I'll point out later, your application must implement all of these entry points for *acl_edit* to work with your ACLs.

Normally, you would implement one set of these manager routines for every ACL manager that your application supports. For the employee database application, for example, you could implement one for the database ACL and one for the database entry ACL. It turns out, however, that the *rdaclif* interface allows the same manager code to support several ACL managers. That is what we'll do for our application.

We will now look at how each of these entry points is implemented for the *emp_db* application. The first one is *rdacl_lookup*.

rdacl_lookup

rdacl_lookup is the remote procedure that *acl_edit* calls to retrieve an object's ACL. This remote procedure takes a reference to an object and returns the ACLs that protect it. Example 7-1 shows our implementation of this routine.

Example 7-1: rdacl_lookup

```
/*
 * Mutex to serialize access to the database.
 */
extern pthread_mutex_t emp_db_mutex;


/*
 * Retrieve the ACL associated with the specified object.
 */
void
rdacl_lookup(
        handle_t                        binding_handle,   ❶
        sec_acl_component_name_t        component_name,   ❷
        uuid_t                          *manager_type,    ❸
        sec_acl_type_t                  sec_acl_type,     ❹
        sec_acl_result_t                *result) {        ❺

        sec_acl_list_t                  *acl_list;

        pthread_mutex_lock (&emp_db_mutex);               ❻

        /* Find the ACL using the component_name as the lookup key. */
        sec_acl_mgr_lookup(NULL,                          ❼
                (sec_acl_key_t) component_name,
                manager_type,
                sec_acl_type,   /* e.g., sec_acl_type_object. */
                &acl_list,
                &result->st);
        /*
         * Copy the ACL to stub managed heap. This routine also
         * frees acl_list.
         */
        acl_store_copy_acl_list_ss (&acl_list,            ❽
                                &result->tagged_union.sec_acl_list);

        pthread_mutex_unlock (&emp_db_mutex);             ❾
}
```

The most complicated parts of this routine are the arguments:

❶   From the perspective of the client that is calling *rdacl_lookup*, the first two arguments specify the object whose ACL you want. *binding_handle* specifies the server that is exporting the ACL manager interface. (Of course, it becomes the binding handle of the client once the call reaches the server.)

❷   *component_name* further specifies the object whose ACL you want.

   This is different from the usual RPC interface where the binding handle by itself specifies the server or object of interest. The *rdacl* routines use both a binding handle and a component name to support namespace junctions. This allows clients to use names of the form

/.:/subsys/emp_db/wei_hu where the *binding_handle* is used to connect to the ACL manager (e.g., */.:/subsys/em_db*) and *component_name* is the unresolved portion of the name (e.g., *wei_hu*) that is used by the ACL manager to look up the actual object.

The manager code should use the component name to look up the right ACL and return it in `result`. If the ACL manager does not support junctions, the component name will be NULL.

❸ The *manager_type* argument specifies the ACL manager UUID. It identifies the ACL manager that handles this call. (This UUID is returned by *rdacl_get_manager_types* and *rdacl_get_manager_types_semantics* to be described later.) This argument is provided so that you use a single set of remote procedures to support multiple ACL managers. The server code can then use the *manager_type* argument to dispatch to the right routine. You'll see an example of this when I show you *rdacl_replace*.

❹ The *sec_acl_type* argument specifies the type of ACL in which the client is interested. A simple object like a file or a printer has a single ACL (*sec_acl_type_object*). The employee database application uses only object ACLs.

A container object (such as a directory) has two additional ACLs. These are the default ACLs that are used as initial ACLs for newly created objects, which allows a newly created file, for example, to automatically inherit the default ACLs from its parent directory. The **default object creation** ACL (*sec_acl_type_default_object*) is the default ACL that is assigned to each simple object that is created within this container (e.g., creating a file in a directory). The **default container creation** ACL (*sec_acl_type_default_container*) is the default ACL given to newly created container objects (e.g., creating a directory in a directory).

❺ Return the output in `result`. The *sec_acl_result_t* structure allows the lookup routine to return an ACL list because there may be multiple ACLs. Since we have one ACL manager, *sec_acl_mgr_lookup* returns a list of one ACL.

❻ The lookup routine starts by locking the *emp_db_mutex*. You need to use a mutex because the ACL table can be accessed by multiple threads at the same time. For example, one client could be looking up an ACL while another is trying to update the same ACL. You must therefore make sure to lock the mutex before accessing the ACL table.

❼ After locking the mutex, call *sec_acl_mgr_lookup* to get the ACL. We implemented this routine in Chapter 6 as part of the reference monitor. Our implementation of *sec_acl_mgr_lookup* uses the *component_name* as the employee name. If *component_name* is not NULL, then *sec_acl_mgr_lookup* returns the ACL associated with that database entry. Otherwise, *sec_acl_mgr_lookup* returns the ACL for the database as a whole.

❽ The ACL list returned by *sec_acl_mgr_lookup* is allocated from heap memory. If you returned it directly to the server stub code, the memory would never be freed. You should call *acl_store_copy_acl_list_ss* to copy the list to stub-managed memory. This allows the RPC runtime to automatically free this memory after the output arguments have been transmitted to the client. (An alternative is to pass an allocator function argument to *sec_acl_mgr_lookup*.)

❾ Unlock the mutex and return to the server stub code.

acl_store_copy_acl_list_ss copies a list of ACLs into a second ACL list whose memory is allocated from stub-managed memory. The code is shown in Example 7-2.

Example 7-2: Copying the ACL List to Stub Managed Memory

```
/*
 * Copy an ACL list to stub allocated storage. The original ACL list
 * is then freed.
 */
extern void
acl_store_copy_acl_list_ss (sec_acl_list_t **IO_src,     /* IN/OUT */
                            sec_acl_list_t **O_dst)      /* OUT */
{
        sec_acl_list_t  *src, *dst;
        unsigned        num_acls, i;
        sec_acl_p_t     acl_p;

        src = *IO_src;
        if (src == NULL) {
                *O_dst = NULL;
                return;
        }

        num_acls = src->num_acls;

        /*
         * Allocate the list header.
         */
        dst = (sec_acl_list_t *)rpc_ss_allocate (
                        sizeof(sec_acl_list_t) +
                        (num_acls - 1)*sizeof(sec_acl_p_t));
        dst->num_acls = num_acls;

        /*
         * Allocate and copy the ACL entries. acl_store_copy_acl also frees
         * the source ACLs.
         */
        for (i=0; i < num_acls; i++) {
```

Example 7-2: Copying the ACL List to Stub Managed Memory (continued)

```
                        acl_store_copy_acl (&src->sec_acls[i],
                                        &dst->sec_acls[i]);
        }

        /*
         * Free the source ACL list.
         */
        free (src);
        *IO_src = NULL;

        *O_dst = dst;
}


/*
 * Copy an ACL to stub allocated storage. The source ACL is freed.
 */
static void
acl_store_copy_acl (sec_acl_t **IO_src_acl,               /* IN/OUT */
                    sec_acl_t **O_dst_acl)                /* OUT */
{
        sec_acl_t       *src_acl, *dst_acl;
        unsigned        num_entries;

        src_acl = *IO_src_acl;

        if (src_acl == NULL) {
                *O_dst_acl = NULL;
                return;
        }

        num_entries = src_acl->num_entries;

        /*
         * Allocate the fixed part of the ACL header.
         */
        dst_acl = (sec_acl_p_t) rpc_ss_allocate (sizeof(sec_acl_t));
        memcpy (dst_acl, src_acl, sizeof(sec_acl_t));

        /*
         * Allocate the ACL entries.
         */
        dst_acl->sec_acl_entries =
                (sec_acl_entry_t *) rpc_ss_allocate (
                        num_entries * sizeof(sec_acl_entry_t));

        memcpy (dst_acl->sec_acl_entries, src_acl->sec_acl_entries,
                num_entries * sizeof(sec_acl_entry_t));

        acl_store_free_acl (IO_src_acl);
        *O_dst_acl = dst_acl;
}
```

This is it for the lookup operation. Let's look at how the update routine is implemented.

rdacl_replace

When you use the *acl_edit* modify or substitute command to replace an ACL, *acl_edit* makes an RPC to the ACL manager's *rdacl_replace* entry point. This call passes in the new ACLs in *sec_acl_list*. The client supplies a single-entry *sec_acl_list* if it wants to replace the ACL on a simple object. The client supplies multiple ACLs (object ACL plus the default creation ACLs) if it is replacing the ACLs on a container object (which you don't have to do). Example 7-3 shows the resulting code.

Example 7-3: rdacl_replace

```
/*
 * Our ACL manager type UUIDs.
 */
extern uuid_t    emp_db_acl_mgr_uuid;                                    ❶
extern uuid_t    emp_db_entry_acl_mgr_uuid;

/*
 * Replace an ACL.
 *
 * ACLs are immutable.  To modify an ACL, an application must read
 * the ACL and then replace it.
 */
void
rdacl_replace(
     handle_t                        binding_handle,
     sec_acl_component_name_t        component_name,
     uuid_t                          *manager_type,
     sec_acl_type_t                  sec_acl_type,
     sec_acl_list_t                  *sec_acl_list,
     error_status_t                  *st) {

     int           i;
     boolean32     found;

     pthread_mutex_lock (&emp_db_mutex);

     if (uuid_equal(&emp_db_acl_mgr_uuid, manager_type, st)) {          ❷
          /*
           * The ACL for the database is stored in reserved
           * location 0 in the emp_db table.
           */
          i = 0;
     }
     else if (uuid_equal(&emp_db_entry_acl_mgr_uuid, manager_type, st)) { ❸

          /*
           * We've got to look for the entry.
```

Example 7-3: rdacl_replace (continued)

```
            */
            found = false;

            for (i=1; i < DATABASE_SIZE; i++) {
                    if (strcmp (emp_database[i].emp_record.emp_name,
                               component_name) == 0) {
                           found = true;
                           break;
                    }
            }

            if (! found) {
                    *st = sec_acl_object_not_found;
                    pthread_mutex_unlock (&emp_db_mutex);
                    return;
            }
    }
    else {
            *st = sec_acl_unknown_manager_type;

            pthread_mutex_unlock (&emp_db_mutex);
            return;
    }

    /*
     * The caller must have control permission to replace an ACL.
     */
```

❹
```
    if (! client_is_authorized(binding_handle, OP_CONTROL, component_name)){

            *st = sec_acl_not_authorized;

            pthread_mutex_unlock (&emp_db_mutex);
            return;
    }

    /*
     * Delete the existing ACL & write the new one back.
     */
```
❺
```
    acl_store_delete_acl (&emp_database[i].compact_acl);
```
❻
```
    acl_store_write_acl (sec_acl_list->sec_acls[0],
                        &emp_database[i].compact_acl);

    pthread_mutex_unlock (&emp_db_mutex);

    *st = rpc_s_ok;
}
```

The code for *rdacl_replace* is a good example of how a single remote procedure can support multiple ACL managers.

❶ For this application, the two ACL managers are identified by the routines *emp_db_acl_mgr_uuid* and *emp_db_entry_acl_mgr_uuid*, which were initialized in *emp_mgr_init.*

❷ Start by looking up the current ACL. To do this, you need to know whether the client wants the database ACL or one of the database entry ACLs. Since these ACLs are managed by different ACL managers, first check the *manager_type.* If the *manager_type* is that of the database ACL, then we get the ACL from the reserved location (index 0) in *emp_database.*

❸ If you are working with one of the database entry ACLs, search *emp_database* using *component_name* as a key. In any case, you wind up with the index of the entry that contains the ACL you want to replace.

❹ Before allowing a client to replace an ACL, check that he or she is authorized to perform the operation. After all, ACLs are not secure if anyone can change them. For a client to modify an ACL, the ACL must grant the him or her *control* permission. We check this by calling *client_is_authorized.* This is the same reference monitor code that the *emp_db* manager code used in Chapter 6. *client_is_authorized* checks the authenticated RPC parameters to make sure that they are acceptable and then calls *sec_acl_mgr_is_authorized* to see if the ACL grants the client the requested permission.

❺ If the client is authorized to replace the ACL, delete the current ACL.

❻ Write the new ACL back.

This routine then releases the mutex and returns.

rdacl_get_access

When you issue the *get_access* command from *acl_edit*, it makes an RPC to the ACL manager's *rdacl_get_access* routine. This routine looks up the ACL and returns the permissions that would be granted to the client that is running *acl_edit.* The results are returned in the *net_rights* argument.

As you might expect, the code that goes through an ACL to look for matching entries is similar to *sec_acl_mgr_is_authorized.* The difference is that *sec_acl_mgr_is_authorized* returns a boolean value (authorized or not) after finding a matching ACL entry. You need to get the actual permission bits; the *sec_acl_mgr* API defines a routine, *sec_acl_mgr_get_access*, that does this. Because the *sec_acl* API did not include a sample implementation of this routine, you must write your own. I wrote this version by modifying *sec_acl_mgr_get_access.* Example 7-4 shows the implementation of *rdacl_test_access.*

Example 7-4: rdacl_get_access

```
/*
 * Determine's the caller's access to the specified object.
 */
void
rdacl_get_access(
        handle_t                          binding_handle,
        sec_acl_component_name_t          component_name,
        uuid_t                            *manager_type,
        sec_acl_permset_t                 *net_rights,
        error_status_t                    *st) {

        unsigned_char_t      *server_principal_name;
        sec_rgy_name_t       client_principal_name;
        sec_id_pac_t         *pac;
        unsigned32           protection_level;
        unsigned32           authn_svc;
        unsigned32           authz_svc;
        unsigned32           status;

        /*
         * Get the client PAC.
         */
        rpc_binding_inq_auth_client (binding_handle,
                (rpc_authz_handle_t *) &pac,
                &server_principal_name, &protection_level, &authn_svc,
                &authz_svc, &status);
        CHECK_STATUS (status, "rdacl_get_access/inq_auth_client failed",
                      ABORT);

•       sec_acl_mgr_get_access (NULL, pac, component_name, manager_type,
                                NULL, NULL, net_rights, st);
}
```

As you can see, *rdacl_get_access* just gets the client PAC and then calls *sec_acl_mgr_get_access* to do the work. The results are returned in *net_rights*.

sec_acl_mgr_get_access is the same as *sec_acl_mgr_check_access* except that you return the permissions that are granted by an ACL instead of comparing them against a permission set. Because the code is so similar, I'll just show an example of how the code differs. The full implementation is available in Appendix D. Example 7-5 shows how the USER ACL entry type is processed by the two routines.

Example 7-5: Processing the USER ACL Entry

```
boolean32
sec_acl_mgr_is_authorized (
      sec_acl_mgr_handle_t     sec_acl_mgr,
      sec_acl_permset_t        desired_access,
      sec_id_pac_t             *accessor_info,
```

Example 7-5: Processing the USER ACL Entry (continued)

```
        sec_acl_key_t            sec_acl_key,
        uuid_t                   *manager_type_p,
        sec_id_t                 *user_obj,
        sec_id_t                 *group_obj,
        error_status_t           *st_p)
{
    ...


    if (user_entry != ENTRY_NOT_FOUND) {
        /* check the permsets to see if access is granted */
        acc_granted = access_granted(sec_acl_p->sec_acl_entries[user_entry], ❶
                            desired_access, &granted);
        acl_store_free_acl(&sec_acl_p);
        return acc_granted;
    }
    ...


}


/*
 * Determine the client's access to the specified object.
 */
void
sec_acl_mgr_get_access (
    sec_acl_mgr_handle_t    sec_acl_mgr,
    sec_id_pac_t            *accessor_info,
    sec_acl_key_t           sec_acl_key,
    uuid_t                  *manager_type_p,                          •
    sec_id_t                *user_obj,
    sec_id_t                *group_obj,
    sec_acl_permset_t       *net_rights,
    error_status_t          *st_p)
{
    ...


    /* USER check */
    if (user_entry != ENTRY_NOT_FOUND) {
        *net_rights = access_granted_by_entry(                       ❷
                sec_acl_p->sec_acl_entries[user_entry]);
        acl_store_free_acl(&sec_acl_p);
        return;
    }
    ...


}
```

❶ *sec_acl_mgr_is_authorized* checks each entry to see whether the requested access is granted by a matching ACL entry and then returns either true or false. The *access_granted* macro does a logical AND of the permissions specified by the ACL entry and those in *desired_access*.

❷ The corresponding statement in *sec_acl_mgr_get_access* returns the permissions specified by the matching ACL entry.

rdacl_test_access

When you issue the *test_access* command from *acl_edit*, it makes an RPC to the ACL manager's *rdacl_test_access* routine. This remote procedure allows a client, the person running *acl_edit* in this case, to check whether he or she has the permissions specified by *desired_permset* to an object. *rdacl_test_access* answers questions of the form, "Does *wei_hu* have write access to this entry?" It allows the client to see what the reference monitor would do when presented with this type of request from the client.

rdacl_test_access should get the client's PAC and compare it against the object's ACL. If all the permission bits specified in *desired_permset* are set, return true; otherwise, return false. Example 7-6 shows how this routine is implemented.

Example 7-6: rdacl_test_access

```
/*
 * See if the caller has the requested access to the object.
 *
 * See if the ACL contains entries grating privileges to the
 * calling process matching those in desired_permset.
 */
boolean32
rdacl_test_access(
    handle_t                    binding_handle,
    sec_acl_component_name_t    component_name,
    uuid_t                      *manager_type,
    sec_acl_permset_t           desired_permset,
    error_status_t              *st) {

    boolean32       is_authorized;

    if (! uuid_equal(&emp_db_acl_mgr_uuid, manager_type, st) &&
        ! uuid_equal(&emp_db_entry_acl_mgr_uuid, manager_type, st)) {
        *st = sec_acl_unknown_manager_type;
        return false;
    }

    pthread_mutex_lock (&emp_db_mutex);

    is_authorized = client_is_authorized (binding_handle, desired_permset,
```

Example 7-6: rdacl_test_access (continued)

```
                component_name);

    pthread_mutex_unlock (&emp_db_mutex);

    *st = rpc_s_ok;
    return is_authorized;
}
```

For the employee database application, this routine is implemented simply as a call to the reference monitor, *client_is_authorized*.

rdacl_test_access_on_behalf

This remote procedure allows a client to find out whether someone else is permitted to access an object. *rdacl_test_access_on_behalf* determines whether the principal named by subject has the permissions specified in *desired_permset* to an object. This allows, for example, *irene_hu* to test whether *kevin_hu* has read access to an object. This routine returns **true** if both the named principal and the caller have the requested access. Example 7-7 shows how to implement this entry point.

Example 7-7: rdacl_test_access_on_behalf

```
/*
 * Determines whether a particular principal has the requested
 * access.  This routine returns true if both the principal and
 * the caller have the requested access to the object.
 */
boolean32
rdacl_test_access_on_behalf(
    handle_t                    binding_handle,
    sec_acl_component_name_t    component_name,
    uuid_t                      *manager_type,
    sec_id_pac_t                *subject,
    sec_acl_permset_t           desired_permset,
    error_status_t              *st) {

    boolean32      is_authorized;

    if (! uuid_equal(&emp_db_acl_mgr_uuid, manager_type, st) &&
        ! uuid_equal(&emp_db_entry_acl_mgr_uuid, manager_type, st)) {
        *st = sec_acl_unknown_manager_type;
        return false;
    }

    pthread_mutex_lock (&emp_db_mutex);

    is_authorized = client_is_authorized (binding_handle, desired_permset, ❶
                                        component_name)
```

Example 7-7: rdacl_test_access_on_behalf (continued)

```
                    &&
                    sec_acl_mgr_is_authorized (NULL, desired_permset,          ❷
                        subject,
                        (sec_acl_key_t) component_name,
                        manager_type,
                        NULL, NULL, st);

    pthread_mutex_unlock (&emp_db_mutex);

    *st = rpc_s_ok;

    return is_authorized;
}
```

❶ Check to see if the client (the principal that is running *acl_edit*) has the right access to the object by calling *client_is_authorized*. This routine also checks the authentication parameters of the RPC.

❷ If the client has the right access to the object, check to see if the principal specified by *subject* has the right access to the object. *subject* is the PAC of the client whose access you want to test. The *desired_permset* argument is a set of permission bits that the client wants to test.

If both checks succeed, return true. Otherwise, we return false.

Note that *acl_edit* currently does not support a *test_on_behalf* command. You can, however, easily implement one.

acl_edit is written to be independent of any particular ACL managers. Everything that *acl_edit* needs to know about your ACL manager is obtained through *rdacl* calls. The next group of manager routines returns various configuration information that *acl_edit* needs. This includes the manager UUIDs, how to print the permission bits, where to go to update an ACL, and which POSIX semantics are supported.

rdacl_get_manager_types

acl_edit calls this remote procedure to find out which ACL managers protect an object. This routine should return the UUIDs of all the ACL managers that support an object. Like most applications, the employee database supports a single ACL manager per object.

The last statement may be a bit confusing. I said earlier that we support two ACL managers. The distinction is that the ACL managers are associated with two different objects—the database and the database entry. Each of these objects have only a single ACL manager. Example 7-8 shows the implementation of *rdacl_get_manager_types*.

Example 7-8: rdacl_get_manager_types

```
/*
 * Return the types of ACLs protecting an object.
 * An ACL manager may put several different ACLs on the same object
 * and use each in a different manner.
 * Each such ACL type would be identified by a different type UUID.
 */
void
rdacl_get_manager_types(
        handle_t                    binding_handle,
        sec_acl_component_name_t    component_name,
        sec_acl_type_t              sec_acl_type,
        unsigned32                  size_avail,
        unsigned32                  *size_used,
        unsigned32                  *num_types,
        uuid_t                      manager_types[],
        error_status_t              *st) {

        *num_types = 1;                                               ❶
        if (size_avail < 1) {                                        ❷
                *size_used = 0;
        }
        else {
                *size_used = 1;
                if (component_name[0] == '\0')
                        manager_types[0] = emp_db_acl_mgr_uuid;       ❸
                else
                        manager_types[0] = emp_db_entry_acl_mgr_uuid; ❹
        }
        *st = rpc_s_ok;
}
```

The caller allocates *size_avail* entries in *manager_types*, and this routine sets the actual number used in *size_used*. The ACL manager UUIDs are then stored in the *manager_types* output argument. The code works as follows:

❶ Set *num_types* to the number of ACL managers that protects this object, 1.

❷ Check to see if the client has allocated enough space in *manager_types*. If so, continue.

❸ If the *component_name* is the null string, the object the client is binding to is the *emp_db* server itself, e.g., */.:/subsys/emp_db*. In this case, return the UUID of the ACL manager for the database as a whole.

❹ Otherwise, if there is a component name, then the client is binding to an entry in the database, e.g., */.:/subsys/emp_db/wei_hu*. In this case, we return the UUID of the ACL manager for the database entry.

Note that you don't need to use a mutex in this call because the configuration information that this routine reads does not change after the server starts up.

rdacl_get_manager_types_semantics

acl_edit calls this remote procedure to get a list of all the ACL managers that are protecting an object. This calls also lets the caller know which POSIX ACL semantics are supported by each ACL manager. As you can see in Example 7-9 below, it is similar to *rdacl_get_mgr_types*.

Example 7-9: rdacl_get_mgr_types_semantics

```
void
rdacl_get_mgr_types_semantics(
        handle_t                        binding_handle,
        sec_acl_component_name_t        component_name,
        sec_acl_type_t                  sec_acl_type,
        unsigned32                      size_avail,
        unsigned32                      *size_used,
        unsigned32                      *num_types,
        uuid_t                          manager_types[],
        sec_acl_posix_semantics_t       posix_semantics[],
        error_status_t                  *st) {

        *num_types = 1;

        if (size_avail < 1) {
                *size_used = 0;
        }
        else {
                *size_used = 1;
                if (component_name[0] == '\0')
                        manager_types[0] = emp_db_acl_mgr_uuid;
                else
                        manager_types[0] = emp_db_entry_acl_mgr_uuid;

                posix_semantics[0] = sec_acl_posix_no_semantics;
        }

        *st = rpc_s_ok;
}
```

The manager types information is returned as before in *manager_types*. In addition, the POSIX semantics that are supported by each ACL manager is returned in the output array, *posix_semantics*. At present, the only values defined are none and support for the POSIX mask object.

This manager routine was defined late in DCE 1.0. Hence, it is not documented in most DCE documentation. However, you must implement it because *acl_edit* calls it.

rdacl_get_printstring

acl_edit needs to know what permissions you have defined in your ACL manager, and how they should be printed. This lets it specify the permissions during a query or change. The call that returns this information to *acl_edit* is *rdacl_get_printstring*. In addition to the permission strings, this routine also returns a string description of the ACL manager itself.

All the output strings are returned in *sec_acl_printstring_t* structures. Example 7-10 shows how these structures are initialized for your ACL managers.

Example 7-10: Printstrings for the Employee Database ACL Manager

```
static sec_acl_printstring_t emp_db_printstrings[] = {           ❶
        { "c",  "control",  sec_acl_perm_control   },
        { "i",  "write",    sec_acl_perm_insert    }
};

static sec_acl_printstring_t emp_db_entry_printstrings[] = {  ❷
        { "c",  "control",  sec_acl_perm_control   },
        { "r",  "read",     sec_acl_perm_read      },
        { "w",  "write",    sec_acl_perm_write     }
};

static sec_acl_printstring_t emp_db_info = {                      ❸
        "emp_db", "emp_db Application.",
        (sec_acl_perm_control | sec_acl_perm_insert )
};

static sec_acl_printstring_t emp_db_entry_info = {               ❹
        "emp_db (entry)", "emp_db Application (entry).",
        (sec_acl_perm_control | sec_acl_perm_read | sec_acl_perm_write )
};
```

❶ Initialize printstrings for each ACL manager.

   emp_db_printstrings shows the printstrings for the ACL manager for the database as a whole. The first entry says that character *c* maps to the *control* permission; the bit representation is *sec_acl_perm_control* (0x00000008).

❷ *emp_db_entry_printstrings* contains the printstrings for the ACL manager that manages the ACL on each database entry. It contains an entry for each of the permissions that are supported for each database entry's ACL.

❸ *emp_db_info* is the manager information printstring for the employee database ACL manager. It states that the ACL manager name is *emp_db*, the help text is *emp_db Application*, and that this ACL manager supports the *control* and *insert* permissions.

❹ *emp_db_entry_info* is the manager information printstring for the employee database entry ACL manager.

Example 7-11 shows how these printstrings are returned to the client.

Example 7-11: rdacl_get_printstring

```
void
rdacl_get_printstring(
        handle_t                binding_handle,              ❶
        uuid_t                  *manager_type,
        unsigned32              size_avail,
        uuid_t                  *manager_type_chain,
        sec_acl_printstring_t   *manager_info,
        boolean32               *tokenize,
        unsigned32              *total_num_printstrings,
        unsigned32              *size_used,
        sec_acl_printstring_t   printstrings[],
        error_status_t          *st) {

        sec_acl_printstring_t   *printstring;
        int                     i, num_printstrings;

        if (uuid_equal(&emp_db_acl_mgr_uuid, manager_type, st)) { ❷
                printstring = emp_db_printstrings;
                num_printstrings = 2;
                *manager_info = emp_db_info;
        }
        else if (uuid_equal(&emp_db_entry_acl_mgr_uuid, manager_type, st)) {
                printstring = emp_db_entry_printstrings;
                num_printstrings = 3;
                *manager_info = emp_db_entry_info;
        }
        else {
                *st = sec_acl_unknown_manager_type;
                return;
        }

        *total_num_printstrings = num_printstrings;
        if (size_avail < num_printstrings)                   ❸
                *size_used = size_avail;
        else
                *size_used = num_printstrings;


        /*
         * This is the only ACL manager for this object.
         */
        uuid_create_nil (manager_type_chain, st);            ❹

        /*
         * Returned permission printstrings are unambiguous and
         * therefore they do not need to be separated when printed.
         */
```

Example 7-11: rdacl_get_printstring (continued)

```
        *tokenize = false;                                  ❺
        for (i=0; i < *size_used; i++)
                printstrings[i] = printstring[i];           ❻

        *st = rpc_s_ok;
}
```

Let's begin begin by looking at the arguments:

❶ You have the usual *binding_handle* and *manager_type* arguments that specify the ACL manager whose information you want. In this case, however, you don't need a component name since the objects this ACL manager is protecting aren't important; the ACL manager itself is.

The *size_avail* argument tells the server how much space is allocated by the client for the output.

The *manager_type_chain* output argument is used when a server uses multiple ACL managers to support more than 32 permission bits. In this case, *manager_type_chain* is the UUID of the ACL manager that supports the next 32 permission bits. (Note that the DCE 1.0 *acl_edit* ignores this argument; it therefore does not support more than 32 permission bits.)

The *manager_info* output argument provides a string description for the ACL manager itself.

The *tokenize* output argument tells the client (i.e., *acl_edit*) whether the print representations of the permission bits need to be separated when printed. If all the print representations are unambiguous (e.g., *r, w, d, t*), then they do not need to be separated and can be printed together (e.g., *rwdt*). Otherwise, they are ambiguous and must be separated when printed out.

The output, *printstrings*, is an array of strings, one per permission bit supported by this ACL manager. *total_num_printstrings* and *size_used*, which are the output arguments, tell the client the number of printstrings supported by the ACL manager and the number returned in the output array. *size_used* can be less than *total_num_printstrings* if the client did not allocate enough storage.

❷ Start by using the *manager_type* to select a ACL manager. Set the permissions printstring and the ACL manager information printstrings.

❸ Check *size_avail* to see how much space the client has allocated in the printstring arrays so that they do not exceed the size available.

❹ xEach of our objects has only a single ACL manager, so we set the *manager_type_chain* to the nil UUID to signify that there is no next ACL manager.

❺ The printstrings are unique and therefore do not need to be separated when printed. *acl_edit* can, for example, print *"rwc"* instead of *"r w c"* when it encounters an ACL entry with all three permissions.

❻ We copy the permission printstrings to the output argument and return.

rdacl_get_referral

rdacl_get_referral returns the binding information for the ACL manager that can update an ACL. *acl_edit* uses this call when it is working with a replicated service where every server can read a database and only a single server (the master replica) can write the database. An example of this is the DCE security registry where updates must take place at the master replica but reads can be done at any security server.

When a secondary server receives a request to update an ACL (e.g., a call to *rdacl_replace*), it should return the status code *sec_acl_site_readonly*. When *acl_edit* gets this status code, it calls *rdacl_get_referral* at the same server to get the binding information for the master replica. *acl_edit* then binds to the master replica and repeats the update operation.

Since the *emp_db* application is not replicated, this capability is not supported. Example 7-12 shows how this routine is implemented.

Example 7-12: rdacl_get_referral

```
/*
 * Return a referral to an update site.  This is only required when
 * we support read-only replicas.
 */
void
rdacl_get_referral(

        handle_t                    binding_handle,
        sec_acl_component_name_t    component_name,
        uuid_t                      *manager_type,
        sec_acl_type_t              sec_acl_type,
        sec_acl_tower_set_t         *towers,
        error_status_t              *st) {

        *st = sec_acl_not_implemented;
}
```

The *towers* output argument is the set of RPC bindings to the master server. A tower is the data structure CDS uses to store RPC binding information.

If your service is replicated, each of your secondary servers should store a copy of the address of the master replica. A secondary server would then obtain a binding to the master server when it starts up. The master server binding information can be stored in a configuration file or in the name service. As you would expect, the binding to the master server should contain the *rdaclif* interface UUID and the object UUID that your ACL manager exports. Once you have the binding, you would convert it into a tower set using *rpc_tower_vector_from_binding*. This is all done when a secondary server starts up.

Once this is done, *rdacl_get_referral* need only copy the tower set into stub-managed storage (via *rpc_ss_allocate*) and return the result.

With this, we've completed our implementation of the *rdaclif* manager code. All we have to do now is change the server *main* program to register and export this interface.

Registering the Interface

The *rdaclif* interface is just like any other RPC interface. Your server main program needs to register this additional interface with the RPC runtime, register it with the endpoint mapper, and export it into the namespace. Example 7-13 shows how to do this.

Example 7-13: Modify Server main to Export the rdaclif Interface

```
extern uuid_t    emp_db_acl_mgr_uuid;
extern uuid_t    emp_db_entry_acl_mgr_uuid;

int
main(
        int                      argc,
        char                     *argv[])
{
    ...


        rpc_binding_vector_t          *bind_vector_p;
        uuid_vector_t                 *obj_uuids;

        /* Establish our own identity */

        establish_identity (&status);
        CHECK_STATUS (status, "cannot establish identity", ABORT);

        /* Initialize local state. */
        emp_db_init();

        /*
         * Register authentication info with RPC.
         */
```

Example 7-13: Modify Server main to Export the rdaclif Interface (continued)

```
rpc_server_register_auth_info(SERVER_PRINC_NAME,
    rpc_c_authn_dce_secret, NULL /*default key retrieval function*/,
    KEYTAB, &status);
CHECK_STATUS (status,"server_register_auth_info failed",ABORT);

/* Register interface with rpc runtime. */

rpc_server_register_if(emp_db_v1_0_s_ifspec, NULL, NULL, &status);
CHECK_STATUS (status,"unable to register emp_db i/f",ABORT);


/* Register the ACL manager interface. */

rpc_server_register_if(rdaclif_v0_0_s_ifspec, NULL, NULL, &status); ❶
CHECK_STATUS (status,"unable to register rdacl i/f",ABORT);

/* We want to use all supported protocol sequences. */

rpc_server_use_all_protseqs(rpc_c_protseq_max_reqs_default, &status);
CHECK_STATUS (status,"use_all_protseqs failed",ABORT);

/* Get our bindings. */

rpc_server_inq_bindings(&bind_vector_p, &status);
CHECK_STATUS (status,"server_inq_bindings failed",ABORT);

/* Register binding information with the endpoint map. */

rpc_ep_register(emp_db_v1_0_s_ifspec, bind_vector_p,
    NULL,
    (unsigned_char_t *)"Employee database server, version 1.0",
    &status);
CHECK_STATUS (status,"ep_register failed",ABORT);

/*
 * Register an object UUID with our manager code.
 */
obj_uuids = (uuid_vector_t *) malloc (sizeof(uuid_vector_t));   ❷
obj_uuids->count = 1;
obj_uuids->uuid[0] = &emp_db_acl_mgr_uuid;
rpc_ep_register(rdaclif_v0_0_s_ifspec,                          ❸
                bind_vector_p,
                obj_uuids,
                "emp_db ACL manager, version 1.0",
                &status);
CHECK_STATUS (status,"ep_register failed",ABORT);

/*
 * Export binding information into the namespace.
 */
rpc_ns_binding_export(rpc_c_ns_syntax_dce, "/.:/subsys/emp_db",
    emp_db_v1_0_s_ifspec, bind_vector_p,
    NULL, &status);
```

Example 7-13: Modify Server main to Export the rdaclif Interface (continued)

```
        CHECK_STATUS (status,"export failed",ABORT);

        /*
         * Export the emp_db ACL manager interfaces.
         */
        rpc_ns_binding_export(rpc_c_ns_syntax_dce, "/.:/subsys/emp_db",     ❹
                rdaclif_v0_0_s_ifspec, bind_vector_p,
                obj_uuids, &status);
        CHECK_STATUS (status, "export failed", ABORT);

        /* Listen for remote calls. */
        fprintf(stderr, "Server ready.\n");
        rpc_server_listen(rpc_c_listen_max_calls_default, &status);        ❺
        CHECK_STATUS (status,"server_listen failed",ABORT);

        /* We don't expect to return from the listen loop. */
        fprintf(stderr, "Unexpected return from rpc_server_listen");
        exit(1);
}
```

❶ Register the ACL management interface along with the *emp_db* inter-
    face. This tells the RPC runtime that this server process will service
    remote calls to both the *emp_db* and the *rdaclif* interfaces.

❷ As I discussed in Chapter 5, you need to include an object UUID in
    the server's bindings so that the endpoint mapper can dispatch incom-
    ing RPCs to our server's *rdaclif* interface when there are multiple
    servers that export the same interface. You could create a separate
    UUID for this purpose, but since the ACL manager UUIDs are already
    handy, just use one of them as the object UUID.

❸ Register this interface and object UUID with the endpoint mapper
    database on the local machine.

❹ Export the binding (along with the object UUID) to the namespace.

❺ As soon as you call *rpc_server_listen*, you can start accepting RPCs on
    both the *emp_db* and the *rdaclif* interfaces.

With these modifications to the server main program, I've shown you all
the code you need. What's left is to compile and link all the modules
together. (Appendix D shows the Makefile that I used to build this application.) We will run this version of our application shortly. But before I
show you how to work with our ACL managers, I thought I'd review how
acl_edit will use the data structures that we've set up in the namespace
and the endpoint map.

ACL Manager Configuration

Our server main program exported the *rdaclif* and *emp_db* interfaces into the namespace entry */.:/subsys/emp_db*. In addition, we also exported an object UUID with the *rdaclif* interface. We did the same thing with the endpoint mapper. Let's see how *acl_edit* uses this to get to the right ACL manager.

The following happens when you use *acl_edit* to list the ACL associated with the object at */.:/subsys/emp_db*:

1. *acl_edit* does an import of the *rdaclif* interface from the CDS entry named */.:/subsys/emp_db*. It gets back a partial binding that specifies the host address of the *emp_db* server. In addition, the binding also contains the object UUID that you exported: it happens to be one of your ACL manager UUIDs. Since the name is fully resolved in the CDS namespace, the component name for the rest of the *rdaclif* calls will be the null string.

2. *acl_edit* now makes an *rdacl_get_mgr_types_semantics* call with the binding obtained in step 1. Since the partial binding contains the host address, the call is dispatched to the right host. At that point, the endpoint mapper (*rpcd*) looks up the *rdaclif* interface and the object UUID in its database to resolve the partial binding. The object UUID would distinguish among servers, if several exported the same *rdaclif* interface. The endpoint mapper adds the server's port number to the binding, making it a fully resolved binding.

3. Since the RPC runtime now has a fully resolved binding, it can forward the call to the *emp_db* server. The RPC runtime dispatches the call to the *rdacl_get_mgr_types_semantics* entry point. Note that at this point, *acl_edit* still does not know what the ACL manager UUIDs are. (Remember, there are two different ACL manager UUIDs.)

4. *rdacl_get_mgr_types_semantics* looks at the entry name and determines that *acl_edit* wants the ACL manager associated with the database as a whole. So it copies the *emp_db_acl_mgr_uuid* into the output argument, *manager_types*. This routine then returns to its caller, the server stub. The server stub transmits the manager type information back to *acl_edit*.

5. Now, finally, *acl_edit* knows the binding and the UUID of the ACL manager that is protecting this object.

6. *acl_edit* calls *rdacl_get_printstring* to get the list of permissions supported by this ACL manager and their printstring representations. As part of the call, it passes in the ACL manager UUID that it obtained from step 5. *rdacl_get_printstring* uses the ACL manager UUID to select the right data to return.

7. *acl_edit* now calls *rdacl_lookup*, which returns the ACL, and *acl_edit* displays it.

As you can see, there was really nothing special about the object UUID that was exported into the namespace and registered with the endpoint mapper. I used one of the ACL manager UUIDs because it was readily available. But I could have used another UUID. All that matters is that no one else exports the *rdaclif* interface with it.

I hope that this gives you a better idea of how the information we put into the namespace and the endpoint map helps *acl_edit* figure out how to reach the right ACL manager. The example also shows how the first call to *rdacl_get_mgr_types_semantics* helps *acl_edit* find the rest of the *rdacl* calls exported by this ACL manager.

With this out of the way, it is time try out our ACL management interface.

Using acl_edit to Manage Our ACLs

At the start of this chapter, I showed you how we can use *acl_edit* to interact with our ACL manager. In that example, I demonstrated the *acl_edit list* and *modify* commands. You should be able to rerun those operations and satisfy yourself that they work.

Example 7-14 shows how some of the other *acl_edit* commands work with your ACLs. This time, you're working with your other ACL manager—the one for the ACL on the database as a whole.

Example 7-14: Using Other acl_edit Commands with emp_db

```
adlman 19% dce_login emp_db_administrator -dce-
adlman 1% acl_edit /.:/subsys/emp_db          ❶
sec_acl_edit> list                            ❷

# SEC_ACL for /.:/subsys/emp_db:
# Default cell = /.../adlman_cell
group:emp_db_user_group:-i
group:emp_db_admin_group:ci
sec_acl_edit> ?
Known commands are:
        ab[ort]        as[sign_file]  d[elete]      ce[ll]
        co[mmit]       g[et_access]   e[xit]        h[elp]
        k[ill_entries] l[ist]         m[odify]      pe[rmissions]
        pu[rge]        sec_acl_entry  su[bstitute]  t[est_access]
        ?
sec_acl_edit> get_access                      ❸
Granted permissions: ci
sec_acl_edit> delete group:emp_db_user_group ❹
sec_acl_edit> list

# SEC_ACL for /.:/subsys/emp_db:
# Default cell = /.../adlman_cell
```

Example 7-14: Using Other acl_edit Commands with emp_db (continued)

```
group:emp_db_admin_group:ci
sec_acl_edit> commit                            ❺
sec_acl_edit> permissions                       ❻
Token   Description
c       control
i       write
sec_acl_edit> test c                            ❼
Access: GRANTED
sec_acl_edit> test w                            ❽
ERROR: SEC_ACL_EDIT - invalid permission string (dce / sad)
sec_acl_edit> modify user:irene_hu:i            ❾
sec_acl_edit> list

# SEC_ACL for /.:/subsys/emp_db:
# Default cell = /.../adlman_cell
user:irene_hu:-i
group:emp_db_admin_group:ci
sec_acl_edit> exit
adlman 2%
```

❶ Log in as the administrator and run *acl_edit* on the *emp_db* database.

❷ List the current ACL. The output shows that you still have the default ACL that was created with the database. It allows members of the *emp_db_users* group *insert* permission and administrators *insert* and *control* permissions.

❸ Test the *get_access* command. It causes *acl_edit* to make an RPC to our *rdacl_get_access* entry point and returns the results. It correctly shows that the administrator has *control* and *insert* permissions.

❹ Delete an ACL entry.

❺ Commit the changes. This causes all of changes to be sent to the remote ACL manager. *acl_edit* will also do this automatically when you exit the program.

❻ Test the *permissions* command. As expected, it shows the supported permissions along with their helpstrings.

❼ Test whether you have the *control* permission: you do.

❽ Test whether you have the *write* permission. As expected, we fail. This is not one of the permissions defined by this ACL manager.

❾ Add an explicit USER ACL entry for *irene_hu* and exit.

As you can see, *acl_edit* works with your ACL manager.

Summary

With this chapter, we've completed the final version of our sample application. The server program now establishes its own identity and uses authenticated RPC for communications. For authorization, our server uses DCE ACLs. Since we added support for the remote ACL management interface, we can use *acl_edit* to configure our ACLs. The client application has remained basically unchanged through all this. It still uses authenticated RPC and checks to make sure that the server is valid by testing its group membership.

Let us now review the complete series of steps for creating a secure DCE application:

1. Design your application with security in mind. Define a security policy and make space for ACLs in your data structures.

2. Write and debug the application without using security.

3. Change your client and server programs to use authenticated RPC. For the client, this involves annotating the binding handle. For the server, it involves making the server a standalone principal and writing a simple reference monitor. You should configure DCE Security for your application at this point.

4. Add ACLs to your application. Create them whenever an object is created and destroy them as the underlying objects are destroyed. Change your reference monitor to check ACLs.

5. Add the *rdaclif* management interface.

You should also build and test your application at the conclusion of each step, as I have done in this book.

There is a lot of work involved. However, I want to emphasize that much of the code is common across applications. For example, the server main program and the *rdaclif* manager code are fairly consistent across applications. Experienced DCE programmers learn to identify blocks of code that are standard and reuse them across applications. They then focus their energies upon those pieces that are unique to their application. I hope that our sample application has given you an idea of what some of these common pieces are.

The ACL manager implemented here is compatible with DCE 1.1. This is because DCE 1.0 ACL managers are upward-compatible. DCE 1.1 provides an ACL manager library that can simplify how you develop your application. However, this does not affect existing implementations because the API does not affect interoperability. I will discuss the DCE 1.1 ACL manager library along with the other DCE 1.1 security enhancements in the next chapter.

8
DCE 1.1 Security Enhancements

Everything we discussed earlier in this book works with DCE 1.0. At the end of 1994 OSF completed a new release, DCE 1.1. In this chapter, I will briefly describe the major security enhancements that are in this release.

Delegation
> A facility that allows a server to act on behalf of a client when calling another server. The final server can reliably determine the identities of the originating client as well as that of the intermediate server(s).

Generic Security Service API
> A subroutine library that allows non-RPC applications to use DCE authentication and authorization.

ACL Library
> A subroutine library that simplifies the task of writing an ACL manager.

Audit API
> A subroutine library that allows an application to record security-relevant activity.

In addition to describing these new features, I will also touch upon some of the administrative enhancements. Not discussed in this chapter are the other security features of DCE 1.1 (such as hierarchical transitive trust, pre-authentication, password management, login denial, and extended login.)

I would like to start by reassuring you that what we've learned so far is still valid. Because DCE 1.0 applications will run unchanged in a DCE 1.1 environment, applications you develop using the calls and techniques presented in this book will work for DCE 1.1. (You need to use DCE 1.1 calls only if you wish to access the new features.) Clearly, you can take the easy way out and just use the DCE 1.0 APIs. This allows your applications to run in both DCE 1.0 and DCE 1.1 environments. But you can improve your applications by using the DCE 1.1 features. Let us now look at what you get with DCE 1.1.

Delegation

In my opinion, **delegation** is the most significant security enhancement in DCE 1.1. It means that one principal allows another principal to act on its behalf while accessing some service. For delegation to work securely, the final server must be able to determine who the original and the intermediate principals are.

The simplest form of delegation involves three parties: a *client* (or *initiator*), an *intermediary* (or *delegate*), and a *target server.* There can actually be a string of intermediaries; that's a more general case. The client makes an RPC to server 1, the intermediary, to request some service. This intermediary then makes another RPC call to server 2, the target server, to complete its remote operation. The intermediary therefore acts as both a client and a server. The final server returns the results to the intermediary, which then returns its results to the client.

Network printing is an example that is frequently used to explain why we need delegation. Let's assume that you want to implement a print server that accepts requests over the network. Figure 8-1 shows the configuration.

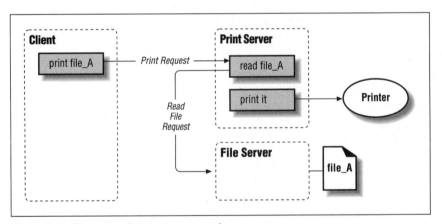

Figure 8-1: The network printing example

A user runs the print client program (e.g., in a UNIX environment, *lp*). The print client program sends a print request with the name of the file (not the file contents) to the print server. When the print server receives the request, it first retrieves the file by issuing a request to a file server. The file server responds by sending the file to the print server, which then prints it.

Now let's look at the security issues. The general problem is that there are now more links in the trust chain, and a chain is only as strong (secure) as its weakest link.

Assume that the client, but not the print server, is authorized to read the file. Unfortunately, since the print server is the one asking for the file, its principal is the one that needs read access. Under DCE 1.0, there is no secure way to grant this *print server acting on behalf of client* access.

The crudest solution would be to give the print server read access to every file. That would allow anyone to print anybody else's file. In effect, everybody would have access to each other's electronic mail, and sensitive corporate documents would become public.

Another workaround would be for the print server to authenticate the client and pass the client's PAC to the file server. The file server could then check the ACL and decide whether the client is authorized to read the file. The trouble with this solution is that the file server has to trust the print server. If someone managed to masquerade as the print server (or otherwise subvert the print server software), they could claim to be printing a file on some client's behalf, when in fact that client never sent a request. The file server would have to expose a file it shouldn't have.

In a small environment, it might be reasonable to make the print server a trusted process. However, in a complex environment where you have multiple servers, it's not feasible to trust all servers. (Remember, in DCE, even the CDS servers are not trusted.) In our example, the file server should not blindly allow a print server to access a client's file unless the client has explicitly authorized the file server to do so, and this chain of permission is what delegation gives you.

Delegation solves the security problem by allowing the client to pass a special delegation credential to the print server. This credential, issued by the security server, certifies that the print server is acting on behalf of the original client. The print server then passes this credential to the file server whenever it accesses a file on behalf of the client. At the file server, the reference monitor:

1. Extracts the identity of the original client and the print server delegate from the credential.

2. Verifies that the client has authorized the print server to act on its behalf.

3. Uses the two sets of security attributes to determine if the read access to the file should be granted or denied.

This is a good solution because it allows you to centralize the access control checks in one place, the file server, where the files are actually managed.

For chain to work, the credential that is passed needs to be unforgeable. Otherwise, an intermediary can pretend to be acting on someone's behalf and gets access to data that the intermediary is not supposed to get. Delegation solves this problem by making the delegation credential part of the security attributes that are exchanged as part of the authentication protocol described in Chapter 2.

Another issue that arises in delegation is controlling the extent to which a client's security attributes are propagated. As I've described it so far, any server that a client calls can assume the client's identity in making further calls. This is usually OK because the objects are protected by ACLs anyway. There are cases, however, when a client may wish to restrict whether a server can act on its behalf to make further calls. The client may also wish to allow an intermediary to assume only some of its security attributes. DCE 1.1 supports this by allowing a client to specify which principals may act on its behalf, which of the client's security attributes to delegate, which target servers can be delegated to, and even whether delegation is allowed at all.

Impersonation is a special, degenerate, form of delegation. It allows an intermediary to assume the identity of the original client in such a way that the target server cannot distinguish between the intermediary and the original client. When an intermediary is impersonating a client, any server that the intermediary calls will think that it is being called directly by the client. Impersonation is conceptually simpler than regular delegation, but less secure because there is no way for you to find out what's wrong if the intermediary is compromised.

With this background out of the way, let's look at how DCE implements delegation. There are two parts to this. First, you need some way to carry the delegation information in the security attributes that are passed to a server. In DCE, this is done through the PAC. Once you've passed the delegation information to the server, the server needs some way to determine whether the delegated access should be granted. This is done through ACLs. Let's look at each in turn.

PAC Extensions to Support Delegation

To support delegation, you must keep track of the security attributes of all the intermediaries a call goes through before it reaches the server. DCE 1.1 stores this information in the client PAC. There is no provision for it in the DCE 1.0 PAC; it had room for only the client's security attributes. So DCE 1.1 uses a new PAC format called an **Extended Privilege Attribute Certificate** (EPAC) or Version 2 PAC. (DCE 1.0 uses Version 1 PACs.) To allow Version 1.0 servers to work, DCE 1.1 clients can also pass a Version 1 PAC.

When a client starts an RPC, an EPAC is created. This EPAC is passed to the intermediate server. The intermediate server extracts the client EPAC as part of its routine authentication. It then tells DCE Security that it wants to act on behalf of the client named in the EPAC. The security server authenticates the intermediary and issues a new EPAC. This EPAC contains both the original client's security attributes and the security attributes of the intermediary. The intermediary then passes this EPAC to next server that it calls.

The next server, if it is also an intermediary, continues the process. It obtains a new EPAC that contains its security attributes in addition to those of the original client and any earlier intermediaries in the call chain. The EPAC is then passed to the next server in the call chain. Eventually, the call gets forwarded to the final server.

The final server receives the RPC and extracts the EPAC from the client binding handle. At this point, the EPAC contains the security attributes of the original client as well as that of each of the intermediaries that forwarded this call. This gives the server all it needs to make its authorization decisions.

ACL Changes to Support Delegation

The EPAC allows a server to get the security attributes of all the principals in a call chain. The target server uses this information to decide whether a given call is authorized. To give accurate information to the server you need a way to specify and check the types of access granted to a principal that is acting on behalf of another principal. In particular, we need to distinguish between the access granted to a principal that is acting on its own behalf (i.e., as an initiator) and the access granted when it is acting on behalf of someone else (i.e., as an intermediary). This is done by extending the ACL facility.

DCE 1.1 adds nine new ACL entry types that relate to delegation.

USER_DELEGATE
FOREIGN_USER_DELEGATE
GROUP_DELEGATE
FOREIGN_GROUP_DELEGATE
OTHER_OBJ_DELEGATE
FOREIGN_OTHER_DELEGATE
ANY_OTHER_DELEGATE
USER_OBJ_DELEGATE
GROUP_OBJ_DELEGATE

For an object to be accessed through intermediaries, its ACL must grant access not only to the initiating client but also to all intermediaries. In our example, a reasonable way to set the ACL on *file_A* would be like that shown in Figure 8-2.

This ACL says that Martin is allowed to read and write this document unconditionally. Furthermore, the print server is allowed to read this document, but only when it is acting as a delegate on behalf of a user who is allowed to read the document.

In this case, the *USER_DELEGATE* entry permits access only if all these conditions are met:

- The *print_server* principal has read access.

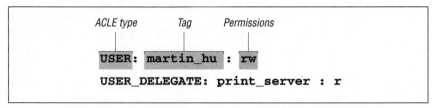

Figure 8-2: Example of USER_DELEGATE entry type

- The client who invoked the print server has read access.

- The client matches the *USER* entry in the ACL.

The reference monitor (*sec_acl_mgr_is_authorized*) checks the initiating client and each of the intermediaries against the ACL and grant access only if they are all authorized for the requested operation.

As you might expect, most of the work in supporting these new ACL entry types lies with the server's reference monitor. In particular, the *sec_acl_mgr_is_authorized* and the *sec_acl_mgr_get_access* routines have been enhanced to take account of these new entries. Let's now program delegation in an application.

Using Delegation

To apply delegation to the network printing example, you need to add calls to the client (the print client program), the intermediary (the print server), and the final server (the file server). Figure 8-3 shows the calls that the print client and the print server need to make.

Print client program

❶ The client starts by calling *sec_login_become_initiator* to allow its identity to be delegated. This call creates a new login context. This call also allows you to place restrictions on how your identity is delegated to the print server.

❷ The client obtains a binding to the print server as usual and then annotates the binding handle with its new (delegatable) login context via *rpc_binding_set_auth_info*.

❸ The client makes the RPC to the print server. This causes the underlying RPC runtime to obtain a delegatable EPAC from the Security Service and pass it to the print server.

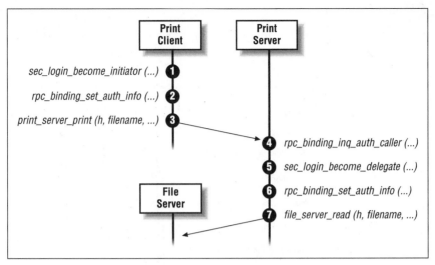

Figure 8-3: Structure of network printing application, part 1

Print server program

❹ When the print server receives the print request, it must first get the client's security attributes. In DCE 1.0, this is done by calling *rpc_binding_inq _auth_client*. This call, however, does not return delegation information. The 1.1 server instead calls a new entry point, *rpc_binding_inq_auth_caller*, to get the EPAC information.

❺ Once the print server gets the client's EPAC, it becomes an intermediary acting on the client's behalf. This is done by calling *sec_login_become_delegate*. This call returns a login context that contains the right delegation information (e.g., print server acting on behalf of principal that is running the print client). Like *sec_login_become_initiator*, *sec_login_become_delegate* allows the caller to restrict how much further the delegated identity itself may be delegated. In any case, the print server can now act on behalf of the client.

❻ The print server now needs to call the file server to read the file. Like any client, it starts by establishing an RPC binding to the file server and annotating it for security (via *rpc_binding_set_auth_info*). The binding handle now contains the security attributes in the modified login context, which includes delegation information.

❼ The print server then uses the binding handle in its RPC to the file server. Because the binding handle contains delegation information, the call passes an EPAC that contains the security attributes of the original client and of the print server.

File server

Figure 8-4 shows how the file server processes the read request from the print server.

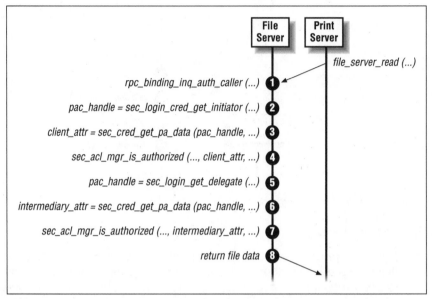

Figure 8-4: Structure of network printing application, part 2

The file server receives the RPC from the print server. It needs to see if this call is authorized, so it calls the reference monitor. The reference monitor does the following:

❶ Calls *rpc_binding_inq_auth_caller* to get the print server's EPAC.

❷ Calls *sec_login_cred_get_initiator* to get a handle to the original client's EPAC.

❸ Calls *sec_cred_get_pa_data* to retrieve the security attributes from that EPAC. Now you have the attributes of the original client: the principal that is running the print client program.

❹ Checks the original client's security attributes against the ACL to look for the entry types USER, GROUP, and so on. If the client is not authorized, you should reject the call. If the check succeeds, check the intermediaries.

❺ Retrieves the security attributes of each intermediary. Start by getting a handle via *sec_login_cred_get_delegate*.

❻ You then get the actual attributes from the EPAC handle by calling *sec_cred_pa_data.*

❼ Checks the intermediary's security attributes against the ACL to look for the new entry types USER_DELEGATE, GROUP_DELEGATE, and so on. If the intermediary is not authorized to act as a delegate (or as an initiator), the call is rejected.

❽ If the intermediary is authorized, process the call and return the data to the caller.

The file server returns the data to the print server. The print server prints the file and then returns control to the original requestor.

I expect delegation to become more important as time goes on. Delegation is needed only when you have nested RPCs to different services. Delegation was not so important during the early days of DCE because there were few services to start with and most servers tended to be fairly simple. As DCE matures and we more services become available, however, you will start to see the equivalent of a distributed runtime library of RPC services. At that point, most RPC servers will be implemented in terms of other services so that when a client calls a server, the server will most likely need to call other servers to complete the requested operation. Delegation will be a significant factor in making this possible.

Generic Security Service API (GSSAPI)

As you have seen, DCE Security is very powerful. It's based on a robust security model embodying encryption and Kerberos authentication. A lot of applications outside of DCE could use this kind of authentication and authorization, for instance, traditional distributed UNIX applications like *rlogin, rsh,* and *sendmail.* It would be really nice, for example, if the r-tools could automatically acquire and send across a ticket for authentication as this would eliminate the need for special files or re-entering passwords.

In theory, you could create secure applications by rewriting them to use DCE RPC. However, that is a pretty major change that makes the application inoperable with non-DCE implementations. A better approach is to incorporate the security message exchange as an extension to the existing protocol. This way, the security module is involved only when you are communicating with a client or server that uses the same security mechanisms. At other times, you would still communicate using the old protocol; the GSSAPI is the link between the old and new ways of communicating.

The GSSAPI Application Model

The GSSAPI allows the client and server programs to request authentication and authorization services from an underlying security service. The API is defined to be independent of the underlying security and communications mechanisms. The interface allows a client to acquire tickets and session keys, for example. The client can then transmit the credentials using any available communications mechanisms (e.g., sockets, streams, or even RPC itself). Once the credentials are received by the server, the server calls into the GSSAPI to verify the credentials and thereby authenticate the client. In effect, the GSSAPI exposes all the internal security calls that are necessary for you to implement your own authenticated communications. One could even reimplement DCE RPC itself to use the GSSAPI.

The GSSAPI assumes that a distributed application goes through four phases in its use of security services:

Establishes global identity
> The client and server processes establish their own global identities and acquire whatever credentials they need to authenticate themselves to other processes. In DCE, this corresponds to a user running *dce_login* or a server establishing its identity.

Establishes a shared security context
> During this phase, the client and server exchange security credentials so that they know each other's authenticated identities. They also pass along whatever information needed to further utilize available security services. For DCE applications, this shared security context contains the authenticated identities of the client and server principals, and a shared session key.

Transfers data
> This is where the client and server programs are actively using the security context to pass data to each other. GSSAPI allows programs to request per-message services that provide integrity and privacy protection to the application data. This corresponds to the integrity and privacy protections offered by DCE RPC.

Destroys the security context
> This is the cleanup phase where the client and server free whatever data structures are allocated.

DCE-izing the GSSAPI

The GSSAPI was originally defined within the Internet Engineering Task Force (IETF) as a means for adding security services to existing Internet protocols. (It is described in Internet RFCs 1508 and 1509.) As you can see from the description, the GSSAPI assumes a very general model of how an application may use security services, which is what makes it possible to implement the GSSAPI over many different security services.

It turns out, however, that the GSSAPI alone is not sufficient for an application to take full advantage of the capabilities of DCE Security because the GSSAPI treats the shared security context as an opaque data structure. DCE authorization requires the server to extract the client EPAC from the security context. In addition, DCE allows clients to select their security attributes (and corresponding credentials) by using alternate login contexts. DCE 1.1 therefore includes some GSSAPI extensions. You can distinguish between the base and extension calls by their prefix. The base GSSAPI entry points start with *gss_* while the DCE extensions start with the prefix *gssdce_*.

Using the GSSAPI

Let us assume that we want to write a client and server program that uses some non-RPC-based transport (e.g., sockets). Figure 8-5 shows what the application needs to do to use DCE authentication and authorization via the GSSAPI.

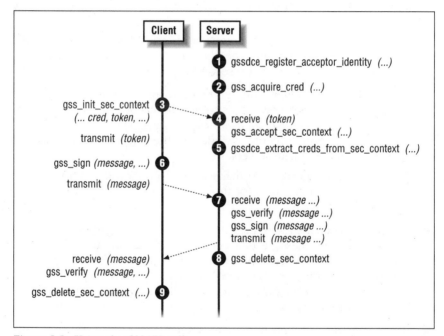

Figure 8-5: Using the GSSAPI calls

❶ The server starts by calling *gssdce_register_acceptor_identity*. This call tells the DCE runtime the location of the server's keytab file. If this call is not made, then DCE will use the systemwide default keytab file in */krb5/srvtab*. You should not do so (unless you are doing systems programming) as this would require the server to run as *root*.

❷ The server calls *gss_acquire_cred*. The call establishes a default GSS-API credential (or server identity) for the server. This, together with the call to *gssdce_register_acceptor_identity*, corresponds to the server-side *rpc_server_register_auth_info* call in DCE.

❸ The client establishes a shared security context with the server. It does so by calling *gss_init_sec_context*. *gss_init_sec_context* returns a security token that the client should pass to the server. In DCE, this is a service ticket encrypted with the secret key of the server. The client then transmits the security token to the server.

❹ The server receives the message from the client and retrieves the security token. The server calls *gss_accept_sec_context* to decode the token. In DCE, this is where the server decrypts the ticket to verify the client's identity and get a copy of the session key.

In the DCE implementation of the GSSAPI, *gss_accept_sec_context* generates an output security token. The server must transmit this token back to the client. The client can then verify this token to authenticate the server. (I have omitted this message exchange in Figure 8-5 for clarity.)

After calls to *gss_init_sec_context* and *gss_accept_sec_context*, the client and server establishes the shared security context. In DCE, this means that they have a shared secret key.

❺ At this point, the client and server have authenticated each other's identities. The server now needs to get the client EPAC. It does so by calling *gssdce_extract_cred_from_sec_context*. This call returns an EPAC containing the security attributes of the original client as well as that of any intermediate servers.

The server uses the EPAC to make its authorization decisions. Assuming the client is authorized for this operation, you now enter the data transfer phase.

❻ The client generates a request message and calls *gss_seal*. This call produces a new message that contains a checksum and the original message (optionally encrypted). This is equivalent to selecting the *pkt_level_integrity* or *pkt_level_privacy* options when calling *rpc_binding_set_auth_info*. In any case, the client gets a message and transmits it to the server.

❼ The server receives the request message. The server calls *gss_unseal* to unpack the message. If the message is integrity protected, this call verifies the checksum to make sure nothing has tampered with or corrupted the message. If the message is privacy protected, it is decrypted.

The server gets the request message, processes it, and generates some output. The server then uses *gss_seal* to protect the message and sends it back to the client. This message exchange between client and server continues until they are done. It is now time to destroy the security context.

❽ The server calls *gss_delete_sec_context* and destroys its half of the security context.

❾ The client also calls *gss_delete_sec_context*.

As you can see, the GSSAPI takes a different approach from authenticated RPC. Authenticated RPC integrates security with communications. The GSS-API explicitly separates out the security mechanisms and relies upon the user application to transfer all the security and encrypted data to its peer.

ACL Library

In Chapter 6, I showed you how to write an application that uses ACLs. We started by creating an ACL storage library and changing the *emp_db* manager code to create, destroy, and check ACLs. We then implemented a reference monitor that uses ACLs and the *rdacl_if* management interface. In the process, we had to write a routine to look up an ACL (*sec_acl_mgr_lookup*) and customize the ACL evaluation routine (*sec_acl_mgr_is_authorized*).

Much of this code can be reused in other ACL managers. In particular, you can reuse the ACL storage library, the *rdacl_if* manager code, and much of our *sec_acl_mgr* routines. To build a new ACL manager using these pieces, you need to:

1. Provide an implementation of *sec_acl_mgr_lookup* so that both the reference monitor and the *rdacl_if* routines can look up your ACLs. This is required because each application names objects and stores ACLs differently.

2. Write the server manager code to create and delete ACLs whenever objects are created and destroyed.

3. Have each of the server's remote procedures call the ACL-based reference monitor to see if the client is authorized to perform the requested operation.

4. Customize the *rdacl_if* entry points by generating a new ACL manager UUID (returned by the *rdacl_get_manager_types_semantics* call) and a set of printstrings that describe your ACL manager and permission bits (these are the constants returned by *rdacl_get_printstring*.)

5. Modify the server main routine to initialize the code and export the interfaces.

As you can see, the amount of ACL manager code you need to write from scratch is fairly small. Most of the code that goes into an ACL manager does not change. DCE 1.1 formalized this by putting the common code into an ACL library for applications to use.

What the ACL Library Provides

The DCE ACL library provides the code that is common across ACL managers. The library includes:

- Functions for storing ACLs in files. (These are in a separate library.)

- Functions to create ACLs. These can be used, for example, to create initial ACLs for newly created objects.

- Routines to get and check the permissions that an ACL grants to a client. These can be used by the reference monitor and some of the *rdacl_if* code.

- An implementation of the *rdacl_if* manager code. This provides the remote management interface to your ACL manager.

Let's take a look at each of these pieces.

Backing store library

The DCE backing store library provides a general facility for storing objects in flat files. You have to determine what format the objects should have in memory, and what format it should have on disk. For instance, in our employee database program you need a full DCE ACL data structure in memory, and a compact format that eliminates redundant fields on the disk.

When you use the backing store library, you need to provide a conversion routine that changes objects to and from the on-disk representation. The library handles the mechanics of storing and retrieving objects. It invokes your conversion routines whenever you ask it to find or store an ACL. In DCE 1.1, you can use the IDL encoding services to automatically generate these conversion routines from an IDL file.

Each object that is stored in a backing store (database) is identified by a unique query key. The query key is a lookup key in the database sense, not a cryptographic key in the security sense. This key can be either a text string or a UUID. The backing store library allows an application to retrieve an entry by using its key or step through all the entries in a database. If you were writing the employee database application to use the backing store library, it would provide the portion of the *ACL_store* and *emp_store* routines that deal with storing objects on disk. The employee database application uses a text string (the employee name) as the lookup key.

I am not going to describe the use of the backing store library in depth because it is fairly straightforward. The backing store library provides an easy way for your applications to store ACLs in persistent storage. The routines are:

dce_db_open
dce_db_close
dce_db_free

dce_db_fetch
dce_db_fetch_by_name
dce_db_fetch_by_uuid
dce_db_store
dce_db_store_by_name
dce_db_store_by_uuid

dce_db_lock
dce_db_unlock

dce_db_iter_start
dce_db_iter_next
dce_db_iter_next_by_name
dce_db_iter_next_by_uuid
dce_db_iter_done

dce_db_inq_count
dce_db_delete
dce_db_delete_by_name
dce_db_delete_by_uuid
dce_db_header_fetch
dce_db_std_header_init

Because the backing store library is designed for storing coarse-grained objects, it is most appropriate when your application uses a small number of ACLs. You should consider a customized backing store if your application has lots of ACLs In any case, the backing store library is definitely a good way to get an application up and running quickly.

Creating ACLs

In the *emp_db* manager code, we call *create_default_db_acl* and *create_default_entry_acl* to create default ACLs whenever a new database or database entry is created. These routines allocate the ACL data structure from heap and then explicitly set all the fields. The DCE ACL library provides a similar set of routines that create and destroy ACLs. They are listed below.

> *dce_acl_obj_init*
> *dce_acl_obj_free_entries*
> *dce_acl_obj_add_user_entry*
> *dce_acl_obj_add_group_entry*
> *dce_acl_obj_add_id_entry*
> *dce_acl_obj_add_unauth_entry*
> *dce_acl_obj_add_any_other_entry*
> *dce_acl_obj_add_obj_entry*
> *dce_acl_obj_add_foreign_entry*
> *dce_acl_copy_acl*

To create an ACL, you would first call *dce_acl_obj_init* and then call the appropriate *dce_acl_obj_add_* routines to add each ACL entry.

Checking an ACL

The third set of routines in the ACL library checks and retrieves the permissions granted by an ACL. They form the core of an application's reference monitor. The prototype for *dce_acl_is_client_authorized* is shown below. This routine checks an ACL to see if the client has the right permissions.

```
void
dce_acl_is_client_authorized (
        handle_t             binding_handle,  ❶
        uuid_t               acl,             ❷
        sec_acl_permset_t    desired_perms,   ❸
        boolean32*authorized,                 ❹
        error_status_t   *st);
```

❶ *binding_handle* identifies the client. It will be used to extract the client EPAC.

❷ *acl* is the UUID of the ACL that we want to check. (The DCE backing store library uses UUIDs as the primary lookup key for objects.)

❸ *desired_perms* contains the permissions that the client is requesting.

❹ *authorized* is the return value of this function. It indicates whether all the requested permissions are granted by the specified ACL.

As you can see, this routine is a variation of *sec_acl_mgr_is_authorized*.

Testing whether a client is authorized is only one of the operations you need. You also need equivalent routines that return the permissions that a client has to an object and so forth. The list below details these permissions.

dce_acl_inq_client_permset
> Returns the set of permissions a client has to an object. It is the equivalent of *sec_acl_mgr_get_access*.

dce_acl_inq_client_creds

Returns the client's EPAC, which is the equivalent of issuing *rpc_binding_inq_auth_caller. dce_acl_inq_client_creds* is better than *rpc_binding_inq_auth_caller* because in the case where the client is unauthenticated, the call doesn't return an error but instead returns dummy creds, which means that all your other functions don't need to special-case that condition.

dce_acl_inq_permset_for_creds

The lowest-level function of the library; all other routines call it. Servers that have their own *rdacl_if* implementation and data storage can use this routine for uniform ACL semantics.

dce_acl_is_unauthenticated

Tells the caller whether the client is unauthenticated. It is used to evaluate the UNAUTHENTICATED ACL entry type.

dce_acl_inq_prin_and_group

Useful for servers with objects that have the concept of an owner (e.g., files).

rdacl_if manager

The last part of the ACL library is an implementation of the *rdacl_if* manager that *acl_edit* calls. The ACL library, for example, supplies entry points for *rdacl_lookup, rdacl_get_manager_types_semantics*, and so forth.

As you might expect, however, you cannot use the exact same implementation of the *rdacl_if* routines for every ACL manager. Some aspects of the manager code are specific to individual ACL managers. Each ACL manager has a different manager type UUID, provides different printstrings, and looks up ACLs differently. The employee database ACL manager, for example, had to supply its own version of *sec_acl_mgr_lookup*. DCE 1.0 solved this problem by supplying a sample ACL manager in source code format so that application developers can customize it for their needs. DCE 1.1 improved upon this by moving all the application-specific information into a single initialization routine. The example below shows the prototype for *dce_acl_register_object_type*. This is the only call you need to make to customize the ACL library's implementation of the *rdacl_if* routines.

```
void
dce_acl_register_object_type (
        dce_db_handle_t        db,                    ❶
        uuid_t                 *manager_type,         ❷
        unsigned32             printstring_size,      ❸
        sec_acl_printstring_t  *printstring,          ❹
        sec_acl_printstring_t  *mgr_help,             ❺
        dce_acl_resolve_func_t *resolver,             ❻
        void                   *resolver_arg,         ❼
        error_status_t         *st);
```

❶ *db* is the handle to the ACL backing store. This is a file descriptor.

❷ *manager_type* is the type UUID for our ACL manager.

❸ *printstring_size* gives the number of entries in *printstring*.

❹ *printstring* contains the permissions supported by this ACL manager and their print representations.

❺ *mgr_help* is a printstring that contains the descriptive text for the ACL manager itself.

❻ *resolver* is a pointer to our ACL lookup routine; i.e., *sec_acl_mgr_lookup*.

❼ *resolver_arg* is provided in order to pass in any additional information to the lookup routine.

Check back to our implementation of the *emp_db* ACL manager to convince yourself, but the input arguments to *dce_acl_register_object_type* are what you need to customize a generic *rdacl_if* routine for a specific ACL manager. This routine combines the information used by *rdacl_get_manager_types_semantics* and *rdacl_get_printstring*. The hardest part of this call, of course, is implementing the resolver function (*sec_acl_mgr_lookup*). But even that is not a lot of work since the ACL library provides two resolver functions: one based on name and one based on UUID.

Using the ACL Library

Using the ACL library to implement an ACL manager involves initializing the ACL manager's *rdacl_if* implementation and then using the other calls in the library in your application to create and check ACLs. The overall steps you take in writing an ACL manager, however, remain the same.

1. Write the application's manager code (e.g., *emp_db*) to use ACLs. Start by storing ACLs with the application's objects. You can either use the DCE backing store library or write your own. Then, make sure to create and destroy ACLs as the associated objects are created and destroyed. This should be done using the ACL creation and deletion routines in the library. Finally, write a reference monitor to check ACLs. This should be based on *dce_acl_is_client_authorized*.

2. Write your version of the *sec_acl_mgr_lookup* function and call *dce_acl_register_object_type* during server initialization. This is used by the callback routines needed by the ACL library; it gives you a complete implementation of the *rdacl_if* manager code.

3. Write the server main program.

At this point, you may wonder why we spent so much time in Chapter 6 and Chapter 7 writing an ACL manager by customizing sample source code when there is an ACL library available. There are several reasons. First, the ACL library is available only under DCE 1.1. You cannot use the ACL library if your application also needs to run under DCE 1.0. Next, the ACL library is designed for simple ACL managers. If your needs are more complex, then it would be easier to rework source code because you have more flexibility and control. And last, I believe that the ACL library obscures a lot of the internal workings of ACL managers. A programmer should see all the steps in order to understand what the program and the Security Service are doing.

Audit API

In computer security, detecting security break-ins are as important as preventing them. **Audit** is a technique for detecting potential and real security break-ins. Auditing means recording security-relevant events in some secure location (typically a log file). Examples of auditable events are: when someone logged in, when someone withdrew money from an account, etc.

Audit can be used to record suspicious activity. So for example, the *dce_login* program could audit all failed login attempts. The audit facility could, in addition to recording the event, raise an alarm if the number of failed login attempts exceeds some configured threshold. These are both examples of audit on failure. Sometimes, applications may audit even when an operation succeeds. For example, an application may want to audit every file access. Then, if some sensitive data were later leaked, you can examine the audit record to narrow down the list of people who could have obtained the information.

There are some obvious issues involved with the design of an audit system. For example, the audit records must be protected against tampering. This prevents someone from removing all the traces of an illegal operation. Also, the information that is audited must identify who the subject (i.e., the principal that is trying to perform an operation), and the object (i.e., the thing that is being operated on) are. This allows you to later figure out what happened should a security breach be discovered. If you are auditing file accesses, for example, you should record the principal's name or UUID and the filename.

The most complex issue involved with audit, however, is making sure that you audit just the right amount of data. Remember, most of the audited events are not break-ins. For example, most incidents of failed login attempts are caused by users mistyping their own passwords. Because most of the information that you audit is innocuous, you have to work hard to avoid having innocuous events drown out the relevant ones. This means not over-auditing.

Fortunately, audit is an area where the computer-security community has a lot of experience. The essential techniques were developed in the course of building secure operating systems. The basic approach involves controlling which events are audited and then supplying audit-reduction tools to search out events of interest after they have been audited. An **audit reduction tool** is a program that scans through the audit records looking for those of interest. You can, for example, comb through the audit file to see if any bank account was getting unusually high volumes of deposits or withdrawals.

Audit-reduction tools are essential because production environments typically have audit logs that are simply too large to go through manually. In addition to searches, sophisticated audit-reduction tools can also assemble low-level events into high-level events that are more meaningful. For example, a good audit-reduction tool might report that "someone has transferred money from one account into another" instead of saying "the account balances on the following accounts do not match" and then leave it to the administrator to piece together what happened.

Now let's look at the audit facility DCE 1.1 provides. Figure 8-6 shows the major components. It consists of the audit daemon, the *dcecp* control program, and the audit logging client library.

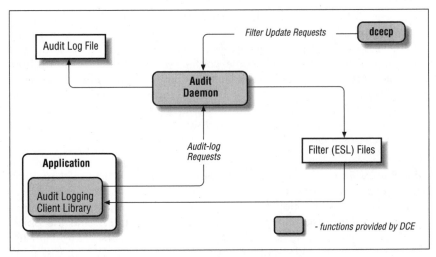

Figure 8-6: Components of the DCE audit facility

An audit daemon exists on every DCE system. Applications audit events by sending RPCs to the audit daemon on the local system. The audit daemon then writes the audit records to the **audit log file**, which stores all the event records so that they can be reviewed later. In addition to the audit log file, the audit daemon also maintains event filters. **Event filters** are data structures that determine which events should be logged. The audit daemon stores event filters in memory and in files called **event selection list (ESL)** files.

The audit daemon exports a management interface that allows a control program to change the event filters. The client of this management interface is the audit part of the *dcecp* control program. *dcecp* works like other DCE management utilities such as *acl_edit*. When an administrator uses *dcecp* to expand the range of events that should be audited, for example, the *dcecp* program makes an RPC to the audit control interface of the audit daemon. The daemon then updates its filters in memory and in the event filter files.

The last part of the audit facility is the **audit-logging client library**. This allows an application to send audit records to the audit daemon. The library communicates with the audit-logging RPC interface of the audit daemon. When an application makes a call to the audit-logging library, the library checks the event filters to see if the event should be audited. If the event filters indicate that the event should not be audited, no RPC is sent to the audit daemon. Thus, the client library is where filtering occurs.

So how does the audit-logging library get the event filters? After all, the filters are maintained by another process, the audit daemon. The answer is that the client library reads the filters from the event filter file. This is done automatically when a client application initiates an audit operation. Since event filters can be changed at anytime by *dcecp*, the client library registers an RPC interface for filter update notifications. Whenever the audit daemon changes the filter files, it notifies all the audit clients on the system. The clients can then check the relevant event filter files to see if they have been changed and update their own copies if necessary.

As you can see, much of the complexity of the audit facility comes from the need to support event filters. The good news, however, is that applications don't need to worry about this. All they need to work with is the audit-logging API. An application must go through just a few steps in order to audit events. The example below shows the calls an application makes to audit an event.

```
dce_aud_start (event... &audit_record,..);           ❶
                                                     ❷
if (audit_record != NULL) {                          ❸

     dce_aud_put_ev_info (audit_record, event_info, ...);  ❹
     .....                                                 ❺
     dce_aud_commit (..., audit_record, ...);
     dce_aud_discard (audit_record.., outcome,.);
}
```

❶ Start by calling *dce_aud_start*. This routine checks the event filters to see if the specified event should be audited. If so, an audit record is initialized and returned to the caller.

❷ If an audit record is returned, this event should be audited.

❸ Add event-specific information to the audit record by making calls to *dce_aud_put_ev_info*. You can make as many calls as necessary to this routine to add needed information to the audit record.

❹ After inserting all event-specific information, call *dce_aud_commit*. This routine examines the outcome of the event to see if it should be audited. If the event should be audited, it is passed to the audit daemon. The caller can also optionally elect to wait until the audit record is written to the audit log file before resuming.

❺ When you're finished with the audit record, free it by calling *dce_aud_discard*.

Enhanced Administration

So far, all the DCE 1.1 enhancements I've described primarily affect application developers. DCE 1.1 has also made some enhancements in administration. In this section, I'll briefly review them.

dcecp

DCE 1.0 has many control programs. DCE 1.1 provides a single control program, *dcecp*, that allows you to administer all the DCE facilities. *dcecp* does almost everything that *rpccp*, *cdscp*, *rgy_edit*, etc. do. For compatibility, the existing control programs are still supported.

The *dcecp* control program is *Tcl*-based. *Tcl* is a command interpreter package that allows users to extend the command set using scripts, which means that administrators can include extensions of their own into the control program. For example, you can implement your own *Tcl* script that searches through the bindings in the namespace to see if they are still valid.

DCE Host Daemon

The DCE host daemon, *dced*, is the remote administration agent that runs on each machine. It allows administrators to remotely modify the configuration files maintained on the host. *dced* also allows administrators to remotely start up servers. The *dced* is meant to combine the functions of all the daemons supplied by DCE for each host.

Extended Registry Attributes

In Chapter 2, I described the information the security registry stores in its databases. For example, DCE stores the local UNIX group and user IDs in the registry. These attributes can then be used to support single logins to UNIX systems. But what if you are running DCE on a non-UNIX system (e.g., an IBM MVS system) where there are different local attributes? In DCE 1.0, you would have to store these values in a separate database. You cannot include them in the DCE security registry because the structure of the data that is stored (i.e., the schema) is fixed.

DCE 1.1 solves this storage problem by allowing you to extend the types of data stored in the security registry. This means that you can now include arbitrary information in the Registry. *dcecp* allows you to define new data structures and then store values of this type in the registry. You can, for example, extend the registry to store disk quota information and have that available when the user logs into a local system that requires this information.

DCE 1.0 stores a fixed set of security attributes in a client's PAC. But in DCE 1.1, the set of security attributes associated with a client can be extended. The EPAC can carry these extended attributes so that they can be used for authorization. So, for example, if the location of the client's workstation is important for your application, it can be passed in the client's EPAC.

Group Override

This file may be useful with single logins. DCE 1.0 allows you to use the information in the security registry to set up your local UNIX account information (e.g., home directory, shell, etc.). To enable you to customize this on a per-system basis, DCE allows you to use a password override file. If the password override file exists, the values in the file replace the default values supplied by the security registry. DCE 1.1 extends this so you can use a group override file to customize the way each system maps the group name to the UNIX group ID.

A

Unauthenticated Version of the Employee Database Application

This version of the employee database application does not use security.

Application Files

Makefile contains the description of how the application is compiled and linked. (See Example A-1.)

emp_db.idl contains the description of the constants, data types, and procedures for the *emp_db* interface. (See Example A-2.)

client.c contains the employee database client code. It establishes a binding to the employee database server and then allows the user to query, modify, delete, and insert records into the database. (See Example A-3.)

server.c initializes the server with a series of standard API calls. It then exports its bindings and goes into a loop waiting for incoming calls. (See Example A-4.)

emp_mgr.c, part of the server, is an implementation of the remote procedures in the *emp_db* interface. (See Example A-5.)

chk_stat.h is a macro that checks the status codes that are returned from DCE calls. (See Example A-6.)

Example A-1: The Makefile for the Employee Database Application

```
# FILE NAME: Makefile
#
# Employee database application, unauthenticated version.

APPL=emp_db
# IDL compiler
```

Example A-1: The Makefile for the Employee Database Application (continued)

```
IDLCMD = /bin/idl -cpp_opt "-D_BSD_COMPAT" -cc_opt "-DDCE_SOURCES -g"

# libraries
LIBS = -ldce

# CC flags
CFLAGS = -g -fullwarn -DDCE_SOURCES -D_BSD_COMPAT

all: interface server client

#
# INTERFACE BUILD
#
interface: $(APPL).h $(APPL)_cstub.o $(APPL)_sstub.o
$(APPL).h $(APPL)_cstub.o $(APPL)_sstub.o: $(APPL).idl
        $(IDLCMD) $(APPL).idl

#
# CLIENT BUILD
#
client: client.o $(APPL)_cstub.o
        $(CC) $(CFLAG) -g -o client client.o $(APPL)_cstub.o $(LIBS)

#
# SERVER BUILD
#
server: server.o $(APPL)_sstub.o emp_mgr.o
        $(CC) $(CFLAG) -g -o server server.o $(APPL)_sstub.o emp_mgr.o $(LIBS)
```

Example A-2: The IDL File for the Employee Database Application

```
/*
 * FILE NAME: emp_db.idl
 */

[uuid(70340588-a9a0-11cd-838b-69076147ce07),
    version(1.0)]
interface emp_db
{
        const unsigned32        emp_s_ok              = 0;
        const unsigned32        emp_s_not_found       = 100;
        const unsigned32        emp_s_exists          = 101;
        const unsigned32        emp_s_nospace         = 102;
        const unsigned32        emp_s_not_authorized  = 103;

        const unsigned32        EMP_DB_MAX_LEN = 40;
        typedef [string] char emp_db_field_t[EMP_DB_MAX_LEN];

        typedef struct {
                emp_db_field_t          emp_name;
                emp_db_field_t          emp_mailstop;
```

Example A-2: The IDL File for the Employee Database Application (continued)

```
                emp_db_field_t          emp_phone_number;
        } emp_record_t;

        void emp_db_insert (
                [in]    handle_t        handle,
                [in]    emp_record_t    emp_record,
                [out]   unsigned32      *emp_status
        );


        void emp_db_modify (
                [in]    handle_t        handle,
                [in]    emp_record_t    emp_record,
                [out]   unsigned32      *emp_status
        );


        void emp_db_delete (
                [in]    handle_t        handle,
                [in]    emp_db_field_t  emp_name,
                [out]   unsigned32      *emp_status
        );


        [idempotent]
        void emp_db_query (
                [in]    handle_t        handle,
                [in]    emp_db_field_t  emp_name,
                [out]   emp_record_t    *emp_record,
                [out]   unsigned32      *emp_status
        );
}
```

Example A-3: Client File of the Grade Server Application

```
/* FILE NAME: client.c
 *
 * Client of the Employee Database Application
 * No authentication and no authorization.
 */

#include <stdio.h>
#include <stdlib.h>
#include "emp_db.h"
#include "chk_stat.h"

void print_status (unsigned  status);

/*
 *      main()
 *
 *      Get started, and main loop.
 */
```

Example A-3: Client File of the Grade Server Application (continued)

```
int
main(
        int                             argc,
        char                            *argv[])
{

        unsigned32                      status;
        handle_t                        binding_handle;
        rpc_ns_handle_t                 import_context;
        emp_db_field_t                  emp_name;
        emp_record_t                    emp_record;
        char                            command[5];

        /*
         * Get server binding from the name space.
         */

        rpc_ns_binding_import_begin(rpc_c_ns_syntax_dce,
                "/.:/subsys/emp_db", emp_db_v1_0_c_ifspec,
                NULL, &import_context, &status);
        CHECK_STATUS (status, "Import begin failed", ABORT);

        rpc_ns_binding_import_next(import_context,
            &binding_handle, &status);
        CHECK_STATUS (status, "Import next failed", ABORT);

        rpc_ns_binding_import_done(&import_context, &status);
        CHECK_STATUS (status, "Import done failed", ABORT);

        /*
         * Enter our command loop.
         */
        while (1) {

                printf ("Ready> ");
                scanf ("%s", &command);

                switch (command[0]) {
                        case 'q':       /* query */
                                printf ("name:");
                                scanf ("%s", (char *)emp_name);
                                emp_db_query (binding_handle,
                                        emp_name, &emp_record, &status);
                                if (status == emp_s_ok)
                                        printf ("mail stop: %s, phone: %s\n",
                                                emp_record.emp_mailstop,
                                                emp_record.emp_phone_number);
                                else
                                        print_status (status);
                                break;

                        case 'i':
                                printf ("name: ");
```

Example A-3: Client File of the Grade Server Application (continued)

```
                        scanf ("%s", emp_record.emp_name);
                        printf ("mailstop: ");
                        scanf ("%s", emp_record.emp_mailstop);
                        printf ("phone: ");
                        scanf ("%s", emp_record.emp_phone_number);
                        emp_db_insert (binding_handle,
                                emp_record, &status);
                        print_status (status);
                        break;

                case 'm':
                        printf ("name: ");
                        scanf ("%s", emp_record.emp_name);
                        printf ("mailstop: ");
                        scanf ("%s", emp_record.emp_mailstop);
                        printf ("phone: ");
                        scanf ("%s", emp_record.emp_phone_number);
                        emp_db_modify (binding_handle,
                                emp_record, &status);
                        print_status (status);
                        break;


                case 'd':
                        printf ("name:");
                        scanf ("%s", emp_name);
                        emp_db_delete (binding_handle,
                                emp_name, &status);
                        print_status (status);
                        break;

                case 'e':
                        exit(0);
                        break;

                default:
                        fflush (stdin);

                        printf ("\n");
                        printf ("q - query emp_name\n");
                        printf (
                          "i - insert emp_name mailstop phone_no\n");
                        printf (
                          "m - modify emp_name mailstop phone_no\n");
                        printf ("d - delete emp_name\n");
                        printf ("e - exit\n");
                        break;


        }
    }
}
```

Example A-3: Client File of the Grade Server Application (continued)

```
void
print_status (unsigned  status)
{
        switch (status) {
                case emp_s_ok:
                        printf ("Ok\n");
                        break;
                case emp_s_not_found:
                        printf ("Record not found\n");
                        break;
                case emp_s_exists:
                        printf ("Record already exists\n");
                        break;
                case emp_s_nospace:
                        printf ("Too many records\n");
                        break;
                case emp_s_not_authorized:
                        printf ("Not authorized for operation\n");
                        break;
                default:
                        printf ("Unknown return code\n");
                        break;
        }
}
```

Example A-4: Server Initialization of the Grade Server Application

```
/* FILE NAME: server.c
 *
 * Server Initialization of the Grade Server Application
 *
 * Server main program.
 *
 * No authentication and no authorization.
 */

#include <stdio.h>
#include <pthread.h>
#include <bstring.h>
#include <string.h>
#include "emp_db.h"
#include "chk_stat.h"

extern void emp_db_init (void);

int
main(
        int                     argc,
        char                    *argv[])
{
        rpc_binding_vector_t            *bind_vector_p;
```

Example A-4: Server Initialization of the Grade Server Application (continued)

```
unsigned32                      status;

/* Initialize local state. */
emp_db_init();

/* Register interface with rpc runtime. */

rpc_server_register_if(emp_db_v1_0_s_ifspec, NULL, NULL, &status);
CHECK_STATUS (status,"unable to register i/f",ABORT);

/* We want to use all supported protocol sequences. */

rpc_server_use_all_protseqs(rpc_c_protseq_max_reqs_default, &status);
CHECK_STATUS (status,"use_all_protseqs failed",ABORT);

/* Get our bindings. */

rpc_server_inq_bindings(&bind_vector_p, &status);
CHECK_STATUS (status,"server_inq_bindings failed",ABORT);

/* Register binding information with the endpoint map. */

rpc_ep_register(emp_db_v1_0_s_ifspec, bind_vector_p,
    NULL,
    (unsigned_char_t *)"Employee database server, version 1.0",
    &status);
CHECK_STATUS (status,"ep_register failed",ABORT);

/*
 * Export binding information into the namespace.
 */
rpc_ns_binding_export(rpc_c_ns_syntax_dce, "/.:/subsys/emp_db",
    emp_db_v1_0_s_ifspec, bind_vector_p,
    NULL, &status);
CHECK_STATUS (status,"export failed",ABORT);

/* Listen for remote calls. */
fprintf(stderr, "Server ready.\n");
rpc_server_listen(rpc_c_listen_max_calls_default, &status);
CHECK_STATUS (status,"server_listen failed",ABORT);
}
```

Example A-5: Server Manager of the Grade Server Application

```
/*
 * FILE NAME: emp_mgr.c
 *
 * Manager routines for the employee database server.
 *
 * No authentication and no authorization.
 */
```

Example A-5: Server Manager of the Grade Server Application (continued)

```
#include <stdio.h>
#include <string.h>
#include <bstring.h>
#include <pthread.h>

#include "emp_db.h"
#include "chk_stat.h"

/*
 * Make our database just an array of DATABASE_SIZE entries.
 */
#define DATABASE_SIZE 1000
emp_record_t    emp_database[DATABASE_SIZE];

/*
 * Some initial entries for the database.
 */
emp_record_t    init_db_entries[] = {
        { "marty_hu", "7L-500", "3-1947" },
        { "kevin_hu", "7L-802", "3-1322" },
        { "kelly_king", "8U-100", "4-1123" },
        { "anthony", "9U-200", "3-1522" },
        { "", "", "" }
};

/*
 * Mutex to serialize access to the database.
 */
pthread_mutex_t emp_db_mutex;


void
emp_db_init (void)
{
        unsigned        i;

        pthread_mutex_init (&emp_db_mutex, pthread_mutexattr_default);

        bzero (emp_database, sizeof(emp_record_t) * DATABASE_SIZE);

        for (i=0; init_db_entries[i].emp_name[0] != '\0'; i++) {
                emp_database[i] = init_db_entries[i];
        }
}


void
emp_db_insert (
        handle_t handle,
        emp_record_t emp_record,
        unsigned32 *emp_status)
{
```

Example A-5: Server Manager of the Grade Server Application (continued)

```
        unsigned        i;

        pthread_mutex_lock (&emp_db_mutex);

        /*
         * Make sure entry is not already in the database.
         */
        for (i=0; i < DATABASE_SIZE; i++) {
                if (strcmp (emp_database[i].emp_name,
                        emp_record.emp_name) == 0) {
                        *emp_status = emp_s_exists;
                        pthread_mutex_unlock (&emp_db_mutex);
                        return;
                }
        }

        /*
         * Now copy the record into the first empty entry.
         */
        for (i=0; i < DATABASE_SIZE; i++) {
                if (emp_database[i].emp_name[0] == '\0') {
                        emp_database[i] = emp_record;
                        *emp_status = emp_s_ok;
                        pthread_mutex_unlock (&emp_db_mutex);
                        return;
                }
        }

        *emp_status = emp_s_nospace;
        pthread_mutex_unlock (&emp_db_mutex);
        return;
}

void
emp_db_modify (
        handle_t handle,
        emp_record_t emp_record,
        unsigned32 *emp_status)
{
        unsigned        i;

        pthread_mutex_lock (&emp_db_mutex);

        for (i=0; i < DATABASE_SIZE; i++) {
                if (strcmp (emp_database[i].emp_name,
                        emp_record.emp_name) == 0) {
                        emp_database[i] = emp_record;
                        *emp_status = emp_s_ok;
                        pthread_mutex_unlock (&emp_db_mutex);
                        return;
                }
        }
```

Example A-5: Server Manager of the Grade Server Application (continued)

```
        *emp_status = emp_s_not_found;

        pthread_mutex_unlock (&emp_db_mutex);
        return;
}


void
emp_db_delete (
        handle_t handle,
        emp_db_field_t emp_name,
        unsigned32 *emp_status)
{
        unsigned        i;

        pthread_mutex_lock (&emp_db_mutex);

        for (i=0; i < DATABASE_SIZE; i++) {
                if (strcmp (emp_database[i].emp_name,
                        emp_name) == 0) {
                        bzero (&emp_database[i], sizeof(emp_record_t));
                        *emp_status = emp_s_ok;
                        pthread_mutex_unlock (&emp_db_mutex);
                        return;
                }
        }

        *emp_status = emp_s_not_found;
        pthread_mutex_unlock (&emp_db_mutex);
        return;
}


void
emp_db_query(
        handle_t handle,
        emp_db_field_t emp_name,
        emp_record_t *emp_record,
        unsigned32 *emp_status)
{
        unsigned        i;

        pthread_mutex_lock (&emp_db_mutex);

        for (i=0; i < DATABASE_SIZE; i++) {
                if (strcmp (emp_database[i].emp_name,
                        emp_name) == 0) {
                        *emp_record = emp_database[i];
                        *emp_status = emp_s_ok;
                        pthread_mutex_unlock (&emp_db_mutex);
                        return;
                }
        }
```

Example A-5: Server Manager of the Grade Server Application (continued)

```
            *emp_status = emp_s_not_found;
            pthread_mutex_unlock (&emp_db_mutex);
            return;

}
```

Example A-6: The Check Error Status Macro

```
#ifndef _CHK_STAT_H
#define _CHK_STAT_H

/*
 * FILE NAME: chk_stat.h"
 *
 * Check return status.
 */
#include <stdio.h>
#include <dce/dce_error.h>

#define RESUME 0
#define ABORT 1

#define CHECK_STATUS(input_status,comment,action) \
{ \
        if(input_status != rpc_s_ok) { \
                dce_error_inq_text(input_status,error_string,&error_stat); \
                fprintf(stderr, "%s %s\n", comment, error_string); \
                if (action == ABORT) \
                        exit(1); \
        } \
}

static int error_stat;
static unsigned char error_string[dce_c_error_string_len];

#include <errno.h>
#define PERROR_EXIT(comment) \
{ \
        perror (comment); \
        exit (1); \
}

#endif /* _CHK_STAT_H */
```

B

Employee Database Application: Authorization by Name

This version of the employee database application uses authenticated RPC and the client's principal name for authorization. The client now annotates the binding handle for security and the server uses a name-based reference monitor.

Application Files

Makefile contains the description of how the application is compiled and linked. (See Example B-1.)

emp_db.idl contains the description of the constants, data types, and procedures for the *emp_db* interface. (See Example B-2.)

client.c contains the employee database client code. It establishes a binding to the employee database server and then annotates it for security. The client program then allows the user to query, modify, delete, and insert records into the database. (See Example B-3.)

server.c initializes the server with a series of standard API calls. Unlike the unauthenticated version, this code now registers the server's principal name and secret key. The server then exports its bindings as before before going into a loop waiting for incoming calls. (See Example B-4.)

emp_mgr.c, part of the server, is an implementation of the remote procedures in the *emp_db* interface. This version makes checks to see if the client is authorized before performing the requested operation. (See Example B-5.)

ref_mon.h contains the declarations for the reference monitor, *client_is_authorized*. (See Example B-6.)

ref_mon.c, part of the server, implements the name-based reference monitor. This version first verifies that the authentication parameters selected by the client are acceptable and then checks the client's principal name to see if the access should be granted. (See Example B-7.)

Example B-1: The Makefile

```
# FILE NAME: Makefile
#
# Employee database application.
# Name-based authorization.

APPL=emp_db

# IDL compiler
IDLCMD = /bin/idl -cpp_opt "-D_BSD_COMPAT" -cc_opt "-DDCE_SOURCES -g"

# libraries
LIBS = -ldce

# CC flags
CFLAGS = -g -fullwarn -DDCE_SOURCES -D_BSD_COMPAT

all: interface server client

#
# INTERFACE BUILD
#
interface: $(APPL).h $(APPL)_cstub.o $(APPL)_sstub.o
$(APPL).h $(APPL)_cstub.o $(APPL)_sstub.o: $(APPL).idl
        $(IDLCMD) $(APPL).idl

#
# CLIENT BUILD
#
client: client.o $(APPL)_cstub.o
        $(CC) -g $(CFLAG) -o client client.o $(APPL)_cstub.o $(LIBS)

#
# SERVER BUILD
#
server: server.o $(APPL)_sstub.o emp_mgr.o ref_mon.o
        $(CC) -g $(CFLAG) -o server server.o $(APPL)_sstub.o emp_mgr.o \
        ref_mon.o $(LIBS)
```

Example B-2: The emp_db IDL File

```
/*
 * FILE NAME: emp_db.idl
 *
 * Copyright (c) 1994, Wei Hu
 */

[uuid(70340588-a9a0-11cd-838b-69076147ce07),
    version(1.0)]
```

Example B-2: The emp_db IDL File (continued)

```
interface emp_db
{
        const unsigned32        emp_s_ok               = 0;
        const unsigned32        emp_s_not_found        = 100;
        const unsigned32        emp_s_exists           = 101;
        const unsigned32        emp_s_nospace          = 102;
        const unsigned32        emp_s_not_authorized   = 103;

        const unsigned32        EMP_DB_MAX_LEN = 40;
        typedef [string] char emp_db_field_t[EMP_DB_MAX_LEN];

        typedef struct {
                emp_db_field_t          emp_name;
                emp_db_field_t          emp_mailstop;
                emp_db_field_t          emp_phone_number;
        } emp_record_t;

        void emp_db_insert (
                [in]    handle_t         handle,
                [in]    emp_record_t     emp_record,
                [out]   unsigned32       *emp_status
        );

        void emp_db_modify (
                [in]    handle_t         handle,
                [in]    emp_record_t     emp_record,
                [out]   unsigned32       *emp_status
        );

        void emp_db_delete (
                [in]    handle_t         handle,
                [in]    emp_db_field_t   emp_name,
                [out]   unsigned32       *emp_status
        );

        [idempotent]
        void emp_db_query (
                [in]    handle_t         handle,
                [in]    emp_db_field_t   emp_name,
                [out]   emp_record_t     *emp_record,
                [out]   unsigned32       *emp_status
        );
}
```

Example B-3: The Client File

```
/* FILE NAME: client.c
 *
 * Client of the Employee Database Application
 * Name-based authorization.
 */

#include <stdio.h>
#include <stdlib.h>
```

Example B-3: The Client File (continued)

```
#include "emp_db.h"
#include "chk_stat.h"

void print_status (unsigned  status);

/*
 *      main()
 *
 *      Get started, and main loop.
 */

int
main(
        int                        argc,
        char                       *argv[])
{

        unsigned32                 status;
        handle_t                   binding_handle;
        rpc_ns_handle_t            import_context;
        emp_db_field_t             emp_name;
        emp_record_t               emp_record;
        char                       command[5];

        /*
         * Get server binding from the name space.
         */

        rpc_ns_binding_import_begin(rpc_c_ns_syntax_dce,
                "/.:/subsys/emp_db", emp_db_v1_0_c_ifspec,
                NULL, &import_context, &status);
        CHECK_STATUS (status, "Import begin failed", ABORT);

        rpc_ns_binding_import_next(import_context,
            &binding_handle, &status);
        CHECK_STATUS (status, "Import next failed", ABORT);

        rpc_ns_binding_import_done(&import_context, &status);
        CHECK_STATUS (status, "Import done failed", ABORT);


#define SERVER_PRINC_NAME "emp_db_server"

        /*
         * Annotate our binding handle for authentication.
         */
        rpc_binding_set_auth_info(binding_handle,
            SERVER_PRINC_NAME, rpc_c_protect_level_default,
            rpc_c_authn_dce_secret, NULL /*default login context*/,
            rpc_c_authz_name, &status);
        CHECK_STATUS (status, "binding_set_auth_info failed", ABORT);

        /*
         * Enter our command loop.
         */
```

Example B-3: The Client File (continued)

```
while (1) {

        printf ("Ready> ");
        scanf ("%s", &command);

        switch (command[0]) {
                case 'q':       /* query */
                        printf ("name:");
                        scanf ("%s", (char *)emp_name);
                        emp_db_query (binding_handle,
                                emp_name, &emp_record, &status);
                        if (status == emp_s_ok)
                                printf ("mail stop: %s, phone: %s\n",
                                        emp_record.emp_mailstop,
                                        emp_record.emp_phone_number);
                        else
                                print_status (status);
                        break;

                case 'i':
                        printf ("name: ");
                        scanf ("%s", emp_record.emp_name);
                        printf ("mailstop: ");
                        scanf ("%s", emp_record.emp_mailstop);
                        printf ("phone: ");
                        scanf ("%s", emp_record.emp_phone_number);
                        emp_db_insert (binding_handle,
                                emp_record, &status);
                        print_status (status);
                        break;

                case 'm':
                        printf ("name: ");
                        scanf ("%s", emp_record.emp_name);
                        printf ("mailstop: ");
                        scanf ("%s", emp_record.emp_mailstop);
                        printf ("phone: ");
                        scanf ("%s", emp_record.emp_phone_number);
                        emp_db_modify (binding_handle,
                                emp_record, &status);
                        print_status (status);
                        break;


                case 'd':
                        printf ("name:");
                        scanf ("%s", emp_name);
                        emp_db_delete (binding_handle,
                                emp_name, &status);
                        print_status (status);
                        break;

                case 'e':
                        exit(0);
                        break;
```

Example B-3: The Client File (continued)

```
                        default:
                                fflush (stdin);

                                printf ("\n");
                                printf ("q - query emp_name\n");
                                printf (
                                  "i - insert emp_name mailstop phone_no\n");
                                printf (
                                  "m - modify emp_name mailstop phone_no\n");
                                printf ("d - delete emp_name\n");
                                printf ("e - exit\n");
                                break;


                }
        }
}


void
print_status (unsigned  status)
{
        switch (status) {
                case emp_s_ok:
                        printf ("Ok\n");
                        break;
                case emp_s_not_found:
                        printf ("Record not found\n");
                        break;
                case emp_s_exists:
                        printf ("Record already exists\n");
                        break;
                case emp_s_nospace:
                        printf ("Too many records\n");
                        break;
                case emp_s_not_authorized:
                        printf ("Not authorized for operation\n");
                        break;
                default:
                        printf ("Unknown return code\n");
                        break;
        }
}
```

Example B-4: Server Main

```
/* FILE NAME: server.c
 *
 * Server Initialization of the Grade Server Application
 *
 * Server main program.
 *
 * This version uses authenticated RPC but does not make
 * the server standalone.
```

Example B-4: Server Main (continued)

```
 */

#include <stdio.h>
#include <pthread.h>
#include <bstring.h>
#include <string.h>
#include "emp_db.h"
#include "chk_stat.h"

extern void emp_db_init (void);

int
main(
        int                     argc,
        char                    *argv[])
{
        unsigned_char_t         *server_name;
        rpc_binding_vector_t    *bind_vector_p;
        unsigned32              status;

        /* Initialize local state. */
        emp_db_init();


#define SERVER_PRINC_NAME "/.:/emp_db_server"
#define KEYTAB "/usr/people/emp_db_server/emp_db_keytab"

        /*
         * Register authentication info with RPC.
         */
        rpc_server_register_auth_info(SERVER_PRINC_NAME,
            rpc_c_authn_dce_secret, NULL /*default key retrieval function*/,
            KEYTAB, &status);
        CHECK_STATUS (status,"server_register_auth_info failed",ABORT);

        /* Register interface with rpc runtime. */

        rpc_server_register_if(emp_db_v1_0_s_ifspec, NULL, NULL, &status);
        CHECK_STATUS (status,"unable to register i/f",ABORT);

        /* We want to use all supported protocol sequences. */

        rpc_server_use_all_protseqs(rpc_c_protseq_max_reqs_default, &status);
        CHECK_STATUS (status,"use_all_protseqs failed",ABORT);

        /* Get our bindings. */

        rpc_server_inq_bindings(&bind_vector_p, &status);
        CHECK_STATUS (status,"server_inq_bindings failed",ABORT);

        /* Register binding information with the endpoint map. */

        rpc_ep_register(emp_db_v1_0_s_ifspec, bind_vector_p,
            NULL,
            (unsigned_char_t *)"Employee database server, version 1.0",
```

Example B-4: Server Main (continued)

```
            &status);
        CHECK_STATUS (status,"ep_register failed",ABORT);


        /*
         * Export binding information into the namespace.
         */
        rpc_ns_binding_export(rpc_c_ns_syntax_dce, "/.:/subsys/emp_db",
            emp_db_v1_0_s_ifspec, bind_vector_p,
            NULL, &status);
        CHECK_STATUS (status,"export failed",ABORT);


        /* Listen for remote calls. */
        fprintf(stderr, "Server ready.\n");
        rpc_server_listen(rpc_c_listen_max_calls_default, &status);
        CHECK_STATUS (status,"server_listen failed",ABORT);
}
```


Example B-5: Server Manager Code

```
/*
 * FILE NAME: emp_mgr.c
 *
 * Manager routines for the employee database server.
 *
 * This version uses name-based authorization.
 */

#include <stdio.h>
#include <string.h>
#include <bstring.h>
#include <pthread.h>

#include "emp_db.h"
#include "ref_mon.h"
#include <dce/dce_cf.h>
#include "chk_stat.h"

/*
 * Make our database just an array of DATABASE_SIZE entries.
 */
#define DATABASE_SIZE 1000
emp_record_t    emp_database[DATABASE_SIZE];

/*
 * Some initial entries for the database.
 */
emp_record_t    init_db_entries[] = {
        { "marty_hu", "7L-500", "3-1947" },
        { "kevin_hu", "7L-802", "3-1322" },
        { "kelly_king", "8U-100", "4-1123" },
        { "anthony", "9U-200", "3-1522" },
        { "", "", "" }
};
```

Example B-5: Server Manager Code (continued)

```c
/*
 * Mutex to serialize access to the database.
 */
pthread_mutex_t emp_db_mutex;

char *emp_db_cell = NULL;


void
emp_db_init (void)
{
        unsigned         i;

        error_status_t   status;

        dce_cf_get_cell_name (&emp_db_cell, &status);
        CHECK_STATUS (status, "dce_cf_get_cell_name failure",ABORT);

        pthread_mutex_init (&emp_db_mutex, pthread_mutexattr_default);

        bzero (emp_database, sizeof(emp_record_t) * DATABASE_SIZE);

        for (i=0; init_db_entries[i].emp_name[0] != '\0'; i++) {
                emp_database[i] = init_db_entries[i];
        }
}


void
emp_db_insert (
        handle_t handle,
        emp_record_t emp_record,
        unsigned32 *emp_status)
{
        unsigned         i;

        pthread_mutex_lock (&emp_db_mutex);

        if (! client_is_authorized (handle, OP_WRITE, emp_record.emp_name)) {
                *emp_status = emp_s_not_authorized;
                pthread_mutex_unlock (&emp_db_mutex);
                        return;
        }

        /*
         * Make sure entry is not already in the database.
         */
        for (i=0; i < DATABASE_SIZE; i++) {
                if (strcmp (emp_database[i].emp_name,
                        emp_record.emp_name) == 0) {
                        *emp_status = emp_s_exists;
                        pthread_mutex_unlock (&emp_db_mutex);
                        return;
                }
        }
```

Example B-5: Server Manager Code (continued)

```
        /*
         * Now copy the record into the first empty entry.
         */
        for (i=0; i < DATABASE_SIZE; i++) {
                if (emp_database[i].emp_name[0] == '\0') {
                        emp_database[i] = emp_record;
                        *emp_status = emp_s_ok;
                        pthread_mutex_unlock (&emp_db_mutex);
                        return;
                }
        }

        *emp_status = emp_s_nospace;
        pthread_mutex_unlock (&emp_db_mutex);
        return;
}

void
emp_db_modify (
        handle_t handle,
        emp_record_t emp_record,
        unsigned32 *emp_status)
{
        unsigned        i;

        pthread_mutex_lock (&emp_db_mutex);

        if (! client_is_authorized (handle, OP_WRITE, emp_record.emp_name)) {
                *emp_status = emp_s_not_authorized;
                pthread_mutex_unlock (&emp_db_mutex);
                return;
        }

        for (i=0; i < DATABASE_SIZE; i++) {
                if (strcmp (emp_database[i].emp_name,
                            emp_record.emp_name) == 0) {
                        emp_database[i] = emp_record;
                        *emp_status = emp_s_ok;
                        pthread_mutex_unlock (&emp_db_mutex);
                        return;
                }
        }

        *emp_status = emp_s_not_found;

        pthread_mutex_unlock (&emp_db_mutex);
        return;
}


void
emp_db_delete (
        handle_t handle,
        emp_db_field_t emp_name,
```

Example B-5: Server Manager Code (continued)

```
        unsigned32 *emp_status)
{
        unsigned        i;

        pthread_mutex_lock (&emp_db_mutex);

        if (! client_is_authorized (handle, OP_WRITE, emp_name)) {
                *emp_status = emp_s_not_authorized;
                pthread_mutex_unlock (&emp_db_mutex);
                return;
        }

        for (i=0; i < DATABASE_SIZE; i++) {
                if (strcmp (emp_database[i].emp_name,
                            emp_name) == 0) {
                        bzero (&emp_database[i], sizeof(emp_record_t));
                        *emp_status = emp_s_ok;
                        pthread_mutex_unlock (&emp_db_mutex);
                        return;
                }
        }

        *emp_status = emp_s_not_found;
        pthread_mutex_unlock (&emp_db_mutex);
        return;
}


void
emp_db_query(
        handle_t handle,
        emp_db_field_t emp_name,
        emp_record_t *emp_record,
        unsigned32 *emp_status)
{
        unsigned        i;

        pthread_mutex_lock (&emp_db_mutex);

        if (! client_is_authorized (handle, OP_READ, emp_name)) {
                *emp_status = emp_s_not_authorized;
                pthread_mutex_unlock (&emp_db_mutex);
                return;
        }

        for (i=0; i < DATABASE_SIZE; i++) {
                if (strcmp (emp_database[i].emp_name,
                            emp_name) == 0) {
                        *emp_record = emp_database[i];
                        *emp_status = emp_s_ok;
                        pthread_mutex_unlock (&emp_db_mutex);
                        return;
                }
        }
```

Example B-5: Server Manager Code (continued)

```
        *emp_status = emp_s_not_found;
        pthread_mutex_unlock (&emp_db_mutex);
        return;

}



/*
 * Local call, for use by reference monitor.
 * This assumes that the caller has the mutex locked.
 */
int
emp_db_present (char    *client_name)
{
        unsigned        i;

        /*
         * Make sure entry is not already in the database.
         */
        for (i=0; i < DATABASE_SIZE; i++) {
                if (strncmp (emp_database[i].emp_name, client_name,
                        EMP_DB_MAX_LEN) == 0)
                        return 1;
        }
        return 0;
}
```

Example B-6: Reference Monitor (ref_mon.b)

```
#ifndef _REF_MON_H
#define _REF_MON_H

typedef enum { OP_READ, OP_WRITE } access_type_t;

extern int client_is_authorized (
        handle_t        handle,
        access_type_t   operation,
        emp_db_field_t  emp_name);

#endif /* _REF_MON_H */
```

Example B-7: Reference Monitor (ref_mon.c)

```
/*
 * FILE NAME: ref_mon.c
 *
 * Reference monitor for the employee database application.
 *
 * This version uses name-based authorization.
 */

#include <stdio.h>
```

Example B-7: Reference Monitor (ref_mon.c) (continued)

```c
#include <stdlib.h>
#include <string.h>
#include <bstring.h>

#include "emp_db.h"
#include "ref_mon.h"
#include "chk_stat.h"

extern int emp_db_present (char    *client_name);
extern char *emp_db_cell;


int
client_is_authorized (
        handle_t        handle,
        access_type_t   operation,
        emp_db_field_t  emp_name)
{
        unsigned_char_t    *server_principal_name;
        unsigned_char_t    *client_principal_name;
        unsigned32         protection_level;
        unsigned32         authn_svc;
        unsigned32         authz_svc;
        unsigned32         status;
        char               *client;

        /*
         * Check the authentication parameters that the client
         * selected for this call.
         */
        rpc_binding_inq_auth_client (handle,
        (rpc_authz_handle_t *) &client_principal_name,
                &server_principal_name, &protection_level, &authn_svc,
                &authz_svc, &status);
        CHECK_STATUS (status, "inq_auth_client failed", ABORT);

        /*
         * Make sure that the caller has specified the required
         * level of protection, authentication, and authorization.
         */
        if (! ((protection_level == rpc_c_protect_level_pkt_integ) &&
                (authn_svc == rpc_c_authn_dce_secret) &&
                (authz_svc == rpc_c_authz_name)))
                return 0;

        /*
         * Strip off the cell name from the client principal name
         * if it matches the local cell name.
         */
        if (strncmp (client_principal_name, emp_db_cell, strlen(emp_db_cell))
                == 0) {
                client = &client_principal_name[strlen(emp_db_cell)+1];
        }
        else
                return 0;
```

Example B-7: Reference Monitor (ref_mon.c) (continued)

```
        /*
         * The administrator can read or write any record.
         */
        if (strcmp (client, "emp_db_administrator") == 0)
                return 1;

        if (operation == OP_READ) {
                /*
                 * We allow read access to any client that is in the
                 * database.
                 */
                return (emp_db_present (client));
        }
        else {
                /*
                 * A client can also update its own record,
                 * provided that the client is already in the
                 * database.
                 */
                return ((emp_db_present (client)) &&
                        ((strcmp (client, emp_name)) == 0));
        }

}
```

C

Employee Database Application: PAC-based Authorization

This version of the employee database application uses the client's PAC for authorization. The server now establishes its own identity and the client also verifies that the server belongs to the right group.

Application Files

Makefile contains the description of how the application is compiled and linked. (See Example C-1.)

emp_db.idl contains the description of the constants, data types, and procedures for the *emp_db* interface. (See Example C-2.)

client.c contains the employee database client code. It establishes a binding to the employee database server and then annotates it for security. In addition, it also queries the server's principal name and verifies that it belongs to the right grooup. The client program then allows the user to query, modify, delete, and insert records into the database. (See Example C-3.)

server.c initializes the server with a series of standard API calls. The server now initializes its own identity by calling *establish_identity*. The server exports its bindings as previously done before going into a loop to wait for incoming calls. (See Example C-4.)

init_identity.c, part of the server initialization code, implements *establish_identity*. This routine makes all the calls required to set up the server's DCE identity. (See Example C-5.)

emp_mgr.c, part of the server, is an implementation of the remote procedures in the *emp_db* interface. This version checks to see if the client is authorized before performing the requested operation. (See Example C-6.)

ref_mon.h contains the declarations for the reference monitor, *client_is_authorized.* (See Example C-7.)

ref_mon.c, part of the server, implements the PAC-based reference monitor. This version first verifies that the authentication parameters selected by the client are acceptable and then checks the client's PAC to see if the access should be granted. (See Example C-8.)

Example C-1: Makefile

```
# FILE NAME: Makefile
#
# PAC-based authorization

APPL=emp_db
# IDL compiler
IDLCMD = /bin/idl -cpp_opt "-D_BSD_COMPAT" -cc_opt "-DDCE_SOURCES -g"

# libraries
LIBS = -ldce

# CC flags
CFLAGS = -g -fullwarn -DDCE_SOURCES -D_BSD_COMPAT

all: interface server client

#
# INTERFACE BUILD
#
interface: $(APPL).h $(APPL)_cstub.o $(APPL)_sstub.o
$(APPL).h $(APPL)_cstub.o $(APPL)_sstub.o: $(APPL).idl
        $(IDLCMD) $(APPL).idl

#
# CLIENT BUILD
#
client: client.o $(APPL)_cstub.o
        $(CC) -g $(CFLAG) -o client client.o $(APPL)_cstub.o $(LIBS)

#
# SERVER BUILD
#
server: server.o $(APPL)_sstub.o emp_mgr.o ref_mon.o init_identity.o
        $(CC) -g $(CFLAG) -o server server.o $(APPL)_sstub.o emp_mgr.o \
        ref_mon.o init_identity.o $(LIBS)
```

Example C-2: The IDL File

```
/*
 * FILE NAME: emp_db.idl
 */

[uuid(70340588-a9a0-11cd-838b-69076147ce07),
    version(1.0)]
interface emp_db
{
        const unsigned32       emp_s_ok               = 0;
        const unsigned32       emp_s_not_found        = 100;
        const unsigned32       emp_s_exists           = 101;
        const unsigned32       emp_s_nospace          = 102;
        const unsigned32       emp_s_not_authorized   = 103;

        const unsigned32       EMP_DB_MAX_LEN = 40;
        typedef [string] char emp_db_field_t[EMP_DB_MAX_LEN];

        typedef struct {
                emp_db_field_t         emp_name;
                emp_db_field_t         emp_mailstop;
                emp_db_field_t         emp_phone_number;
        } emp_record_t;

        void emp_db_insert (
                [in]    handle_t       handle,
                [in]    emp_record_t   emp_record,
                [out]   unsigned32     *emp_status
        );

        void emp_db_modify (
                [in]    handle_t       handle,
                [in]    emp_record_t   emp_record,
                [out]   unsigned32     *emp_status
        );

        void emp_db_delete (
                [in]    handle_t       handle,
                [in]    emp_db_field_t emp_name,
                [out]   unsigned32     *emp_status
        );

        [idempotent]
        void emp_db_query (
                [in]    handle_t       handle,
                [in]    emp_db_field_t emp_name,
                [out]   emp_record_t   *emp_record,
                [out]   unsigned32     *emp_status
        );
}
```

Example C-3: The Client

```
/* FILE NAME: client.c
 *
 * Client of the Employee Database Application,
 * PAC based authorization.
 */

#include <stdio.h>
#include <stdlib.h>
#include "emp_db.h"
#include "chk_stat.h"

#include <dce/binding.h>
#include <dce/pgo.h>
#include <dce/secidmap.h>

void print_status (unsigned  status);

/*
 *      main()
 *
 *      Get started, and main loop.
 */

int
main(
        int                     argc,
        char                    *argv[])
{

        unsigned32              status;
        handle_t                binding_handle;
        rpc_ns_handle_t         import_context;
        emp_db_field_t          emp_name;
        emp_record_t            emp_record;
        char                    command[5];
        sec_rgy_handle_t        rgy_handle;
        unsigned_char_t         *server_princ_name;
        sec_rgy_name_t          princ_name;
        int                     is_member;

        /*
         * Get server binding from the name space.
         */

        rpc_ns_binding_import_begin(rpc_c_ns_syntax_dce,
                "/.:/subsys/emp_db", emp_db_v1_0_c_ifspec,
                NULL, &import_context, &status);
        CHECK_STATUS (status, "Import begin failed", ABORT);

        rpc_ns_binding_import_next(import_context,
                &binding_handle, &status);
        CHECK_STATUS (status, "Import next failed", ABORT);
```

Example C-3: The Client (continued)

```
rpc_ns_binding_import_done(&import_context, &status);
CHECK_STATUS (status, "Import done failed", ABORT);

/*
 * Determine the server's principal name.
 */
rpc_ep_resolve_binding (binding_handle, emp_db_v1_0_c_ifspec,
        &status);
CHECK_STATUS (status, "resolve_binding failed", ABORT);

rpc_mgmt_inq_server_princ_name (binding_handle,
        rpc_c_authn_dce_secret,
        &server_princ_name, &status);
CHECK_STATUS (status, "inq_princ_name failed", ABORT);

/*
 * Find out if the principal is a member of the emp_db_server
 * group.
 */

/*
 * Open a registry site for query.
 */
sec_rgy_site_open ("/.:", &rgy_handle, &status);
CHECK_STATUS (status, "rgy_site_open failed", ABORT);

/*
 * Ask the Security registry to translate the global principal
 * name into a simple principal name.
 */
sec_id_parse_name (rgy_handle, server_princ_name,
        NULL, NULL, princ_name, NULL, &status);
CHECK_STATUS (status, "sec_id_parse_name failed", ABORT);

/*
 * The group membership check.
 */
is_member = sec_rgy_pgo_is_member (rgy_handle,
        sec_rgy_domain_group, "emp_db_server",
        princ_name, &status);
CHECK_STATUS (status, "is_member failed", ABORT);

/*
 * We are done with the registry; we can release the rgy_handle.
 */
sec_rgy_site_close(rgy_handle, &status);
CHECK_STATUS (status, "rgy_site_close failed", ABORT);

if (! is_member) {
        fprintf (stderr, "Got an imposter, please report this!\n");
        exit (1);
}
```

Example C-3: The Client (continued)

```
/*
 * Annotate our binding handle for authentication.
 */
rpc_binding_set_auth_info(binding_handle,
    server_princ_name, rpc_c_protect_level_default,
    rpc_c_authn_dce_secret, NULL /*default login context*/,
    rpc_c_authz_dce, &status);
CHECK_STATUS (status, "binding_set_auth_info failed", ABORT);

/*
 * Enter our command loop.
 */
while (1) {

        printf ("Ready> ");
        scanf ("%s", &command);

        switch (command[0]) {
                case 'q':       /* query */
                        printf ("name:");
                        scanf ("%s", (char *)emp_name);
                        emp_db_query (binding_handle,
                                emp_name, &emp_record, &status);
                        if (status == emp_s_ok)
                                printf ("mail stop: %s, phone: %s\n",
                                        emp_record.emp_mailstop,
                                        emp_record.emp_phone_number);
                        else
                                print_status (status);
                        break;

                case 'i':
                        printf ("name: ");
                        scanf ("%s", emp_record.emp_name);
                        printf ("mailstop: ");
                        scanf ("%s", emp_record.emp_mailstop);
                        printf ("phone: ");
                        scanf ("%s", emp_record.emp_phone_number);
                        emp_db_insert (binding_handle,
                                emp_record, &status);
                        print_status (status);
                        break;

                case 'm':
                        printf ("name: ");
                        scanf ("%s", emp_record.emp_name);
                        printf ("mailstop: ");
                        scanf ("%s", emp_record.emp_mailstop);
                        printf ("phone: ");
                        scanf ("%s", emp_record.emp_phone_number);
                        emp_db_modify (binding_handle,
                                emp_record, &status);
                        print_status (status);
```

Example C-3: The Client (continued)

```
                                          break;

                        case 'd':
                                printf ("name:");
                                scanf ("%s", emp_name);
                                emp_db_delete (binding_handle,
                                        emp_name, &status);
                                print_status (status);
                                break;

                        case 'e':
                                exit(0);
                                break;

                        default:
                                fflush (stdin);

                                printf ("\n");
                                printf ("q - query emp_name\n");
                                printf (
                                  "i - insert emp_name mailstop phone_no\n");
                                printf (
                                  "m - modify emp_name mailstop phone_no\n");
                                printf ("d - delete emp_name\n");
                                printf ("e - exit\n");
                                break;


                }
        }
}


void
print_status (unsigned  status)
{
        switch (status) {
                case emp_s_ok:
                        printf ("Ok\n");
                        break;
                case emp_s_not_found:
                        printf ("Record not found\n");
                        break;
                case emp_s_exists:
                        printf ("Record already exists\n");
                        break;
                case emp_s_nospace:
                        printf ("Too many records\n");
                        break;
                case emp_s_not_authorized:
                        printf ("Not authorized for operation\n");
                        break;
                default:
```

Example C-3: The Client (continued)

```
                          printf ("Unknown return code\n");
                          break;
        }
}
```

Example C-4: The Server Main Program

```c
/* FILE NAME: server.c
 *
 * Server Initialization of the Grade Server Application
 *
 * server main program.
 *
 * This version establishes the server's own identity.
 */

#include <stdio.h>
#include <pthread.h>
#include <bstring.h>
#include <string.h>
#include "emp_db.h"
#include "chk_stat.h"

extern void emp_db_init (void);
extern void establish_identity (error_status_t *o_status);


int
main(
        int                       argc,
        char                      *argv[])
{
        unsigned_char_t           *server_name;
        rpc_binding_vector_t      *bind_vector_p;
        unsigned32                status;

        establish_identity (&status);
        CHECK_STATUS (status, "cannot establish identity", ABORT);

        /* Initialize local state. */
        emp_db_init ();


#define SERVER_PRINC_NAME "emp_db_server"
#define KEYTAB "/usr/people/emp_db_server/emp_db_keytab"

        /*
         * Register authentication info with RPC.
         */
        rpc_server_register_auth_info(SERVER_PRINC_NAME,
            rpc_c_authn_dce_secret, NULL /*default key retrieval function*/,
```

Example C-4: The Server Main Program (continued)

```
        KEYTAB, &status);
    CHECK_STATUS (status,"server_register_auth_info failed",ABORT);

    /* Register interface with rpc runtime. */

    rpc_server_register_if(emp_db_v1_0_s_ifspec, NULL, NULL, &status);
    CHECK_STATUS (status,"unable to register i/f",ABORT);

    /* We want to use all supported protocol sequences. */

    rpc_server_use_all_protseqs(rpc_c_protseq_max_reqs_default, &status);
    CHECK_STATUS (status,"use_all_protseqs failed",ABORT);

    /* Get our bindings. */

    rpc_server_inq_bindings(&bind_vector_p, &status);
    CHECK_STATUS (status,"server_inq_bindings failed",ABORT);

    /* Register binding information with the endpoint map. */

    rpc_ep_register(emp_db_v1_0_s_ifspec, bind_vector_p,
        NULL,
        (unsigned_char_t *)"Employee database server, version 1.0",
        &status);
    CHECK_STATUS (status,"ep_register failed",ABORT);

    /*
     * Export binding information into the namespace.
     */
    rpc_ns_binding_export(rpc_c_ns_syntax_dce, "/.:/subsys/emp_db",
        emp_db_v1_0_s_ifspec, bind_vector_p,
        NULL, &status);
    CHECK_STATUS (status,"export failed",ABORT);

    /* Listen for remote calls. */
    fprintf(stderr, "Server ready.\n");
    rpc_server_listen(rpc_c_listen_max_calls_default, &status);
    CHECK_STATUS (status,"server_listen failed",ABORT);

    /* We don't expect to return from the listen loop. */
    fprintf(stderr, "Unexpected return from rpc_server_listen");
    exit(1);
}
```

Example C-5: Initializing the Server Identity

```
/* FILE NAME: init_identity.c
 *
 * Initialize server identity.
 */
```

Example C-5: Initializing the Server Identity (continued)

```
#include <pthread.h>
#include <stdio.h>
#include <dce/rpc.h>
#include "chk_stat.h"

#define SERVER_PRINC_NAME "emp_db_server"
#define KEYTAB "/usr/people/emp_db_server/emp_db_keytab"


/*
 * establish_identity.
 *
 * Establish this server as a principal.
 */
#include <dce/sec_login.h>
#include <dce/keymgmt.h>

void establish_identity (error_status_t *o_status)
{
        sec_login_handle_t  login_context;
        sec_login_auth_src_t auth_src;
        void               *server_key;
        error_status_t      status;
        boolean32           identity_valid;
        boolean32           reset_passwd;
        pthread_t               refresh_login_context_thread;
        pthread_t           key_mgmt_thread;
        void                refresh_login_context_rtn ();
        void                key_mgmt_rtn ();

        /*
         * Set up the network identity for this server principal.
         * The network credentials obtained are seald and must be
         * unsealed with the server's secret key before they can
         * be used.
         */
        sec_login_setup_identity(SERVER_PRINC_NAME,
                                 sec_login_no_flags,
                                 &login_context, &status);
        CHECK_STATUS (status,"unable to set up identity",ABORT);

        /*
         * Retrieve the server's secret key from the private keytab
         * file.
         */
        sec_key_mgmt_get_key(rpc_c_authn_dce_secret, KEYTAB,
                        SERVER_PRINC_NAME,
                        0,  /* return most recent version */
                        &server_key, &status);
        CHECK_STATUS (status,"unable to retrieve key",ABORT);

        /*
         * Unseal the network identity using the server's secret key.
```

Example C-5: Initializing the Server Identity (continued)

```
        */
        identity_valid = sec_login_validate_identity(login_context,
                    server_key, &reset_passwd, &auth_src, &status);

        /*
         * Free the secret key as soon as we are done with it.
         */
        sec_key_mgmt_free_key (&server_key, &status);
        CHECK_STATUS (status,"unable to free key",ABORT);

        if (identity_valid) {
                /*
                 * Make sure that the server identity was validated by
                 * the network -
                 * i.e., the security server, instead of local data.
                 */
                if (auth_src != sec_login_auth_src_network) {
                        fprintf (stderr, "Server has no network credentials\n");
                        exit (1);
                }

                /*
                 * We make this login context the default for this process.
                 */
                sec_login_set_context(login_context, &status);
                CHECK_STATUS (status,"unable to set login context",ABORT);

                /*
                 * Start up a thread to refresh the login context when it
                 * expires.
                 */
                if (( pthread_create (&refresh_login_context_thread,
                        pthread_attr_default,
                        (pthread_startroutine_t) refresh_login_context_rtn,
                        (pthread_addr_t)login_context) ) == -1)
                        exit (1);

                /*
                 * Start up a thread to manage our secret key.
                 */
                if (( pthread_create (&key_mgmt_thread, pthread_attr_default,
                        (pthread_startroutine_t) key_mgmt_rtn,
                        (pthread_addr_t)NULL) ) == -1)
                        exit (1);


                *o_status = status;
        }
        else {
                error_status_t temp_status;

                CHECK_STATUS (status,"unable to validate network identity",
                            RESUME);
```

Example C-5: Initializing the Server Identity (continued)

```
                /* Reclaim the storage */
                sec_login_purge_context (&login_context, &temp_status);
                CHECK_STATUS (temp_status, "unable to purge login context",
                              ABORT);

                *o_status = status;
                return;
        }
}

/*
 * A thread to periodically change the server's secret key.
 */
void key_mgmt_rtn ()
{
        error_status_t  status;

        fprintf (stderr, "key mgmt thread started up\n");

        sec_key_mgmt_manage_key (rpc_c_authn_dce_secret,
                        KEYTAB, SERVER_PRINC_NAME, &status);
        CHECK_STATUS (status,"key mgmt failure",ABORT);
}

/*
 * A thread to periodically refresh the credentials contained in a
 * login context.
 */
#include <sys/time.h>

void refresh_login_context_rtn (sec_login_handle_t  login_context)
{
        struct timeval  current_time;
        struct timezone tz;
        struct timespec delay;
        signed32                expiration;
        signed32                delay_time;
        unsigned32              used_kvno;
        boolean32               reset_passwd;
        boolean32               identity_valid;
        void            *server_key;
        sec_login_auth_src_t auth_src;
        error_status_t  status;

#define MINUTE 60

        fprintf (stderr, "refresh login context thread started up\n");

        while (1) {

                /*
                 * Wait until shortly before the login context expires...
```

Example C-5: Initializing the Server Identity (continued)

```
                */

#ifdef _BSD_COMPAT
                /* BSD version of gettimeofday has a timezone parameter. */
                gettimeofday (&current_time, &tz);
#else
                gettimeofday (&current_time);
#endif

                sec_login_get_expiration (login_context, &expiration, &status);
                if ((status != rpc_s_ok) &&
                    (status != sec_login_s_not_certified)) {
                        fprintf (stderr,
                                "Cannot get login context expiration time\n");
                        exit (1);
                }

                delay_time = expiration - current_time.tv_sec - (10*MINUTE);

                if (delay_time > 0) {
                        delay.tv_sec = delay_time;
                        delay.tv_nsec = 0;
                        pthread_delay_np (&delay);
                }

                /*
                 * Refresh the login context.
                 */
                sec_login_refresh_identity (login_context, &status);
                CHECK_STATUS (status, "cannot refresh identity", ABORT);

                /*
                 * Retrieve the server's secret key from the private keytab
                 * file.
                 */
                sec_key_mgmt_get_key(rpc_c_authn_dce_secret, KEYTAB,
                        SERVER_PRINC_NAME,
                        0,  /* return most recent version */
                        &server_key, &status);
                CHECK_STATUS (status,"unable to retrieve key",ABORT);

                /*
                 * The refreshed login context still needs to be validated.
                 */
                identity_valid = sec_login_validate_identity(login_context,
                        server_key, &reset_passwd, &auth_src, &status);

                /*
                 * Free the secret key as soon as we are done with it.
                 */
                sec_key_mgmt_free_key (&server_key, &status);
                CHECK_STATUS (status,"unable to free key",ABORT);
```

Example C-5: Initializing the Server Identity (continued)

```
                    if (! identity_valid) {
                            error_status_t temp_status;

                            /* Reclaim the storage */
                            sec_login_purge_context (&login_context, &temp_status);
                            CHECK_STATUS (temp_status,
                                    "unable to purge login context",ABORT);

                            /* Report original error. */
                            CHECK_STATUS (status,
                                    "unable to validate network identity",ABORT);
                    }

            }
}
```

Example C-6: The Server Manager

```
/*
 * FILE NAME: emp_mgr.c
 *
 * Manager routines for the employee database server.
 * This version uses PAC-based authorization.
 *
 */

#include <stdio.h>
#include <string.h>
#include <bstring.h>
#include <pthread.h>
#include <dce/dce_cf.h>

#include "emp_db.h"
#include <dce/binding.h>
#include <dce/pgo.h>
#include <dce/secidmap.h>
#include "ref_mon.h"
#include "chk_stat.h"

/*
 * Make our database just an array of DATABASE_SIZE entries.
 */
#define DATABASE_SIZE 1000
emp_record_t    emp_database[DATABASE_SIZE];

/*
 * Some initial entries for the database.
 */
emp_record_t    init_db_entries[] = {
        { "marty_hu", "7L-500", "3-1947" },
        { "kevin_hu", "7L-802", "3-1322" },
```

Example C-6: The Server Manager (continued)

```
                { "kelly_king", "8U-100", "4-1123" },
                { "anthony", "9U-200", "3-1522" },
                { "", "", "" }
};

/*
 * Mutex to serialize access to the database.
 */
pthread_mutex_t emp_db_mutex;

/*
 * Cached copy of the cell name.
 */
char *emp_db_cell = NULL;

/*
 * Cached pointer to the Security Registry.
 */
sec_rgy_handle_t  emp_db_rgy_handle = NULL;

/*
 * uuid for the emp_db_admin and emp_db_user groups.
 */
uuid_t  emp_db_admin_group_uuid;
uuid_t  emp_db_user_group_uuid;


void
emp_db_init (void)
{
        unsigned        i;
        error_status_t  status;

        pthread_mutex_init (&emp_db_mutex, pthread_mutexattr_default);

        dce_cf_get_cell_name (&emp_db_cell, &status);
        CHECK_STATUS (status, "dce_cf_get_cell_name failure",ABORT);

        /*
         * Establish a binding to the registry interface of the
         * Security Server.
         */
        sec_rgy_site_open ("/.:", &emp_db_rgy_handle, &status);
        CHECK_STATUS (status, "rgy_site_open failed", ABORT);

        /*
         * Convert the group names into UUIDs and save it for
         * later use by the reference monitor.
         */
        sec_rgy_pgo_name_to_id (emp_db_rgy_handle,
                sec_rgy_domain_group,
                "emp_db_user_group",
                &emp_db_user_group_uuid,
```

Example C-6: The Server Manager (continued)

```
                        &status);
        CHECK_STATUS (status, "pgo_name_to_id failed", ABORT);

        sec_rgy_pgo_name_to_id (emp_db_rgy_handle,
                sec_rgy_domain_group,
                "emp_db_admin_group",
                &emp_db_admin_group_uuid,
                &status);
        CHECK_STATUS (status, "pgo_name_to_id failed", ABORT);


        bzero (emp_database, sizeof(emp_record_t) * DATABASE_SIZE);

        for (i=0; init_db_entries[i].emp_name[0] != '\0'; i++) {
                emp_database[i] = init_db_entries[i];
        }
}


void
emp_db_insert (
        handle_t handle,
        emp_record_t emp_record,
        unsigned32 *emp_status)
{
        unsigned        i;

        pthread_mutex_lock (&emp_db_mutex);

        if (! client_is_authorized (handle, OP_WRITE, emp_record.emp_name)) {
                *emp_status = emp_s_not_authorized;
                pthread_mutex_unlock (&emp_db_mutex);
                return;
        }

        /*
         * Make sure entry is not already in the database.
         */
        for (i=0; i < DATABASE_SIZE; i++) {
                if (strcmp (emp_database[i].emp_name,
                        emp_record.emp_name) == 0) {
                        *emp_status = emp_s_exists;
                        pthread_mutex_unlock (&emp_db_mutex);
                        return;
                }
        }

        /*
         * Now copy the record into the first empty entry.
         */
        for (i=0; i < DATABASE_SIZE; i++) {
                if (emp_database[i].emp_name[0] == '\0') {
                        emp_database[i] = emp_record;
```

Example C-6: The Server Manager (continued)

```
                                *emp_status = emp_s_ok;
                                pthread_mutex_unlock (&emp_db_mutex);
                                return;
                        }
                }

                *emp_status = emp_s_nospace;
                pthread_mutex_unlock (&emp_db_mutex);
                return;
        }


void
emp_db_modify (
        handle_t handle,
        emp_record_t emp_record,
        unsigned32 *emp_status)
{
        unsigned        i;

        pthread_mutex_lock (&emp_db_mutex);

        if (! client_is_authorized (handle, OP_WRITE, emp_record.emp_name)) {
                *emp_status = emp_s_not_authorized;
                pthread_mutex_unlock (&emp_db_mutex);
                return;
        }

        for (i=0; i < DATABASE_SIZE; i++) {
                if (strcmp (emp_database[i].emp_name,
                        emp_record.emp_name) == 0) {
                        emp_database[i] = emp_record;
                        *emp_status = emp_s_ok;
                        pthread_mutex_unlock (&emp_db_mutex);
                        return;
                }
        }

        *emp_status = emp_s_not_found;
        pthread_mutex_unlock (&emp_db_mutex);
        return;
}


void
emp_db_delete (
        handle_t handle,
        emp_db_field_t emp_name,
        unsigned32 *emp_status)
{
        unsigned        i;

        pthread_mutex_lock (&emp_db_mutex);
```

Example C-6: The Server Manager (continued)

```
        if (! client_is_authorized (handle, OP_WRITE, emp_name)) {
                *emp_status = emp_s_not_authorized;
                pthread_mutex_unlock (&emp_db_mutex);
                return;
        }

        for (i=0; i < DATABASE_SIZE; i++) {
                if (strcmp (emp_database[i].emp_name,
                        emp_name) == 0) {
                        bzero (&emp_database[i], sizeof(emp_record_t));
                        *emp_status = emp_s_ok;
                        pthread_mutex_unlock (&emp_db_mutex);
                        return;
                }
        }

        *emp_status = emp_s_not_found;
        pthread_mutex_unlock (&emp_db_mutex);
        return;
}


void
emp_db_query(
        handle_t handle,
        emp_db_field_t emp_name,
        emp_record_t *emp_record,
        unsigned32 *emp_status)
{
        unsigned        i;

        pthread_mutex_lock (&emp_db_mutex);

        if (! client_is_authorized (handle, OP_READ, emp_name)) {
                *emp_status = emp_s_not_authorized;
                pthread_mutex_unlock (&emp_db_mutex);
                return;
        }

        for (i=0; i < DATABASE_SIZE; i++) {
                if (strcmp (emp_database[i].emp_name,
                        emp_name) == 0) {
                        *emp_record = emp_database[i];
                        *emp_status = emp_s_ok;
                        pthread_mutex_unlock (&emp_db_mutex);
                        return;
                }
        }

        *emp_status = emp_s_not_found;
        pthread_mutex_unlock (&emp_db_mutex);
        return;
```

Example C-6: The Server Manager (continued)

```
}


/*
 * Local call, for use by reference monitor.
 * This assumes that the caller has the mutex locked.
 */
int
emp_db_present (char     *client_name)
{
        unsigned          i;

        /*
         * Make sure entry is not already in the database.
         */
        for (i=0; i < DATABASE_SIZE; i++) {
                if (strncmp (emp_database[i].emp_name, client_name,
                        EMP_DB_MAX_LEN) == 0)
                        return 1;
        }
        return 0;
}
```

Example C-7: The Reference Monitor (ref_mon.h)

```
#ifndef _REF_MON_H
#define _REF_MON_H

typedef enum { OP_READ, OP_WRITE } access_type_t;

extern uuid_t emp_db_user_group_uuid;
extern uuid_t emp_db_admin_group_uuid;
extern sec_rgy_handle_t   emp_db_rgy_handle;

extern int client_is_authorized (
        handle_t          handle,
        access_type_t     operation,
        emp_db_field_t    emp_name);

#endif /* _REF_MON_H */
```

Example C-8: The Reference Monitor (ref_mon.c)

```
/*
 * FILE NAME: ref_mon.c
 *
 * Reference monitor for the employee database application.
 * PAC-based authorization.
 *
 */
```

Example C-8: The Reference Monitor (ref_mon.c) (continued)

```
#include <stdio.h>
#include <stdlib.h>
#include <string.h>
#include <bstring.h>

#include "emp_db.h"
#include "chk_stat.h"

#include <dce/binding.h>        /* binding to registry */
#include <dce/pgo.h>            /* registry i/f */
#include <dce/secidmap.h>       /* translate global name -> princ name */

#include <dce/id_base.h>

#include "ref_mon.h"

extern int emp_db_present (char    *client_name);
extern char *emp_db_cell;


/*
 * See if group_uuid is among the local group list in the pac.
 */
int
is_member (sec_id_pac_t                *pac,
           uuid_t                      *group_uuid)
{
        int             i;
        sec_id_t        *group;
        unsigned32      status;

        group = pac->groups;
        for (i=0; i < pac->num_groups; i++) {
                if (uuid_equal (&group->uuid, group_uuid, &status))
                        return 1;
                CHECK_STATUS (status, "uuid_equal failed", ABORT);
                group++;
        }
        return 0;
}


int
client_is_authorized (
        handle_t        handle,
        access_type_t   operation,
        emp_db_field_t  emp_name)
{
        unsigned_char_t     *server_principal_name;
        sec_rgy_name_t      client_principal_name;
        sec_id_pac_format_v1_t *pac;
        unsigned32          protection_level;
```

Example C-8: The Reference Monitor (ref_mon.c) (continued)

```
unsigned32          authn_svc;
unsigned32          authz_svc;
unsigned32          status;
char                *client;

/*
 * Check the authentication parameters that the client
 * selected for this call.
 */
rpc_binding_inq_auth_client (handle,
        (rpc_authz_handle_t *) &pac,
        &server_principal_name, &protection_level, &authn_svc,
        &authz_svc, &status);
CHECK_STATUS (status, "inq_auth_client failed", ABORT);

/*
 * Make sure that the caller has specified the required
 * level of protection, authentication, and authorization.
 */
if (! ((protection_level == rpc_c_protect_level_pkt_integ) &&
        (authn_svc == rpc_c_authn_dce_secret) &&
        (authz_svc == rpc_c_authz_dce)))
        return 0;

/*
 * An administrator can read or write any record.
 */
if (is_member (pac, &emp_db_admin_group_uuid)) {
        return 1;
}


if (operation == OP_READ) {
        /*
         * We allow read access to any client that is in the
         * database.
         */
        return (is_member (pac, &emp_db_user_group_uuid));
}
else {
        /*
         * A client can also update its own record,
         * provided that the client is already in the
         * database.
         */

        /*
         * Convert the principal uuid into a name.
         * Note that this call returns a cell-relative name.
         */
        sec_rgy_pgo_id_to_name (emp_db_rgy_handle,
                        sec_rgy_domain_person,
                        &(pac->principal.uuid),
```

Example C-8: The Reference Monitor (ref_mon.c) (continued)

```
                         client_principal_name,
                         &status);
          CHECK_STATUS (status, "pgo_id_to_name failed", ABORT);

          return ((is_member (pac, &emp_db_user_group_uuid)) &&
                  ((strcmp (client_principal_name, emp_name)) == 0));
     }

}
```

D

Employee Database Application: ACL-based Authorization

This version of the employee database application uses DCE ACLs for authorization. The server now exports both the *emp_db* and the *rdaclif* interfaces. In addition, the server also stores the database and ACLs in a backing store.

Application Files

Makefile contains the description of how the application is compiled and linked. (See Example D-1.)

emp_db.idl contains the description of the constants, data types, and procedures for the *emp_db* interface. (See Example D-2.)

client.c contains the employee database client code. It establishes a binding to the employee database server and then annotates it for security. In addition, it also queries the server's principal name and verifies that it belongs to the right group. The client program then allows the user to query, modify, delete, and insert records into the database. (See Example D-3.)

server.c initializes the server with a series of standard API calls. The server initializes its own identity by calling *establish_identity*, initializes the database from the file, and then sets up the ACL manager. (See Example D-4.)

init_identity.c, part of the server initialization code, implements *establish_identity*. This routine makes all the calls required to set up the server's DCE identity. (See Example D-5.)

emp_mgr.c, part of the server, is an implementation of the remote procedures in the *emp_db* interface. This version creates and deletes ACLs when database entries get created and deleted. This version of the manager code calls an ACL-based reference monitor. (See Example D-6.)

empstore.h, contains the declarations for the employee database backing store. (See Example D-7.)

empstore.c, part of the server, implements the backing store for the employee database. (See Example D-8.)

aclstore.h contains the declarations for the ACL backing store. (See Example D-9.)

aclstore.c, part of the server, implements the backing store for ACLs. (See Example D-10.)

ref_mon.h contains the declarations for the reference monitor, *client_is_authorized*. This version uses the permission bits defined by our ACL manager. (See Example D-11.)

ref_mon.c, part of the server, implements the ACL-based reference monitor. This version contains *client_is_authorized, sec_acl_mgr_is_authorized, sec_acl_mgr_get_access*, and *sec_acl_mgr_lookup*. These routines are called from both the *emp_db* manager code and the *rdaclif* manager code. (See Example D-12.)

rdaclmgr.c, part of the server, implements the remote ACL management interface. (See Example D-13.)

Example D-1: The Makefile

```
# FILE NAME: Makefile
#
# ACL based version of the employee database application.
#

APPL=emp_db

# IDL compiler
IDLCMD = /bin/idl -cpp_opt "-D_BSD_COMPAT" -cc_opt "-DDCE_SOURCES -g"

# libraries
LIBS = -ldce

# CC flags
CFLAGS = -g -fullwarn -DDCE_SOURCES -D_BSD_COMPAT

all: interface server client

#
# INTERFACE BUILD
#
interface: $(APPL).h $(APPL)_cstub.o $(APPL)_sstub.o
$(APPL).h $(APPL)_cstub.o $(APPL)_sstub.o: $(APPL).idl
        $(IDLCMD) $(APPL).idl

#
```

Example D-1: The Makefile (continued)

```
# CLIENT BUILD
#
client: client.o $(APPL)_cstub.o
        $(CC) -g $(CFLAG) -o client client.o $(APPL)_cstub.o $(LIBS)


#
# SERVER BUILD
#
server: server.o $(APPL)_sstub.o empstore.o aclstore.o emp_mgr.o \
        ref_mon.o init_identity.o rdaclmgr.o rdaclif_sstub.o
        $(CC) -g $(CFLAG) -o server server.o $(APPL)_sstub.o \
        aclstore.o empstore.o emp_mgr.o ref_mon.o init_identity.o \
        rdaclmgr.o rdaclif_sstub.o $(LIBS)

rdaclif_sstub.o: rdaclif.idl rdaclif.acf
        $(IDLCMD) rdaclif.idl
```

Example D-2: The emp_db IDL File

```
/*
 * FILE NAME: emp_db.idl
 */

[uuid(70340588-a9a0-11cd-838b-69076147ce07),
    version(1.0)]
interface emp_db
{
        const unsigned32      emp_s_ok              = 0;
        const unsigned32      emp_s_not_found       = 100;
        const unsigned32      emp_s_exists          = 101;
        const unsigned32      emp_s_nospace         = 102;
        const unsigned32      emp_s_not_authorized  = 103;

        const unsigned32      EMP_DB_MAX_LEN  = 40;
        typedef [string] char emp_db_field_t[EMP_DB_MAX_LEN];

        typedef struct {
                emp_db_field_t        emp_name;
                emp_db_field_t        emp_mailstop;
                emp_db_field_t        emp_phone_number;
        } emp_record_t;

        void emp_db_insert (
                [in]    handle_t        handle,
                [in]    emp_record_t    emp_record,
                [out]   unsigned32      *emp_status
        );

        void emp_db_modify (
                [in]    handle_t        handle,
                [in]    emp_record_t    emp_record,
```

Example D-2: The emp_db IDL File (continued)

```
                [out]    unsigned32      *emp_status
        );

        void emp_db_delete (
                [in]     handle_t        handle,
                [in]     emp_db_field_t   emp_name,
                [out]    unsigned32      *emp_status
        );

        [idempotent]
        void emp_db_query (
                [in]     handle_t        handle,
                [in]     emp_db_field_t   emp_name,
                [out]    emp_record_t     *emp_record,
                [out]    unsigned32      *emp_status
        );
}
```

Example D-3: The Client

```
/* FILE NAME: client.c
 *
 * Client of the Employee Database Application
 */

#include "emp_db.h"
#include "chk_stat.h"
#include <stdio.h>
#include <stdlib.h>

#include <dce/binding.h>
#include <dce/pgo.h>
#include <dce/secidmap.h>

void print_status (unsigned  status);

/*
 *      main()
 *
 *      Get started, and main loop.
 */

int
main(
        int                     argc,
        char                    *argv[])
{

        unsigned32              status;
        handle_t                binding_handle;
        rpc_ns_handle_t         import_context;
```

Example D-3: The Client (continued)

```
emp_db_field_t              emp_name;
emp_record_t                emp_record;
char                        command[5];
sec_rgy_handle_t            rgy_handle;
unsigned_char_t             *server_princ_name;
sec_rgy_name_t              princ_name;
int                         is_member;

/*
 * Get server binding from the name space.
 */

rpc_ns_binding_import_begin(rpc_c_ns_syntax_dce,
        "/.:/subsys/emp_db", emp_db_v1_0_c_ifspec,
        NULL, &import_context, &status);
CHECK_STATUS (status, "Import begin failed", ABORT);

rpc_ns_binding_import_next(import_context,
    &binding_handle, &status);
CHECK_STATUS (status, "Import next failed", ABORT);

rpc_ns_binding_import_done(&import_context, &status);
CHECK_STATUS (status, "Import done failed", ABORT);

/*
 * Determine the server's principal name.
 */
rpc_ep_resolve_binding (binding_handle, emp_db_v1_0_c_ifspec,
        &status);
CHECK_STATUS (status, "resolve_binding failed", ABORT);

rpc_mgmt_inq_server_princ_name (binding_handle,
        rpc_c_authn_dce_secret,
        &server_princ_name, &status);
CHECK_STATUS (status, "inq_princ_name failed", ABORT);

/*
 * Find out if the principal is a member of the emp_db_server
 * group.
 */

/*
 * Open a registry site for query.
 */
sec_rgy_site_open ("/.:", &rgy_handle, &status);
CHECK_STATUS (status, "rgy_site_open failed", ABORT);

/*
 * Ask the Security registry to translate the global principal
 * name into a simple principal name.
 */
sec_id_parse_name (rgy_handle, server_princ_name,
        NULL, NULL, princ_name, NULL, &status);
```

Example D-3: The Client (continued)

```
CHECK_STATUS (status, "sec_id_parse_name failed", ABORT);

/*
 * The group membership check.
 */
is_member = sec_rgy_pgo_is_member (rgy_handle,
        sec_rgy_domain_group, "emp_db_server",
        princ_name, &status);
CHECK_STATUS (status, "is_member failed", ABORT);

/*
 * We are done with the registry; we can release the rgy_handle.
 */
sec_rgy_site_close(rgy_handle, &status);
CHECK_STATUS (status, "rgy_site_close failed", ABORT);

if (! is_member) {
        fprintf (stderr, "Got an imposter, please report this!\n");
        exit (1);
}

/*
 * Annotate our binding handle for authentication.
 */
rpc_binding_set_auth_info(binding_handle,
    server_princ_name, rpc_c_protect_level_default,
    rpc_c_authn_dce_secret, NULL /*default login context*/,
    rpc_c_authz_dce, &status);
CHECK_STATUS (status, "binding_set_auth_info failed", ABORT);

/*
 * Enter our command loop.
 */
while (1) {

        printf ("Ready> ");
        scanf ("%s", &command);

        switch (command[0]) {
                case 'q':        /* query */
                        printf ("name:");
                        scanf ("%s", (char *)emp_name);
                        emp_db_query (binding_handle,
                                emp_name, &emp_record, &status);
                        if (status == emp_s_ok)
                                printf ("mail stop: %s, phone: %s\n",
                                        emp_record.emp_mailstop,
                                        emp_record.emp_phone_number);
                        else
                                print_status (status);
                        break;

                case 'i':
```

Example D-3: The Client (continued)

```
                        printf ("name: ");
                        scanf ("%s", emp_record.emp_name);
                        printf ("mailstop: ");
                        scanf ("%s", emp_record.emp_mailstop);
                        printf ("phone: ");
                        scanf ("%s", emp_record.emp_phone_number);
                        emp_db_insert (binding_handle,
                                emp_record, &status);
                        print_status (status);
                        break;

                case 'm':
                        printf ("name: ");
                        scanf ("%s", emp_record.emp_name);
                        printf ("mailstop: ");
                        scanf ("%s", emp_record.emp_mailstop);
                        printf ("phone: ");
                        scanf ("%s", emp_record.emp_phone_number);
                        emp_db_modify (binding_handle,
                                emp_record, &status);
                        print_status (status);
                        break;


                case 'd':
                        printf ("name:");
                        scanf ("%s", emp_name);
                        emp_db_delete (binding_handle,
                                emp_name, &status);
                        print_status (status);
                        break;

                case 'e':
                        exit(0);
                        break;

                default:
                        fflush (stdin);

                        printf ("\n");
                        printf ("q - query emp_name\n");
                        printf (
                          "i - insert emp_name mailstop phone_no\n");
                        printf (
                          "m - modify emp_name mailstop phone_no\n");
                        printf ("d - delete emp_name\n");
                        printf ("e - exit\n");
                        break;


        }
    }
}
```

Example D-3: The Client (continued)

```
void
print_status (unsigned  status)
{
        switch (status) {
                case emp_s_ok:
                        printf ("Ok\n");
                        break;
                case emp_s_not_found:
                        printf ("Record not found\n");
                        break;
                case emp_s_exists:
                        printf ("Record already exists\n");
                        break;
                case emp_s_nospace:
                        printf ("Too many records\n");
                        break;
                case emp_s_not_authorized:
                        printf ("Not authorized for operation\n");
                        break;
                case emp_s_unknown_name:
                        printf ("Unknown name\n");
                        break;
                default:
                        printf ("Unknown return code\n");
                        break;
        }
}
```

Example D-4: The Server Main Program

```
/* FILE NAME: server.c
 *
 * Server Initialization of the Grade Server Application
 * ACL version.
 *
 * server main program.
 *
 */

#include <stdio.h>
#include <pthread.h>
#include <string.h>
#include "emp_db.h"
#include "chk_stat.h"

extern void emp_db_init (void);
extern void establish_identity (error_status_t *o_status);

#include "rdaclif.h"
```

Example D-4: The Server Main Program (continued)

```
extern uuid_t    emp_db_acl_mgr_uuid;
extern uuid_t    emp_db_entry_acl_mgr_uuid;

int
main(
        int                           argc,
        char                          *argv[])
{
        unsigned_char_t               *server_name;
        rpc_binding_vector_t          *bind_vector_p;
        unsigned32                    status;
        uuid_vector_t                 *obj_uuids;

        establish_identity (&status);
        CHECK_STATUS (status, "cannot establish identity", ABORT);

        /* Initialize local state. */
        emp_db_init();


#define SERVER_PRINC_NAME "/.:/emp_db_server"
#define KEYTAB "/usr/people/emp_db_server/emp_db_keytab"

        /*
         * Register authentication info with RPC.
         */
        rpc_server_register_auth_info(SERVER_PRINC_NAME,
            rpc_c_authn_dce_secret, NULL /*default key retrieval function*/,
            KEYTAB, &status);
        CHECK_STATUS (status,"server_register_auth_info failed",ABORT);

        /* Register interface with rpc runtime. */

        rpc_server_register_if(emp_db_v1_0_s_ifspec, NULL, NULL, &status);
        CHECK_STATUS (status,"unable to register emp_db i/f",ABORT);


        /* Register the ACL manager interface. */

        rpc_server_register_if(rdaclif_v0_0_s_ifspec, NULL, NULL, &status);
        CHECK_STATUS (status,"unable to register rdacl i/f",ABORT);

        /* We want to use all supported protocol sequences. */

        rpc_server_use_all_protseqs(rpc_c_protseq_max_reqs_default, &status);
        CHECK_STATUS (status,"use_all_protseqs failed",ABORT);

        /* Get our bindings. */

        rpc_server_inq_bindings(&bind_vector_p, &status);
        CHECK_STATUS (status,"server_inq_bindings failed",ABORT);

        /* Register binding information with the endpoint map. */
```

Example D-4: The Server Main Program (continued)

```
rpc_ep_register(emp_db_v1_0_s_ifspec, bind_vector_p,
    NULL,
    (unsigned_char_t *)"Employee database server, version 1.0",
    &status);
CHECK_STATUS (status,"ep_register failed",ABORT);

/*
 * Register an object UUID with our manager code.
 */
obj_uuids = (uuid_vector_t *) malloc (sizeof(uuid_vector_t));
obj_uuids->count = 1;
obj_uuids->uuid[0] = &emp_db_acl_mgr_uuid;
rpc_ep_register(rdaclif_v0_0_s_ifspec,
                bind_vector_p,
                obj_uuids,
                "emp_db ACL manager, version 1.0",
                &status);
CHECK_STATUS (status,"ep_register failed",ABORT);

/*
 * Export binding information into the namespace.
 */
rpc_ns_binding_export(rpc_c_ns_syntax_dce, "/.:/subsys/emp_db",
    emp_db_v1_0_s_ifspec, bind_vector_p,
    NULL, &status);
CHECK_STATUS (status,"export failed",ABORT);

/*
 * Export the emp_db ACL manager interfaces.
 */
rpc_ns_binding_export(rpc_c_ns_syntax_dce, "/.:/subsys/emp_db",
        rdaclif_v0_0_s_ifspec, bind_vector_p,
        obj_uuids, &status);
CHECK_STATUS (status, "export failed", ABORT);

/* Listen for remote calls. */
fprintf(stderr, "Server ready.\n");
rpc_server_listen(rpc_c_listen_max_calls_default, &status);
CHECK_STATUS (status,"server_listen failed",ABORT);

/* We don't expect to return from the listen loop. */
fprintf(stderr, "Unexpected return from rpc_server_listen");
exit(1);
}
```

Example D-5: Initialize Server Identity

```
/* FILE NAME: init_identity.c
 *
 * Initialize server identity.
 */

#include <pthread.h>
#include <stdio.h>
#include <dce/rpc.h>
#include "chk_stat.h"

#define SERVER_PRINC_NAME "emp_db_server"
#define KEYTAB "/usr/people/emp_db_server/emp_db_keytab"


/*
 * establish_identity.
 *
 * Establish this server as a principal.
 */
#include <dce/sec_login.h>
#include <dce/keymgmt.h>

void establish_identity (error_status_t *o_status)
{
        sec_login_handle_t   login_context;
        sec_login_auth_src_t auth_src;
        void            *server_key;
        error_status_t  status;
        boolean32               identity_valid;
        boolean32               reset_passwd;
        pthread_t               refresh_login_context_thread;
        pthread_t               key_mgmt_thread;
        void            refresh_login_context_rtn ();
        void            key_mgmt_rtn ();

        /*
         * Set up the network identity for this server principal.
         * The network credentials obtained are seald and must be
         * unsealed with the server's secret key before they can
         * be used.
         */
        sec_login_setup_identity(SERVER_PRINC_NAME,
                                 sec_login_no_flags,
                                 &login_context, &status);
        CHECK_STATUS (status,"unable to set up identity",ABORT);

        /*
         * Retrieve the server's secret key from the private keytab
         * file.
         */
        sec_key_mgmt_get_key(rpc_c_authn_dce_secret, KEYTAB,
                             SERVER_PRINC_NAME,
                             0,  /* return most recent version */
```

Example D-5: Initialize Server Identity (continued)

```
                            &server_key, &status);
        CHECK_STATUS (status,"unable to retrieve key",ABORT);

        /*
         * Unseal the network identity using the server's secret key.
         */
        identity_valid = sec_login_validate_identity(login_context,
                    server_key, &reset_passwd, &auth_src, &status);

        /*
         * Free the secret key as soon as we are done with it.
         */
        sec_key_mgmt_free_key (&server_key, &status);
        CHECK_STATUS (status,"unable to free key",ABORT);

        if (identity_valid) {
                /*
                 * Make sure that the server identity was validated by
                 * the network -
                 * i.e., the security server, instead of local data.
                 */
                if (auth_src != sec_login_auth_src_network) {
                        fprintf (stderr, "Server has no network credentials\n");
                        exit (1);
                }

                /*
                 * We make this login context the default for this process.
                 */
                sec_login_set_context(login_context, &status);
                CHECK_STATUS (status,"unable to set login context",ABORT);

                /*
                 * Start up a thread to refresh the login context when it
                 * expires.
                 */
                if (( pthread_create (&refresh_login_context_thread,
                        pthread_attr_default,
                        (pthread_startroutine_t) refresh_login_context_rtn,
                        (pthread_addr_t)login_context) ) == -1)
                        exit (1);

                /*
                 * Start up a thread to manage our secret key.
                 */
                if (( pthread_create (&key_mgmt_thread, pthread_attr_default,
                        (pthread_startroutine_t) key_mgmt_rtn,
                        (pthread_addr_t)NULL) ) == -1)
                        exit (1);


                *o_status = status;
        }
```

Example D-5: Initialize Server Identity (continued)

```
        else {
                error_status_t temp_status;

                CHECK_STATUS (status,"unable to validate network identity",
                             RESUME);

                /* Reclaim the storage */
                sec_login_purge_context (&login_context, &temp_status);
                CHECK_STATUS (temp_status, "unable to purge login context",
                             ABORT);

                *o_status = status;
                return;
        }
}

/*
 * A thread to periodically change the server's secret key.
 */
void key_mgmt_rtn ()
{
        error_status_t  status;

        fprintf (stderr, "key mgmt thread started up\n");

        sec_key_mgmt_manage_key (rpc_c_authn_dce_secret,
                        KEYTAB, SERVER_PRINC_NAME, &status);
        CHECK_STATUS (status,"key mgmt failure",ABORT);
}

/*
 * A thread to periodically refresh the credentials contained in a
 * login context.
 */
#include <sys/time.h>

void refresh_login_context_rtn (sec_login_handle_t  login_context)
{
        struct timeval   current_time;
        struct timezone tz;
        struct timespec delay;
        signed32                expiration;
        signed32                delay_time;
        unsigned32              used_kvno;
        boolean32               reset_passwd;
        boolean32               identity_valid;
        void            *server_key;
        sec_login_auth_src_t auth_src;
        error_status_t  status;

#define MINUTE 60

        fprintf (stderr, "refresh login context thread started up\n");
```

Example D-5: Initialize Server Identity (continued)

```
        while (1) {

                /*
                 * Wait until shortly before the login context expires...
                 */

#ifdef _BSD_COMPAT
                /* BSD version of gettimeofday has a timezone parameter. */
                gettimeofday (&current_time, &tz);
#else
                gettimeofday (&current_time);
#endif

                sec_login_get_expiration (login_context, &expiration, &status);
                if ((status != rpc_s_ok) &&
                    (status != sec_login_s_not_certified)) {
                        fprintf (stderr,
                                "Cannot get login context expiration time\n");
                        exit (1);
                }

                delay_time = expiration - current_time.tv_sec - (10*MINUTE);

                if (delay_time > 0) {
                        delay.tv_sec = delay_time;
                        delay.tv_nsec = 0;
                        pthread_delay_np (&delay);
                }

                /*
                 * Refresh the login context.
                 */
                sec_login_refresh_identity (login_context, &status);
                CHECK_STATUS (status, "cannot refresh identity", ABORT);

                /*
                 * Retrieve the server's secret key from the private keytab
                 * file.
                 */
                sec_key_mgmt_get_key(rpc_c_authn_dce_secret, KEYTAB,
                                SERVER_PRINC_NAME,
                                0,  /* return most recent version */
                                &server_key, &status);
                CHECK_STATUS (status,"unable to retrieve key",ABORT);

                /*
                 * The refreshed login context still needs to be validated.
                 */
                identity_valid = sec_login_validate_identity(login_context,
                                server_key, &reset_passwd, &auth_src, &status);

                /*
```

Example D-5: Initialize Server Identity (continued)

```
                    * Free the secret key as soon as we are done with it.
                    */
                    sec_key_mgmt_free_key (&server_key, &status);
                    CHECK_STATUS (status,"unable to free key",ABORT);

                    if (! identity_valid) {
                            error_status_t temp_status;

                            /* Reclaim the storage */
                            sec_login_purge_context (&login_context, &temp_status);
                            CHECK_STATUS (temp_status,
                                    "unable to purge login context",ABORT);

                            /* Report original error. */
                            CHECK_STATUS (status,
                                    "unable to validate network identity",ABORT);
                    }

            }
}
```

Example D-6: The emp_db Manager Code

```
/*
 * FILE NAME: emp_mgr.c
 *
 * Manager routines for the employee database server.
 *
 */

#include <pthread.h>
#include <stdio.h>
#include <string.h>
#include <dce/dce_cf.h>

#include <dce/binding.h>
#include <dce/pgo.h>
#include <dce/secidmap.h>

#include "emp_db.h"
#include "aclstore.h"
#include "empstore.h"
#include "ref_mon.h"
#include "chk_stat.h"

/*
 * The in-memory copy of the employee database.
 */
emp_store_record_t      emp_database[DATABASE_SIZE];

static unsigned32 create_default_entry_acl (char *db_entry_name,
```

Example D-6: The emp_db Manager Code (continued)

```
            compact_acl_t *compact_acl);

static void create_default_db_acl (compact_acl_t *compact_acl);

/*
 * Mutex to serialize access to the database.
 */
pthread_mutex_t emp_db_mutex;

/*
 * Cached binding to the Security Registry.
 */
sec_rgy_handle_t  emp_db_rgy_handle = NULL;

/*
 * UUIDs for the emp_db_admin and emp_db_user groups.
 */
uuid_t  emp_db_admin_group_uuid;
uuid_t  emp_db_user_group_uuid;

#define EMP_DB_USER_GROUP "emp_db_user_group"
#define EMP_DB_ADMIN_GROUP "emp_db_admin_group"

/*
 * Our cell name and UUID.
 */
static char           *emp_db_cell_name;
static uuid_t          emp_db_cell_uuid;

/*
 * ACL manager type UUIDs for our ACL managers.
 */
static char emp_db_acl_mgr_uuid_str[] =
        "73c3d2fc-0966-11ce-9968-69076147ce07";
static char emp_db_entry_acl_mgr_uuid_str[] =
        "b5a7d9ac-0966-11ce-82e5-69076147ce07";
uuid_t  emp_db_acl_mgr_uuid;
uuid_t  emp_db_entry_acl_mgr_uuid;


void
emp_db_init (void)
{
        int            initial_db;
        error_status_t status;

        pthread_mutex_init (&emp_db_mutex, pthread_mutexattr_default);

        /*
         * Establish a binding to the registry interface of the
         * Security Server.
         */
        sec_rgy_site_open ("/.:", &emp_db_rgy_handle, &status);
```

Example D-6: The emp_db Manager Code (continued)

```
CHECK_STATUS (status, "rgy_site_open failed", ABORT);

/*
 * Convert the group names into UUIDs and save it for
 * later use by the reference monitor.
 */
sec_rgy_pgo_name_to_id (emp_db_rgy_handle,
        sec_rgy_domain_group,
        EMP_DB_USER_GROUP,
        &emp_db_user_group_uuid,
        &status);
CHECK_STATUS (status, "pgo_name_to_id failed", ABORT);

sec_rgy_pgo_name_to_id (emp_db_rgy_handle,
        sec_rgy_domain_group,
        EMP_DB_ADMIN_GROUP,
        &emp_db_admin_group_uuid,
        &status);
CHECK_STATUS (status, "pgo_name_to_id failed", ABORT);

/*
 * Initialize our cell name & UUID.
 */
dce_cf_get_cell_name (&emp_db_cell_name, &status);
CHECK_STATUS (status, "dce_cf_get_cell_name failed", ABORT);

sec_id_parse_name (emp_db_rgy_handle, emp_db_cell_name, NULL,
                &emp_db_cell_uuid, NULL, NULL, &status);
CHECK_STATUS (status, "sec_id_parse_name failed", ABORT);

/*
 * Read the ACLs in from the backing store.
 */
acl_store_init();

/*
 * Read the emp_db database itself in from the backing store
 * into emp_database. If the database does not exist, zeroes
 * the emp_database.
 */
emp_store_init(emp_database, &initial_db);

/*
 * Set up the ACL manager UUIDs.
 */
uuid_from_string (emp_db_acl_mgr_uuid_str,
        &emp_db_acl_mgr_uuid, &status);
CHECK_STATUS (status, "uuid_from_string failed", ABORT);

uuid_from_string (emp_db_entry_acl_mgr_uuid_str,
        &emp_db_entry_acl_mgr_uuid, &status);
CHECK_STATUS (status, "uuid_from_string failed", ABORT);
```

Example D-6: The emp_db Manager Code (continued)

```
        /*
         * If this is a new database, create the default database ACL.
         * We store the database ACL in reserved location 0 of the
         * employee database.
         */
        if (initial_db) {
                strcpy (emp_database[0].emp_record.emp_name, "emp_db_server");
                create_default_db_acl (&emp_database[0].compact_acl);
        }
}


void
emp_db_insert (
        handle_t handle,
        emp_record_t emp_record,
        unsigned32 *emp_status)
{
        unsigned        i;

        pthread_mutex_lock (&emp_db_mutex);

        /*
         * Check the creation ACL on the database. We don't care which db
         * entry gets created, so we pass in NULL for the entryname.
         */
        if (! client_is_authorized (handle, OP_INSERT, NULL)) {
                *emp_status = emp_s_not_authorized;
                pthread_mutex_unlock (&emp_db_mutex);
                return;
        }

        /*
         * Make sure entry is not already in the database.
         *
         * Note how we start from index 1; index 0 is reserved for holding
         * the creation ACL for the database as a whole.
         */
        for (i=1; i < DATABASE_SIZE; i++) {
                if (strcmp (emp_database[i].emp_record.emp_name,
                        emp_record.emp_name) == 0) {
                        *emp_status = emp_s_exists;
                        pthread_mutex_unlock (&emp_db_mutex);
                        return;
                }
        }

        /*
         * Now copy the record into the first empty entry.
         */
        for (i=1; i < DATABASE_SIZE; i++) {
                if (emp_database[i].emp_record.emp_name[0] == '\0') {
                        /*
```

Example D-6: The emp_db Manager Code (continued)

```
                                * Update the incore database.
                                */
                            emp_database[i].emp_record = emp_record;
                            *emp_status = create_default_entry_acl (
                                    emp_record.emp_name,
                                    &emp_database[i].compact_acl);

                            if (*emp_status == emp_s_ok) {
                                    /*
                                     * Write to the backing stores.
                                     */
                                    emp_store_write (i);
                            }
                            pthread_mutex_unlock (&emp_db_mutex);
                            return;
                    }
            }

        *emp_status = emp_s_nospace;
        pthread_mutex_unlock (&emp_db_mutex);
        return;
}

void
emp_db_modify (
        handle_t handle,
        emp_record_t emp_record,
        unsigned32 *emp_status)
{
        unsigned        i;

        pthread_mutex_lock (&emp_db_mutex);

        if (! client_is_authorized (handle, OP_WRITE, emp_record.emp_name)) {
                *emp_status = emp_s_not_authorized;
                pthread_mutex_unlock (&emp_db_mutex);
                return;
        }

        for (i=1; i < DATABASE_SIZE; i++) {
                if (strcmp (emp_database[i].emp_record.emp_name,
                        emp_record.emp_name) == 0) {

                        emp_database[i].emp_record = emp_record;
                        emp_store_write (i);

                        *emp_status = emp_s_ok;
                        pthread_mutex_unlock (&emp_db_mutex);
                        return;
                }
        }

        *emp_status = emp_s_not_found;
```

Example D-6: The emp_db Manager Code (continued)

```
                pthread_mutex_unlock (&emp_db_mutex);
                return;
}


void
emp_db_delete (
        handle_t handle,
        emp_db_field_t emp_name,
        unsigned32 *emp_status)
{
        unsigned        i;

        pthread_mutex_lock (&emp_db_mutex);

        if (! client_is_authorized (handle, OP_WRITE, emp_name)) {
                *emp_status = emp_s_not_authorized;
                pthread_mutex_unlock (&emp_db_mutex);
                return;
        }

        for (i=1; i < DATABASE_SIZE; i++) {
                if (strcmp (emp_database[i].emp_record.emp_name,
                        emp_name) == 0) {

                        /*
                         * Delete the ACL and the database entry.
                         */
                        acl_store_delete_acl (&emp_database[i].compact_acl);
                        emp_store_delete (i);
                        memset (&emp_database[i], 0, sizeof(emp_record_t));

                        *emp_status = emp_s_ok;
                        pthread_mutex_unlock (&emp_db_mutex);
                        return;
                }
        }

        *emp_status = emp_s_not_found;
        pthread_mutex_unlock (&emp_db_mutex);
        return;
}


void
emp_db_query(
        handle_t handle,
        emp_db_field_t emp_name,
        emp_record_t *emp_record,
        unsigned32 *emp_status)
{
        unsigned        i;
```

Example D-6: The emp_db Manager Code (continued)

```
                pthread_mutex_lock (&emp_db_mutex);

                if (! client_is_authorized (handle, OP_READ, emp_name)) {

                        /*
                         * Explicitly clear the output argument for those
                         * cases where we have nothing to return.
                         */
                        memset (emp_record, 0, sizeof(emp_record_t));
                        *emp_status = emp_s_not_authorized;
                        pthread_mutex_unlock (&emp_db_mutex);
                        return;
                }

                for (i=1; i < DATABASE_SIZE; i++) {
                        if (strcmp (emp_database[i].emp_record.emp_name,
                                    emp_name) == 0) {
                                *emp_record = emp_database[i].emp_record;
                                *emp_status = emp_s_ok;
                                pthread_mutex_unlock (&emp_db_mutex);
                                return;
                        }
                }

                memset (emp_record, 0, sizeof(emp_record_t));
                *emp_status = emp_s_not_found;
                pthread_mutex_unlock (&emp_db_mutex);
                return;

}


/*
 * Create the default ACL for an entry in the database. It allows:
 *    1. members of the emp_db_users group read access.
 *    2. members of the emp_db_admin group read+write+control access.
 *    3. the person named in this database entry read+write+control access.
 */
static unsigned32
create_default_entry_acl (char            *db_entry_name,
                  compact_acl_t           *compact_acl)
{
        sec_acl_t       acl;
        sec_acl_entry_t *acl_entry_p;
        error_status_t  status;

        /*
         * Initialize an ACL of 3 entries.
         */
        acl.num_entries = 3;
        acl.sec_acl_entries = acl_entry_p =
                (sec_acl_entry_t *) malloc (
                        acl.num_entries * sizeof(sec_acl_entry_t));
```

Example D-6: The emp_db Manager Code (continued)

```
/*
 * Fill in the default realm.
 */
acl.default_realm.name = strdup (emp_db_cell_name);
acl.default_realm.uuid = emp_db_cell_uuid;

/*
 * Allow "r" access to emp_db_users group.
 */
acl_entry_p->perms = sec_acl_perm_read;
acl_entry_p->entry_info.entry_type = sec_acl_e_type_group;
acl_entry_p->entry_info.tagged_union.id.uuid = emp_db_user_group_uuid;
acl_entry_p->entry_info.tagged_union.id.name = (idl_char *) "";

/*
 * Allow "rwc" access to emp_db_admin group.
 */
acl_entry_p++;
acl_entry_p->perms = sec_acl_perm_read | sec_acl_perm_write |
                     sec_acl_perm_control;
acl_entry_p->entry_info.entry_type = sec_acl_e_type_group;
acl_entry_p->entry_info.tagged_union.id.uuid = emp_db_admin_group_uuid;
acl_entry_p->entry_info.tagged_union.id.name = (idl_char *) "";

/*
 * Allow the person named in the database entry "rwc" access.
 */
acl_entry_p++;
acl_entry_p->perms = sec_acl_perm_read | sec_acl_perm_write |
                     sec_acl_perm_control;
acl_entry_p->entry_info.entry_type = sec_acl_e_type_user;
sec_rgy_pgo_name_to_id (emp_db_rgy_handle,
        sec_rgy_domain_person,
        db_entry_name,
        &acl_entry_p->entry_info.tagged_union.id.uuid,
        &status);
if (status != rpc_s_ok)
        return emp_s_unknown_name;

acl_entry_p->entry_info.tagged_union.id.name = (idl_char *) "";

/*
 * Write this ACL to the ACL table and backing store.
 */
acl_store_write_acl (&acl, compact_acl);

/*
 * Since we now have the compact_acl, we don't need the full ACL
 * any more.
 */
free (acl.sec_acl_entries);
```

```
        return emp_s_ok;
}


/*
 * Create the default ACL for the database as a whole. It allows:
 *    1. members of the emp_db_users group "w" access.
 *    2. members of the emp_db_admin group "wc" access.
 */
static void
create_default_db_acl (compact_acl_t    *compact_acl)
{
        sec_acl_t        acl;
        sec_acl_entry_t *acl_entry_p;
        error_status_t   status;

        /*
         * Initialize an ACL of 2 entries.
         */
        acl.num_entries = 2;
        acl.sec_acl_entries = acl_entry_p =
                (sec_acl_entry_t *) malloc (
                        acl.num_entries * sizeof(sec_acl_entry_t));

        /*
         * Fill in the default realm.
         */
        acl.default_realm.name = strdup (emp_db_cell_name);
        acl.default_realm.uuid = emp_db_cell_uuid;

        /*
         * Note that we do not bother to fill in the ACL manager UUID
         * since we can infer it when we read the ACL back.
         */

        /*
         * Allow "i" access to emp_db_users group.
         */
        acl_entry_p->perms = sec_acl_perm_insert;
        acl_entry_p->entry_info.entry_type = sec_acl_e_type_group;
        acl_entry_p->entry_info.tagged_union.id.uuid = emp_db_user_group_uuid;
        acl_entry_p->entry_info.tagged_union.id.name = (idl_char *) "";

        /*
         * Allow "ic" access to emp_db_admin group.
         */
        acl_entry_p++;
        acl_entry_p->perms = sec_acl_perm_insert | sec_acl_perm_control;
        acl_entry_p->entry_info.entry_type = sec_acl_e_type_group;
        acl_entry_p->entry_info.tagged_union.id.uuid = emp_db_admin_group_uuid;
        acl_entry_p->entry_info.tagged_union.id.name = (idl_char *) "";

        /*
```

Example D-6: The emp_db Manager Code (continued)

```
                * Write this ACL to the ACL table and backing store.
                */
               acl_store_write_acl (&acl, compact_acl);

               /*
                * Since we now have the compact_acl, we don't need the full ACL
                * any more.
                */
               free (acl.sec_acl_entries);
}
```

Example D-7: The emp_db Backing Store (empstore.h)

```
#ifndef _EMP_STORE_H
#define _EMP_STORE_H
/*
 * emp_store.h
 *
 * Backing store for the employee database application.
 */
#include <dce/aclbase.h>
#include "emp_db.h"
#include "aclstore.h"

/*
 * Internal definitions.
 */

typedef struct {
        emp_record_t     emp_record;
        compact_acl_t    compact_acl;
} emp_store_record_t;

#define DATABASE_SIZE 500
extern emp_store_record_t emp_database[DATABASE_SIZE];

/*
 * Initialize the emp_db database from the backing store
 */
extern void
emp_store_init (emp_store_record_t emp_database[],
                int                           *initial_db);

/*
 * Write an emp_db record to the backing store.
 */
extern void
emp_store_write (unsigned        emp_index);

/*
 * Delete an emp_db record from the backing store.
```

Example D-7: The emp_db Backing Store (empstore.h) (continued)

```
*/
extern void
emp_store_delete (unsigned      emp_index);

#endif /* _EMP_STORE_H */
```

Example D-8: The emp_db Backing Store (empstore.c)

```c
/*
 * emp_store.c
 *
 * Backing store for the employee database.
 */
#include <dce/aclbase.h>
#include "emp_db.h"
#include "aclstore.h"
#include "empstore.h"
#include "chk_stat.h"

#include <sys/types.h>
#include <sys/stat.h>
#include <unistd.h>
#include <fcntl.h>
#include <string.h>
#include <errno.h>

#define EMP_DB_FILE "/usr/people/emp_db_server/emp_db_file"

static int emp_db_fd;

/*
 * Initialize the emp_db database from the backing store
 */
void
emp_store_init (emp_store_record_t emp_database[],
                int                        *initial_db)
{
        int     n, db_size, fd;

        db_size = DATABASE_SIZE*sizeof(emp_store_record_t);

        /*
         * If the file exists, read it in. Otherwise, create one.
         */
        fd = open (EMP_DB_FILE, O_RDWR|O_SYNC);
        if (fd != -1) {
                /*
                 * File exists, read it in.
                 */
                n = read (fd, emp_database, db_size);
                if ((n == -1) || (n < db_size))
```

Example D-8: The emp_db Backing Store (empstore.c) (continued)

```
                              PERROR_EXIT ("emp_store_init, open failed");
                *initial_db = 0;
        }
        else if (errno == ENOENT) {
                /*
                 * File does not exist; create it.
                 */
                if ((fd = creat (EMP_DB_FILE, S_IRUSR|S_IWUSR)) == -1)
                        PERROR_EXIT ("emp_store_init, create failed");

                memset (emp_database, 0, db_size);
                n = write (fd, emp_database, db_size);
                if ((n == -1) || (n < db_size))
                        PERROR_EXIT ("emp_store_init, write failed");
                *initial_db = 1;
        }
        else {
                PERROR_EXIT ("emp_store_init, open failed");
        }

        /*
         * Save the file descriptor to the backing store for later use.
         */
        emp_db_fd = fd;
}

/*
 * Write an emp_db record to the backing store.
 */
void
emp_store_write (unsigned      emp_index)
{
        int     offset, n;

        offset = emp_index * sizeof(emp_store_record_t);
        if (lseek (emp_db_fd, offset, SEEK_SET) == -1)
                PERROR_EXIT ("emp_store_write, seek failed");

        n = write (emp_db_fd, &emp_database[emp_index],
                   sizeof(emp_store_record_t));
        if ((n == -1) || (n < sizeof(emp_store_record_t)))
                PERROR_EXIT ("emp_store_write, write failed");

}

/*
 * Delete an emp_db record from the backing store.
 */
extern void
emp_store_delete (unsigned      emp_index)
{
        /*
         * We assume that the incore entry has already been cleared.
```

Example D-8: The emp_db Backing Store (empstore.c) (continued)

```
         */
        emp_store_write (emp_index);
}
```

Example D-9: The ACL Backing Store (aclstore.h)

```
#ifndef _ACL_STORE_H
#define _ACL_STORE_H
/*
 * acl_store.h
 *
 * Backing store for ACLs.
 */
#include <dce/aclbase.h>

#define ACL_STORE_SIZE 500

typedef struct acl_table_entry_s {
        sec_acl_entry_t acl_entry;
        int             ref_count;
} acl_table_entry_t;


#define MAX_ACLS_PER_OBJ 10

typedef struct {
        sec_acl_id_t    default_realm;
        int             num_entries;
        int             acl_indices[MAX_ACLS_PER_OBJ];
} compact_acl_t;


/*
 * Initialize the ACL store.
 */
extern void
acl_store_init (void);

/*
 * Read in an ACL.
 */
extern void
acl_store_read_acl (uuid_t          *acl_mgr_type,      /* IN */
                    compact_acl_t   *compact_acl,       /* IN */
                    sec_acl_t       **acl_p);           /* OUT */

/*
 * Write an ACL.
 */
extern void
acl_store_write_acl (sec_acl_t      *acl,               /* IN */
```

Example D-9: The ACL Backing Store (aclstore.b) (continued)

```
                              compact_acl_t        *compact_acl);           /* OUT */


/*
 * Delete an ACL.
 */
extern void
acl_store_delete_acl (compact_acl_t        *compact_acl);          /* IN */


/*
 * Free an ACL
 */
extern void
acl_store_free_acl    (sec_acl_t             **acl_p);             /* IN/OUT */


/*
 * Copy an ACL list to stub allocated storage. The original ACL list
 * is then freed.
 */
extern void
acl_store_copy_acl_list_ss (sec_acl_list_t **IO_src_acl_list,    /* IN/OUT */
                            sec_acl_list_t **O_dst_acl_list);    /* OUT */


#endif /* _ACL_STORE_H */
```

Example D-10: The ACL Backing Store (aclstore.c)

```
/*
 * acl_store.c
 *
 * Backing store for ACLs.
 */

#include <sys/types.h>
#include <dce/uuid.h>
#include <sys/stat.h>
#include <unistd.h>
#include <stdlib.h>
#include <stdio.h>
#include <fcntl.h>
#include <string.h>
#include <errno.h>

#include <dce/rpc.h>
#include <dce/aclbase.h>
#include <dce/dce_cf.h>
#include <dce/binding.h>
#include <dce/secidmap.h>
#include <dce/idlbase.h>
```

Example D-10: The ACL Backing Store (aclstore.c) (continued)

```c
#include "chk_stat.h"
#include "aclstore.h"


static acl_table_entry_t acl_table[ACL_STORE_SIZE];

#define ACL_DB_FILE "/usr/people/emp_db_server/acl_db_file"
static int acl_db_fd;


/*
 * Initialize the ACL store.
 */
void
acl_store_init (void)
{
        int                     n, db_size, fd;

        db_size = ACL_STORE_SIZE*sizeof(acl_table_entry_t);

        /*
         * If the file exists, read it in. Otherwise, create one.
         */
        fd = open (ACL_DB_FILE, O_RDWR|O_SYNC);
        if (fd != -1) {
                /*
                 * File exists, read it in.
                 */
                n = read (fd, acl_table, db_size);
                if ((n == -1) || (n < db_size))
                        PERROR_EXIT ("acl_store_init, open failed");
        }
        else if (errno == ENOENT) {
                /*
                 * File does not exist; create it.
                 */
                if ((fd = creat (ACL_DB_FILE, S_IRUSR|S_IWUSR)) == -1)
                        PERROR_EXIT ("acl_store_init, create failed");

                memset (acl_table, 0, db_size);
                n = write (fd, acl_table, db_size);
                if ((n == -1) || (n < db_size))
                        PERROR_EXIT ("acl_store_init, write failed");
        }
        else {
                PERROR_EXIT ("acl_store_init, open failed");
        }

        /*
         * Save the file descriptor for later use.
         */
        acl_db_fd = fd;
}
```

Example D-10: The ACL Backing Store (aclstore.c) (continued)

```
/*
 * Read in an ACL.
 */
extern void
acl_store_read_acl (uuid_t              *acl_mgr_type,   /* IN */
                    compact_acl_t       *compact_acl,    /* IN */
                    sec_acl_t           **acl_p)         /* OUT */
{
        sec_acl_t       *acl;
        unsigned        i, acl_table_index, size;
        sec_acl_entry_t *acl_entry_p;
        unsigned32      st;

        /*
         * Allocate space for the ACL.
         */
        acl = (sec_acl_t *) malloc(sizeof(sec_acl_t));
        memset (acl, 0, sizeof(sec_acl_t));

        /*
         * Allocate space for the ACL entries.
         */
        acl->num_entries = compact_acl->num_entries;
        size = compact_acl->num_entries * sizeof(sec_acl_entry_t);
        acl_entry_p = acl->sec_acl_entries =
                (sec_acl_entry_t *)malloc (size);
        memset (acl_entry_p, 0, size);

        /*
         * Fill in the ACL entries with information from the ACL table.
         */
        for (i=0; i < compact_acl->num_entries; i++) {
                acl_table_index = compact_acl->acl_indices[i];
                memcpy (&acl_entry_p[i], &acl_table[acl_table_index],
                        sizeof(sec_acl_entry_t));
        }

        acl->default_realm = compact_acl->default_realm;
        if (acl_mgr_type)
                acl->sec_acl_manager_type = *acl_mgr_type;
        else
                uuid_create_nil (&acl->sec_acl_manager_type, &st);

        *acl_p = acl;
}


/*
 * Internal procedure to write an ACL entry and update the backing store.
 * This routine returns the ACL table index to which this ACL entry was
 * written.
```

Example D-10: The ACL Backing Store (aclstore.c) (continued)

```c
    */
static void
acl_store_write_acl_entry (sec_acl_entry_t    *acl_entry,    /* IN */
                           int                 *acl_index)    /* OUT */
{
        unsigned       i, found;
        int            n;

        /*
         * See if entry is already in the table.
         */
        found = 0;
        for (i=0; i < ACL_STORE_SIZE; i++) {
                if (memcmp (acl_entry, &acl_table[i].acl_entry,
                        sizeof(sec_acl_entry_t)) == 0) {
                        /*
                         * It exists, just increment the reference count.
                         */
                        acl_table[i].ref_count++;
                        *acl_index = i;
                        found = 1;
                        break;
                }
        }

        if (! found) {
                /*
                 * This acl entry does not exist in the table; add it.
                 */
                for (i=0; i < ACL_STORE_SIZE; i++) {

                        /*
                         * Free entries have reference counts of 0.
                         */
                        if (acl_table[i].ref_count == 0) {
                                memcpy (&acl_table[i].acl_entry, acl_entry,
                                        sizeof(sec_acl_entry_t));
                                acl_table[i].ref_count = 1;
                                *acl_index = i;
                                found = 1;
                                break;
                        }
                }

                if (! found)
                        PERROR_EXIT (
                          "acl_store_write_acl_entry, no space in acl_table");
        }

        /*
         * Write the acl entry to the backing store.
         */
        if (lseek (acl_db_fd, i*sizeof(acl_table_entry_t), SEEK_SET) == -1)
```

Example D-10: The ACL Backing Store (aclstore.c) (continued)

```
                    PERROR_EXIT ("acl_store_write_acl_entry, seek failed");

        n = write (acl_db_fd, &acl_table[i], sizeof(acl_table_entry_t));
        if ((n == -1) || (n < sizeof(acl_table_entry_t)))
                PERROR_EXIT ("acl_store_write_acl_entry, write failed");

}


/*
 * Write an ACL.
 */
extern void
acl_store_write_acl (sec_acl_t          *acl,            /* IN */
                     compact_acl_t      *compact_acl)    /* OUT */
{
        unsigned        i;
        sec_acl_entry_t *acl_entry_p;

        acl_entry_p = acl->sec_acl_entries;
        for (i=0; i < acl->num_entries; i++) {
                acl_store_write_acl_entry (&acl_entry_p[i],
                        &compact_acl->acl_indices[i]);
        }
        compact_acl->num_entries = acl->num_entries;
        compact_acl->default_realm = acl->default_realm;
}


/*
 * Internal procedure to delete an ACL entry.
 */
static void
acl_store_delete_acl_entry (int        acl_index)        /* IN */
{
        int     n;

        /*
         * Decrement the reference count. A reference count of 0
         * implicitly frees this entry.
         */
        acl_table[acl_index].ref_count--;
        if (acl_table[acl_index].ref_count == 0)
                memset (&acl_table[acl_index], 0, sizeof(acl_table_entry_t));

        /*
         * Write the empty acl entry to the backing store.
         */
        if (lseek (acl_db_fd, acl_index*sizeof(acl_table_entry_t), SEEK_SET)
            == -1)
                PERROR_EXIT ("acl_store_delete_acl_entry, seek failed");
```

Example D-10: The ACL Backing Store (aclstore.c) (continued)

```
        n = write (acl_db_fd, &acl_table[acl_index], sizeof(acl_table_entry_t));
        if ((n == -1) || (n < sizeof(acl_table_entry_t)))
                PERROR_EXIT ("acl_store_delete_acl_entry, write failed");

}

/*
 * Delete an ACL.
 */
extern void
acl_store_delete_acl (compact_acl_t      *compact_acl)              /* IN */
{
        unsigned        i;

        for (i=0; i < compact_acl->num_entries; i++) {
                acl_store_delete_acl_entry (compact_acl->acl_indices[i]);
        }
        memset (compact_acl, 0, sizeof(compact_acl_t));
}

/*
 * Free an ACL
 */
extern void
acl_store_free_acl (sec_acl_t          **acl_p)                     /* IN/OUT */
{
        sec_acl_t       *acl;
        unsigned        i, acl_table_index, size;
        sec_acl_entry_t *acl_entry_p;
        unsigned32      st;

        free ((*acl_p)->sec_acl_entries);
        free (*acl_p);
        *acl_p = NULL;
}

/*
 * Copy an ACL to stub allocated storage. The source ACL is freed.
 */
static void
acl_store_copy_acl (sec_acl_t **IO_src_acl,                 /* IN/OUT */
                    sec_acl_t **O_dst_acl)                  /* OUT */
{
        sec_acl_t       *src_acl, *dst_acl;
        unsigned        num_entries;

        src_acl = *IO_src_acl;

        if (src_acl == NULL) {
                *O_dst_acl = NULL;
                return;
        }
```

Example D-10: The ACL Backing Store (aclstore.c) (continued)

```
        num_entries = src_acl->num_entries;

        /*
         * Allocate the fixed part of the ACL header.
         */
        dst_acl = (sec_acl_p_t) rpc_ss_allocate (sizeof(sec_acl_t));
        memcpy (dst_acl, src_acl, sizeof(sec_acl_t));

        /*
         * Allocate the ACL entries.
         */
        dst_acl->sec_acl_entries =
                (sec_acl_entry_t *) rpc_ss_allocate (
                        num_entries * sizeof(sec_acl_entry_t));

        memcpy (dst_acl->sec_acl_entries, src_acl->sec_acl_entries,
                num_entries * sizeof(sec_acl_entry_t));

        acl_store_free_acl (IO_src_acl);
        *O_dst_acl = dst_acl;
}

/*
 * Copy an ACL list to stub allocated storage. The original ACL list
 * is then freed.
 */
extern void
acl_store_copy_acl_list_ss (sec_acl_list_t **IO_src,     /* IN/OUT */
                            sec_acl_list_t **O_dst)      /* OUT */
{
        sec_acl_list_t  *src, *dst;
        unsigned        num_acls, i;
        sec_acl_p_t     acl_p;

        src = *IO_src;
        if (src == NULL) {
                *O_dst = NULL;
                return;
        }

        num_acls = src->num_acls;

        /*
         * Allocate the list header.
         */
        dst = (sec_acl_list_t *)rpc_ss_allocate (
                        sizeof(sec_acl_list_t) +
                        (num_acls - 1)*sizeof(sec_acl_p_t));
        dst->num_acls = num_acls;

        /*
         * Allocate and copy the ACL entries. acl_store_copy_acl also frees
         * the source ACLs.
```

Example D-10: The ACL Backing Store (aclstore.c) (continued)

```
        */
        for (i=0; i < num_acls; i++) {
                acl_store_copy_acl (&src->sec_acls[i],
                                    &dst->sec_acls[i]);
        }

        /*
         * Free the source ACL list.
         */
        free (src);
        *IO_src = NULL;

        *O_dst = dst;
}
```

Example D-11: The Reference Monitor (ref_mon.h)

```
#ifndef _REF_MON_H
#define _REF_MON_H

/*
 * FILE: ref_mon.h
 *
 * ACL based reference monitor.
 */
typedef enum { OP_READ, OP_WRITE } access_type_t;
#define OP_READ sec_acl_perm_read
#define OP_WRITE sec_acl_perm_write
#define OP_INSERT sec_acl_perm_insert
#define OP_CONTROL sec_acl_perm_control

extern int client_is_authorized (
        handle_t                handle,
        sec_acl_permset_t       operation,
        emp_db_field_t          emp_name);

#endif /* _REF_MON_H */
```

Example D-12: The Reference Monitor (ref_mon.c)

```
/*
 * FILE NAME: ref_mon.c
 *
 * Reference monitor for the employee database application.
 *
 */

#include <stdio.h>
#include <stdlib.h>
#include <string.h>
```

Example D-12: The Reference Monitor (ref_mon.c) (continued)

```
#include "emp_db.h"
#include "empstore.h"
#include "aclstore.h"
#include "chk_stat.h"

#include <dce/binding.h>        /* binding to registry */
#include <dce/pgo.h>            /* registry i/f */
#include <dce/secidmap.h>       /* translate global name -> princ name */

#include <dce/id_base.h>
#include <dce/daclmgr.h>

#include "ref_mon.h"


int
client_is_authorized (
        handle_t                handle,
        sec_acl_permset_t       desired_access,
        emp_db_field_t          emp_name)
{
        unsigned_char_t    *server_principal_name;
        sec_rgy_name_t     client_principal_name;
        sec_id_pac_t       *pac;
        unsigned32         protection_level;
        unsigned32         authn_svc;
        unsigned32         authz_svc;
        unsigned32         status;
        boolean32          authorized;

        /*
         * Check the authentication parameters that the client
         * selected for this call.
         */
        rpc_binding_inq_auth_client (handle,
                (rpc_authz_handle_t *) &pac,
                &server_principal_name, &protection_level, &authn_svc,
                &authz_svc, &status);
        CHECK_STATUS (status, "inq_auth_client failed", ABORT);

        /*
         * Make sure that the caller has specified the required
         * level of protection, authentication, and authorization.
         */
        if (! ((protection_level == rpc_c_protect_level_pkt_integ) &&
                (authn_svc == rpc_c_authn_dce_secret) &&
                (authz_svc == rpc_c_authz_dce)))
                return 0;

        authorized = sec_acl_mgr_is_authorized (NULL, desired_access,
                pac, emp_name, NULL, NULL, NULL, &status);
```

Example D-12: The Reference Monitor (ref_mon.c) (continued)

```
        /*
         * We can get sec_acl_object_not_found if the ACL is not found.
         * This can happen since we call the reference monitor before we
         * look up the entry in the emp_db.
         */
        if ((status != rpc_s_ok) && (status != sec_acl_object_not_found))
                CHECK_STATUS (status, "sec_acl_mgr_is_authorized failed",
                                      ABORT);

        return authorized;

}


/* access_granted
 *
 * Private routine to compare an ACL entry permset against the desired
 * access permset, to determine if access should be granted
 */

boolean32
access_granted (
    sec_acl_entry_t      entry,
    sec_acl_permset_t    desired,
    sec_acl_permset_t    *granted)
{
    boolean32 grant_access = false;

    switch (entry.entry_info.entry_type) {
        case sec_acl_e_type_any_other:
        case sec_acl_e_type_user:
        case sec_acl_e_type_group:
        case sec_acl_e_type_other_obj:
        case sec_acl_e_type_foreign_other:
        case sec_acl_e_type_foreign_user:
        case sec_acl_e_type_foreign_group:
        case sec_acl_e_type_extended:
            *granted = entry.perms & desired;
            break;

        case sec_acl_e_type_group_obj:
        case sec_acl_e_type_user_obj:
        case sec_acl_e_type_mask_obj:
        case sec_acl_e_type_unauthenticated:
        default:
            /*
             * We do not support POSIX-compatibility or the
             * UNAUTHENTICATED ACL entry types.
             */
            *granted = (sec_acl_permset_t) 0;
    }
    if ( *granted == desired )
        grant_access = true;
```

Example D-12: *The Reference Monitor (ref_mon.c)* *(continued)*

```
        return grant_access;
}


/* s e c _ a c l _ m g r _ i s _ a u t h o r i z e d
 *
 * The basic operation in the authorization package, this function will
 * yield true if the principal (as described in the privilege attribute
 * certificate referred to by "accessor_info") is authorized to perform
 * the requested operation.  The dacl controlling this decision is
 * not passed directly to this function, but is referred to via the
 * sec_acl_key and the sec_acl_type parameters (Generally objects will
 * only be protected by a dacl_type_object dacl, but specifying the
 * sec_acl_type on the call will allow for future enhancement)
 *
 * NOTE:
 *    We supply two implementations of this routine. The first one
 *    does all the access checks in-line. This is the version described
 *    in the book. It is useful for illustrating the access control
 *    algorithm.
 *    The second, simpler implementation uses sec_acl_mgr_get_access().
 *    You should use the second version because it allows you to
 *    isolate the ACL entry checks in a single routine.
 */

/* Compare default realm with accessor's realm */
#define default_realm_eq(entry) uuid_equal(&accessor_info->realm.uuid, \
                                   &sec_acl_p->default_realm.uuid, \
                                   &st)

/* Compare foreign realm with accessor's realm */
#define foreign_realm_eq(entry) uuid_equal(&accessor_info->realm.uuid, \
   &sec_acl_p->sec_acl_entries[entry].entry_info.tagged_union. \
   foreign_id.realm.uuid, &st)

#define ENTRY_NOT_FOUND -1
#define MAX_PERMISSIONS ~0


boolean32
sec_acl_mgr_is_authorized (
     sec_acl_mgr_handle_t    sec_acl_mgr,
     sec_acl_permset_t       desired_access,
     sec_id_pac_t            *accessor_info,
     sec_acl_key_t           sec_acl_key,
     uuid_t                  *manager_type_p,
     sec_id_t                *user_obj,
     sec_id_t                *group_obj,
     error_status_t          *st_p)
{
     sec_acl_list_t      *sec_acl_list;
     sec_acl_t           *sec_acl_p;
     int                 i;                /* For traversing entry list. */
```

Example D-12: The Reference Monitor (ref_mon.c) (continued)

```
unsigned int          j;              /* For traversing entry list. */
int                   user_entry,     /* For keeping track of entries... */
                      foreign_user_entry,
                      other_obj_entry,
                      foreign_other_entry,
                      any_other_entry;
sec_id_t              *group_id, *realm_id;
error_status_t        st;
sec_acl_permset_t     granted, group_access;
boolean32             chk_loc_groups = false, one_group_found = false;
boolean32             acc_granted;

/*
 * Retrieve the ACL for this key.
 */

sec_acl_mgr_lookup(NULL, sec_acl_key, manager_type_p,
                   sec_acl_type_object, &sec_acl_list, st_p);
if (*st_p != rpc_s_ok) {
    return false;
}
else
    sec_acl_p = sec_acl_list->sec_acls[0];

/*
 * We will check for each of the following ACL types. Only
 * one entry of each will match the client.
 */
user_entry = foreign_user_entry = other_obj_entry =
foreign_other_entry = any_other_entry = ENTRY_NOT_FOUND;

/*
 * Now find each type in the ACL, if it exists. Only one entry
 * in the ACL matches each type.
 */
for (i = 0; i < sec_acl_p->num_entries; i++) {

    /*
     * Check for existence of each type of entry, and keep track
     * of where each type was found in the entry list.
     * Don't mark type as found if the associated realm id's
     * are not the same.
     */
    switch(sec_acl_p->sec_acl_entries[i].entry_info.entry_type) {

        case sec_acl_e_type_user:
            if ((uuid_equal(&accessor_info->principal.uuid,
                            &sec_acl_p->sec_acl_entries[i].entry_info.
                            tagged_union.id.uuid,
                            &st)) && (default_realm_eq(i)))
                    user_entry = i;
                break;
```

Example D-12: The Reference Monitor (ref_mon.c) (continued)

```
            case sec_acl_e_type_foreign_user:
                if ((uuid_equal(&accessor_info->principal.uuid,
                              &sec_acl_p->sec_acl_entries[i].entry_info.
                               tagged_union.foreign_id.id.uuid,
                              &st)) && (foreign_realm_eq(i)))
                    foreign_user_entry = i;
                break;

            case sec_acl_e_type_other_obj:
                if (default_realm_eq(i))
                    other_obj_entry = i;
                break;

            case sec_acl_e_type_foreign_other:
                if ( uuid_equal( &accessor_info->realm.uuid,
                        &sec_acl_p->sec_acl_entries[i].entry_info.
                         tagged_union.id.uuid, &st))
                    foreign_other_entry = i;
                break;

            case sec_acl_e_type_any_other:
                any_other_entry = i;
                break;

            default:
                break;
        }
    }
    /*
     * Now that we know which entries match the user described in the PAC,
     * check the permissions corresponding to each entry until access is
     * granted or denied by one of them.
     */

    /*
     * USER check
     */
    if (user_entry != ENTRY_NOT_FOUND) {
        /* check the permsets to see if access is granted */
        acc_granted = access_granted(sec_acl_p->sec_acl_entries[user_entry],
                            desired_access, &granted);
        acl_store_free_acl(&sec_acl_p);
        return acc_granted;
    }

    /*
     * FOREIGN_USER check
     */
    if (foreign_user_entry != ENTRY_NOT_FOUND) {
        /* check the permsets to see if access is granted */
        acc_granted =
                access_granted(sec_acl_p->sec_acl_entries[foreign_user_entry],
                            desired_access, &granted);
```

Example D-12: The Reference Monitor (ref_mon.c) (continued)

```
        acl_store_free_acl(&sec_acl_p);
        return acc_granted;
    }

    /*
     * GROUP checks
     */

    /*
     * Initialize mask where we will store all permissions that we find.
     */
    group_access = (sec_acl_permset_t) 0;

    for (i = 0; i < sec_acl_p->num_entries; i++) {

        switch(sec_acl_p->sec_acl_entries[i].entry_info.entry_type) {

            case sec_acl_e_type_group:
            case sec_acl_e_type_foreign_group:

                if (sec_acl_p->sec_acl_entries[i].entry_info.entry_type
                                            == sec_acl_e_type_group) {
                    /*
                     * The PAC has 2 group lists: one for the local groups
                     * to which the client belongs and one for the foreign
                     * groups to which the client belongs. Figure out which
                     * one we need to search as follows:
                     *
                     * If the client belongs to this ACL's default (local)
                     * cell, then we need to look in the PAC's list of
                     * local groups for a match. Otherwise, look in the
                     * PAC's foreign group list.
                     */
                    chk_loc_groups = default_realm_eq(i);

                    /*
                     * The group that we want to match is stored in the
                     * ACL entry and the cell is the ACL's default cell.
                     */
                    group_id = &sec_acl_p->sec_acl_entries[i].entry_info.
                            tagged_union.id;
                    realm_id = &sec_acl_p->default_realm;

                } else {        /* sec_acl_e_type_foreign_group */

                    /*
                     * If the client belongs to the same cell as that
                     * specified by the ACL entry, then we need to
                     * look in the PAC's local group list. Otherwise,
                     * look in the PAC's foreign group list.
                     */
                    chk_loc_groups = foreign_realm_eq(i);
                    group_id = &sec_acl_p->sec_acl_entries[i].entry_info.
```

Example D-12: The Reference Monitor (ref_mon.c) (continued)

```
                        tagged_union.foreign_id.id;
        realm_id = &sec_acl_p->sec_acl_entries[i].entry_info.
                        tagged_union.foreign_id.realm;
}

/*
 * Check either the PAC's list of local groups or the
 * PAC's list of foreign groups.
 */
if (chk_loc_groups) {

  /*
   * We are checking the PAC's local group list.
   *
   * First, check the primary group.
   */
  if (uuid_equal(&accessor_info->group.uuid,
                      &group_id->uuid, &st) ) {

    /* then check the perms to see if access is granted */
    if (access_granted(sec_acl_p->sec_acl_entries[i],
                          desired_access, &granted)) {
        acl_store_free_acl(&sec_acl_p);
        return true;
    }
    else {
        one_group_found = true;
        group_access = (group_access | granted);
    }
  }

  /*
   * Check the secondary groups.
   */
  for (j = 0; j < accessor_info->num_groups; j++) {

    if (uuid_equal(&accessor_info->groups[j].uuid,
                      &group_id->uuid, &st) ) {

      /* check the perms to see if access granted */
      if (access_granted(sec_acl_p->sec_acl_entries[i],
                            desired_access, &granted)) {
          acl_store_free_acl(&sec_acl_p);
          return true;
      }
      else {
          one_group_found = true;
          group_access = (group_access | granted);
      }
    }
  }
} else {
```

Example D-12: The Reference Monitor (ref_mon.c) (continued)

```
                /*
                 * We are checking the PAC's foreign group list.
                 */
                for (j = 0; j < accessor_info->num_foreign_groups; j++) {

                    if ((uuid_equal(&accessor_info->foreign_groups[j].id.uuid,
                                &group_id->uuid, &st)) &&
                        (uuid_equal(&accessor_info->foreign_groups[j].realm.uuid,
                                    &realm_id->uuid, &st)) ) {

                        /* check the perms to see if access granted */
                        if (access_granted(sec_acl_p->sec_acl_entries[i],
                                        desired_access, &granted)) {
                            acl_store_free_acl(&sec_acl_p);
                            return true;
                        }
                        else {
                            one_group_found = true;
                            group_access = (group_access | granted);
                        }
                    }
                }
                break;

            default:
                break;

        } /* switch (entry type) */

        /* See if the union of multiple group entries granted access */
        if ((group_access & desired_access) == desired_access) {
            acl_store_free_acl(&sec_acl_p);
            return true;
        }

    } /* GROUP check */

    /*
     * At this point, we've gone through all the groups in the PAC without
     * having granted the client access. If we've gotten a matching group
     * entry, then deny any access.
     */
    if (one_group_found) {
        acl_store_free_acl(&sec_acl_p);
        return false;
    }

    /* OTHER_OBJ check */
    if (other_obj_entry != ENTRY_NOT_FOUND) {
        /* check the permsets to see if access is granted */
        acc_granted = access_granted(
                            sec_acl_p->sec_acl_entries[other_obj_entry],
```

Example D-12: The Reference Monitor (ref_mon.c) (continued)

```
                                    desired_access, &granted);
            acl_store_free_acl(&sec_acl_p);
            return acc_granted;
        }


        /* FOREIGN_OTHER check */
        if (foreign_other_entry != ENTRY_NOT_FOUND) {
            /* check the permsets to see if access is granted */
            acc_granted = access_granted(
                                sec_acl_p->sec_acl_entries[foreign_other_entry],
                                desired_access, &granted);
            acl_store_free_acl(&sec_acl_p);
            return acc_granted;
        }


        /* ANY_OTHER check */
        if (any_other_entry != ENTRY_NOT_FOUND) {
            /* check the permsets to see if access is granted */
            acc_granted = access_granted(sec_acl_p->sec_acl_entries[any_other_entry],
                            desired_access, &granted);
            acl_store_free_acl(&sec_acl_p);
            return acc_granted;
        }

        /*
         * No matching ACL entries were found, deny access.
         */
        acl_store_free_acl(&sec_acl_p);
        return false;

    }



/*
 * An alternative implementation of sec_acl_mgr_is_authorized that
 * uses sec_acl_mgr_get_access().
 */
boolean32
sec_acl_mgr_is_authorized_alternative (
    sec_acl_mgr_handle_t    sec_acl_mgr,
    sec_acl_permset_t       desired_access,
    sec_id_pac_t            *accessor_info,
    sec_acl_key_t           sec_acl_key,
    uuid_t                  *manager_type_p,
    sec_id_t                *user_obj,
    sec_id_t                *group_obj,
    error_status_t          *st_p)
{
    error_status_t      st;
    sec_acl_permset_t   access_granted;

    /*
     * First, find what kind of access our client has to the object.
```

Example D-12: The Reference Monitor (ref_mon.c) (continued)

```
     */
     sec_acl_mgr_get_access (
         sec_acl_mgr, accessor_info, sec_acl_key, manager_type_p,
         user_obj, group_obj, &access_granted, st_p);

     if (*st_p != rpc_s_ok)
         return false;

     /*
      * Now see if desired_access is in access_granted.
      */
     return ((access_granted & desired_access) == desired_access);
}


/*
 * Retrieve the ACL associated with the object named by sec_acl_key.
 */
void
sec_acl_mgr_lookup(
        sec_acl_mgr_handle_t    sec_acl_mgr,
        sec_acl_key_t           sec_acl_key,
        uuid_t                  *manager_type,
        sec_acl_type_t          sec_acl_type,
        sec_acl_list_t          **sec_acl_list,
        error_status_t          *st)
{
        sec_acl_t               *acl_p;
        sec_acl_list_t          *acl_list;
        unsigned                i, found;

        if ((sec_acl_key == NULL) ||
            (((char *)sec_acl_key)[0] == '\0')) {
                /*
                 * We are looking up the ACL for the database as a whole.
                 * It is stored in reserved location 0 of the emp_database[].
                 */
                acl_store_read_acl (manager_type,
                                    &emp_database[0].compact_acl, &acl_p);
                found = 1;
        }
        else {
                /*
                 * We are looking up the ACL for a single database entry.
                 */
                found = 0;
                for (i=0; i < DATABASE_SIZE; i++) {
                        if (strcmp (emp_database[i].emp_record.emp_name,
                                    sec_acl_key) == 0) {

                                acl_store_read_acl (manager_type,
                                        &emp_database[i].compact_acl, &acl_p);
                                found = 1;
```

Example D-12: The Reference Monitor (ref_mon.c) (continued)

```
                                 break;
                        }
                }

                if (! found) {
                        *st = sec_acl_object_not_found;
                        *sec_acl_list = NULL;
                        return;
                }
        }
        acl_list = malloc (sizeof(sec_acl_list_t));
        acl_list->num_acls = 1;
        acl_list->sec_acls[0] = acl_p;

        *sec_acl_list = acl_list;

        *st = rpc_s_ok;
}


/*
 * access_granted_by_entry
 *
 * Private routine to return the permissions granted by an ACL entry.
 */

static sec_acl_permset_t
access_granted_by_entry (
    sec_acl_entry_t      entry)
{
    switch (entry.entry_info.entry_type) {
        case sec_acl_e_type_any_other:
        case sec_acl_e_type_user:
        case sec_acl_e_type_group:
        case sec_acl_e_type_other_obj:
        case sec_acl_e_type_foreign_other:
        case sec_acl_e_type_foreign_user:
        case sec_acl_e_type_foreign_group:
        case sec_acl_e_type_extended:
            return entry.perms;

        case sec_acl_e_type_group_obj:
        case sec_acl_e_type_user_obj:
        case sec_acl_e_type_mask_obj:
        case sec_acl_e_type_unauthenticated:
        default:
            /*
             * We do not support POSIX-compatibility or the
             * UNAUTHENTICATED ACL entry types.
             */
            return (sec_acl_permset_t) 0;
    }
}
```

Example D-12: The Reference Monitor (ref_mon.c) (continued)

```
/*
 * Determine the client's access to the specified object.
 */
void
sec_acl_mgr_get_access (
     sec_acl_mgr_handle_t    sec_acl_mgr,
     sec_id_pac_t            *accessor_info,
     sec_acl_key_t           sec_acl_key,
     uuid_t                  *manager_type_p,
     sec_id_t                *user_obj,
     sec_id_t                *group_obj,
     sec_acl_permset_t       *net_rights,
     error_status_t          *st_p)
{
     sec_acl_list_t      *sec_acl_list;
     sec_acl_t           *sec_acl_p;
     int                 i;              /* For traversing entry list. */
     unsigned int        j;              /* For traversing entry list. */
     int                 user_entry,     /* For keeping track of entries... */
                         foreign_user_entry,
                         other_obj_entry,
                         foreign_other_entry,
                         any_other_entry;
     sec_id_t            *group_id, *realm_id;
     error_status_t      st;
     sec_acl_permset_t   granted, group_access;
     boolean32           chk_loc_groups = false, one_group_found = false;

     /* Retrieve the sec_acl for this key */

     sec_acl_mgr_lookup(NULL, sec_acl_key, manager_type_p,
                        sec_acl_type_object, &sec_acl_list, st_p);
     if (*st_p != rpc_s_ok) {

         if (*st_p == emp_s_not_found)
                 *st_p = emp_s_ok;
         *net_rights = (sec_acl_permset_t) 0;
         return;
     }
     else
         sec_acl_p = sec_acl_list->sec_acls[0];

     /*
      * Only one of each type of entry could possibly match this
      * principal id, so keep a running tab on if/where each
      * type of entry is found in the list
      */
     user_entry = foreign_user_entry = other_obj_entry =
     foreign_other_entry = any_other_entry = ENTRY_NOT_FOUND;

     /* PRE-PROCESS the acl entries so we only have to loop
```

Example D-12: The Reference Monitor (ref_mon.c) (continued)

```
    * through once looking for specific types of entries
    *
    * Note, the accessor may be a member of multiple {foreign_}groups.
    * Therefore, the *group checks must be done below, in a separate
    * pass through the entry list.
    */
   for (i = 0; i < sec_acl_p->num_entries; i++) {

       /* Check for existence of each type of entry, and keep track
        * of where each type was found in the entry list.
        * Don't mark type as found if the associated realm id's
        * are not the same
        */
       switch(sec_acl_p->sec_acl_entries[i].entry_info.entry_type) {

           case sec_acl_e_type_user:
               if ((uuid_equal(&accessor_info->principal.uuid,
                               &sec_acl_p->sec_acl_entries[i].entry_info.
                                tagged_union.id.uuid,
                                &st)) && (default_realm_eq(i)))
                   user_entry = i;
               break;

           case sec_acl_e_type_foreign_user:
               if ((uuid_equal(&accessor_info->principal.uuid,
                               &sec_acl_p->sec_acl_entries[i].entry_info.
                                tagged_union.foreign_id.id.uuid,
                                &st)) && (foreign_realm_eq(i)))
                   foreign_user_entry = i;
               break;

           case sec_acl_e_type_other_obj:
               if (default_realm_eq(i))
                   other_obj_entry = i;
               break;

           case sec_acl_e_type_foreign_other:
               if ( uuid_equal( &accessor_info->realm.uuid,
                       &sec_acl_p->sec_acl_entries[i].entry_info.
                        tagged_union.id.uuid, &st))
                   foreign_other_entry = i;
               break;

           case sec_acl_e_type_any_other:
               any_other_entry = i;
               break;

           default:
               break;
       }
   }

   /* Now that we know which entries match the user described in the PAC,
```

Example D-12: The Reference Monitor (ref_mon.c) (continued)

```
     * check the permissions corresponding to each entry until access is
     * granted or denied by one of them.
     */

    /* USER check */
    if (user_entry != ENTRY_NOT_FOUND) {
        *net_rights = access_granted_by_entry(
                sec_acl_p->sec_acl_entries[user_entry]);
        acl_store_free_acl(&sec_acl_p);
        return;
    }


    /* FOREIGN_USER check */
    if (foreign_user_entry != ENTRY_NOT_FOUND) {
        *net_rights = access_granted_by_entry(
                sec_acl_p->sec_acl_entries[foreign_user_entry]);
        acl_store_free_acl(&sec_acl_p);
        return;
    }

    /* GROUP checks */
    group_access = (sec_acl_permset_t) 0;
    for (i = 0; i < sec_acl_p->num_entries; i++) {

        switch(sec_acl_p->sec_acl_entries[i].entry_info.entry_type) {

            case sec_acl_e_type_group:
            case sec_acl_e_type_foreign_group:

            if (sec_acl_p->sec_acl_entries[i].entry_info.entry_type
                                        == sec_acl_e_type_group) {
                /*
                 * The PAC has 2 group lists: one for the local groups
                 * to which the client belongs and one for the foreign
                 * groups to which the client belongs. Figure out which
                 * one we need to search:
                 *
                 * If the client belongs to this ACL's default (local)
                 * cell, then we need to look in the PAC's list of
                 * local groups for a match. Otherwise, look in the
                 * PAC's foreign group list.
                 */
                chk_loc_groups = default_realm_eq(i);

                /*
                 * The group that we want to match is stored in the
                 * ACL entry and the cell is the ACL's default cell.
                 */
                group_id = &sec_acl_p->sec_acl_entries[i].entry_info.
                        tagged_union.id;
                realm_id = &sec_acl_p->default_realm;

            } else {        /* sec_acl_e_type_foreign_group */
```

Example D-12: The Reference Monitor (ref_mon.c) (continued)

```
            /*
             * If the client belongs to the same cell as that
             * specified by the ACL entry, then we need to
             * look in the PAC's local group list. Otherwise,
             * look in the PAC's foreign group list.
             */
            chk_loc_groups = foreign_realm_eq(i);
            group_id = &sec_acl_p->sec_acl_entries[i].entry_info.
                        tagged_union.foreign_id.id;
            realm_id = &sec_acl_p->sec_acl_entries[i].entry_info.
                        tagged_union.foreign_id.realm;
        }

        /*
         * Check either the PAC's list of local groups or the
         * PAC's list of foreign groups.
         */
        if (chk_loc_groups) {

            /*
             * We are checking the PAC's local group list.
             *
             * First, check the primary group.
             */
            if (uuid_equal(&accessor_info->group.uuid,
                            &group_id->uuid, &st) ) {

                granted = access_granted_by_entry(
                            sec_acl_p->sec_acl_entries[i]);
                group_access = (group_access | granted);
                one_group_found = true;
            }

            /*
             * Check the secondary groups.
             */
            for (j = 0; j < accessor_info->num_groups; j++) {

                if (uuid_equal(&accessor_info->groups[j].uuid,
                                &group_id->uuid, &st) ) {

                    granted = access_granted_by_entry(
                                sec_acl_p->sec_acl_entries[i]);
                    group_access = (group_access | granted);
                    one_group_found = true;
                }
            }
        } else {

            /*
             * We are checking the PAC's foreign group list.
             */
```

Example D-12: The Reference Monitor (ref_mon.c) (continued)

```
                for (j = 0; j < accessor_info->num_foreign_groups; j++) {

                    if ((uuid_equal(&accessor_info->foreign_groups[j].id.uuid,
                                    &group_id->uuid, &st)) &&
                        (uuid_equal(&accessor_info->foreign_groups[j].realm.uuid,
                                    &realm_id->uuid, &st)) ) {

                        granted = access_granted_by_entry(
                                sec_acl_p->sec_acl_entries[i]);
                        group_access = (group_access | granted);
                        one_group_found = true;
                    }
                }
            }
            break;

        default:
            break;

    } /* switch (entry type) */

} /* GROUP check */

/*
 * At this point, we've gone through all the groups in the PAC.
 * If we've gotten any matching group entres, then
 * group_access specifies the access granted.
 */
if (one_group_found) {
    *net_rights = group_access;
    acl_store_free_acl(&sec_acl_p);
    return;
}

/* OTHER_OBJ check */
if (other_obj_entry != ENTRY_NOT_FOUND) {
    *net_rights = access_granted_by_entry(
            sec_acl_p->sec_acl_entries[user_entry]);
    acl_store_free_acl(&sec_acl_p);
    return;
}

/* FOREIGN_OTHER check */
if (foreign_other_entry != ENTRY_NOT_FOUND) {
    *net_rights = access_granted_by_entry(
            sec_acl_p->sec_acl_entries[user_entry]);
    acl_store_free_acl(&sec_acl_p);
    return;
}

/* ANY_OTHER check */
if (any_other_entry != ENTRY_NOT_FOUND) {
    *net_rights = access_granted_by_entry(
```

Example D-12: The Reference Monitor (ref_mon.c) (continued)

```
                sec_acl_p->sec_acl_entries[user_entry]);
        acl_store_free_acl(&sec_acl_p);
        return;
    }

    /*
     * No matching ACL entries were found, no access.
     */
    acl_store_free_acl(&sec_acl_p);
    *net_rights = (sec_acl_permset_t) 0;

}
```

Example D-13: Remote ACL management interface

```
/*
 * File: rdaclmgr.c
 *
 * Manager code for the rdaclif (remote ACL management)
 * interface.
 */
#include <pthread.h>
#include <dce/rdaclif.h>
#include <dce/secidmap.h>
#include <dce/daclmgr.h>
#include <stdlib.h>
#include <stdio.h>
#include <string.h>
#include "aclstore.h"
#include "emp_db.h"
#include "empstore.h"
#include "ref_mon.h"
#include "chk_stat.h"


/* Declare the entrypoint vector for this interface. */
rdaclif_v0_0_epv_t rdaclif_v0_0_manager_epv = {
        rdacl_lookup,
        rdacl_replace,
        rdacl_get_access,
        rdacl_test_access,
        rdacl_test_access_on_behalf,
        rdacl_get_manager_types,
        rdacl_get_printstring,
        rdacl_get_referral,
        rdacl_get_mgr_types_semantics
};


/*
 * Mutex to serialize access to the database.
```

Example D-13: Remote ACL management interface (continued)

```
 */
extern pthread_mutex_t emp_db_mutex;

/*
 * Our ACL manager type UUIDs.
 */
extern uuid_t   emp_db_acl_mgr_uuid;
extern uuid_t   emp_db_entry_acl_mgr_uuid;


/*
 * Retrieve the ACL associated with the specified object.
 */
void
rdacl_lookup(
        handle_t                        binding_handle,
        sec_acl_component_name_t        component_name,
        uuid_t                          *manager_type,
        sec_acl_type_t                  sec_acl_type,
        sec_acl_result_t                *result) {

        sec_acl_list_t          *acl_list;

        pthread_mutex_lock (&emp_db_mutex);

        /* Find the ACL using the component_name as the lookup key. */
        sec_acl_mgr_lookup(NULL,
                (sec_acl_key_t) component_name,
                manager_type,
                sec_acl_type,     /* e.g., sec_acl_type_object. */
                &acl_list,
                &result->st);
        /*
         * Copy the ACL to stub managed heap. This routine also
         * frees acl_list.
         */
        acl_store_copy_acl_list_ss (&acl_list,
                                &result->tagged_union.sec_acl_list);

        pthread_mutex_unlock (&emp_db_mutex);
}

/*
 * Replace an ACL.
 *
 * ACLs are immutable.  To modify an ACL, an application must read
 * the ACL and then replace it.
 */
void
rdacl_replace(
        handle_t                        binding_handle,
        sec_acl_component_name_t        component_name,
        uuid_t                          *manager_type,
```

Example D-13: Remote ACL management interface (continued)

```
            sec_acl_type_t              sec_acl_type,
            sec_acl_list_t              *sec_acl_list,
            error_status_t              *st) {

        int             i;
        boolean32       found;

        pthread_mutex_lock (&emp_db_mutex);

        if (uuid_equal(&emp_db_acl_mgr_uuid, manager_type, st)) {
                /*
                 * The ACL for the database is stored in reserved
                 * location 0 in the emp_db table.
                 */
                i = 0;
        }
        else if (uuid_equal(&emp_db_entry_acl_mgr_uuid, manager_type, st)) {

                /*
                 * We've got to look for the entry.
                 */
                found = false;

                for (i=1; i < DATABASE_SIZE; i++) {
                        if (strcmp (emp_database[i].emp_record.emp_name,
                                    component_name) == 0) {
                                found = true;
                                break;
                        }
                }

                if (! found) {
                        *st = sec_acl_object_not_found;
                        pthread_mutex_unlock (&emp_db_mutex);
                        return;
                }
        }
        else {
                *st = sec_acl_unknown_manager_type;

                pthread_mutex_unlock (&emp_db_mutex);
                return;
        }

        /*
         * The caller must have control permission to replace an ACL.
         */

        if (! client_is_authorized (binding_handle, OP_CONTROL,
                                    component_name)) {

                *st = sec_acl_not_authorized;
```

Example D-13: Remote ACL management interface (continued)

```
                    pthread_mutex_unlock (&emp_db_mutex);
                    return;
         }

         /*
          * Delete the existing ACL & write the new one back.
          */
         acl_store_delete_acl (&emp_database[i].compact_acl);

         acl_store_write_acl (sec_acl_list->sec_acls[0],
                              &emp_database[i].compact_acl);

         pthread_mutex_unlock (&emp_db_mutex);

         *st = rpc_s_ok;
}

/*
 * Determine's the caller's access to the specified object.
 */
void
rdacl_get_access (
         handle_t                       binding_handle,
         sec_acl_component_name_t       component_name,
         uuid_t                         *manager_type,
         sec_acl_permset_t              *net_rights,
         error_status_t                 *st) {

         unsigned_char_t     *server_principal_name;
         sec_rgy_name_t      client_principal_name;
         sec_id_pac_t        *pac;
         unsigned32          protection_level;
         unsigned32          authn_svc;
         unsigned32          authz_svc;
         unsigned32          status;

         /*
          * Get the client PAC.
          */
         rpc_binding_inq_auth_client (binding_handle,
                 (rpc_authz_handle_t *) &pac,
                 &server_principal_name, &protection_level, &authn_svc,
                 &authz_svc, &status);
         CHECK_STATUS (status, "rdacl_get_access/inq_auth_client failed",
                       ABORT);

         sec_acl_mgr_get_access (NULL, pac, component_name, manager_type,
                                 NULL, NULL, net_rights, st);
}

/*
 * See if the caller has the requested access to the object.
 *
```

Example D-13: Remote ACL management interface (continued)

```
 * See if the ACL contains entries grating privileges to the
 * calling process matching those in desired_permset.
 */
boolean32
rdacl_test_access(
        handle_t                        binding_handle,
        sec_acl_component_name_t        component_name,
        uuid_t                          *manager_type,
        sec_acl_permset_t               desired_permset,
        error_status_t                  *st) {

        boolean32       is_authorized;

        if (! uuid_equal(&emp_db_acl_mgr_uuid, manager_type, st) &&
            ! uuid_equal(&emp_db_entry_acl_mgr_uuid, manager_type, st)) {
                *st = sec_acl_unknown_manager_type;
                return false;
        }

        pthread_mutex_lock (&emp_db_mutex);

        is_authorized = client_is_authorized (binding_handle, desired_permset,
                component_name);

        pthread_mutex_unlock (&emp_db_mutex);

        *st = rpc_s_ok;
        return is_authorized;
}


/*
 * Determines whether a particular principal has the requested
 * access.  This routine returns true if both the principal and
 * the caller have the requested access to the object.
 */
boolean32
rdacl_test_access_on_behalf(
        handle_t                        binding_handle,
        sec_acl_component_name_t        component_name,
        uuid_t                          *manager_type,
        sec_id_pac_t                    *subject,
        sec_acl_permset_t               desired_permset,
        error_status_t                  *st) {

        boolean32       is_authorized;

        if (! uuid_equal(&emp_db_acl_mgr_uuid, manager_type, st) &&
            ! uuid_equal(&emp_db_entry_acl_mgr_uuid, manager_type, st)) {
                *st = sec_acl_unknown_manager_type;
                return false;
        }
```

Example D-13: Remote ACL management interface (continued)

```
        pthread_mutex_lock (&emp_db_mutex);

        is_authorized = client_is_authorized (binding_handle, desired_permset,
                                              component_name)
                        &&
                        sec_acl_mgr_is_authorized (NULL, desired_permset,
                                subject,
                                (sec_acl_key_t) component_name,
                                manager_type,
                                NULL, NULL, st);

        pthread_mutex_unlock (&emp_db_mutex);

        *st = rpc_s_ok;

        return is_authorized;
}


/*
 * Return the types of ACLs protecting an object.
 * An ACL manager may put several different ACLs on the same object
 * and use each in a different manner.
 * Each such ACL type would be identified by a different type UUID.
 */
void
rdacl_get_manager_types(
        handle_t                        binding_handle,
        sec_acl_component_name_t        component_name,
        sec_acl_type_t                  sec_acl_type,
        unsigned32                      size_avail,
        unsigned32                      *size_used,
        unsigned32                      *num_types,
        uuid_t                          manager_types[],
        error_status_t                  *st) {

        *num_types = 1;
        if (size_avail < 1) {
                *size_used = 0;
        }
        else {
                *size_used = 1;
                if (component_name[0] == '\0')
                        manager_types[0] = emp_db_acl_mgr_uuid;
                else
                        manager_types[0] = emp_db_entry_acl_mgr_uuid;
        }
        *st = rpc_s_ok;
}


/*
 * Return the printable representations for the permission bits
```

Example D-13: Remote ACL management interface (continued)

```
* that are supported.
*/

static sec_acl_printstring_t emp_db_printstrings[] = {
        { "c",  "control",  sec_acl_perm_control   },
        { "i",  "write",    sec_acl_perm_insert    }
};

static sec_acl_printstring_t emp_db_entry_printstrings[] = {
        { "c",  "control",  sec_acl_perm_control   },
        { "r",  "read",     sec_acl_perm_read      },
        { "w",  "write",    sec_acl_perm_write     }
};

static sec_acl_printstring_t emp_db_info = {
        "emp_db", "emp_db Application.",
        (sec_acl_perm_control | sec_acl_perm_insert )
};

static sec_acl_printstring_t emp_db_entry_info = {
        "emp_db (entry)", "emp_db Application (entry).",
        (sec_acl_perm_control | sec_acl_perm_read | sec_acl_perm_write )
};

void
rdacl_get_printstring(
        handle_t                binding_handle,
        uuid_t                  *manager_type,
        unsigned32              size_avail,
        uuid_t                  *manager_type_chain,
        sec_acl_printstring_t   *manager_info,
        boolean32               *tokenize,
        unsigned32              *total_num_printstrings,
        unsigned32              *size_used,
        sec_acl_printstring_t   printstrings[],
        error_status_t          *st) {

        sec_acl_printstring_t   *printstring;
        int                     i, num_printstrings;

        if (uuid_equal(&emp_db_acl_mgr_uuid, manager_type, st)) {
                printstring = emp_db_printstrings;
                num_printstrings = 2;
                *manager_info = emp_db_info;
        }
        else if (uuid_equal(&emp_db_entry_acl_mgr_uuid, manager_type, st)) {
                printstring = emp_db_entry_printstrings;
                num_printstrings = 3;
                *manager_info = emp_db_entry_info;
        }
        else {
                *st = sec_acl_unknown_manager_type;
                return;
```

Example D-13: Remote ACL management interface (continued)

```
        }

        *total_num_printstrings = num_printstrings;
        if (size_avail < num_printstrings)
                *size_used = size_avail;
        else
                *size_used = num_printstrings;


        /*
         * This is the only ACL manager for this object.
         */
        uuid_create_nil (manager_type_chain, st);

        /*
         * Returned permission printstrings are unambiguous and
         * therefore they do not need to be separated when printed.
         */
        *tokenize = false;
        for (i=0; i < *size_used; i++)
                printstrings[i] = printstring[i];

        *st = rpc_s_ok;
}


/*
 * Return a referral to an update site.  This is only required when
 * we support read-only replicas.
 */
void
rdacl_get_referral(

        handle_t                        binding_handle,
        sec_acl_component_name_t        component_name,
        uuid_t                          *manager_type,
        sec_acl_type_t                  sec_acl_type,
        sec_acl_tower_set_t             *towers,
        error_status_t                  *st) {

        *st = sec_acl_not_implemented;
}


void
rdacl_get_mgr_types_semantics(
        handle_t                        binding_handle,
        sec_acl_component_name_t        component_name,
        sec_acl_type_t                  sec_acl_type,
        unsigned32                      size_avail,
        unsigned32                      *size_used,
        unsigned32                      *num_types,
        uuid_t                          manager_types[],
```

Example D-13: Remote ACL management interface (continued)

```
        sec_acl_posix_semantics_t        posix_semantics[],
        error_status_t                   *st) {

        *num_types = 1;

        if (size_avail < 1) {
                *size_used = 0;
        }
        else {
                *size_used = 1;
                if (component_name[0] == '\0')
                        manager_types[0] = emp_db_acl_mgr_uuid;
                else
                        manager_types[0] = emp_db_entry_acl_mgr_uuid;

                posix_semantics[0] = sec_acl_posix_no_semantics;
        }

        *st = rpc_s_ok;
}
```

Index

E

F

About the Author

Wei Hu is one of the original designers of DCE. At Digital, Wei was the project leader for the team that worked with Hewlett-Packard Co. to deliver DCE RPC to the Open Software Foundation. Wei's team developed the connection-oriented RPC protocols, authenticated RPC, and the name service interfaces to the DCE Cell Directory Service. Wei also worked with the OSF and the other DCE technology providers to integrate this software into DCE.

Prior to DCE, Wei worked on the VAX Security Kernel, a virtual machine operating system designed for the A1 rating (the highest security rating defined by the U.S. government). In addition to working on various aspects of the kernel, Wei invented a new approach for eliminating a class of security flaws that were previously thought intractable; he then led the team that implemented these safeguards.

Before joining Digital, Wei worked for five years at Honeywell Information Systems where he experienced first-hand the challenges involved in building heterogeneous distributed applications without the benefits of a DCE. Wei worked on a number of products including electronic mail, distributed calendars, and gateways.

Wei and his wife Irene practice growth through change. Within a six-month period they had a second child, started writing books, changed jobs, and moved across the country to Silicon Valley. Wei is now with Silicon Graphics Computer Systems working on server technologies for multimedia and high availability.

Wei received his bachelor's and master's degrees in electrical engineering and computer science from the Massachusetts Institute of Technology in Cambridge, Massachusetts. In addition to this book, Wei coauthored the second edition of the *Guide to Writing DCE Applications*, also by O'Reilly & Associates, and has published numerous papers on distributed applications and computer security. He also holds four patents based on his work with the security and distributed computing.

Programming

UNIX, C and MULTI-PLATFORM

Books from O'Reilly & Associates, Inc.

Summer 1995

C Programming Libraries

Practical C++ Programming

By Steve Oualline
1st Edition August 1995 (est.)
500 pages (est.), ISBN 1-56592-139-9

Fast becoming the standard language of commercial software development, C++ is an update of the C programming language, adding object-oriented features that are very helpful for today's larger graphical applications.

Practical C++ Programming is a complete introduction to the C++ language for the beginning programmer, and also for C programmers transitioning to C++. Unlike most other C++ books, this book emphasizes a practical, real world approach, including how to debug, how to make your code understandable to others, and how to understand other people's code. Topics covered include good programming style, C++ syntax (what to use and what not to use), C++ class design, debugging and optimization, and common programming mistakes. At the end of each chapter are a number of exercises you can use to make sure you've grasped the concepts. Solutions to most are provided.

Practical C++ Programming describes standard C++ features that are supported by all UNIX C++ compilers, including gcc, DOS/Windows and NT compilers including Microsoft Visual C++, and Macintosh compilers.

Porting UNIX Software

By Greg Lehey
1st Edition September 1995 (est.)
430 pages (est.), ISBN 1-56592-126-7

If you work on a UNIX system, a good deal of your most useful software comes from other people—your vendor is not the source. This means, all too often, that the software you want was written for a slightly different system and that it has to be ported. Despite the best efforts of standards committees and the admirable people who write the software (often giving it away for free), something is likely to go wrong when you try to compile their source code.

This book deals with the whole life cycle of porting, from obtaining the software to correcting platform differences and even building the documentation. It exhaustively discusses the differences between versions of UNIX and the areas where porters tend to have problems. The assumption made in this book is that you just want to get a package working on your system; you don't want to become an expert in the details of your hardware or operating system (much less an expert in the system used by the person who wrote the package!). Many problems can be solved without a knowledge of C or UNIX, while the ones that force you to deal directly with source code are explained as simply and concretely as possible.

POSIX.4

By Bill Gallmeister
1st Edition January 1995 (est.)
570 pages, ISBN 1-56592-074-0

A general introduction to real-time programming and real-time issues, this book covers the POSIX.4 standard and how to use it to solve "real-world" problems. If you're at all interested in real-time applications— which include just about everything from telemetry to transaction processing—this book is for you. An essential reference.

POSIX Programmer's Guide

By Donald Lewine
1st Edition April 1991
640 pages, ISBN 0-937175-73-0

Most UNIX systems today are POSIX compliant because the federal government requires it for its purchases. Given the manufacturer's documentation, however, it can be difficult to distinguish system-specific features from those features defined by POSIX. The *POSIX Programmer's Guide*, intended as an explanation of the POSIX standard and as a reference for the POSIX.1 programming library, helps you write more portable programs.

"If you are an intermediate to advanced C programmer and are interested in having your programs compile first time on anything from a Sun to a VMS system to an MSDOS system, then this book must be thoroughly recommended." —*Sun UK User*

Understanding and Using COFF

By Gintaras R. Gircys
1st Edition November 1988
196 pages, ISBN 0-937175-31-5

COFF—Common Object File Format—is the formal definition for the structure of machine code files in the UNIX System V environment. All machine code files are COFF files. This handbook explains COFF data structure and its manipulation.

Practical C Programming

By Steve Oualline
2nd Edition January 1993
396 pages, ISBN 1-56592-035-X

C programming is more than just getting the syntax right. Style and debugging also play a tremendous part in creating programs that run well. *Practical C Programming* teaches you not only the mechanics of programming, but also how to create programs that are easy to read, maintain, and debug. There are lots of introductory C books, but this is the Nutshell Handbook®! In this edition, programs conform to ANSI C.

"This book is exactly what it states—a practical book in C programming. It is also an excellent addition to any C programmer's library."
—Betty Zinkarun, *Books & Bytes*

Using C on the UNIX System

By Dave Curry
1st Edition January 1989
250 pages, ISBN 0-937175-23-4

This is the book for intermediate to experienced C programmers who want to become UNIX system programmers. It explains system calls and special library routines available on the UNIX system. It is impossible to write UNIX utilities of any sophistication without understanding the material in this book.

"A gem of a book.... The author's aim is to provide a guide to system programming, and he succeeds admirably. His balance is steady between System V and BSD-based systems, so readers come away knowing both." —*SUN Expert*

Programming with curses

By John Strang
1st Edition 1986
76 pages, ISBN 0-937175-02-1

Curses is a UNIX library of functions for controlling a terminal's display screen from a C program. This handbook helps you make use of the curses library. Describes the original Berkeley version of curses.

C Programming Tools

Applying RCS and SCCS

By Don Bolinger & Tan Bronson
1st Edition September 1995 (est.)
500 pages (est.), ISBN 1-56592-117-8

Applying RCS and SCCS tells you how to manage a complex software development project using RCS and SCCS. The book tells you much more than how to use each command; it's organized in terms of increasingly complex management problems, from simple source management, to managing multiple releases, to coordinating teams of developers on a project involving many files and more than one target platform. Few developers use RCS or SCCS alone; most groups have written their own extensions for working with multi-person, multi-platform, multi-file, multi-release projects. Part of this book, therefore, discusses how to design your own tools on top of RCS or SCCS, both covering issues related to "front-ending" in general, and by describing TCCS, one such set of tools (available via FTP). This book also provides an overview of CVS, SPMS, and other project management environments.

Programming with GNU Software

By Mike Loukides
1st Edition September 1995 (est.)
250 pages (est.), ISBN 1-56592-112-7

It is no surprise that the most popular programming tools on UNIX are free. Not only are they easy to get and easy to customize, they are better than most tools put out by vendors. And the source code is publicly available. These free software tools offer a great deal of power within an operating system that can be customized and tuned in almost unlimited ways.

This book and CD combination is a complete package for programmers who are new to UNIX or who would like to make better use of the system. The tools come from the Free Software Foundation, which directs the GNU project, and from Cygnus Support, Inc., a well-known company that provides support for free software. Contents include GNU Emacs, *gcc*, C and C++ libraries, *gdb*, RCS, GNATS, and *make*. The book provides an introduction to all these tools for a C programmer. Previous experience with UNIX is not required.

Microsoft RPC Programming Guide

By John Shirley & Ward Rosenberry, Digital Equipment Corp.
1st Edition March 1995
254 pages, ISBN 1-56592-070-8

Remote Procedure Call (RPC) is the glue that holds together MS-DOS, Windows 3.x, and Windows NT. It is a client-server technology—a way of making programs on two different systems work together like one. The advantage of RPC is that you can link two systems together using simple C calls, as in a single-system program. Like many aspects of Microsoft programming, RPC forms a small world of its own, with conventions and terms that can be confusing. This book is an introduction to Microsoft RPC concepts combined with a step-by-step guide to programming RPC calls in C. Topics include server registration, interface definitions, arrays and pointers, context handles, and basic administration procedures. This edition covers version 2.0 of Microsoft RPC. Four complete examples are included.

Power Programming with RPC

By John Bloomer
1st Edition February 1992
522 pages, ISBN 0-937175-77-3

RPC, or remote procedure calling, is the ability to distribute the execution of functions on remote computers. Written from a programmer's perspective, this book shows what you can do with RPCs, like Sun RPC, the de facto standard on UNIX systems. It covers related programming topics for Sun and other UNIX systems and teaches through examples.

lex & yacc

By John Levine, Tony Mason & Doug Brown
2nd Edition October 1992
366 pages, ISBN 1-56592-000-7

Shows programmers how to use two UNIX utilities, *lex* and *yacc*, in program development. The second edition contains completely revised tutorial sections for novice users and reference sections for advanced users. This edition is twice the size of the first, has an expanded index, and covers Bison and Flex.

Software Portability with imake

By Paul DuBois
1st Edition July 1993
390 pages, ISBN 1-56592-055-4

imake is a utility that works with *make* to enable code to be compiled and installed on different UNIX machines. *imake* makes possible the wide portability of the X Window System code and is widely considered an X tool, but it's also useful for any software project that needs to be ported to many UNIX systems.

This Nutshell Handbook®—the only book available on *imake*—is ideal for X and UNIX programmers who want their software to be portable. The book is divided into two sections. The first section is a general explanation of *imake*, X configuration files, and how to write and debug an *Imakefile*. The second section describes how to write configuration files and presents a configuration file architecture that allows development of coexisting sets of configuration files. Several sample sets of configuration files are described and are available free over the Net.

Managing Projects with make

By Andrew Oram & Steve Talbott
2nd Edition October 1991
152 pages, ISBN 0-937175-90-0

make is one of UNIX's greatest contributions to software development, and this book offers the clearest description of *make* ever written. It describes all the basic features of *make* and provides guidelines on meeting the needs of large, modern projects. Also contains a description of free products that contain major enhancements to *make*.

Checking C Programs with lint

By Ian F. Darwin
1st Edition October 1988
84 pages, ISBN 0-937175-30-7

The *lint* program is one of the best tools for finding portability problems and certain types of coding errors in C programs. This handbook introduces you to *lint*, guides you through running it on your programs, and helps you interpret *lint's* output.

Fortran/Scientific Computing

Migrating to Fortran 90

By James F. Kerrigan
1st Edition November 1993
389 pages, ISBN 1-56592-049-X

This book is a practical guide to Fortran 90 for the current Fortran programmer. It provides a complete overview of the new features that Fortran 90 has brought to the Fortran standard, with examples and suggestions for use. Topics include array sections, modules, file handling, allocatable arrays and pointers, and numeric precision.

"This is a book that all Fortran programmers eager to take advantage of the excellent features of Fortran 90 will want to have on their desk." —*FORTRAN Journal*

UNIX for FORTRAN Programmers

By Mike Loukides
1st Edition August 1990
264 pages, ISBN 0-937175-51-X

This handbook lowers the UNIX entry barrier by providing the serious scientific programmer with an introduction to the UNIX operating system and its tools. It familiarizes readers with the most important tools so they can be productive as quickly as possible. Assumes some knowledge of FORTRAN, none of UNIX or C.

High Performance Computing

By Kevin Dowd
1st Edition June 1993
398 pages, ISBN 1-56592-032-5

Even if you never touch a line of code, *High Performance Computing* will help you make sense of the newest generation of workstations. A must for anyone who needs to worry about computer performance, this book covers everything, from the basics of modern workstation architecture, to structuring benchmarks, to squeezing more performance out of critical applications. It also explains what a good compiler can do—and what you have to do yourself. The author also discusses techniques for improving memory access patterns and taking advantage of parallelism.

Database

Multi-Platform Programming

ORACLE Performance Tuning

By Peter Corrigan & Mark Gurry
1st Edition September 1993
642 pages, ISBN 1-56592-048-1

The ORACLE relational database management system is the most popular database system in use today. ORACLE offers tremendous power and flexibility, but at some cost. Demands for fast response, particularly in online transaction processing systems, make performance a major issue. With more organizations downsizing and adopting client-server and distributed database approaches, performance tuning has become all the more vital. Whether you're a manager, a designer, a programmer, or an administrator, there's a lot you can do on your own to dramatically increase the performance of your existing ORACLE system. Whether you are running RDBMS Version 6 or Version 7, you may find that this book can save you the cost of a new machine; at the very least, it will save you a lot of headaches.

"This book is one of the best books on ORACLE that I have ever read.... [It] discloses many Oracle Tips that DBA's and Developers have locked in their brains and in their planners.... I recommend this book for any person who works with ORACLE, from managers to developers. In fact, I have to keep [it] under lock and key, because of the popularity of it." —Mike Gangler

ORACLE PL/SQL Programming

By Steven Feuerstein
1st Edition September 1995 (est.)
1000 pages (est.), Includes diskette, ISBN 1-56592-142-9

PL/SQL is a procedural language that is being used more and more with ORACLE, particularly in client-server applications. It offers such features as block structures, a myriad of data types, functions, packages, and exception handlers. *ORACLE PL/SQL Programming* fills a huge gap in the ORACLE market. The book provides developers with a single, comprehensive guide to building applications with PL/SQL— and building them the right way. It's packed with strategies, code architectures, tips, techniques, and fully realized code.

Guide to Writing DCE Applications

By John Shirley, Wei Hu & David Magid
2nd Edition May 1994
462 pages, ISBN 1-56592-045-7

A hands-on programming guide to OSF's Distributed Computing Environment (DCE) for first-time DCE application programmers. This book is designed to help new DCE users make the transition from conventional, nondistributed applications programming to distributed DCE programming. Also includes practical programming examples.

"This book will be useful as a ready reference by the side of the novice DCE programmer." —;login

Distributing Applications Across DCE and Windows NT

By Ward Rosenberry & Jim Teague
1st Edition November 1993
302 pages, ISBN 1-56592-047-3

This book links together two exciting technologies in distributed computing by showing how to develop an application that simultaneously runs on DCE and Microsoft systems through remote procedure calls (RPC). Covers the writing of portable applications and the complete differences between RPC support in the two environments.

Understanding DCE

By Ward Rosenberry, David Kenney & Gerry Fisher
1st Edition October 1992
266 pages, ISBN 1-56592-005-8

A technical and conceptual overview of OSF's Distributed Computing Environment (DCE) for programmers, technical managers, and marketing and sales people. Unlike many O'Reilly & Associates books, *Understanding DCE* has no hands-on programming elements. Instead, the book focuses on how DCE can be used to accomplish typical programming tasks and provides explanations to help the reader understand all the parts of DCE.

DCE Security Programming

By Wei Hu
1st Edition July 1995 (est.)
450 pages (est.), ISBN 1-56592-134-8

Security is critical in network applications since an outsider can so easily gain network access and pose as a trusted user. Here lies one of the greatest strengths of the Distributed Computing Environment (DCE) from the Open Software Foundation (OSF). DCE offers the most complete, flexible, and well-integrated network security package in the industry. The only problem is learning how to program it.

This book covers DCE security requirements, how the system fits together, what is required of the programmer, and how to figure out what needs protecting in an application. It will help you plan an application and lay the groundwork for Access Control Lists (ACLs), as well as use the calls that come with the DCE security interfaces. Using a sample application, increasingly sophisticated types of security are discussed, including storage of ACLs on disk and the job of writing an ACL manager. This book focuses on version 1.0 of DCE. However, issues in version 1.1 are also discussed so you can migrate to that interface.

Multi-Platform Code Management

By Kevin Jameson
1st Edition August 1994
354 pages, Includes two diskettes, ISBN 1-56592-059-7

For any programmer or team struggling with builds and maintenance, this book—and its accompanying software (available for fifteen platforms, including MS-DOS and various UNIX systems)—can save dozens of errors and hours of effort. A "one-stop-shopping" solution for code management problems, it shows you how to structure a large project and keep your files and builds under control over many releases and platforms. The building blocks are simple: common-sense strategies, public-domain tools that you can obtain on a variety of systems, and special utilities developed by the author. The book also includes two diskettes that provide a complete system for managing source files and builds.

Encyclopedia of Graphics File Formats

By James D. Murray & William vanRyper
1st Edition July 1994
928 pages, Includes CD-ROM
ISBN 1-56592-058-9

The computer graphics world is a veritable alphabet soup of acronyms; BMP, DXF, EPS, GIF, MPEG, PCX, PIC, RIFF, RTF, TGA, and TIFF are only a few of the many different formats in which graphics images can be stored. *The Encyclopedia of Graphics File Formats* is the definitive work on file formats—the book that will become a classic for graphics programmers and everyone else who deals with the low-level technical details of graphics files. It includes technical information on nearly 100 file formats, as well as chapters on graphics and file format basics, bitmap and vector files, metafiles, scene description, animation and multimedia formats, and file compression methods. Best of all, this book comes with a CD-ROM that collects many hard-to-find resources. We've assembled original vendor file format specification documents, along with test images and code examples, and a variety of software packages for MS-DOS, Windows, OS/2, UNIX, and the Macintosh that will let you convert, view, and manipulate graphics files and images.

Understanding Japanese Information Processing

By Ken Lunde
1st Edition September 1993
470 pages, ISBN 1-56592-043-0

Understanding Japanese Information Processing provides detailed information on all aspects of handling Japanese text on computer systems. It brings all of the relevant information together in a single book and covers everything from the origins of modern-day Japanese to the latest information on specific emerging computer encoding standards. Appendices provide additional reference material, such as a code conversion table, character set tables, mapping tables, an extensive list of software sources, a glossary, and more.

"A programmer interested in writing a computer program [that] will handle the Japanese language will find the book indispensable." —*Multilingual Computing*